BRETT PERKINS

FRANTIC
FRANCIS

How One Coach's
Madness Changed
Football

UNIVERSITY OF NEBRASKA PRESS
LINCOLN & LONDON

Library of Congress Cataloging-in-Publication Data
Perkins, Brett.
Frantic Francis : how one coach's madness changed
football / Brett Perkins.
p. cm.
Includes bibliographical references and index.
ISBN 978-0-8032-1894-9 (pbk. : alk. paper)
1. Schmidt, Francis (Francis Albert), 1886–1944.
2. Football coaches—United States—Biography.
3. Coaches (Athletics)—United States—Biography.
I. Title.
GV939.S34P47   2009
796.332092—dc22
[B]
2009009247

Set in ITC New Baskerville.

To my wife, Colleen.
Where would I be without her endless faith?

CONTENTS

ILLUSTRATIONS

PREFACE

Amazingly, despite his unusual personality and the important influence he had on the game of football, Francis Schmidt has never before been the subject of a book. Even those who study football history know little about him. Sportswriters—the initial gatekeepers of a coach's legacy—were entertained by Schmidt, but after time they were also alienated by him, and a coach must sell himself to the press if he wishes to secure his legacy in writing. Schmidt, however, despite his many attributes, was unable to do this. He was too preoccupied with his relentless thoughts, too caustic with his opinions, and his unusual sense of humor could only make up for so much. Additionally, Schmidt's unpopular habit of running up scores, his short stay on college football's main stage, and his inability to build an iconic relationship with one school hindered his reputation. Despite having a mountain of friends, Schmidt had no *close* friends. Furthermore, Schmidt and his wife, Evelyn, never had any children. When all hope for a well-earned legacy seems lost, a loyal child can often provide the last line of offense, usually with a well-slanted article or book.

For a multiplicity of reasons, there isn't a lot of information about Francis Schmidt to be found in one spot. Capturing his story required the melding of many bits and pieces from various sources both great and small. Such a foolhardy project could never have been completed without a great deal of help, and I wish to thank those who kindly contributed their piece to this fascinating puzzle.

Those in the business of running special collections and

university archives are a patient, organized lot indeed. I was fortunate enough to be helped by Susan Swain at Texas Christian University, Julie Monroe at the University of Idaho, Brenda Brown at Tulsa University, I. Marc Carlson at the University of Tulsa, and Carmella Orosco at the University of Nebraska–Lincoln. I am deeply indebted to the professional staff at the University Archives of The Ohio State University; special thanks go to Bertha Ihnat and Michelle Drobik.

Others who were kind enough to help me were Langston Rogers and Daniel Snowden at the University of Mississippi; Earl Hawkey at the University of Nebraska–Lincoln; Ginna Langston at the University of Tulsa; Stephen Charter at Bowling Green State University; Karen Fox at the Fairbury, Nebraska, public library; and Robin Sandwina and Pat Thomas at the Arkansas City, Kansas, public library.

Thank you to Nadine Kantola for her help in locating information on Evelyn Keesee Schmidt, Sean Sheehan for sharing his knowledge of Buckeye football with me, William Roman at football-videos.com for facilitating my viewing of 1930s Ohio State game footage, Melody Kohl for helping me when I was clueless, and Todd Tobias—the expert on all things Sid Gillman—for being generous enough to share his vast collection of information as well as for securing for me a photo of Sir Sid.

To get an authentic feel for Francis Schmidt and the 1930s I needed to talk with some of Schmidt's players from that period. Cecil Souders was glad to recount his unusual moments with Schmidt. Tom Kinkade was still a fun-loving rascal nearly seventy years after his Buckeye days. Campbell Graf was kind enough to invite me into his home and offer insights into Schmidt's unusual organizational skills. Jack Graf and his wife, Kay (who is still as beautiful as the day she was named Ohio State's homecoming queen), were a delight, and I'm grateful that Jack not only kept many plays and notes from his days as a Schmidt quarterback but was nice enough to let me copy the entire collection. And the picture certainly wouldn't have been complete without my spending a few hours with another Schmidt quarterback: the intelligent and charismatic Tippy Dye. Spending a day with this great man and his loving daughter and son-in-law, Penny and Roger Carnegie, with whom Tippy is blessed to share a home, was indeed my utmost pleasure.

This project is fortunate to have received the magic touch of my editors, Rob Taylor, Ann Baker, and Ann Harrington. I appreciate all of the assistance and hard work given by the team at the University of Nebraska Press.

How incredibly thankful I am to have an agent like Kate McKean of the Howard Morhaim Literary Agency. I forgive her for being an unrelenting Florida Gator fan and choose instead to appreciate her talent, humor, and class. Her greatness is a perfect tribute to her wonderful father, Thomas Albert McKean.

Like most writers who bite off more than they can chew, I am indebted to my family. This book could never have existed without the guidance of my cousin, Justin Martin. His wisdom and authorial advice were invaluable toward keeping me on the right path. Liza Charlesworth encouraged and assisted me when I needed it most. My in-laws, Herb and Shirley McCrorey, exercised boundless patience and an even greater amount of faith. And if I've accomplished nothing else in finishing this project, I will be satisfied to have made my father, Randy Perkins, proud that our dream was realized and to have relieved my mother, Diane Caldwell, of the fear that I might never finish anything.

Finally, I thank my wife, Colleen, and my son, Cy. They are still a little unsure of how Francis Schmidt became such an integral part of their lives, but they never questioned his years-long "visit" nor did they ever criticize my fascination. Colleen's joy in eagerly reading each chapter and Cy's measured approval were both priceless to me.

INTRODUCTION

A Man Ahead of His Time

Part of what makes the sport of football so interesting is the sheer number of tactical choices available on every play. These strategic possibilities come in hundreds of forms with just as many names and variations. They range from the wildly conservative to the shrewdly dangerous. Football coaches—who are deified for various reasons—are often celebrated for the type of tactical decisions that help define their style. Yet after nearly 150 years, the proliferation of ball-moving schemes is so great that the method known to define one coach is really the intertwined cunning of dozens of coaches before him, who in turn borrowed from dozens before them. Thus any sort of breakthrough system is ephemeral, lasting only long enough to have its choicest parts "borrowed" and added to other treasure maps. That's why, in football, true long-lasting influence is a philosophy, not an item.

Francis Schmidt had a playbook that was ten times larger than those used by other coaches before him. Among those many plays were things fantastic, beautiful, over-engineered, and standard. Schmidt's playbook was long ago stripped like an abandoned car in Queens, its parts scattered among other playbooks, clinics, and hungry coaches. But Schmidt's great influence lay not in the exact implementation of his plays but rather manifests itself as a philosophy—a philosophy that says: consider the entire spectrum of offensive football and then shoot the works. It's a philosophy that was completely at odds with the football establishment during Schmidt's career, and only through a chain of followers has this futuristic concept fulfilled its promise. Schmidt constantly commented on how much fans enjoyed open football. Fans jumping to their feet and roaring with pleasure at the perfect execution of an intricate play was his great satisfaction as well as a tribute to his great legacy. Today's game of football—the most popular spectator sport in America—is so revered in part because of the innumerable possibilities on every play. And if there is one thing that makes Schmidt important, it was his obsessive, groundbreaking exploration of possibilities.

I am aware that every book ever written about a football coach makes a claim for the importance of that coach. Nearly every one of those books would have you believe that the coach in question not only made every one of his players a better man but that he made the game of football better with his many strategic breakthroughs. This, however, usually reflects the wishful thinking of someone who happens to be a rabid fan of the team by which this coach achieved his fame. I have never been a particular fan or follower of any school that employed Schmidt during his career. Rather, it is my love of football history that brought me to Francis Schmidt.

The reason I've written about Francis Schmidt is twofold: He was an eccentric, colorful man in a profession noted for stoic leaders, and he has been nearly forgotten as a truly influential strategist. Neither of these items is based solely on my opinion but on the recorded opinions of others. The final chapter of this book will connect the dots in making a case for Schmidt's important legacy. The preceding chapters tell the story of Schmidt's hypomanic mind, which lead him to the top of his profession before crashing his career. The mindset that led to his importance also brought about his demise. He was funny and charismatic. He was aloof and frustrating. For better or worse, he was just plain different.

Perhaps the greatest challenge in describing Schmidt and his football is that his story takes place against a backdrop unfamiliar to current followers of the game. Schmidt coached between the two world wars, a period usually defined by visual cues like leather helmets without facemasks, 200-pound linemen, fistfights, and long-sleeved jerseys covered in mud. But to understand Schmidt's novelty—and thus his legacy—one has to explore a few of the era's quirks in both strategy and rule.

It was a time before platoon football; offensive players would simply switch to defense after a punt or turnover. Many players would play an entire game without being replaced by a substitute. Moreover, thanks to the stubborn attitude of coaches and rulemakers alike, it was a time when forward passing was still considered too risky to be a featured part of offense. Many viewed Schmidt as foolishly daring for his extreme stance on offensive football.

Even beyond these strategic differences, one has to note the difference in social views between then and now. During Schmidt's career college football was still treated as an amateur ideal by wishful fans and writers who hated for the game's purity to be corrupted by something as insipid as money. The truth is that the college game had long ago been shaped by cash, but most folks clung to the appearance of amateurism. When Schmidt coached, full scholarships that paid for classes, room, and board were nonexistent. Those were a thinly veiled form of professionalism, and pro football was still considered vulgar and uninspired.

As hard as it is to imagine, NFL football in the 1920s and 1930s was far less popular than the college version, which ruled virtually unopposed for the first fifty years of the game's existence. The NFL, which began in 1920, was playing catch-up, and with just a handful of financially shaky teams concentrated in the Northeast it was far from being guaranteed a national success story. In Schmidt's era the college game received media coverage almost exclusively.

Finally, Schmidt's time at Ohio State took place during the 1930s, a time known more commonly as the Depression. Although one wouldn't normally make a connection between the nation's economic condition and football strategy, a valid cause and effect can be found there. In this pretelevision era, a football program's profits were generated almost entirely from ticket sales. And in many cases, the schools were depending on football profits to either pay for other school needs—which were countless in the Depression—or to service debt on the large stadiums built during the boom economy of the previous decade. Having a winning team was one way to attract more customers, but an even more foolproof method was to field a team that played wide-open exciting offense. Win or lose, a certain percentage of fans would attend games if there was a practical assurance of thrills to be had.

These oddities—an integral part of football between the wars— are interesting from a history enthusiast's standpoint and are important for anyone seeking to define Schmidt's place in the game. Francis Schmidt was an interesting character who stood out during an interesting time. I hope this book will make Schmidt an essential part of the football conversation as he rightly deserves to be.

FRANTICFRANCIS

One. Something Stirring on the Prairie

Because Francis Schmidt operated somewhere between odd-ness and madness, it has always been difficult to determine which stories about him are true and which are myths. Everything he did had a manic quality, making even the outlandish tales hard to dismiss. But the truth is fascinating enough. He worked eighteen hours a day, devoting most of his waking thought to football, and even a few hours of sleep failed to interrupt his passion. He kept a pad and pencil hanging from his bedpost so he could jot down ideas that came to him in the night. Besides coaching his own team during the football season, Schmidt attended as many football games as possible, whether they were at a university, a teachers' college, or an all-black high school. He filled notebooks with endless notes on what he saw, always looking for variations of plays or formations that might be new to him. There weren't many. The diagramming—or creating—of football plays was his most famous obsession. Schmidt worked at creating plays the way a chain smoker works a cigarette. Using Xs and Os to represent players and arrows and dashes to represent movement, Schmidt was a mad scientist seeking a cure for touchdown deficiency. His mind seemed unable to disengage from this pursuit, and he frustrated all who knew him by mentally disappearing during conversations, parties, and bridge games. There had to be a million possible plays, and Schmidt seemed determined to discover and document every one in a notebook, on a napkin, or on random scraps of paper. This prodigious output was always his blessing as well as his curse.

Schmidt certainly looked the part of a zealot, with lazy eyelids barely concealing dark, knowing eyes that hinted at maniacal possibilities. Those same eyes displayed dark circles and bags, the result of hours of obsessing instead of sleeping. He had a long, hawk-like nose and a mouth that always seemed on the verge of smiling at a cynical joke of which only he was aware. His short, prematurely graying hair was parted on the left with great precision and combed to the sides. The whole look was underscored by his trademark bow ties. He was a curious vision by most standards and one unlikely to be missed. Standing 6 feet 2 inches, which was quite tall for the time, Schmidt was usually the tallest man in the room.

Francis Schmidt was absentminded and myopic, often oblivious to his surroundings, which included other folks. People were a curiosity to him, and his dealings with them were devoid of subtlety. He was often referred to as "plainspoken," and usually not in a complimentary sense. Telling reporters that an upcoming opponent was lucky and possibly undeserving of their win was the sort of plain speaking most coaches avoided. Francis Schmidt was confident—almost to the point of delusion—and full of raw sarcasm, but he was not angry or mean-spirited; he just struggled subconsciously to reconcile the minutiae of social custom with a zeal for getting to the point. He was not an intellectual but he was clever and imaginative, and his mind worked relentlessly, unable to slow itself. Mentally, he was a bull in a china shop.

Schmidt's players understood this. They loved him even while he was mispronouncing—and then forgetting—their names and confusing them with other teammates. They were wide-eyed and amused by his staggering use of profanity, a habit that kept school officials constantly wincing. The players even found Schmidt's sarcasm and caustic wit fascinating, verbal curiosities the young men were unaccustomed to hearing from a professional adult. Schmidt had both a great sense of humor and an unintentionally humorous personality. The players smiled as they shook their heads at his antics.

His practices on the field were long and arduous. They were also confusing as Schmidt ruled with a capricious fist, tinkering with lineups and introducing newly devised plays even though the team had yet to fully grasp plays from the previous day's lesson. He was a hands-on coach, giving animated demonstrations on the proper running of each play, but he was too impatient to delegate, leaving his assistants feeling frustrated and useless. He talked fast, machine-gun style. The players learned to accept the on-field version of Schmidt as a lovable caricature of obtrusive fervency. Off the field he remained mysterious, continuously vacillating between ebullience and unapproachable thought.

In the spring of 1933 Francis Schmidt was finishing his fourth year as head coach at Texas Christian University (TCU). The Fort Worth school was a member of the Southwest Conference (SWC), an athletic association made up of seven Texas universities and a stray, the University of Arkansas. It was a highly competitive bunch, but these teams were considered a minor collection by the national media. Fans in the East or Upper Midwest, where "important" football was played, may have recognized the names of the SWC members or even have been aware of their proclivity for an open style of play, but few northerners knew any specifics about these tumbleweed institutions.

Although best known as TCU's head football coach, Schmidt was also in charge of basketball and handled part of the athletic director's duties. He had to wear several hats in order to justify his annual salary of $5,500 (the Depression had forced a small cut from his original $6,000 salary). It was a large sum of money for a struggling private school in an economically depressed country. The school's board had hoped Schmidt could build a successful athletic program at TCU so as to raise interest and attract more students. Plus, in Texas, providing students with an education was admirable, but providing a good football team was sacred, especially a team that could humble its rivals. Anyone could teach a class, but how many could beat Southern Methodist University (SMU) or Texas A&M? Through four years Schmidt hadn't disappointed.[1]

Under his guidance the Horned Frogs football team had already won the first two conference titles in school history. The title they had just won was especially forceful; the Horned Frogs finished 10-0-1 and ranked as high as fourth nationally in the season-ending rankings. It was their third unofficial top-ten ranking under Schmidt and the highest national ranking achieved by an SWC member to date. Eight of the Frogs' eleven starters were first-team all-conference, including six linemen, a feat that has never been matched by any team, anywhere, at anytime. The season's biggest win had come against the Texas Longhorns. It was only the second time in school history that TCU had toppled the state's goliath program, and the students had so much fun celebrating that a weekend wasn't sufficient to contain the whole of it. They unofficially declared a holiday the following Monday by blocking classroom and office doors with benches, crates, and wire. The school president, after entering his office through a window, was pleased to make the "holiday" official.[2]

It was quite an accomplishment for the smallest school in a "minor" conference. TCU's total enrollment was only 1,245, and of those students only 634 were men. That was almost a third fewer than the next-smallest school. Southern Methodist, another private school in the SWC had sixteen hundred male students to choose from. State-funded universities like Texas A&M (two thousand men) and the University of Texas (four thousand men) had much larger pools of male students from which to find players. And while the state schools received most of their money from the Texas government, TCU survived solely on tuition, and there wasn't much of that to collect during the Depression. She was barely solvent, just hoping to survive until the economy inevitably recovered. In the meantime TCU needed all the profit and exposure it could possibly wring from its football program, and if anyone could make something out of nothing, Schmidt was just the man to do it.[3]

Schmidt's manic personality was the great equalizer. His tireless efforts in the areas of strategizing and recruiting simply overwhelmed everything in his way. Away from the field, he studied the science of advancing the ball with contrarian intensity, discarding nothing and attempting everything. He had come to believe that brains trumped brawn, and that deception, used as standard practice, allowed any team, no matter the size or strength, to collect touchdowns in bulk.

So far Schmidt's record was indeed impressive. During his tenure the Horned Frogs had outscored the rest of the SWC by a wide margin. Their average of 20.6 points per game was 52 percent more than the 13.6 points averaged by the rest of the conference members. Just as impressively, where the much-tougher conference games were concerned, the Frogs under Schmidt scored 55 percent more points than the other conference foes when they played each other. It was a staggering difference, especially since the SWC had already earned a reputation for aggressive offenses. The 1932 Frogs lead the nation in scoring, averaging 25.7 points per game while the national average was just about half that at 12.8 points.[4]

Schmidt's imaginative strategies played a large part in his success, but he left nothing to chance. Having talented players was the safest way to ensure victories, and again Schmidt's mania paid dividends. He pursued high school football talent as if his life depended on it. He talked quickly and passionately—a pigskin zealot—hypnotizing many a talented young high schooler who had been undecided on college. Lon Evans, a Schmidt recruit who had developed into one of the all-conference linemen, summed Schmidt up best: "He was dynamic and personally spectacular without intending to be. He exuded energy, temperament, and originality." Plenty of schoolboys simply surrendered to Schmidt's overwhelming personality.[5]

And Schmidt wasn't just recruiting football players. He was known as one of the top basketball coaches in the entire nation. In the last eight years (including his previous regime at Arkansas) his hoops squads had won 82 percent of their games, 5 conference titles, and held virtually every scoring mark in the swc, both individual- and team-related. Schmidt was a leading basketball expert at coaching clinics held all over the country. He also had a knack for convincing springy, six-footers that they needed to enroll at his school.

Being dynamic helped in an era when full athletic scholarships were forbidden by almost all conferences. It would be years until the issuance of scholarships became the standard practice we know today. At this time the swc technically allowed only work scholarships for athletes, meaning that the school could facilitate jobs for the players but not cover their tuition, books, room, or board. Even at that, TCU was threadbare and couldn't offer much work. More incoming students needed work than there were campus jobs to give them. Alumni were usually good about offering jobs, but again, TCU's small size and smaller number of graduates worked against the school. Using the risky tactic of trading present for future, the school often wrote its own loans to students, a practice that only further jeopardized its perilous cash position. As the school's athletic gatekeeper, Francis Schmidt was apportioned some of these meager resources, but he had to be much more judicious with their use than other athletic directors in the conference. While other schools could provide "help" for prospects in individual sports, TCU had to stretch its juice, meaning an athlete needed to be capable of playing multiple sports to ensure that the school would get the most return on its investment. Schmidt was a master at capturing such talent, but the process of actually evaluating who was worthy of being captured had always been an inexact science. Some school boys blossomed late or weren't given the right opportunities in high school to utilize their skills. Oftentimes procuring the right player involved quite a bit of luck.

Leo "Dutch" Meyer was sure he had lucked onto just such a player. Dutch was the athletic department's jack-of-all-trades. His most high-profile jobs were as freshman football coach and varsity baseball coach, and it was while performing the duties of the latter that he'd found a kid with some real ability. He wanted badly to enroll the youngster at TCU, but the kid's ability was in baseball, a varsity sport lower on the athletic department's voracious food chain. Football was—and would always be—king. It was the university's most popular and most profitable sport, and to get financial aid it was rather important that, first and foremost, a prospective athlete be able to do his part on the gridiron. Help was not available for those whose prowess was confined to baseball. But Dutch was smitten and had been working on a sales presentation since he left Abilene.

He had discovered the young infielder during a spring barnstorming trip—an annual trek wherein he rounded up a dozen of his varsity baseball players and hit the highway, competing with amateur and semipro teams from around the state. This way the boys could round themselves into shape before their regular college schedule started. They headed west in the athletic department's motor pool, which consisted of two cars—a Chevy with a jump seat and an old Cadillac.[6]

One of their stops was a tournament in Abilene where they met up with a semipro outfit named the Mose Sims' Oilers. The two teams played each other over the course of a couple days, and

Dutch became fascinated by the skills of the Oilers' third baseman, Sammy Baugh. He was a high school senior from a scrawny little town called Sweetwater, thirty miles west of Abilene. "He was quick as a cat," recalled Dutch, "And the way he could throw that baseball—whew! And he could hit. I wanted him bad, but the trouble was I didn't have any baseball scholarship to offer him." Ignoring reality and embracing covetousness, Dutch approached Baugh after the last game and told him he'd like to have him play at TCU but would have to see what could be worked out with Francis Schmidt, the dispenser of athletic aid. When Dutch asked if he played any other sports, Baugh mentioned that he could hold his own in both basketball and football and enjoyed playing each. Dutch assured Baugh he could get Schmidt to allow the necessary tryouts. Like everyone in Sweetwater, Baugh and his family were poor, certainly too poor to pay for college. Some sort of financial arrangement would be necessary; Dutch promised to get back to Baugh with an answer and, hopefully, an offer. Baugh probably forgot to mention that a teammate who was going to play baseball at Washington State in the fall was currently working to facilitate a baseball scholarship for him to attend the eastern Washington school. A young third baseman with a cannon for an arm can never have enough options, and it was best not to show all his cards to just anyone.[7]

When Dutch returned to Fort Worth he met with his boss. They were a funny-looking duo: Schmidt—towering and slump-shouldered, Dutch—the pugnacious bantam. Dutch recalls telling Schmidt he'd "found a kid named Baugh out in west Texas who was a real fine basketball player, was also a baseball player, and maybe could play a little football too." Leading with one of Schmidt's sports (basketball) and casually squeezing the baseball part in was savvy strategy, but just as Dutch feared, the football portion hung up the deal. Schmidt, the football junkie, knew every recruit in the region, including Baugh and his Sweetwater High School football team. The squad had been very successful in 1932, but the problem was that Red Sheridan—not Baugh—was the team's star. Baugh had been used primarily as a wingback with few ballhandling responsibilities. He could punt with the best of them but was probably too skinny to play every down in college. With work scholarships and loans at a premium, Schmidt couldn't afford to waste resources or take chances on skinny one-sport stars if multi-sport prized prospects were available. Only when Schmidt had thoroughly exhausted the prime stuff did he begin seriously eyeing the next layer. Baugh's teammate Red Sheridan fit this bill, thus he was nearer the top of Schmidt's wish list. Dutch needed some luck to get his third baseman, and to some extent it was tied to Sheridan. If he and a couple other blue chips enrolled elsewhere, Baugh, being near the top of the second stratus, might score an offer from TCU. Sheridan had his pick of schools in the state, and word on the street was that he was considering the University of Texas Longhorns—flagship program of the Lone Star State—but hadn't committed just yet. In this era players didn't sign papers of intent. Often a coach didn't know he had secured a recruit until that first day of classes when the athlete walked into the registrar's office and enrolled.[8]

By the end of the summer things got even more complicated for Baugh. During one of his semipro baseball games, he hurt his knee sliding into second base. It appeared to be cartilage damage. The doctor, in true prairie fashion, prescribed a mud pack. Hearing that Baugh was unable to fully straighten his leg, Washington State got spooked and bailed on the idea of a scholarship offer. However, "Slingin' Sammy"—as he was nicknamed for his live baseball arm—was far from being out of options. As it turned out, Red Sheridan did decide to play for the Longhorns, and the trickle-down effect was such that some TCU financial help was now available for Baugh. The problem Dutch faced was that Baugh himself was now being pursued by the Longhorns. Probably on a tip

from Sheridan, "Uncle Billy" Disch, the Longhorns' iconic baseball coach had called Baugh and asked if he would be interested in
playing baseball in Austin, and if so, if he would like to come visit.
He was indeed interested as the state college was held in high es-
teem by the citizens of Sweetwater. Longhorn prestige held sway,
and Billy Disch was damn near a saint in state baseball circles, on
his way to winning 20 conference titles since having taken the job
in 1911.[9]

With the start of school drawing near, Baugh visited Austin, and
his campus tour seemed to be a success for everyone. He liked what
he saw and heard and had all but decided to be a Longhorn when
Uncle Billy threw a wrench in the works. In answer to Baugh's in-
quiry about playing football, Uncle Billy had to shake his head "no,"
indicating that the scholarship offer was for baseball only. This caveat caught Baugh by surprise. He needed to rethink his feelings.
He wandered the Austin campus alone, debating his collegiate future. Serendipitously, Baugh ended up at the football field where
the Texas football team was practicing. It was a big team with big-
name players. It was also a hot day, so Baugh sat down alone in the
stands and observed. The sounds of football practice drifted up to
him—grunting and laughing and coaches' whistles—and he felt a
longing course through him. Although baseball was Baugh's true
love and he hoped to be a major-league baseball player one day,
watching the boys practice made him realize he wasn't quite ready
to give up football. Games would be starting soon, and he wanted
to be part of them. The feeling was strong enough that he gave TCU
renewed consideration, putting Uncle Billy on ice and returning
home. Then he surprised Dutch with a phone call.[10]

Uncle Billy took the news well. Perhaps he was slightly relieved
given the state of Baugh's knee. He even loaned the kid money so
he could afford to travel the two hundred miles from Sweetwater to
Fort Worth, where he enrolled at rival TCU that fall. Down in Texas
they took care of one another.

Baugh received a partial scholarship, and what it didn't cover he agreed to pay back by signing a note. Shortly thereafter he made the freshman football team—known as the Pollywogs—where he and TCU made an instant impression on each other. The staff found that the third baseman's arm could really fling a football, and Baugh discovered a world of football unknown to most, one that fit his skills.[11]

As coach of the Pollywogs, Dutch was responsible for immersing the youngsters into the TCU football system, and that system, as dreamed up by Schmidt, was enough to drown a Pollywog. There was so much strategy, and there were so many plays—beyond anything happening anywhere else in the world of football. But Dutch was savvy—a good man for the job—and he laid out a strategy that focused on the core elements of Schmidt's imaginative attack, things that freshmen could absorb. It had a profound effect on Baugh.

"In my first team meeting," remembered Baugh, "Dutch wrote three S's on the board, and no one knew what the hell they meant. They stood for 'short, safe, and sure.' That was his theory. I had never thought of the passing game that way, but it made a lot of sense. Dutch's offense was about timing, precision, and ball control."[12]

Forward passing had always been viewed as a gimmick by the traditional coaching establishment. It was something to be used as an occasional surprise or a play of desperation when things were bad and time was running out. Unlike the current passing game with its intricate patterns and beautiful spirals, the old method lacked substance and was generally used fewer than ten times per game.

As a college coach Schmidt had always included the controlled passing game as one of the many elements in his trailblazing, versatile offense. During his five years of learning Schmidt's diverse system, Dutch had been particularly taken by the short passing portion. It was a fascinating hybrid that combined the relative safety of running plays with the high rewards of pass plays. "We would just move the ball right down the field hitting short passes—with little risk of interception—and nobody could figure out how to stop it," recalled Baugh. It was to become the centerpiece of a long and successful career for Dutch and would also play a significant role in Slingin' Sammy's future, which in turn would play a major part in the evolution of football from a bland Victorian game to a wide-open affair that today thrills millions of fans every fall.[13]

In Baugh's freshman season, the Pollywogs won all three of their games against freshman squads from other schools, and Slingin' Sammy developed his ticket to football greatness: the forward pass. The team trainer continued to carefully wrap Baugh's knee, but it never did heal completely, and Sammy simply adjusted to the new feel. Francis Schmidt and Dutch Meyer enjoyed the pleasant surprise of an emerging phenom and looked forward to seeing what the kid could do using Schmidt's aggressive tactics on the varsity squad.[14]

Meanwhile, Schmidt and the varsity team turned out another stellar season. Despite losing ten of eleven starters to graduation, new guys were plugged into the system, and the Horned Frogs finished a surprising 9-2-1, second in the conference. And for the fourth time in five seasons, the Frogs scored more than 200 points—something only two other swc teams had even done twice in that same period, and one of them, the Arkansas Razorbacks, were coached by a Schmidt protégée.[15]

In February the Frogs also won another basketball title. They even beat the New York Celtics, a traveling professional team that was considered the preeminent squad in the nation. It was the Celtics' only defeat in 50 games against collegiate teams that year. Schmidt was given a loving cup trophy from his squad with the inscription: "To our coach—a man."[16]

The athletic merriment in Fort Worth had reached unknown

heights thanks to Francis Schmidt, but his time in Texas was about to end suddenly in a way no one would have expected. Schmidt was always looking for a new challenge—more money, bigger stakes. Perhaps as the son of a restless photographer he had also been imbued with a need for new sights. Although the previous spring he had agreed to coach for three more years at TCU (even accepting a reduced salary to help the school in light of its bad financial state) he had since engaged in some heavy flirting with Oregon State, Missouri, and the University of Texas and claimed to have received some "colorful offers" from other schools, but nothing had been consummated. Even though his eye was wandering, however, Schmidt wasn't expecting the opportunity of a lifetime to come looking for him. But that's exactly what was about to happen.[17]

And though he would be leaving the Southwest for good, he had already put into motion a philosophy of football that would help change the sport and make it the most popular in America. Dutch Meyer, John Vaught, and Sammy Baugh would be a few of Schmidt's agents of change, and all would eventually join Schmidt—their mentor—as members of the College Football Hall of Fame, each of them contributing something to the style of football we enjoy today. Speed, deception, and variety—lots of variety—were the cornerstones of Schmidt's teachings, and those same elements help make football the enjoyable and profitable game it is today, but what Schmidt really contributed to football was his relentless creativity. His followers—and there were more to come—hastened the game's evolution by borrowing from Schmidt's spectrum and fearlessly striking out on their own, emboldened by the anything-goes approach of their frantic mentor.

But that's getting a bit ahead of ourselves. In February of 1934, Francis Schmidt was still mostly unknown to a nation of football followers, his reputation for magic and mayhem having, up to that point, been confined to the prairies.

Two. Frantic Francis

Francis Albert Schmidt was born on December 3, 1886, in Downs, Kansas, one of many stops for the Schmidt family. Their hometown was really the Great Plains since they lived, for short periods, in places all throughout Oklahoma, Arkansas, Texas, Kansas, and Nebraska. Their migratory lifestyle could be attributed to the head of the household, Francis Walter Schmidt, who worked as an itinerant studio photographer. It was difficult on the prairie to find folks with the means or the willingness to dress up and sit down for photos more than once or twice in a lifetime, so the elder Schmidt was forced to pull up stakes and find a fresh customer base every few years. Fortunately, his family was small enough to move relatively easily. Besides Francis the father and Francis the son (neither used a distinguishing suffix) the Schmidt family included the mother, Emma Morbacher Schmidt, and a little sister, Katherine, who was born on Christmas Day, 1889, in Lebanon, Kansas.

The Schmidt family did manage to stay put long enough for young Francis to attend high school in the town of Fairbury, Nebraska, where he graduated in 1903. During this period in American history small towns thrived, thanks in part to the fact that the majority of the nation's jobs were related to the farm or the railroad, which in turn thrived on open space. Thus Fairbury offered a fairly normal, steady scene with its rural pace, dependence on a railroad (the Rock Island Railroad), and a solitary schoolhouse that serviced all grades. Schmidt's senior class totaled twenty-one students, of which twelve were boys—an unusual ratio. Since college-educated professionals made up such a thin slice of society, it was a common, reasonably accepted practice for boys to drop out of high school and get on with the business of making a living. Within this small pond Francis was a relatively large fish. His energetic, large persona made him a natural for president of his class as well as for the athletic association. As a student he wasn't exactly an over-achiever. "Well I guess I did all right," he recalled, "At least I got out." Like many a boy before—and since—Schmidt was more inter-ested in sports than in academics. He was the captain of the foot-ball team, and this position carried some weight. Paid coaches were still rare in rural America, and so were male teachers, meaning the running of the team fell to the captain. The Fairbury football team had Mr. Fetz for mentoring, but Schmidt was responsible for strat-egy and other details. Schmidt's first act as captain was to send for a new football since none were sold locally. Physically, Schmidt was large for his age and, by relative standards, athletically inclined. Be-sides football he played basketball and baseball and also ran track. During the statewide fall track meet his senior year Schmidt had broken the state record in the broad jump, and during regional meets the following spring he medaled in eight separate events. At the state finals in Lincoln, he and his teammate Blaine McCul-ley—an army of two—nearly won the team title for Fairbury, losing by one point to a team of eight from the big city. Schmidt blamed himself for their second-place finish, recalling that during one hur-dles event he had "cleared those hurdles with too much room to spare."[1]

While track titles were pretty cut and dried, football titles were not so easily determined. League No. 3 of the Nebraska Interscholastic

Athletic Association was made up of four schools: Fairbury, Be-
atrice, Hebron, and Crete. During the 1902 football season Fairbury's entire regular-season schedule consisted of home and away
games against these same schools. With Schmidt playing fullback
and primary kicker, Fairbury easily went undefeated and hosted
the big-city boys of Lincoln High for the unofficial title of Nebraska
state champion. Fairbury's entire roster consisted of eleven enrolled boys plus a couple substitutes from town. They had never
practiced against a defense. The Lincoln boys, also undefeated, not
only had a second team, but they honed their skills against a schedule including the University of Nebraska's scrubs. On Thanksgiving
Day, playing before an emotional crowd at the fairgrounds, Lincoln
dashed Fairbury's hopes with a 21–12 victory. Like a good mother
hen, Fairbury's local newspaper accused Lincoln of bad taste for using an academically ineligible player (a "crack halfback") while the
local heroes had benched one of their wayward academics in good
faith. Also, years later, Schmidt was quick to remind others that his
team had entered the game still suffering from injuries incurred
during their final league game. Although Fairbury had not pulled
the stunning upset, there were obviously those who forever claimed
victory in their biased small-town hearts.[2]

Schmidt was also quite busy musically, using his obsessive personality to learn the playing of many instruments. In the spring of his
senior year, he put his musical talents on display, singing with the
boys' quartet and playing a bass solo during the annual class program. Other seniors used oratorical gifts by giving thought-provok-
ing speeches on women's rights and on whether the Philippines
should be retained as a U.S. territory. On May 29, 1903, at the
Christian Church, Schmidt and his classmates graduated, receiving their diplomas from school board president, Mr. Hole. What
they received in reality was a rolled-up newspaper tied with a piece
of ribbon because the actual diplomas had been consumed in a

recent fire that burned part of the school. This commencement exercise included a speech on "the negro problem" and was followed by a banquet featuring cold ham, butter sandwiches, pickles, and potato salad. Such reckless living could only be topped by a collegiate stint away from home, but Francis Schmidt had to wait a year. He already had the ambition—wanting to earn a law degree—but he needed money and spent the year after graduation amassing college funds. The following fall, on September 20, 1904, he finally enrolled at the University of Nebraska.[3]

Even though Schmidt never ranked among the academic elite, he was still a hypomanic, pursuing his law degree with full force and fulfilling class requirements—including undergraduate work—in three years. During the fall semesters when he was playing football, he averaged seven classes. During the spring he completed nine classes per semester. For the last two years, in which he took mostly upper-level law courses, his average course score was 81.1 percent. His grades were far from spectacular but were a perfect representation of how his mind worked. Unless Schmidt was particularly interested in something or saw great value in it, he struggled to give more than was minimally necessary. For him the ends always justified the means, and shades of gray meant nothing.[4]

Schmidt played football at Nebraska and lettered twice (he couldn't letter during his freshman year because freshmen were not eligible for varsity play), but he was not a standout. He mostly played end and some halfback but rarely started. Like everyone else he played both offense and defense. Teammate Earl Eager remembered him this way: "Schmitty was a good-natured chap of about twenty years. He was always anxious to get in there and give all there was in him, and—funny thing—he never seemed to get injured. He played every game and often he and I swapped places. . . . He seldom carried the ball, being content to make the way for the other fellow. Schmitty was tall and had the physique to stay with the best of them." The school yearbook described Schmitty this way: "Schmidt has the grit and physical hardihood to endure a long and continuous attack without tiring or playing with any less fierceness than at the outset."[5]

The Cornhuskers' head coach in Schmidt's final season was the newly hired Amos Foster, a recent graduate of Dartmouth who was working on his law degree while he coached. This season, 1906, marked the legalization of the forward pass as well as the implementation of the rule allowing 4 downs to gain 10 yards (The previous rule had allowed 3 downs to gain 5 yards). The game opened up a bit, and Foster had his boys use some passes, but not enough to really matter. If Schmidt took anything from this time with Foster it was the idea of possibilities rather than the experience of radical implementation. Nothing during this time hints at Schmidt's future obsession with football strategy.

The final game of Schmidt's playing career was also his most memorable. Playing on Thanksgiving Day, Schmidt and the Huskers overwhelmed Cincinnati 41–0; Schmidt scored 3 touchdowns. Perhaps Schmidt was unusually inspired, and perhaps Foster gave him extra opportunities to score as a way of rewarding the hardworking senior for his years of dogged blocking.

While he was at the university Schmidt also won a varsity letter for playing first base on the baseball team during his second spring semester. He also played basketball but never lettered. For some reason during interviews throughout his coaching career, Schmidt always seemed to mention playing one of the two sports in conjunction with football but rarely both, and he never seemed to favor one over the other. Coincidently, he was also very reluctant to reveal his age, leaving many reporters to estimate, which they usually did toward the younger side.[6]

During his time at Nebraska he was an active member of the

Sigma Alpha Epsilon fraternity, an association Schmidt would earnestly maintain for the rest of his life and cultivate at the various schools along his career's path. As the pursuer of a law degree, it made sense that he was also a member of the Phi Delta Phi honorary legal fraternity. On June 13, 1907, Schmidt graduated with his LLB degree. He fully intended to pursue a career as an attorney—further proof that football had not yet hijacked his mind—but fate intervened, and Schmidt found himself back home.[7]

Schmidt's mother, Emma, had become very ill, and Francis chose to help care for her. At this point his father could not afford time off from his studio, and his sister, heading into her senior year in high school, was in no position to put her life on hold. Francis joined his family who were now living in Arkansas City, Kansas. He and his father took turns caring for Emma and running the photography studio. Young Francis had proven himself a quality photographer, and this arrangement was workable, but sadly, Emma passed away late that summer, leaving everyone a bit lost.

For now, while he sorted out his feelings, young Francis looked out for his sister Katherine and continued to help at the family photo studio on North Summit Street. The two small tasks combined were not nearly enough to feed his hyper mind, and he began taking walks about town to settle his restlessness. One of these walks changed his life forever. He observed the Arkansas City High School football team as they began fall practice. He noted that they were without an adult leader, and, not coincidently, their practices were a little on the ragged side. Francis's passion for athletics was reawakened, and he interrupted their practice, volunteering to "assist" them. In retrospect, Schmidt claimed his intention was not to become a coach, but to simply "help the boys out a little." But since he never did anything on a little scale, he instantly threw himself into the middle of everything from organizing practices to implementing strategy. Not being one to "assist" from the sidelines and being too impatient for mail-order shoulder pads, Schmidt had a local leather worker fashion a set of pads that allowed him to join in the scrimmages. Though the football team finished the season in the middle of the pack, they had improved from the previous year, and Schmidt was hooked.[8]

Once Schmidt finished with the football season he was anxious to keep coaching and stay busy. Coaching fit him, and he was confident he could make any team a winner. Soon he had taken over as basketball coach for both the girls' and boys' teams. The girls' team was captained by his sister, Katherine, who started at center. She also played some steady defense, allowing forward Ruth Horton to concentrate on offense and lead the team in scoring. The Arkansas City girls only averaged 18.8 points per game as a team but they held opponents to a miniscule 6.3 points. The town was thrilled to watch their girls go undefeated and win the Kansas state championship.[9]

Having proven himself a great teacher and impressing all with a larger-than-life personality, Schmidt was offered the position of athletic director, a previously nonexistent position at Arkansas City (as it was at most small schools). His new duties were primarily coaching, both physical education and extracurricular. Principal Gilliland would still arrange the scheduling of games with other schools. There was a catch, however, to Schmidt's new offer: the position wasn't a paid one. If he accepted, the school promised to work on the fact that no funds were allotted for him in the budget. Already smitten by this line of work, Schmidt agreed and dove right into the job. It was the first in a series of improving job offers that would define his professional life, and in every instance he grabbed at the next rung without hesitation. Oddly, he never haggled over salary even though he had a reputation for enjoying the company of money.

Content that the salary issue would be resolved, Schmidt focused his manic mind on the work put before him. He was more prepared for some jobs than others. His first real class involved teaching aesthetic dancing to girls as part of their physical education. Nothing in his background prepared him for this task, but he hit the books and learned all the steps needed to teach the girls anyway. He also continued with school-sponsored extracurricular activities and added to that the directing of a local band, "sometimes doubling in brass on the cornet, trombone, or bass horn." Schmidt was not a master of one instrument but he was incredibly versatile, able to play the piano, guitar, banjo, violin, and many others. Before the year was over it was arranged for him to join the district's payroll, and his career as a *professional* instructor was begun.[10]

Now that Schmidt had officially chosen the path of physical education, his desire for knowledge on the subject bloomed. He was particularly interested in football strategy. With all the rule changes that the sport was undergoing, plus its innate capacity for cunning and tactics, Schmidt had been awakened to a new life. His approach to thinking had always slanted toward against-the-flow contrarianism, hence his attraction to the study of law with its arguments and loopholes. Anybody could battle on even terms, but that provided little thrill for Schmidt. Let others memorize things or base their plans on fundamentals. Schmidt preferred imagination, the most underrated form of intellectual pursuit, the path less traveled, a shortcut to success. As to what causes a man to favor this stratagem, the answer is the same for nearly all traits: a dash of genetics and a sprinkle of social influence. Schmidt's father had chosen to fill small photography vacuums on the prairie rather than fight toe-to-toe with picture takers in populous cities. The price was a nomadic lifestyle, and because his family moved frequently, young Francis spent much time alone, entertaining himself, observing others, and exercising his imagination. That Schmidt would enjoy

thinking backward was almost inevitable. Thus, as he began studying football strategy, he noted a delicious number of tactical ideas
that were deemed too risky for a "smart" coach to employ with any
consistency. He did not immediately become a zealot for the wide-
open football game, but his development of an open game had begun and would continue to grow for the next thirty years. For now
he simply had an edge, and his second football team, the 1910
squad, only lost one game. The 1911 team won the highest honor
available: championship of southern Kansas and northern Oklahoma. Because high school football had no championship tournament like basketball did, a team claimed mythical rule by virtue of
defeating all neighboring teams. In this case the regional title they
claimed was over a vast barren area that encompassed parts of two
states but had no governing body or league name. Schmidt's 1912
squad was expected to rule this zone again, but lost to the big-city
boys of Wichita, a team that Arkansas City had beaten in their previous three meetings.[11]

Schmidt had so much energy that often he seemed to be in two
places at once, and never were these fanatical efforts more evident
than the day in 1914 when his five basketball teams won a total
of nine games on the same day. It started at the Arkansas Valley
League tournament, a round-robin affair in Wichita. Schmidt's varsity and junior varsity girls' teams along with his second-string boys'
team won all seven games they entered, with each of them winning
the championship in their division. Later that afternoon, Schmidt
drove back to Arkansas City, dropped off his champions, and took
the reins as coach of the school's eighth-grade team as well as the
varsity boys' team. They each won, awarding Schmidt a perfect day.
This great basketball season came on the heels of another undefeated football season and another claim of superiority over southern Kansas and northern Oklahoma. In his own hyper-dynamic way,

Schmidt had parlayed some volunteer help into a multisport powerhouse, and it was about to lead to his next big break.[12]

Three of Schmidt's star football players, "Rube" Leekley, "Puny"
Blevens, and Ivan Grove had graduated and made their way 120
miles south to tiny Henry Kendall College in Tulsa, Oklahoma—a
small, private Presbyterian school named after a man who had dedicated his life to mission work in New York. In a few years it would
be renamed Tulsa University and be on its way to notability, but in
1915 it was a speck on the plains with an enrollment of about 150.
One reason for the boys' interest in Kendall was the school's recent
emphasis on football, due largely to Kendall's head coach, a full-
time banker named Sam McBirney.

McBirney, as well as his brother Jim before him, had been lured
to Tulsa as ringers for the local baseball team, but over time the
brothers' adult lives began to outgrow semipro baseball. Sam joined
his brother in a new banking venture, and by 1911 he was the head
cashier, working under Jim who was now the bank's president. Two
years later Sam married Nettie Williams, supervisor of home eco-
nomics for the nearby Muskogee public school system (She would
later gain national notoriety as "Aunt Chick," writer of a syndicated
cooking column). All the while, as his life improved, Sam continued his involvement with athletics by coaching football. The sport
became his greatest passion, and over time this coaching "hobby"
gained him a measure of local renown. He mentored the Tulsa
high school team to new heights, culminating with a mythical state
title in 1913. That squad, led by a fantastic athlete named John
Young, won every one of their games, including a 27–6 thrashing
of local Henry Kendall College (this on the heels of a 44–3 beating
administered to the Kendall squad the year before). McBirney and
his players were the toast of Tulsa. Several people close to Sam felt

his coaching prowess might benefit the city even more if he were to mentor at Henry Kendall, the city's growing flagship college, instead of serving the school with embarrassing football losses. McBirney agreed, and after some simple negotiating it came to pass. One of McBirney's first acts was to persuade John Young to join him at Kendall—no small feat considering that Michigan and Oklahoma, among other schools, also wished to secure the boy's services.[13]

Until McBirney's arrival Kendall's football history had been rather lean. They had only played one intercollegiate game between 1900 and 1912. But in McBirney's first season they scheduled eight games and finished 6-2. Because of the size of the school and its location, worthy opponents were difficult to find, resulting in some lopsided wins over lesser competition, including a junior college and a high school. During the next season, 1915, eight more games were scheduled, and this time they finished 6-1-1. In both seasons they had played Oklahoma and Oklahoma A&M, the biggest schools in the state, but had failed to beat them. The program was exceeding expectations, but for McBirney the next step was problematic.

In order for Kendall to step up to the next level, McBirney needed to devote more time to the program. And as much as Sam loved coaching, his banking responsibilities were growing. His brother Jim had been the driving force in organizing the Bank of Commerce, and with Sam's help the institution had grown into the city's largest bank. Sam knew he could not juggle college football and banking much longer. He had previously asked for an assistant coach to be groomed for the head job, but Kendall didn't have the money. Fortunately for McBirney, the school's fortunes improved at just the right time. Thanks in part to the exposure generated by a successful football program, Kendall's enrollment ballooned from 150 to 400 in 1916. With this sudden increase in school population, Kendall could now scrape together enough funds to hire someone as a full-time physical education instructor and assistant football coach. When the school consulted with McBirney about filling the new position, McBirney definitely had a name in mind.[14]

For two years he had been listening to stories told by the boys who'd come from Arkansas City. Most of these tales involved Francis Schmidt, their hurly-burly high school coach, and McBirney had become interested in the colorful Schmidt. More important, he'd heard about some of the clever strategy they had learned under Schmidt. So definite was the praise from these players that McBirney decided Schmidt would be his choice for replacement when the time was right. Now was that time, and Henry Kendall College offered the job to Francis Schmidt, who immediately accepted. The salary was "meager," but Schmidt had become fascinated with the idea of coaching as a career. He loved athletics and felt like he had the sort of mind that was daring and creative enough to lead him to success.

When Schmidt arrived late in the summer of 1916 he was also assigned the duties of coaching both baseball and basketball, but this was no big deal for a man with an unusually high amount of energy. McBirney also made it clear to Schmidt that he intended to concentrate on banking after the upcoming season and hoped Schmidt would be his successor. Right away, the two men connected. Both had a boundless passion for football and couldn't get enough of it. Mary McBirney, Sam's daughter, remembered paying the price for her father's interest. "We were always going to football games, sitting in the cold. We always had to sit on the top row so he could see all of the plays." Anyone who has ever sat in the highest row of the bleachers on a miserable fall day will understand Mary's discomfort, due to the lack of protection from the wind and the absence of body warmth from surrounding spectators. For Sam, though, it was necessary. He loved football strategy and needed the best view to absorb every detail, something McBirney and Schmidt had in common. Now, as a newly formed brain trust, they were truly something to behold. Opponents soon discovered that Schmidt and McBirney were not only masters of offensive football, they were also brothers when it came to mercy or, more precisely, the lack of it.[15]

Besides having two strategists in charge who loved deception and unique play calling, the Hurricane football program had two bona fide star players entering their upper-class years. John Young and Ivan Grove might have starred at universities with enrollments twenty times larger than Henry Kendall, yet here they were, conjoined at little Kendall, entering the peak of their collegiate prowess. Regional observers expected a banner season from this conglomeration, but nobody was prepared for the actual scoreboard carnage. Henry Kendall College outscored their opponents 566–40 including nasty mismatches against Ozarks (81–0), NW Oklahoma State (60–7), St. Gregory's (82–0), and Missouri–Rolla (117–0). During the latter game, Schmidt had the boys break out their "tower play," a maneuver they had dreamed up in practice where Grove threw a forward pass to little Vergil Jones as he sat on the shoulders of Puny Blevens. They scored a touchdown with the play, which made the national rounds as a minor curiosity (it was outlawed the next year).[16]

This squad, however, was more than an abuser of the helpless. On the way to an undefeated season and a conference championship, Kendall beat Oklahoma A&M 17–13 and, even more shocking, they traveled to Norman and defeated the Oklahoma Sooners 16–0, ending the Sooners' thirty-four-game winning streak. Additionally it was the Sooners' first football loss to another state team in school history.

Ivan Grove was particularly impressive; his enormous talent had greatly benefited from a reunion with the strategy of his high school coach, Schmidt. Consequently, Grove led the nation in scoring with

196 points. One element that had been revived in Grove was his forward passing. Schmidt was fond of the short passing game, which in the hands of Grove was unusually successful for this period. In one game, after returning the opening kick, Grove locked into the short passing game, completing 12 consecutive passes before finishing off the perfect drive with a touchdown pass. This type of controlled passing would later be absorbed and perfected by Dutch Meyer and Sammy Baugh.

After the season Sam McBirney did indeed step down as the head coach. Not only were his banking responsibilities increasing—he would later become vice president for the Bank of Commerce—but it was obvious that Schmidt was a force to be reckoned with.

The 1917 team was poised to set unreachable standards with a fully unleashed Schmidt instructing a talented nucleus of seniors. But everything changed when the United States entered World War I in early April 1917. Players Ivan Grove, John Young, and Vergil Jones all quickly signed up with the Forty-second Division, an ambulance company that would soon see action in France. Schmidt was equally as anxious to help the American wartime cause. With the Kaiser's army on a killing spree, it behooved any man with the blatantly German name of "Schmidt" to prove his allegiance rather hastily. Schmidt officially enlisted April 30, 1917, three weeks after Congress voted to declare war. When he first went to sign up, the thirty-year-old who had no military experience was offered roles serving with either the engineer or ambulance corps, neither of which appealed to him. Instead he applied for officers' training and was accepted. He was assigned to bayonets and received his training at a wartime pace. After just three months he was assigned to Fort Still (Oklahoma) as an instructor, and after proving himself there he was shipped to Camp Pyke (Arkansas) where he was commissioned Captain and named the division bayonet instructor in charge of the Eighty-seventh Infantry. He eventually spent some time in France but was brought home because it was decided he was of more value as a trainer stateside. This time he was assigned to the Fiftieth Infantry at Camp Dix, New Jersey, where at one point he had under his command one of the largest companies in the entire army. That's where Schmidt was when Germany surrendered, ending the First World War. Almost twenty-nine months to the day since he had enlisted, Schmidt was honorably discharged on September 29, 1919—just in time for football season. He was anxious to experiment with some strategies and plays he had thought up in the interim.[17]

College football had continued during the war, but it limped badly. At Kendall the 1917 team only had two returning varsity players. McBirney was forced back into limited service as an assistant to Hal Mefford, an Illinois import. The program was so desperate for players that they dipped into their resident high school, Kendall Academy, for manpower. All the scrambling was for naught as they went 0-8-1 and suffered Sooner revenge by the score of 0–80. The following year, only three games could be scrapped up, and the harmless Hurricanes managed to score but 9 total points.

Amazingly, all of Kendall's star players had survived the war unharmed, and most were ready to enjoy the rest of their eligibility. In some respects it was as though nothing had happened. The same coach and many of the same players began practicing football just as they had done three years earlier. The reality, of course, was that all of these men had been changed by the war. Some had seen and done things no man should ever have to, and all of them had sacrificed valuable years for the fight. Now, older in both years and experience, they returned to campus restless, anxious, and cynical. Football was more of a game to them than ever, and those involved could hardly wait to trade some hits and laugh while savoring their newfound security. Other schools may have lost young men over-seas or had lesser talent to begin with, but Kendall returned to the postwar football scene strong and deep. Over the next two seasons, Kendall went 18-0-2, won two more conference titles, and beat the Sooners in Norman again.

What really caught everyone's attention, though, was Schmidt's continued willingness to let his boys romp when they played lesser competition. The first postwar game set the pace, with Kendall mis-treating Oklahoma Baptist to the tune of 152–0. During the 1919 and 1920 seasons, the Hurricanes continually left destruction in their wake, scoring 60 or more points in two-thirds of their games and outscoring their opponents by the obscene margin of 1212–48 overall. It was both awesome and bothersome and it helped forge Schmidt's reputation.

Today, running up the score is most often viewed with disdain, somewhere between poor sportsmanship and a breach of morality. In 1920 such poor treatment of the vanquished wasn't exactly cele-brated but wasn't cause for outrage either. On the whole, society was tougher then, with fewer feelings of entitlement and much thicker skin. Tough blue collar jobs were the norm rather than the excep-tion, and many a man took pride in surviving because there was lit-tle other reward to be had in life. One of Schmidt's players, Harold Balcom, claimed that despite the lopsided scores, "there weren't any bad feelings between us and the other team." Even so, one can be certain the other team didn't exactly enjoy the spanking.[18]

No simple answer exists as to why Schmidt allowed such outra-geous scores. For one thing, he saw football contests from a purely pragmatic point of view; namely, when you agree to a game and step on the field, you agree to the consequences, be they good or bad. If your team is bad, perhaps you should schedule games against other bad teams. Additionally, Schmidt had an underdeveloped sense of empathy. It just didn't occur to him to walk in another man's shoes.

He'd always been a loner, didn't readily cultivate intimate friendships, didn't have a brother, and never had any children. He lived in his own little world even while he was boisterously engaged on the outside. Another factor that influenced Schmidt's allowance of lopsided scores was his self-aggrandizement. Schmidt didn't consider himself an elite intellectual but he did consider himself to be superior by virtue of imagination and contrarian cleverness. He wanted others to view him as he viewed himself, and these outrageous scores provided tangible proof of his unique cunning.

In his defense—what little there is—Schmidt always adhered to blowout etiquette by inserting waves of substitutes. Indeed, throughout his career, he substituted more than almost any other coach, regardless of the score. But because he substituted more than most, Kendall's second string was nearly interchangeable with the starters from a talent standpoint; thus, his substitutes offered opponents little relief compared to the drop-off in execution that most school's substitutes provided. Schmidt's system of offense also presented a problem as it was specifically designed to be versatile and dynamic. Even when players from the bottom of the depth chart were on the field, they wanted to make a good showing, proving themselves capable of running the system's standard plays, which just happened to be more aggressive than most. Even considering all of this, an authoritative coach with manners might demand that whoever is on the field representing his team during the latter stages of an administered blow-out should make minimal effort toward advancing the ball. Schmidt, however, showed no genuine desire to restrict the pillaging. As he moved up the coaching ladder and the level of competition increased, running up scores became less of a factor because the opportunity became rarer, but Schmidt almost never stood in the way of a good rout, thus deservedly earning his future "shut the gates of mercy" sobriquet.

Schmidt claimed he "had probably the best passing team in the

United States" during his time at Kéndall—a rather large boast that is impossible to judge. No one kept official statistics during this period, and very few unofficial statistics can be unearthed either. Additionally, television was yet to be available, meaning a comment like Schmidt's was based on what he saw in person or heard from other sources. However, although Schmidt coached in a remote part of the country, he was obsessed with the game and made efforts to attend far more games than most. He was also a serial attendee at football clinics and talked with many coaches. So perhaps Schmidt had an unusually wide berth of knowledge on which to base his opinion, but the opinion is still highly subjective and far from provable. What does seem to be certain is that he was a leading proponent of forward passing when it was still considered experimental and risky.[19]

Due more to the oil industry than to football, the city of Tulsa was growing quickly, was feeling increasingly important, and wanted its flagship college to reflect this. So on February 8, 1921, Henry Kendall College was renamed the University of Tulsa. If nothing else, naming the school after the city made *all* Tulsa citizens—and their checkbooks—feel a civic inclusion. It was a good move, and the school and city have flourished ever since, although the remainder of 1921 was not so joyful. A few months later, on the last day of May, a race riot erupted between blacks and whites. Consequently, thirty-five blocks were burned, more than eight hundred people were injured, and anywhere from thirty-six (the original estimate) to three hundred people were killed. Schmidt—the photographer's son—recorded some of the devastation, including charred bodies and blacks' being arrested. Some of his photos are still prominent in the University's documentation of the sixteen-hour ugliness.[20]

That fall, Schmidt and his team contributed to Tulsa's period of gloom by failing to meet expectations. They finished 6-3 and were

shut out by Texas Christian and Haskell Institute. In Schmidt's defense the team's upperclassmen—a collection that had been assembled during his war absence—were not overly talented. Since returning he had added some quality prospects, but they were still a
little too green to save the 1921 season. Because those postwar recruits would be upperclassmen the following year, the good folks
of Tulsa were sure that the 1922 season would feature a return to
regional dominance. What they didn't know was that a rift between
Schmidt and the college had grown.

Despite his outstanding record, Schmidt's salary had not improved much, and Tulsa claimed they could afford no more. While
this was possibly true, it may also have been a way for Tulsa to hint
that Schmidt's antics were beginning to outweigh his goodwill. He
had returned from the war a changed man. He was still humorous, but his humor was now vitriolic. He had never been patient,
but his tendency toward gentler prodding was missing now as well.
This change was most evident in his language. It seems that the otherwise reasonably refined man had picked up the use of profanity
while in the army. This was not the least bit unusual, and many veterans came home not only swearing but smoking and boozing as
well. The combination of a manly military culture and the devil-
may-care attitude necessary when mentally processing the daily fear
of death and destruction made the adoption of such coarse habits
inevitable. For most soldiers, especially the highly educated ones,
this habit abated as they assimilated back into a normal society of
refined jobs, women, and children. But while Schmidt was able to
restrain his language to some degree when he was away from football, his swearing on the practice field was appalling. Perhaps it had
to do with similarities between football and the military. Both involved physical toughness, exact training, and a strong male presence. Schmidt had learned his habit in this setting, and maybe in
his mind the setting and the habit were forever linked. Perhaps it

had to do with the extremism that permeated Schmidt's life. He wasn't a crazy driver, he was the *craziest*. He didn't start thinking about football strategy as much as he *never quit* thinking about it. Other men swore in what they considered acceptable environments (bars, poker games, etc.), but Schmidt went too far—a college practice field was not as acceptable a place as he might have thought. Educated instructors were not supposed to be agents of corruption, if for no other reason than that the school was taking tuition money from parents who didn't want their kids trained in the ways of a pirate (at least that was the case in the 1920s. Today, many a professor considers it a badge of coolness to speak more outlandishly than his students). School officials were more apt to hide their displeasure when Schmidt's teams were winning regularly, piling up ticket receipts, and earning the school notoriety. However, when the team struggled, the administration began to consider the prudence of distancing themselves from their salty, eccentric coach. The school's claim that it had no money for a raise may have been part of its watch-and-wait plan for handling Schmidt. Whatever the truth, Schmidt was getting anxious to move on. He was so intent on escaping that he had entered negotiations with the Missouri School of Mines in Rolla, seeking a job as its football coach. Thankfully, before he could complete this career-killing decision, a plum job fortuitously became available.[21]

During Tulsa's postwar reign of terror on regional gridirons, one of the victimized was the University of Arkansas Razorbacks. They had suffered a 63–7 thumping at the hands of Schmidt's boys in 1919, a beating that must have stuck in the mind of Arkansas's president, John C. Futrall. The former professor of classic languages was nobody's one-dimensional bookworm. In his first year as a teacher at Arkansas Futrall had put together the school's first football team and led them for three seasons. He was actively involved in organizing the swc, which debuted in 1914, and he continued to influence Razorback athletics long afterward. When the Razorback coaching position opened up, Schmidt was contacted, and on March 21, 1922, Futrall announced the school's hiring of Francis Schmidt. The Fayetteville institution had received some forty applications for the vacant head-coaching position before deciding on the man who had given Arkansas a black eye just three years earlier.[22]

Tulsa administrators were not surprised and showed no hard feelings upon hearing the news of Schmidt's departure. "Not only myself but everybody at the school will deeply regret the loss of Coach Schmidt," declared Tulsa's president, Dr. Gordon. Schmidt's former boss, Sam McBirney, saw it as a practical matter and applauded the move. "Schmidt is a great football coach, and as for all-around ability, he's without equal in this part of the country. While I regret to see him leave Tulsa, I'm mighty glad to see him better himself. As the head of athletics in a state university he will have much more material to work with and will gain a great deal more prestige."[23]

McBirney was correct; the Razorback job was a large opportunity. The number of students registered at Arkansas was only 960, but that was far more than Tulsa could claim, and Arkansas was ambitious. It wasn't just a state school, it was the state's *only* major school. Unlike some states that had multiple colleges competing for citizen loyalty, the state of Arkansas had one big fish taking up nearly all the water in the pond. The Fayetteville institution represented an entire state population, and folks were getting anxious to compete with neighboring state schools that had already established large programs. There is no quicker or more impassioned way to make a name for oneself as a school than to become somebody in the world of college football. President Futrall had already taken the first step toward legitimacy, gaining the Razorbacks entrance into the swc. The swc wasn't nationally prestigious yet, but it was gaining in stature, and the University of Arkansas had wisely fought to be included. The bad news was that Arkansas had achieved only fringe status. Because of its remote location and small stadium it had trouble scheduling home games with other conference teams. Most of the SWC football games—when Arkansas was able to schedule them—were road games that were not as profitable or as easy to win. But even if this hadn't been the case, Arkansas was still miles from the big league. Schmidt had just accepted a job at a university without a gymnasium or even a varsity basketball team. Its football team had not won more than five games in a season since 1913. The Arkansas Razorbacks had mighty potential, but they were playing catch-up and needed a man just like Schmidt; someone who somehow could squeeze two days' work out of twenty-four hours.[24]

Schmidt secured even more help when he hired Ivan Grove, his star pupil, to join him in Fayetteville as an assistant coach. It was the first time a full-time athletic assistant was employed by the University of Arkansas, and it would be the only time that Schmidt ever imported an assistant when taking over a new program.

During all of this, Schmidt continued to aggressively recruit as usual. Never one to pass up the slightest advantage, he immediately began using every prairie trick he knew in order to improve his hand. Among the varsity players he added were "ex-college men" brought to Fayetteville "to finish work." If you had some talent and a little eligibility remaining, Coach Schmidt was willing to "improve your education," so to speak. The freshman team that Schmidt claimed to be "the best that ever reported" was captained by Elza Renfro—a Wagoner, Oklahoma import who Schmidt had convinced to attend Tulsa before convincing him to attend Arkansas. Schmidt, when he wanted something, could be dynamic, and he saved much of his magnetism for getting young players to join him in the quest for touchdowns and wins.[25]

Still, for a football program to flourish within a big-time

conference, one man cannot do it all. Therefore he must establish a network encompassing alumni and local businesses. With conference restrictions against full athletic scholarships and brazen coach–recruit negotiations, the alumni and businessmen were responsible for exploiting loopholes, scouting, and providing jobs. And because the Arkansas program was so raw, Schmidt had to remodel the network he found. He needed unified assertiveness, and there was no time for a delicate plea. Schmidt went straight to the *Fayetteville (Arkansas) Daily Democrat* and had them write an article requesting local businessmen to notify him if they had job openings for college men. In case the point was missed, the article spelled it out: "Coach Schmidt is in correspondence with a number of high school football stars who would like to try for the Razorback football squad this fall if they get financial assistance." Not just a couple of ordinary players, mind you, but a number of *stars*.[26]

Despite Schmidt's urgency, a team network takes time to build, with its first recruiting class two seasons away from seriously impacting the varsity's fortunes. For the 1922 season Schmidt would have to make do with a varsity team of ex-collegians, transfers, and holdovers. Not surprisingly, Schmidt's first football season was a mixed bag.

The season's low point was a 13–60 beating inflicted by Baylor in Waco. It was one of Frank Bridges's best squads, led by the amazing duo of Wesley Bradshaw and Russell Blailock and on its way to an swc title. Even though the score was lopsided, the action was fast and furious throughout, with the Bear duo's breaking off broken field runs and the Arkansas team's attempting a wide variety of plays. The spectators were thrilled by Arkansas's heavy use of forward passing. The Razorbacks completed 12 of 17 for 160 yards and both touchdowns, very large numbers for this era. In contrast Baylor attempted 4 forward passes all day. This type of play that thrilled fans was a Schmidt trademark—one he took pride in. He did not take pride in being blown out but he knew his turn would come.[27]

And when it happened, it happened quickly. The next week Arkansas pummeled Louisiana State by the count of 40–7. It was all part of a wild season full of unexpected wins and losses. When the season had finally come to rest with one wheel in the ditch and steam pouring from the radiator, the Razorbacks' program had seemingly made little progress, finishing 4-5—the only losing season in Schmidt's football coaching career.

It was an unusually optimistic group that met at the Arkansas booster club smoker to honor the Razorback football teams of 1922. Besides handing out 18 varsity letters, a dozen blankets to graduating players, and "numerals" to a staggering 29 freshmen, Schmidt and Grove gave happy speeches. Not only did the club members enjoy smoking donated cigars and cigarettes (hence the smoker designation) and hearing about football, they were also treated to a magic show, four rounds of boxing, and a wrestling match. As if that wasn't enough, T. C. Carlson, the athletic board secretary, announced that the football program had produced a record profit of $5,500 during the 1922 season. This seemed to contradict the team's pedestrian win-loss record, but Schmidt continued to generate record attendance, receipts, and profits for his employers throughout his career. His brand of open football was a spectacle that always drew crowds.[28]

The whole athletic vibe at Fayetteville had been percolating since Schmidt's arrival. The man was too energetic, had too much imagination, and was too impatient. In the midst of his first football season he added to his workload the task of having a gymnasium approved, planned, paid for, and built from scratch. And he was expecting to have it done by January so the Razorbacks could field their first-ever varsity basketball team.

In October Schmidt began visiting the Rotary club, the chamber of commerce, and other businesses in an effort to raise money. The cost of the "temporary" structure was pegged at around $5,000. He managed to get $2,500 from the University, and students had donated another $1,500 a few dollars at a time. Schmidt had drawn up the gymnasium's design himself. Although he wasn't a professional architect, he used his "down time" to teach himself various skills such as watch repair or basic architectural design. Using the latter, Schmidt drew up plans for a starter gym that would seat six hundred spectators around a 40-by-9 wood floor and that would include badly needed dressing rooms and showers. Visiting athletes currently had to change and bathe in the tiny basement room of one of the men's dormitories. While the school was still collecting funds, Schmidt was playing a dangerous game of chicken, contacting swc opponents and arranging tentative scheduling. By mid-November his plan was in desperate need of full funding, but despite his pleas there just wasn't enough cash available on such short notice. Schmidt was forced to delay plans for the gym and the varsity basketball program for another year. In the meantime he used the 1922–23 winter to organize a freshman basketball team. Their home games and practices were played on the school's outdoor court.[29]

In the midst of planning his gym, Schmidt was also laying the groundwork for track and field. He invited all the high school principals in northwest Arkansas to a meeting where they arranged a spring track meet featuring all of the region's schools. Around the same time, Schmidt won the rights for the University of Arkansas to host the Southwestern Interscholastic Conference track meet, a giant gathering in May that boasted some of the best high school talent throughout the Southwest.[30]

He also found time to manage the Razorback baseball team, but that was one sport he did not prove successful in running. Perhaps the pace was too slow for him, or maybe it's just that baseball

doesn't really allow room for original, contrarian strategy. Whatever the reasons, he posted a poor record for baseball leadership.
In seven years as the manager of Arkansas varsity baseball, his teams
went 38-64, giving him the lowest winning percentage (.373) for a
manager in Razorback history.

All of Schmidt's recruiting efforts toward football began to pay
off in his second season. His dominant group of freshman recruits
from the first year bolstered the varsity football squad, and they improved to 6-2-1. Scheduling was still a major issue, but the Hogs did
manage to get two conference teams to visit Fayetteville in 1923,
which was one more than usually could be arranged. They beat
Rice and lost to Baylor. Excited about Schmidt's regime and what
its success could mean to the University and thus the state, others
began to get involved in the effort to attract better opponents. The
Little Rock chamber of commerce did its part by attempting to line
up a big game between the Hogs and some major southern school
such as Tennessee or Alabama, but the plans didn't work out. The
Hogs' program would have to walk before it could run.[31]

Arkansas did make progress on one front, however. The new
gym was completed and was nicknamed "Schmidt's Barn," a tribute to its guiding force but not exactly a tribute to his architectural
prowess. Schmidt announced that the school's first-ever varsity basketball practices would start while there were still two weeks left in
the football season. While Schmidt had the enthusiasm to pull off
such a double dipping, it's unlikely the athletes who played both
sports were thrilled. Schmidt also declared that the new team would
practice through the Christmas break with scrimmages against the
YMCA, American Legion, or any other group he could talk into a
holiday skirmish. A full slate of swc games had been set up for the
season, which in this era did not officially begin until early January after the students had returned from winter break. Ultimately,
the Razorback hoopsters finished seventh in the conference, but

their final record of 17-11 exceeded expectations for the inaugural season.

After another great year of football in 1924 (7-2-1) Schmidt and the Razorbacks turned in consecutive mediocre years in 1925 (4-4-1) and 1926 (5-5) just when they should have been peaking. This first "slump" in Schmidt's football coaching career came as a surprise to him. The talent seemed to be there, and he was creating more and more plays that should have helped but didn't. Some blamed Schmidt's capricious nature and disdain for proven methods of strategy; he spent too much time thinking about new plays and he kept the players on edge with his churning of the depth chart. He was often undecided about half the spots in his starting lineup as game day approached. The two consecutive seasons of mediocrity had fans restless, and the once-strong love affair between coach and students was shaky. Glen Rose, who enrolled at Fayetteville in the fall of 1926 recalled: "When I enrolled in school there, you'd walk around the campus and see where the students had written 'fire Schmidt' all over the sidewalks." But president Futrall stuck by his unusual coach and defended him.[32]

Also defending Schmidt was his bride, Evelyn Keesee, formerly of Midlothian, Texas. They were married June 9, 1926, when he was forty years old and she was twenty-nine. Evelyn attended Tulsa University and had known Schmidt many years before they finally married. They were a perfect match and adored each other until death parted them. Evelyn was charming, quiet, and optimistic— a perfect counterweight to Schmidt's bluster. She also thoroughly enjoyed football. "I go on all the football trips with the team and have a grand time," said Evelyn, "for I'm as interested in the team as Francis is." She also attended many school functions and actually reveled in the college atmosphere. "You must associate with young people, look at their problems from their angle, and join in the fun." Her belief was that the college campus could be a "fountain of youth" for anyone willing to immerse herself in the culture. Francis and Evelyn never had any children but were always surrounded by youth.[33]

About the same time Francis gained a wife, he lost his trusted lieutenant. Ivan Grove accepted the head coaching job at Hendrix College, a small Methodist college located about 150 miles southeast in Conway, Arkansas. The two men had known each other since Grove was in high school, and there was no other man for whom Schmidt felt more pride. Grove would remain at Hendrix for thirty years, eventually rising to the position of athletic director and cementing his status on campus as someone students and faculty revered.

Ultimately, Grove was replaced by Fred Thomsen, a fellow Nebraska alumnus. The former Cornhusker end was a high school coach in Gothenburg, Nebraska when Schmidt contacted him. A bit of a free spirit with a gift for storytelling, Thomsen would eventually replace Schmidt as head coach of the Razorbacks and do a fine job.[34]

While the Razorback football team was fighting through a lull, the new basketball team became a runaway success. After a third-place finish in the conference in 1925 the Razorbacks won the conference title in 1926—an amazing feat for a program that had no gym and no varsity team when Schmidt arrived. Even more amazing was that Arkansas won the conference again in 1927. Then again in 1928. And yet again in 1929, for its fourth consecutive title. During that reign Schmidt's hoopsters won 42 out of 46 conference games and, not surprisingly, they did it with offense. They set and reset scoring records using a combination of speed, movement, and physicality unknown to most of the country. During this period in basketball history there was no shot clock and no dunking, and instead of jump shots the players took set shots from the waist while their feet remained on the ground. The game featured far more passing and far less scoring than is seen today. Personal fouls, called more closely back then, often outnumbered field goals. A major college team in the 1920s might score about 35 points a game. Schmidt's Porkers averaged 52. During a two-week period in 1929 they broke their own single-game record by scoring 66 against TCU and then rebroke it with 73 against Baylor. So prolific was Arkansas' scoring machine that the conference's two leading individual scorers were both Hogs—Wear Schoonover (runner-up) and Rom Pickell (leader). In addition, all of this happened during a period without shot clocks when many teams would play "stall ball," a form of keep-away designed to aid underdogs by keeping the game a tight, low-scoring affair. Schmidt's teams were a popular target for stall ball, and he worked hard to gain legislation against it when he was named to the national rules committee.[35]

For Schmidt basketball represented relaxation from football. "I always considered it a letdown when basketball started after the football season," he reminisced. "It's a lot easier to keep a family of ten than it is to keep a family of thirty, isn't it? The pressure on you is so much less. Nobody expects you to win all your games in basketball. In football everybody does, apparently." If Schmidt was relaxing, the players couldn't tell. One of them, Eugene Lambert, recalled the team's fascination with notes Schmidt made in his scorebook next to the names of opposing players. "It was quite caustic. We fought to get in that book after a game. It was very entertaining."[36]

In 1927 and 1928 the football program began to find its stride as well, winning 15 of 18 games and outscoring opponents by a composite score of 469–139. Both squads missed the conference title by a single game, but the play on the field was still only half the battle for Schmidt. Because of the distance (it was nearly three days roundtrip between Fayetteville and the Texas schools) and the small gate receipts (The Hogs' playing field could only hold about four thousand), Arkansas was still only able to get one swc opponent to visit Fayetteville each year. Even including road games, the Hogs played just 19 contests with swc teams during Schmidt's seven years, meaning less than 3 conference games per season. That wasn't even enough to qualify for a conference crown, so it was agreed that games with nonconference teams like Mississippi and Louisiana State University (LSU) would count toward Arkansas's minimum.[37]

Schmidt was never able to fully clear such hurdles. He didn't possess the diplomacy skills needed to change Arkansas's situation, nor was he organized enough to fully develop a strong network. Fred Thomsen, who assumed head coaching duties when Schmidt left, had much more success playing the necessary political games required of a program seeking upper-tier status. It was under his direction that the Razorbacks were able to negotiate a full conference schedule, the key first step in progressing.

Still, Schmidt had been wildly successful with the basketball team, and his football teams in 1927 and 1928 had come close to winning conference titles. Arkansas backers had never been more excited. Consequently, nobody in Arkansas was prepared for Schmidt's sudden announcement that he was leaving. TCU had just lost Matty Bell—their head football coach—to Texas A&M, who had just lost Schmidt's old friend Dana Bible to Nebraska. Anxious to profit from this game of musical chairs, Schmidt contacted TCU. The school was very interested in the "miracle man," and further discussion was arranged.

On Thursday, February 7, 1929, while Schmidt and the Razorback basketball team were in Fort Worth to play a conference game against TCU, Schmidt spent part of his afternoon at a clandestine job interview. The meeting was a great success, and the two parties agreed to a contract. Schmidt requested that his signing not be announced until Saturday night after Arkansas and the Texas Long-horns had finished playing so that his team would not be distracted from clinching its fourth consecutive conference title. All were in agreement on this plan, but the news was too much for somebody, and rumors broke immediately. By the time Schmidt met his team at TCU's gymnasium, a reporter was already asking him about the TCU job. He flatly denied any dialogue, let alone an actual signing. But the rumors were relentless, and they followed the team on their trip to Austin the next day. The players were curious and unsettled by the talk, and Schmidt finally decided he could no longer hide the truth from them. He sent a telegram to TCU's athletic director, L. C. Wright, saying that he was about to tell his players the truth and that TCU could make an official announcement if they wished. By the time the basketball game was over that night everyone knew. Schmidt told reporters, "I hate to leave Arkansas but it's a question of money." Both the president and athletic director at Arkansas received the news by telegram and were said to be quite surprised at Schmidt's acceptance of another post. Others on campus refused to believe the news upon hearing it.[38]

At first glance, the job at TCU didn't seem like much of an up-grade over the Arkansas position. TCU was the smallest school in the conference and had never seriously contended for any SWC titles in football or basketball since becoming a late addition to the conference in 1923. TCU was also a private school, meaning it had available only a small portion of the resources that most of the other SWC colleges enjoyed. Still, TCU had a couple advantages over Arkansas. Located in Texas where all the conference action was centered, it had a wealthy benefactor in Amon Carter, an insatiable Fort Worth booster. Carter was a newspaperman who had built the *Fort Worth (Texas) Star-Telegram* into the largest paper in the South, which had in turn spun off a popular radio station. He desperately wanted to see TCU make the locals proud and prayed for the day when its football team finally beat the University of Texas, the largest school in the state. Schmidt liked that a more polished network was already in place, liked that Texas was teeming with great recruits, and loved that he would be making more money.

Upon returning from the basketball road trip, Schmidt tendered his resignation at Arkansas. The Hogs, spurned and hurting, chose to find a replacement and release Schmidt as soon as possible rather than force him to finish out his contract. The Ark "A" Club, a group comprised of school lettermen, knew who they wanted as a replacement and submitted a signed petition asking for assistant Fred Thomsen to take over "based on the grounds that Thomsen . . . is familiar with Schmidt's style and will carry on without a break." As much as the administration was feeling betrayed by Schmidt, they couldn't deny that his system was special, and they agreed to promote Schmidt's protégée.[39]

On Monday afternoon, March 3, 1929, less than a month after agreeing to the TCU job, Francis Schmidt stepped off the train in Fort Worth. Those who were curious as to whether Schmidt was as insanely frantic as was rumored received their answer quickly. Within two hours he'd met with the athletic director, two assistant coaches, and the entire body of athletes at the university before donning his football coaching uniform and beginning spring football practice. For the next month he amazed onlookers with his boundless energy. George White, sportswriter for the *Dallas (Texas) Morning News* was equally amazed at Schmidt's whirlwind style, especially where recruiting was concerned. Schmidt was "doing more missionary work in a week than his predecessors have in all their time," wrote White. "The first week he opened spring training he visited every high school in the city and shook hands with practically all of those high school gridsters." Schmidt was like a hurricane, and local observers were always impressed with him in the beginning. Only later would they note that his gale-force methods blew right past fundamentals, rules, and—occasionally—cordiality.[40]

Of all the wide-eyed observers were two men with more at stake than others: the assistant coaches, Leo "Dutch" Meyer and Raymond "Bear" Wolf. These two coaches represented the largest, most knowledgeable staff Schmidt had ever been blessed to work with, and they would be of great help in building TCU's greatest stretch of athletic success.

Dutch Meyer was a TCU mainstay. He had served as a water boy for the football team when he was a child and later graduated from the school amid much athletic acclaim. After a failed stint as a pitcher with the Cleveland Indians he had returned to TCU as coach for several sports. Of all the sports he coached at TCU, football seemed to fit his personality best. The results were hard to refute. The freshman footballers, known as "pollywogs," had established a composite record of 29-4 during Dutch's eleven years at the helm. Although the youngsters practiced all season they only played three games against outsiders. The rest of the time they spent serving the football program's larger needs. On a weekly basis the freshman team played the role of scout squad, meaning they scrimmaged against the varsity boys, using the formations of the varsity's upcoming opponent. When not being pounded by the upperclassmen, they prepared for the day when they would themselves be varsity men. It was Dutch's job to not only ingrain fundamentals to the frosh but to introduce them to the rudimentary nuances of Francis Schmidt's varsity playbook. In this capacity Dutch was receiving a wide-eyed education in unorthodox football strategy. Trying to keep up with Schmidt's football imagination was a difficult task, but it would prove to be a valuable one for Dutch.

Bear Wolf, the other assistant, was beginning his first season on the staff. Like Dutch, Wolf seemed destined to be a part of TCU.

He grew up in Fort Worth and graduated from the city's North Side high. At 174 pounds, Wolf had been a small lineman in high school, but he was a fighter and had no trouble making the football team at TCU, joining the varsity in 1925. Wolf quit school after his junior year to play baseball with the Cincinnati Reds organization, but a knee injury ended that dream. He had eventually returned to TCU and was now set to be the varsity line coach. This had been arranged before Schmidt arrived, and a new head coach might have nixed Wolf in favor of his own choice, but Schmidt was satisfied and left things as they were. Wolf would prove to be a wonderful line coach, greatly responsible for the slew of all-conference linemen turned out by TCU during the Schmidt regime.[41]

The two assistants were knowledgeable football men, and they were both passionate about the sport, hence they were instantly entranced by Schmidt, a man who took football knowledge and passion to impossible heights. It was a virtual certainty that this threesome would turn out some great football.

The first spring practice was less populated than Schmidt had hoped. Only seven of TCU's twelve returning lettermen reported, the other five were playing baseball. This was a typical problem at TCU where the three dozen or so athletes were expected to play multiple sports in return for being set up with loans or jobs to cover their schooling expenses. Schmidt filled the holes with reserves and freshmen and began his usual obsession with offense. He declared, "We may get beaten badly, but we're going to be out there making an awful effort to score ourselves. I intend to go in strongly for an offense this year." His standard philosophy was to score like hell and see if the other guy could keep up. Dutch and Wolf ate this philosophy up.[42]

Schmidt was used to making any town a home, but he felt especially comfortable in Fort Worth. It helped that Evelyn had grown up in Midlothian, just south of the Dallas–Fort Worth area.

Her mother, Lina, who was in poor health, had moved in with the Schmidts, making it feel even more like home. And even though Francis was not one to develop many close relationships, he found Fort Worth to be a city where he could cultivate his standing within the many social groups of which he was a member. Included in this collection were the American Legion, Elks, Shriners, Masons, and both Scottish Rite and Knights Templar. He was also a member of the Presbyterian Church.[43]

As his first summer in Texas came to a close, and the latest crop of high school graduates began making final plans for college, Schmidt stepped up his recruiting. Besides tapping into the rich reserves of Texas prep talent, he landed a handful of Arkansas and Louisiana recruits that he'd been working on before the job switch. All in all, the 1929 freshman class at TCU was loaded. Besides three members of Abilene High's championship team, there were also surefire stars like "Ad" Dietzel and "Buster" Brannon.

The varsity team that Schmidt inherited had some talent of its own, but not enough to wow anybody. The prognosticators figured TCU for a middle-of-the-pack team. What they didn't figure on was Schmidt's system, which utilized a wide variety of talents, including some that didn't always fit snuggly into other traditional schemes. For example, one player who immediately intrigued Schmidt was Cy Leland, a junior halfback. He was a track man, a sprinter—one of the fastest in Texas—but Matty Bell had never figured out how to use him. Cy had appeared in only one game his sophomore year. Schmidt had a series of plays for everything, including some that would give Leland space to make something happen.

From the start, the Horned Frogs were constantly running offensive plays, sometimes in slow motion as they learned them and other times at breakneck speeds to test game-like responses from the defense. Usually these play rehearsals, known as signal drills, did not involve any sort of tackling. Schmidt did not like "scrimmages" or simulated games because of the possibility they presented for injury and because he thought it ruined players' confidence in learning new plays. From a scientific standpoint Schmidt liked to see his creations evolve slowly and purely so he could monitor the translation from his brain to paper to action. Also, in a scrimmage environment, one wily defender might break up a new play, causing the quarterback to become uneasy in calling for it again and causing Schmidt the frustration of not knowing how the play might have otherwise resolved itself.[44]

TCU played its first three games of the 1929 season against weak competition that would normally offer little in the way of indicating the strength of a new regime. After all, these lesser teams had been scheduled specifically for their lack of threat. But TCU's first game under Schmidt made a statement, nonetheless, as they ran roughshod over tiny Daniel Baker College of Brownwood, Texas. The Frogs' 61–0 victory included 26 first downs and 515 yards from scrimmage. The Hillbillies (yes, that was their real nickname) were denied their only first down until the fourth quarter. This lopsided win was followed by easy victories over Hardin-Simmons and Centenary. Having won the three games by a cumulative score of 109–0, the Frogs were prepared to get down to business. The conference opener was a beauty: at home against Texas A&M and their new coach, Matty Bell.[45]

An estimated 16,600 spectators packed TCU's Clark Field, including 3,600 that sat on the temporary wood bleachers behind the north goal post. As the band played before the game, Schmidt gave the Frogs a locker room speech—one of his few memorable efforts. He finished by pointing to a couple of neglected holdovers from the previous year's squad, saying, "You and you weren't good enough to play for Matty Bell, but you're plenty good enough to play for me. You can lick 'em and you're not going to fail today." Then addressing the entire team he declared, "I never had, and never want, any better football players." The Frogs in their white uniforms poured onto the field while the hometown fans roared. Drama filled the air, and the game did not disappoint.[46]

It was a wild and wooly battle the entire way. The Frogs had taken a 13–7 lead in the second half thanks to a play call of dubious sportsmanship. With Cy Leland lined up wide as a wingback, the Frogs' right tackle stood up complaining he could no longer endure the pain in his finger, which had been knocked out of joint. He asked the opposing linemen if they would pull it back into place. While two of them obliged, the ball was snapped, and a quick screen was thrown to Leland. He shot through the space where the linemen stood and raced 45 yards for a touchdown. It was the kind of trickery that could occasionally be found during this era, especially in the South and Southwest, where winning justified the means. Faking injuries and hiding men along the sideline were favorite traps. With less than two minutes remaining in the game TCU was still clinging to the 13–7 lead, but the Aggies had the ball, driving ever closer to a touchdown. Here, Schmidt made a curious move. He pulled star quarterback/safety Howard Grubbs from the game and replaced him with a 145-pound sophomore named Paul Snow who had not played all day. Two plays later, Texas A&M threw a pass to the 6-yard line, and leaping over players from both squads was Paul Snow. Like some sort of scrawny superhero he intercepted the pass, sealing victory to the delight of a delirious crowd. If ever Schmidt wanted to underscore his reputation as a miracle man, the Paul Snow substitution was a good move. The afternoon's drama didn't end with the final whistle either. Five minutes after the game had ended, as fans were beginning to exit, a hailstorm broke loose, sending spectators scurrying in every direction, their shrieks barely audible above the thud of ice pelting the wooden stands. Things were rarely dull on a fall Saturday in the SWC, and Schmidt was right at home.[47]

The amazing Frogs were 7-0 when they traveled to Austin for a game with the undefeated Texas Longhorns on November 16. If this was truly to be a miracle season, the Frogs would need to conquer Texas for the first time ever. The Longhorns controlled the first quarter, and early in the second they scored a touchdown to lead 6–0, but Cy Leland changed the momentum in a hurry. He took the following kickoff on his 10-yard line and started up the middle before bursting to the left and catching everyone on the wrong foot. Using his world-class speed he blazed down the sideline, untouched. Both teams scored another touchdown in the second quarter, but only TCU converted an extra point, giving them a wild 13–12 lead at halftime. In the second half the Frogs began to control the game's pace but were unable to capitalize. Twice they were just feet from a touchdown but missed out because of poor execution and penalties. They finally scored on a safety because the Longhorns' punter stepped over the end line. After that, the Frogs used Howard Grubb passes and Cy Leland end runs to run out the clock for a 15–12 win. It was the school's greatest football victory ever, and Fort Worth absolutely lost its mind for the next three days.[48]

The star of the game, Cy Leland, though just a small man, left a big impression on the Horns. Besides boasting incredible speed (9.6 in the 100-yard dash was elite in 1929) he had learned a stiff-arm technique from Schmidt that was just as dangerous. After the game Eddie Beular, the Longhorns' fullback, told reporters, "I've had my pan hit and pushed many times, but never in my life have I seen any straight arm that would compare to Leland's."[49]

Following a 34–7 trouncing of Baylor, the Horned Frogs had only one game left against SMU (6-0-3), and the winner would be crowned conference champion. It figured to be a wide-open game as offensive gurus Schmidt and Ray Morrison were meeting for the first time in four years. Because the championship was being decided at tiny Clark Field, tickets were being scalped at unprecedented prices. It was the Dallas-Fort Worth showdown that city boosters had been dreaming about. The Frogs appeared on the field wearing their lucky white jerseys; although due to intense use they were now more of a "frayed gray." Before the season started the athletic department had purchased some "gaudy purple" jerseys for the season but, not wanting to jinx their winning streak, had stuck with the white ones. Mother Nature squelched plans for the offensive fireworks that had been expected; the weather was terrible, with rain and a fierce wind that made passing nearly impossible. The sloppy field limited running, and with few offensive options, neither team had scored by halftime. It wasn't until midway through the third quarter that the wind temporarily mellowed, and both teams took advantage. SMU connected on a long 58-yard pass to lead 7–0, and then Howard Grubbs began completing passes for the Frogs. They got within a yard of the end zone where SMU stonewalled them. But after a punt, TCU drove again, and this time Grubbs knifed over. Sophomore Harks Green coolly split the uprights on the subsequent extra-point attempt, tying the score. After that, neither team could maintain their burst of momentum, and the game ended 7–7. Because TCU's conference record was unblemished coming into the game, a tie gave them their first-ever SWC football title. Schmidt, during his first season in Fort Worth, had taken a supposedly mediocre squad and delivered an undefeated championship to the smallest school in the conference.[50]

While Schmidt was immensely pleased he wasn't one to savor things at great length. His brain just couldn't sit still for that long, so four days after the gun sounded on football he announced the start of varsity basketball practice. For those playing both sports, such as Noble Atkins, that didn't make for much of an off-season. Schmidt, however, did approach basketball practice differently than he did football, and the proof was in his first day's fare. With football, he couldn't wait to run plays and see his diagramming come to life from the start, but with basketball, where play calling is a minor task, Schmidt spent the first day lecturing "the fundamentals of guarding, pivoting, and stance."[51]

Schmidt was not able to lead the Frogs to a conference basketball title in his first year at TCU. They finished with a record of 7-10 and placed a dismal sixth place in the conference standings, the lowest finish in school history. Had he lost his touch or did he just need time for his recruits to blossom? For now, he could take some pride in the fact that Arkansas had won the championship. It was their fifth straight title, validating Schmidt, the architect and recruiter who had built the powerful Razorback program. But to really cement his reputation as one of the nation's best basketball coaches Schmidt needed to perform a miracle or two in Fort Worth. This he did in his second season there when the Horned Frogs won their first-ever conference hoops title with a record of 18-4. The biggest star of the team, Ad Dietzel, set a conference record for points scored in a season. The next season he broke his own mark by averaging a then-whopping 15.9 points per game.[52]

Over the next four seasons, Schmidt's football and basketball teams would finish first or second in the conference every year except one (the 1930 football squad finished third), a remarkable feat of consistency, especially considering the school's size. But beyond his achieving success in the standings, Schmidt continued to build on his reputation for other things as well.

Aside from Schmidt's distinction as an influential strategist, he was known as a man difficult to understand. The swearing, caustic humor, and obsessive nature were enchanting in their own way, but one had to get used to his quirks. TCU Lineman Lon Evans recalled one example involving his roommate and fellow guard, Johnny Vaught: "One day during practice, Coach gave us a play in which we were to pull out of the line and lead interference. Well, when we pulled out, we were supposed to be going the same direction around the line, but we didn't. We went different directions and hit head-on, each taking a terrific blow to the face. I said, 'Coach, where do you want me to go on this play?' He said, 'You can go straight to hell as far as I'm concerned—you're not doing me a bit of good.'"[53]

Such talk from a mentor to one of his players would be considered over-the-top today, but it was positively taboo in the 1930s. The thing is, with Schmidt it was almost comical. The bombastic talk on the football field was just part of his strange persona, and over time people came to accept—but not endorse—the fact that his on-field persona as an intense madman was the height of entertainment. Phil Handler, one of Schmidt's Frogs and later a stalwart in Chicago's NFL scene, remembered a game against Baylor: "Cy Leland dropped a long pass in the end zone. Coach Schmidt rose from the bench, threw his hands in the air, and yelled, 'Ten thousand fans in the stands rose up and hollered phooey!' It seemed almost everyone in the park heard him and burst out laughing. Even the players of both teams guffawed."[54]

It was as though he was in his own world, and the things around him that he couldn't control drove him batty. Perhaps his caustic behavior was so enthralling because it seemed more like an out-of-control soliloquy than calculated anger. And to confuse the issue even more, there was the off-the-field Schmidt who, though still sarcastic, was energetic, quick witted, and full of song. He seemed to love life; he just couldn't get it to cooperate all the time.

And then there was the unabashed hypocrisy. Nobody was sure if he was naïve or just a lawyer at heart, but he certainly could be absurd. A case in point was the Arkansas debacle of 1933. The Razorbacks, led by Schmidt's protégée Fred Thomsen, were one game away from winning their first-ever SWC football title when it was discovered they had inadvertently used an ineligible player for a few minutes of three games. This led to some discussion within the conference, and while the swc tried to decide the matter, Schmidt, the former friend and colleague of Arkansas, went public with the view that the Hogs had become a soulless football mercenary, sinking to the use of recruiting from junior colleges and even establishing a "training house." They should forfeit the three games in question, he added. In response to the hypocritical attack from his former friend, Arkansas's president Futrall responded: "I have seen the statement of Coach Francis Schmidt . . . regarding the ineligibility. To those who know Mr. Schmidt and his methods of conducting athletics, the statement is amusing." Amusing indeed. Francis Schmidt was not above any method of program building and had used his imagination to create any number of questionable tricks along this line. He was vindictive, competitive, crazy, and hopelessly tactless. That his Horned Frogs stood to benefit from Arkansas's forfeits was no excuse for trashing the reputation of his former assistant.[55]

Schmidt even knew how to frustrate seemingly unflappable professionals. In a 1933 basketball game against the barnstorming New York Celtics, Schmidt and the boys turned the tables. Today's basketball is a contact sport; pushing and shoving in the low post has become accepted as part of the game. This wasn't so in the 1930s. The sport was still basically officiated as a noncontact sport involving lots of passing in order to create opportunities for scoring. The Celtics, featuring the legendary Joe Lapchick, were the premier basketball team in America, and since there was no NBA, they traveled the country playing top college and semipro teams (the games against colleges were somehow accepted as exhibitions). Not only were the pros from New York tall and gifted, they were known for playing a none-too-gentle brand of basketball. Imagine the Celtics' surprise when it became apparent that the young Frogs were even more practiced in the art of rough play than they were.

Joe Lapchick, the Celtics' captain, had been enjoying success during the game when Schmidt decided to turn up the heat by sending in John Vaught. Referred to as "hatchet man" by his teammates, Vaught was directed by Schmidt to use his skills on Lapchick in particular. As Vaught recalls it, he got the job done: "We got into a brawl under the basket, and the officials ejected both of us. The Celtics had lost their star." Joe Lapchick took a time out and protested this behavior to Schmidt, even threatening to quit. Schmidt just told Lapchick to deal with it. If the Celtics quit they would also forfeit their gate guarantee. The game was resumed, and when it was all over, the Horned Frogs had won 36–35, giving the Celtics their only defeat of the season. For someone who would build his legacy on razzle-dazzle, Schmidt was not opposed to the occasional foray into bullying tactics.[56]

So it was that Schmidt left his mark on the prairie as both an innovator and an oddball. But underneath all the controversy lay some enviable results that still stand up today.

Immediately following Schmidt's departure, TCU's basketball team finished last in the conference for seven straight seasons, not finishing in the top two until 1951 when the program was turned around by Buster Brannon, a former Schmidt player. Over seventy years later, Schmidt still holds the records for the highest winning percentage of any basketball coach in TCU history (.750), Arkansas history (.837), and the second highest in Tulsa history (.737).[57]

After winning the school's first conference football title in 1929, the Schmidt-led Frogs won another title in 1932. This second championship team was the SWC's smallest squad (thirty-five men) and it was the first SWC team to defeat every other conference team in a single season. They also led the nation in scoring, churning out 25.7 points per game, more than double the national average. Schmidt's winning percentage as a football coach is the highest in the history of TCU (.868) and Tulsa (.889) and is the fifth best at Arkansas (.669).[58]

Some skeptics doubted that Schmidt's insane approach would flourish outside of the prairie. He just didn't seem to focus enough on fundamentals or discipline, the cornerstones of good football since its birth. Had Schmidt created the better mouse trap? The answer would be a resounding yes *and* no. The bright side of Schmidt's obsession is that it pushed the sport forward, helping to make football a viewable extravaganza, the most watched team sport in America today. The darker side of Schmidt's obsession would unfold over the next few years, proving that the open-game movement was not sustainable without a practical foundation. Football would heed this lesson and trailblaze smarter. Schmidt wouldn't, and he would pay personally.

Three. The Man from Nowhere

Given a distant, backward glance, the Great Depression is often viewed in the simplest terms. People dressed in rags, standing in soup lines or fleeing ruined farms. Indeed, all of this occurred with unprecedented veracity, and the suffering was real, but it wasn't the only reality. In the 1930s the Marx Brothers made America laugh, Amelia Earhart awed everyone with her aeronautical feats by breaking both flying records and female boundaries, Dr. Seuss delighted children with his books of rhyme, Duke Ellington was swinging, Astaire and Rogers were dancing, and Dale Carnegie was winning friends and influencing people. The 1930s also saw the large-scale construction of some of our country's most enduring objects: the Hoover Dam, the Golden Gate Bridge, Mount Rushmore, and the Empire State Building—testaments to the fact that although America was *down*, it certainly was not *out*.

Ironically, the Depression produced a handful of collateral benefits including the increase in students' educational participation and involvement. Thanks to a brutal unemployment rate (21.7 percent in 1934) high school students were less inclined to drop out of school in favor of seeking a job with its promise of instant money because there were no appropriate jobs to be found. Work that a high school dropout might have acquired in the Roaring Twenties was now fair game for better qualified, more experienced men who otherwise wouldn't have stooped to such work.[1]

As a result, public high schools were bulging at the seams, short on teachers, short on class rooms, and begging for more money from local and state governments who in turn were dealing with declining revenues of their own. And with the high school graduation rate ballooning in the 1930s and fewer entry-level jobs in the workplace, this led to an obvious domino effect wherein higher education was being inundated with students' pursuing the path of least resistance. Many high school graduates simply had nowhere else to go and nothing else to do. Many of the state universities, with their lower fees, were being hit the hardest by this tidal wave of students who had stayed in school during the worst part of the Depression and were now graduating en masse.

Ohio State University, for one, was being swamped. The Columbus school's freshman class of 1934 had an enrollment of 2,871, the largest in the institution's history. It was a staggering 30 percent increase over the size of the previous freshman crop. Unused space within the bowels of Ohio Stadium had already been turned into discount housing for some of the needier students. Offices were being used as classrooms, and closets were being used for offices. It seemed as though only bathrooms and birdhouses were spared from campus re-zoning, but with no guarantees for the future.[2]

While the administration was surely pleased to educate these young souls, the financial realities were making the job extremely difficult. Because the Depression had forced the state government to slash its budget, Ohio State University's annual income from state appropriations—which were supposed to offset operating expenses—had shrunk from $4 million in 1930 to under $2.8 million in 1934. And during the initial part of the Depression—the darkest part—Ohio State had been forced to drop 229 full-time teachers and trim 480 classes, which constituted 10 percent of the total curriculum. So now, with resources at their worst, Ohio State was being forced to facilitate the first of several consecutive, massive freshman classes. This unprecedented collision of circumstances meant that even with increased class sizes and senior professors' covering a frosh course or two where possible, there were still fifty-seven class sections without a teacher. The school was scrambling to add twenty-five "new people, instructors, assistants, and graduate assistants" to cover the courses. These new teachers, some of whom would be added to the staff "rather quickly and without much knowledge of their capacity," came more cheaply than experienced teachers, yet still added $10,000 to a groaning budget. Such was the sad state of affairs campus wide, that even the heretofore profitable football program was getting a little threadbare around the cuffs, and anyone who knows anything about Ohio State football knows that to be a serious matter.[3]

All athletics at OSU fell under the umbrella of the board of athletic control, a body separate from the school budget and one charged with paying its own way. Football, which generated far more cash than any other sport (as was the case at most major universities) was the lynchpin to OSU's athletic cartel, its profits paying for tennis, golf, polo, and all intramural sports, plus occasionally aiding basketball when it couldn't pull black numbers. Since the Depression had erased much of the public's discretionary spending, attendance was lagging, and football was struggling to pay for itself, let alone for the satellite sports. Football ticket prices had been reduced at the start of the 1931 season based on a combination of compassion, marketing strategy, and desperation on the part of the administration, but attendance still dropped, leaving a $31,000 shortfall in the budget. The entire athletic budget was cut to the bone; spring sports were reduced, and personnel were whacked. In 1932 and 1933 the average attendance for OSU home games fell below 28,000 to its lowest totals since Ohio Stadium was christened in 1922. This drop in attendance was adversely affecting the whole sports scene at the school. And it wasn't just the money.[4]

You see, within the borders of Ohio there is a passion for Buckeye football that percolates and bubbles year-round. Football is more important than politics and religion and twice as controversial. Columbus is the epicenter of this fanaticism, and during football season the city leaves a lasting impression on the brave visitors who enter. That's how it was in 1934 (and it's still the case today). Henry McLemore, a well-known syndicated sportswriter from New York during this period, traveled to all the major cities to cover all the major sports, and he thought the good citizens of Columbus were:

> Without any doubt . . . the most fanatical backers of football in this country. The entire city, from the furthermost suburb to the mayor's cloakroom, starts trembling violently with the first kickoff of the season, and doesn't settle down to normal until the last whistle. On Friday and Saturday nights the intersection of High and Broad, and the lobbies of the Neil House and the Deshler-Wallick are a combination of insane asylum, Wild West rodeo, the retreat from Moscow, and Halloween in Hell. If a man hasn't seen Columbus in the midst of a football fever he might think that a town like Knoxville takes its football seriously, or that Detroit when the Tigers are in the World Series is tops in civic lunacy. But when Columbus goes into high gear there is nothing quite like it.[5]

He wasn't kidding. It was in this town that an Ohio State pep rally turned into a two-hour riot requiring sixty cops to intervene with tear gas after bricks had been thrown and trolley poles had been knocked over. And that was the day *before* the game.[6]

Exhausted from two months of decadent celebration each fall, Columbus would generally lapse into a short period of quiet conversations and holiday shopping before renewing her lust for Buckeye football and filling the next ten months with speculation, rumors, debates, agendas, lies, and prayers. Many of these addicts could be found working or living near a major Columbus thoroughfare that paralleled the university and were therefore appropriately known as the "High Street crowd" or "Downtown quarterbacks." Often they were simply referred to as "the wolves." Most of this mob were alumni, but many were simply sports enthusiasts who loved their hometown boys. No single description sufficiently summed up the wolves. One influential pack was the Quarterback Club, a select group of intellectual football nuts, founded by Karl Pauly, a political journalist for the *Ohio State Journal* (Columbus). The Club studied Buckeye football under a microscope at their serious meetings and then pronounced their findings to anyone who would listen. For football talk that was a little less highbrow but just as intense, a good debate could always be found in the back of Ben Ratner's legendary sporting goods store. Few fan bases were as intense as Ohio State's, and almost none received less success for all its passion. Despite always being in contention, the Buckeyes had not won a Big 10 football championship since 1920, and this insatiable band of supporters was getting testy.

Nobody understood this better than Lynn Wilbur "Saint" St. John, Ohio State's athletic director. He was the man in charge of finding a new head football coach. For only the second time in twenty-two years the position had become vacant, and for the wolves, waiting on a new coach held all the drama and importance of a papal election.

The anticipation had officially begun on January 30, 1934, when Sam Willaman, the Buckeyes' head coach for the previous five seasons, resigned his position and almost simultaneously accepted a similar post at Western Reserve College, a much smaller school in

Cleveland. For months fans had speculated that Willaman would resign or be fired, but only those behind the scenes knew what an audacious, brazen campaign had been conducted by St. John and Ohio State in order to reach this point.

Willaman had been a popular choice when he was hired in 1929. He was a former star player for the Buckeyes, thirty-eight years old at the time of hiring, and looked like he was still in perfect playing condition. After five seasons Willaman still seemed fit on the outside, but inside he was faltering. For one thing, he was suffering from a chronic intestinal condition that left him in constant pain and actually led to his death a year later. His psyche wasn't much better, his support having eroded on all sides. Although the Buckeyes' record during Willaman's tenure was a solid 26-10-5, and although they had only lost twice in the last two seasons, those two losses had been his final undoing. In both instances his squad had been shut out by their hated rival, Michigan. Not winning a single conference title was bad enough, but twice being shut out by the Michigan Wolverines—the mother of all rivals—was a cardinal sin in Ohio. If a coach was already on shaky ground due to his practices or personality, then losing often and badly to the Wolverines was standard grounds for divorce. Only the purest saints in Ohio would argue otherwise.[7]

Following the third game of the 1933 season—a loss to Michigan in which the Buckeyes had managed just 3 first downs the entire game—Willaman refused to be interviewed by the press. Already having alienated some board members as well as the vocal High Street crowd, the papers now turned on him, and rumors of his demise began in earnest.

A week after the Michigan game (it was not until 1935 that osu and Michigan began meeting on the final weekend of the schedule) St. John had an old friend stay at his house; together the two men began the plot to dump Ohio State's coach.[8]

The old friend was John L. "Major" Griffith, commissioner of the Big 10 conference. The Big 10 was a collection of large Midwest universities that worked together for the good of their sports programs, and the "Major" was their spokesman and backroom dealer. Griffith had been elected to this figurehead (quasi-marketing) position a decade earlier with the help of a special committee that included St. John. The two had been friends since they were young coaches a decade before that. Griffith ran the Big 10's headquarters from the Hotel Sherman in Chicago where he facilitated communication between conference schools and took care of things like referee schedules, publicity, and squabbling amongst the members.

Over that weekend, St. John confided to his old friend the commissioner that Willaman had to go. Saint had been bothered by Willaman's laid-back style for some time. The previous winter he had approached a head coach at another school, feeling him out as to whether he would like to take over the reins at Ohio State. That coach, Tuss McLaughry of Brown University, had then embarrassed St. John and the whole Buckeye program by telling newspapers he had been approached but was staying back east. Caught with his hand in the cookie jar, St. John had backed off from replacing Willaman, but the Michigan debacle was now the catalyst for revisiting change. The problem was that St. John and the board didn't have the nerve to fire a physically ill former player who had lost only two games in two years. Saint would have to tread lightly behind the scenes to fix the coaching situation, and he sought the advice of Griffith, a master manipulator.[9]

Three days later, after returning home and thinking about what he had heard, Griffith sent a letter to St. John that he recommended be destroyed, and for good reason. He was passing on information about a replacement for Willaman who was so good that Buckeye fans would no longer care about Willaman. It seems the talented football coach at Minnesota (another Big 10 member) was

being asked to take a pay cut and was not too happy about it. Perhaps a school such as osu could tempt him to leave by matching
his current salary. The coach, Bernie Bierman, was good—damn
good—and Griffith thought that "he may be willing to take a different job if the same [salary] were offered to him inside the next
month or so." It was a completely unethical use of information at
the expense of another conference member whose interests were
supposed to be treated equally by the commissioner. This idea was
a little too conspicuous for St. John's taste, and nothing came of it,
but a month later he and the Buckeye machine came up with their
own solution: they would pawn Willaman off as a hand-me-down to
a lesser school.[10]

It went down this way: St. John turned to one of his loyal boosters—a man named Floyd—to do the dirty work. Floyd, who was employed as the directing supervisor of the Cleveland board of education, took some time off one day to visit Carl Davis, the athletic
director at Western Reserve, a local college. Floyd asked Davis if he
wanted his football coach to return next year. When Davis inquired
as to why Floyd was asking, Floyd responded, "From my observa-
tions of Western Reserve teams over the past three years I [can] not
help but feel that there [are] many coaches available who would do
more for Western Reserve . . . than [has] been done by the present
coach." And just in case damning the coach's professional ability
wasn't enough, Floyd added that "he had no personal knowledge
of the situation [but] there was a great deal of rather pointed talk
about the habits and manner of living of the present football coach,
particularly in regard to his use of intoxicating beverages." When
Davis agreed that a change would be best for the Western Reserve
program, Floyd innocently told Davis that he "in no way, wished to
influence his judgment but simply to present to him for his consideration the point of view of a highly interested outsider." He then
boldly pitched the idea of Sam Willaman's coaching at Western

Reserve. By most definitions this was a serious attempt to "influence" not one but two schools. In unabashed fashion Floyd assured Davis that Willaman was careful with his language, didn't use tobacco, and was a very efficient worker. He didn't spend much time explaining why OSU wanted to get rid of Willaman. As it turned out, Davis didn't really need to be sold on the idea. He claimed that his current coach, Tom Keady, had undermined him and sought to have him fired so that he himself could be promoted to the position of athletic director. Therefore, moving Willaman to Western Reserve would make everyone happy—everyone, that is, except for the coup-minded coach with the alleged drinking problem. Davis said he would talk to his school president. Floyd, the innocent outsider, said he could help here as well by arranging for Willaman to meet secretly with the Western Reserve president. Hell, Floyd even knew someone who knew Judge Friebolin, who sat on the Western Reserve board of trustees, if that would help expedite things. So concerned was Ohio State about Western Reserve's coaching problem that they were evidently willing to take care of most of the sordid details. The entire arrangement was as crooked as any backroom state senate deal, but with much higher stakes. This was Ohio State football, after all, not some bureaucratic issue like crime or education.[11]

Apparently, Willaman had already told St. John he would leave and refrain from making waves as long as Ohio State helped him land another job. After his conversation with the Western Reserve athletic director, Floyd had written a recap for St. John and even sent a copy to Willaman.[12]

Finally, on the evening of January 30, the switch was set in motion when Western Reserve announced that its football coach of three years, Tom Keady, would not be re-signed. "We are unable to offer Keady a contract at the figure we have been paying," explained the school's athletic committee. The next day Willaman resigned as coach at Ohio State before traveling to Cleveland where he was—the same day—announced as the new coach at Western Reserve.[13]

After a couple days of respectful restraint, St. John began looking for Willaman's replacement. At the top of his list was Clark Shaughnessy, who had replaced the iconic Amos Alonzo Stagg at the University of Chicago the previous year. The problem with Saint's chasing Shaughnessy was twofold: Chicago was a fellow Big 10 school, and Shaughnessy had only been coaching there for one year. While not illegal, for Saint to be trolling his own conference for a coach was akin to finding a new spouse by dating your friends' wives. And from Shaughnessy's standpoint, hopping into bed with three programs in three years might make him look like a bit of a tramp, even if Ohio State—the wayward seducer—was partly to blame.

Still, the University of Chicago football program was making it difficult for Shaughnessy to be loyal. He was just beginning to fully grasp what a mess he had walked into. His predecessor, Stagg, the coach since 1892 (!), had not kept up with the increasingly shrewd and aggressive recruiting practices of big-time football. And worse yet, as Stagg was rendering himself irrelevant, the school was in the midst of an academic revival that increased scholastic standards to a level not conducive for attracting phenomenal bodies with marginal minds. Football was quietly being deemphasized. The seventy-year-old, lame-duck Stagg had been forced out by school age-limit policy and replaced by Shaughnessy, who had initially been excited about hooking up with a Big 10 school. But the environment surrounding Chicago Maroon football was becoming fatally dysfunctional, and Shaughnessy was questioning the wisdom of their relationship after only one year. Concerned about his future, he'd just met quietly with a faction of the school's trustees who still wanted to redeem the football program. They had promised Shaughnessy they would take care of his security no matter what the team's record and even offered to raise his salary some 14 percent to $8,000 per year. Sticking with Chicago seemed the right thing to do, but Shaughnessy was a bit worried and was still disillusioned over being talked into holding the bag as Maroon football edged closer to its grave.[14]

Only someone with insider knowledge would know that Shaughnessy was conflicted *and* possibly available; someone like commissioner Griffith, who worked in Chicago and knew all the inner workings of the Maroon program. And Griffith didn't just pass on his insider information to dear old St. John. Taking collusion to new heights, Griffith actually contacted Shaughnessy directly and advised him to check out Ohio State before agreeing to stay at Chicago. Following this discussion, Griffith wrote to Saint, saying, "I told Clark that I thought he should not make a definite decision until he had visited you at Columbus, and he said he would. . . . He wanted me, however, to make it clear to you that his present hunch was that he should stay where he is, so that he would be treating you fairly. Perhaps after he has seen your layout he will lean the other way."[15]

St. John sought permission from the athletic board to make an $8,000 offer to Shaughnessy when they met a week later, but ultimately it was a moot request; Shaughnessy remained loyal to Chicago. St. John never did publicly confirm any sort of interest in the Chicago coach, but the backstreet affair was so poorly hidden that Shaughnessy felt compelled to declare to the press on February 11, "I will remain in Chicago." Shaughnessy wanted to publicly acknowledge his loyalty, but also, he probably didn't mind the Chicago school officials' knowing he had turned somebody's head.[16]

One week later the Buckeyes were running low on pride thanks to a second public rejection. Again it was a Big 10 coach. This time it was Noble Kizer, current Purdue head coach and former Notre Dame stalwart. St. John traveled to Chicago for a visit with Mr. Kizer, but "well-informed sources" claimed that, among other things, money was a stumbling block. Kizer wanted $9,000 annually, which was probably more than St. John had been authorized to informally offer. The following day Kizer denied he was a candidate. "I'll be at Purdue next year, unless they kick me out," he said. His being booted was hardly likely, with a record of 28-4-2 in his four years in West Lafayette. Unlike the apathetic Chicago followers, the Purdue alumni associations were outraged that St. John was trying to poach on conference land. They launched a barrage of telegrams at Ohio State president Dr. George W. Rightmire protesting this breach of unwritten etiquette. Twice the Buckeyes had been caught sneaking; twice they had been rejected. The scolding they were now receiving was embarrassing to Buckeye followers who considered their program to have proud standing and elite possibilities. St. John didn't abandon his stealth methods, but he wisely decided to hunt a little farther from the pack.[17]

By now Ohio football fans were working themselves into a frenzy. The names of prospective coaches were flying everywhere.

Ernie Godfrey, the Buckeyes' line coach had a loyal following, and many boosters pressed for him, but he had in the past expressed misgivings about holding a head coaching job. Coaches from all around the country sent in unsolicited résumés that were often followed by corresponding letters of reference. Alumni groups all over Ohio weighed in with their suggestions. St. John, however, was as comfortable ignoring "advice" as he was receiving it. He listened to certain confidantes but dismissed the pressure from outsiders who had no inside knowledge of the situation. The clock was ticking. Spring practice was closing in, and it had been nearly a full month since Willaman had resigned. St. John, however, was determined to find what he was looking for; he wanted someone with a winning record, a reputation for offense, experience, and a little charisma, just for good measure.

St. John had once coached the Ohio State basketball team (1911–19) and was a member of the national basketball rules committee. A district chairman who sat on the committee with Saint had always intrigued him. His name was Francis Schmidt, and he coached at Texas Christian. He was a helluva basketball coach and was well known on the committee for pushing rules that encouraged fast-break hoops. From what St. John had gathered, Schmidt was just as good and just as interested in excitement when it came to football. An alumnus named Campbell "Honus" Graf, the OSU football captain in 1914 and now part of Saint's inner circle, had also mentioned Schmidt at one point, having learned about him through knowledgeable contacts acquired during his job as a referee. The only thing that troubled St. John was that Schmidt was from the SWC. Saint had never seen Schmidt's teams in action, and people in Ohio had never even heard of him. Even if Schmidt was the right guy, would St. John be able to convince the alumni, reporters, and wolves to give the guy a break? Could he even convince the athletic board to hire him? St. John had a couple of trustworthy contacts in Texas, and he inquired of them as to Schmidt's ability and reputation. The responses were so positive that St. John sent a telegram on February 15, 1934:[18]

> Francis A. Schmidt,
> Texas Christian University,
> Fort Worth, Texas.
>
> Would you be interested football coaching position here?
> What salary necessary to move you? Send me full
> personal history, airmail, special. This is great league,
> but salaries generally are not high. Tell me something
> about offensive system you are using.
>
> (signed)
> L. W. St. John.[19]

That evening, Schmidt telegrammed back his single-line answer:

> Am greatly interested. Letter follows. Single wing double wing
> punt = F. A. Schmidt.

Those who knew Schmidt would not be surprised that half the words were devoted to the "offensive system" question that St. John surely expected to be answered in the letter. And for those who knew St. John, his preemptive claim as to poor pay in the Big 10 was completely in character.[20]

The next day Schmidt sent his follow-up letter by airmail as instructed. "I of course consider your position a big promotion," he wrote in the cover letter, "and would work like the devil to 'pin their ears back' as I have tried to do here." Enclosed was a freeform résumé he called "the dope on my record." He listed three heavyweights as personal references: Pop Warner, Robert Zuppke, and Dana Bible. Schmidt wasn't overly tight with Zuppke or Warner, but they were big names, and Schmidt had impressed them with his knowledge of strategy when attending clinics or conferences they had attended. Dana Bible was a highly respected and popular coach who had successfully managed programs at Texas A&M and Nebraska. He and Schmidt knew each other very well, having run summer clinics together in Texas. After listing these three esteemed references Schmidt added, "Or any coach in the Southwest Conference," apparently convinced that the vanquished would speak highly of their conqueror.[21]

Meanwhile, St. John had continued checking with friends and acquaintances in the Southwest as to Schmidt's true character. It was obvious that Schmidt's teams had prospered, but St. John wanted to know if there were personal problems or traits that would make for an embarrassing or untenable relationship. So far, he liked what he'd heard in regard to Schmidt's intensity and work habits, which starkly contrasted Willaman, who had once proudly declared, "At

Ohio State the boys still have fun playing in games and they still have fun practicing." Such a utopian outlook was admirable, but only if held while one was beating Michigan and winning titles, otherwise it was just idealistic cooing interpreted as a sign of apathy. Schmidt couldn't be apathetic if he tried.[22]

After receiving final reports from multiple sources, St. John identified two Schmidt traits of some concern, which he related to a bigwig Toledo alumnus: "One is to the effect that he [Schmidt] gets a little overgenerous at times in his use of language in his enthusiasm and driving tactics with the football squad. The other is that he has been a little overactive in going after good high school material." St. John was delighted with these problems. "I think that we will be able to keep Schmidt well within bounds," he added, "and the qualities which these criticisms would be indicative of are really pretty worthwhile qualities when it comes to the matter of successful football coaching." It sounded like he had found the right antidote to Willaman's languid ways.[23] Saint was satisfied with his choice. Schmidt was entertaining, affordable, and anxious to capitalize on a big opportunity. His football record was exemplary, and his offense was exciting.

An advisory committee was technically responsible for recommending a final candidate to the athletic board, but they were really just a vehicle for St. John. Upon his asking, they too had done a cursory background check on Schmidt, and, finding no cause for alarm, had recommended the hiring. A telegram was sent to Fort Worth requesting the coach's appearance in Columbus. Schmidt knew it was serious when he received a second telegram from the athletic department's public relations sector requesting, "Please bring all scrapbook material you happen to have. Also, best possible collection and variety of pictures of self." The pictures would be necessary for the newspapers should Schmidt be hired.[24]

St. John would have preferred that Schmidt arrive in Columbus before the news broke, but before that could happen, Ohio and Texas papers were both identifying the unknown Texan as a serious candidate. Any number of people with insider knowledge may have tipped them off. Telegraph operators were especially notorious for moonlighting as anonymous informants. Most Buckeye fans were shocked, having never heard of Schmidt. Some in Texas were surprised as well, and local reporters confronted Schmidt, wanting the scoop. He handled the ambush like it was a hot potato. "I don't know what to say," he told them. "I don't know whether they want anything said about it or not. . . . Yes, we have had some correspondence about my taking a job up there, but nothing has been closed." On Monday night he coached the TCU basketball team in their last game of the season. They trounced Rice 42–25, clinching the second conference title in the school's history, both under Schmidt. The next morning he boarded a train for Ohio. Before stepping onto the train Schmidt explained his visit to the assembled reporters: "Coaching is a profession just like any other. When a man gets a chance at a promotion he should take it. I think everyone will agree with me on that."[25]

Francis Schmidt arrived at Union Station in Columbus via the Pennsylvania Railroad on the evening of Wednesday, February 28. He was met at the depot by St. John and Thomas French, a member of the athletic board. They took him directly to the Deshler-Wallick Hotel, a thousand-room beauty located downtown at the corner of High and Broad streets where all the action happened.[26]

After a nice dinner, Schmidt was taken to one of the hotel's meeting rooms for a small, prearranged assembly. It had been organized by St. John and included all the local newspapermen, some regular faculty, athletic department faculty, coaches, and choice alumni. It was evident to Schmidt that this was no mixer, but rather a thinly veiled combination of job interview and press conference.

Schmidt would have to draw on his bombastic charm, knowing the impression he made was of utmost importance, affecting the athletic board when they met for a vote in the morning.

Schmidt was offered a "hot seat" where he sat alone, surrounded by folding chairs filled with curious onlookers. He was the unknown stranger on display. Cigarette and cigar smoke filled the air, a tangible sign that they had been there waiting for him for some time. Some initial chitchat ensued about the weather and the train trip as each side awkwardly proved its harmlessness. Then, ever so innocently, the conversation turned to the SWC. Now it was chitchat with a purpose. Those assembled were gauging Schmidt's relative success, and he was selling Texas football in an effort to sell himself. Soon, football—the real reason for this meeting—was out in the open. The conversation picked up pace, and the questions to Schmidt became more pointed. Football was Schmidt's obsession, and now he was the picture of deftness and magnetism. When he wanted to be, he could be a star, and tonight he was giving them all he had. Ed Penisten, sportswriter for the *Columbus (Ohio) Dispatch*, had initially felt bad that Schmidt was being ambushed by a bunch of gawkers but quickly fell prey to Schmidt's spell. "His reactions were quick," Penisten wrote. "He talks rapidly and to the point. He never feels around for an answer. His frankness was refreshing." When asked what system of offense he used, Schmidt told them he preferred the "touchdown system," which made everyone laugh. They also got a kick out of his abundant use of slang such as "lookee" and the way he called people "guys." His was not the usual stiff talk of a coach. As the conversation moved more deeply into football strategy Schmidt became more and more animated. The idea that this was a quasi–job interview gave way to his unbridled appetite for Xs and Os. So great was his obsession with football strategy that he temporarily lost his grip on standard interview decorum. Here, Penisten and the rest got their first glimpse of the madness that was Schmidt.[27]

In his three-piece suit and bow tie, Schmidt dropped to his knees on the floor of the hotel room and pulled out a handful of coins, which he scattered on the carpet. These nickels and dimes now represented football players, and he proceeded to preach at breakneck speed the many points of his offensive football system while moving the coins through formations and plays. He turned everything up a notch—his speech, his gestures, his mind. He was a zealot, full of excitement, confidence, and quirks—a cross between John the Baptist and Nero. Converts began to join him on the floor, including osu assistant football coaches Ernie Godfrey and Floyd Stahl. For over an hour he talked football strategy and moved the nickels and dimes around like a kaleidoscope. In his frantic desire to promote his offense, he often reduced his commentary to include descriptions such as, "This guy gets the ball; these guys come around here and get these guys right here; this guy goes through," and so on.[28]

Penisten had never seen anyone so immersed in football strategy and didn't fully understand everything Schmidt was talking about. When the session finally broke up, Penisten looked for and found Godfrey on the way out. Godfrey, the line coach, loved football in his own right and was highly respected by the local writers, so Penisten knew he could get a valid opinion from him. "This guy is good," said a dead-serious Godfrey.[29]

The next day, at noon, the advisory committee offered up their official recommendation of Francis A. Schmidt to the athletic board. Usually, the board accepted and voted accordingly, but on this day, two of the board's eleven members withheld their approval, thwarting a unanimous vote, which they had all agreed earlier would be necessary. Apparently the two abstainers were running a backdoor campaign for another coaching candidate and wanted the rest of the day to make a final pitch, either to the candidate or to St. John. When the meeting adjourned the writers gathered around Saint for news of the Schmidt hiring, but Saint covered for his board and claimed there was a delay because *he himself* "wanted more time to talk things over" with Schmidt. The board would meet again the next day.[30]

Stuck in interview purgatory, Schmidt took a tour of the campus that afternoon. A late-winter storm had left snow on the ground, something Schmidt had not had to worry about much at his previous coaching venues. He made his way to the enormous Ohio Stadium, nicknamed "The Horseshoe" for its open-ended shape. Schmidt envisioned himself on the sidelines, leading Ohio State in battle against some of the nation's best teams as a loyal crowd roared with approval. The Horseshoe's permanent seating capacity (not including temporary stands) was 62,210, three times greater than that of Amon Carter Stadium where Texas Christian hosted its games. If Schmidt was intimidated by the weather or grandeur it didn't show. He was jovial and confident, declaring himself to be "sold" on Ohio State. Now it was just a matter of Ohio State's being sold on him.[31]

The Ohio State athletic board met again the next day, March 2, and after more debating the two dissenting board members fell in line. Everyone agreed to offer Schmidt a contract. The school's president and the board of trustees still had to approve the hiring, but there was almost no chance they would not. The contract would officially commence on July 1—a three-year contract, which was an unprecedented departure from the annual contract offered to most school employees or coaches. The athletic board reasoned that this would keep the wolves at bay while the new coach built his program. It was also a sign of the times. In the increasingly mad rush to get what were considered the best coaches, many colleges had begun to offer multi-year contracts as an additional incentive, something that had been previously frowned upon as it made the schools appear to be overemphasizing football, which indeed they were (there was, and still is, too much money involved in big-time college football to pretend it isn't a great commercial fundraiser. Girl Scouts sell cookies, and colleges sell football). Many raised their eyebrows at Schmidt's three-year deal, but mostly they were satisfied that Ohio State was keeping pace in the collegiate football arms race.[32]

Schmidt's agreed-upon salary was $7,500 annually, with the promise of $500 yearly raises should the budget permit. These figures were not officially released, and the newspapers, left to surmise or trust faulty sources, incorrectly pegged Schmidt's salary somewhere between $6,000 and $7,000. Schmidt's actual pay was near the bottom of the Big 10 salary spectrum. According to St. John (thanks to inside information from Griffith, undoubtedly), Doc Spears at Wisconsin was making $10,000, Ossie Solem was just hired at Iowa for $8,000, Illinois was paying Robert Zuppke $10,400 before the Depression and $9,000 now, and Dick Hanley was being paid $9,000 at Northwestern. Still, Schmidt's OSU salary was a nice raise from his TCU pay and was an exceptional amount of money considering the Depression. Taking inflation into account, Schmidt's $7,500 in 1934 was equal to about $119,000 in 2008. To further put it in perspective, recall that the school was paying only $10,000 to hire twenty-five new entry-level teachers for the fall.[33]

Because of this perceived inequity, St. John worked a little deal with the university whereby Schmidt got $6,500 of his pay from the athletic department (thus the newspaper estimate), with the other $1,000 being quietly paid from university funds in order to spread things out and lessen the envy. Many school academics were already alarmed that a veritable ruffian (the way most coaches were viewed) should get a three-year contract and several thousand dollars for merely conducting a sport. Additionally, this head coach would be named the director of physical education, technically deeming him "Professor Schmidt."[34]

The physical education department was a relatively new development at most colleges, and some academics were still getting used to the idea that one could earn a degree on the basis of such a shallow discipline. Worse yet, the football coach often had rather free reign over half this department, whose simple requirements attracted many athletes of dubious intellect or ambition. Not so pleased with this arrangement were the noncoaching, quasi-academic men responsible for running the other half of the department as a legitimate educational pursuit.

Afternoon papers carried the news of Francis Schmidt's hiring on the front page. As word of the Buckeyes' new football coach spread across Ohio it was received with more curiosity than celebration. Bill Snypp, sports editor of the *Lima (Ohio) News*, offered a backhanded endorsement: "All other sources apparently exhausted, Ohio State has turned to Fort Worth for its successor for Sam Willaman. . . . Little is known in Ohio of Texas Christian educationally or athletically, hence there can be little written of Mr. Schmidt." Having consulted his old *Spalding's Official Foot Ball Guide*, Snypp was at least able to buoy his readers with the fact that Schmidt's teams had flourished in the swc, whatever the hell that meant. Both editor and reader struggled to get used to the idea that an unknown outsider would take over such a precious and important thing as their Buckeye football program. It was as though some yahoo in chaps and spurs had just been elected president. Unlike all the other coaches in the Big 10, Schmidt had no previous connection to the conference as a player, coach, friend, or relative. "He is a strange face in a strange land," wrote Snypp. "A coach of nineteen years' experience but new to his latest assignment. We hope the 'wolves' give him the break he deserves."[35]

The sports editors at the two Fort Worth daily newspapers were sad to see Schmidt go and were quick to offer unsolicited information to their Ohio counterparts. Schmidt had left a lasting impression on the Texas writers, and they wanted Ohio to understand they were getting someone special. "You're in for the thrill of your life," declared the ancient Pop Boone of the *Fort Worth (Texas) Press.* "[Schmidt] started out last fall with a firm determination to delete his practice language because some of the dear brethren deplored rumors that he used terrible language. But it was a no go." Boone also passed along an example of Schmidt's obsession for thinking up football plays: "They tell of a bridge game he was in— three tables in his own home. He fell to studyin' a hand. Minute after minute ticked by. All three tables finally fell silent. All at once he stirred, scratched his head, and bellered: 'Aw, shit, that won't work.' . . . He never misses a game—high school, junior college, or any other kind when he can make them."[36]

Flem Hall, editor of the *Fort Worth (Texas) Star-Telegram*, praised him even further: "An omnivorous reader of papers and magazines, Schmidt is familiar with every football player and coach, both high school and university, in Texas." As for a general description, Hall wrote that "[Schmidt] is a dynamo walking. His rather sharp face with prominent nose and keen eyes only hints at the remarkable mental alertness and nervous energy it masks. He is never quiet. Whether he is strumming his mandolin or scrimmaging on the gridiron he is likely to have his coat off, sleeves up, and collar open, sweating and going like he is fighting a fire."[37]

Even though they were losing their beloved, eccentric coach the Fort Worth editors described Schmitty with pride. Not only was he their local guy, he had been born and raised on the prairie. His move to Ohio State validated the SWC. His promotion deemed him the banner carrier for the entire region's brand of football. After all, Schmidt's new home, the Big 10, was considered by experts to be the home of the nation's best football, not just for its quality of play, but for its history, size, and prestige as well.

The Big 10 was founded in 1896 and is today the oldest surviving Division I athletic conference in America. It was created in order to regulate eligibility and recruiting amongst its members and to promote the caretaking of amateurism. Its official name is "The Intercollegiate Conference of Faculty Representatives," but that proved a bit bulky, so it was soon nicknamed "The Western Conference," its western-ness being relative to the era. Not long afterward, it acquired a second nickname—the "Big 7"—and over the years as its membership increased it became the "Big 9" and finally the "Big 10" when Michigan rejoined in 1917 after a decade of absence. Today the conference has eleven members but continues to be known almost exclusively as the "Big 10."[38]

The "big" part of Big 10 was very appropriate and getting more so every day as the conference's student population grew with abandon. Based on full-time students in residence during the mid 1930s, five of the conference's schools (Minnesota, Illinois, Ohio State, Michigan, and Wisconsin) were among the nation's ten largest, with Northwestern and Chicago among the next ten. With the conference's football teams being assembled from such a staggering amount of students, the odds favored their superiority on the gridiron.[39]

Besides the great teams and huge campus populations, the Big 10 also had a reputation for enforcing the strongest code of conduct for amateur athletics among major conferences. Bob Zuppke of Illinois called the Big 10 "the anchor of amateur athletics in America." This reputation was a big deal before the 1950s. Not only was amateurism held to a higher standard at that time, but conferences were in charge of self-policing where morality was concerned. The NCAA, which rules today with absolute power and draconian sensibilities, existed in 1934 merely as a purveyor of opinions. It had little bark and even less bite.[40]

Of course everyone knows that written codes of ethics are really just a set of challenges to be overcome on the way to accomplishing goals of greed, and the Big 10 members abused the spirit of their code with gusto and imagination. But as far as the public was concerned, and as far as the papers pretended to be, the Big 10 was the ultimate caretaker of amateur sports in all of academia. St. John could only cross his fingers and hope that his new head coach of football would not embarrass the school or the Big 10 by importing any of the maverick morals he'd learned on the notoriously loose prairie.

Late the next morning, March 3, the newly appointed Schmidt held court in his hotel room at the Deshler-Wallick. The reporters who crowded his room came bearing gifts, namely a schedule and a roster. Schmidt, busy with touring and talking, had not had the time to calmly appraise the logistics of his new venture, and the reporters were anxious to study his reactions. Sitting in an easy chair, Schmidt first looked over the schedule. It was mean—conference play out of the gate, and only one genuine patsy the whole season. "Lookee, that's plenty tough," Schmidt declared, endearing himself to the crowd with his slang. At TCU he had always opened the season with three or four lesser opponents. It was good for the team's record, boosted their confidence, and allowed a margin of error while new players and plays were being introduced. Then again, TCU played a dozen games a year. Ohio State, under Big 10 law, could only play eight, and St. John intended to make each one of those both interesting and profitable.[41]

After further complaining about the schedule, Schmidt moved on to some good news: the Buckeyes' roster. It was twice the size of TCU's, and the players as a whole were much bigger than anything he'd enjoyed before. Although only four of eleven starters would be returning in the fall, the reporters assured Schmidt that his sophomore class would be strong. As for freshman, The Big 10 did not allow them to play on the varsity squad or to play games against freshman squads from other schools.[42]

After enjoying Schmidt's assessments, the writers began to ask questions of the "husky, bronzed Nebraskan." What about Ohio State's current assistant coaches? They will all stay, Schmidt thought. (The only change in staff possible was the addition of "Bear" Wolf, his line coach at TCU, but that was far from being decided yet.[43]) What was Schmidt's chief hobby? Football, he replied. Okay, how about just plain recreation? The movies.[44] Was he worried about the notoriously demanding followers of Buckeye football? "They tell me this is a tough spot," admitted Schmidt, "but I'm firmly convinced that Columbus and Ohio State are no worse than hundreds of other college towns." He would be firmly convinced otherwise down the road.[45]

What about Michigan? They wanted to know if this outsider fully appreciated the intensity of OSU's rivalry with the Wolverines. Schmidt smiled and replied, "They put their pants on one leg at a time, the same way we do." It was a folksy colloquialism he'd picked up from the Plains, and the gathered reporters loved it. They furiously scribbled down the gem on their little tablets. It was the perfect blend of humor, irreverence, and arrogance. The statement instantly became part of the rivalry's lore, and before the year was done it would spawn the Gold Pants Club, an Ohio State tradition celebrating victories over the Wolverines by issuing little golden trouser-shaped charms to those participating in the conquest. Engraved on the front are both the score of the game and the year in which the victory took place. The little pants are deeply treasured and are not intended for the open market where they could fetch thousands of dollars.[46]

For the time being, Schmidt was the picture of unflappable confidence. The boys from the papers found themselves mesmerized by his combination of humor, bluster, and slang. He was like some sort of fictional character who had walked off the pages of a screwball novel. He was either a brilliant coach or an insane imposter, but either way their jobs had suddenly become much more interesting.

Having delivered some good copy, Schmidt excused himself, explaining that he needed to make his way to the university's faculty club. There, at a noon luncheon in the North Wicker Room, Schmidt was officially introduced as Ohio State's new director of football. All the important people in the Buckeyes' football universe were there for the unofficial coronation, a group that included everyone from president Rightmire to athletic board chairman Clarence Laylin to Sid Gillman, last fall's team captain. Schmidt, impressed with Gillman's knowledge and passion for football, would talk the senior into being part of the coaching staff during spring football.[47]

The next day Schmidt boarded a train for his two-day trip back to Fort Worth. He left having promised he would arrange to be in Columbus for spring practice by securing a leave of absence from TCU. This he did upon arrival in Fort Worth, submitting his letter of resignation at the same time.

Meanwhile, back in Columbus, St. John caught up on all the correspondence he had been forced to neglect during Schmidt's hiring frenzy. He needed to write letters to those coaching candidates who had been passed over and thank-you notes to the many alumni who had kindly offered up their advice on who should fill the coaching vacancy. To all of them, St. John offered his gratitude along with assurances that Schmidt was the right choice.

There was no guarantee, of course, that Schmidt would make him look good, but St. John was pleased to find on his desk congratulatory telegrams from luminaries like Ray Morrison and Phog Allen, who declared Schmidt's hiring a triumph for Ohio State. Even the great Bob Zuppke was "very enthusiastic and quite complimentary" about the signing. The affirmation of such successful minds had to be valued. But lest St. John get too confident, he also received counterweight messages like the note from a Texas friend who laughingly reminded the athletic director, "You'll have the job of Christian missionary to convert the heathen Texan."[48]

St. John may even have suffered a small twinge of remorse a week later, after Schmidt had returned to Fort Worth and got behind on his correspondence. This caused the pair's letters to cross in the mail, which lead to a disjointed and frustrating postal conversation (long-distance phone calls were still expensive and doubly difficult to justify in a Depression-fueled budget mess). Not only did Schmidt get behind, but he was always in such a hurry to get his letters posted that he would forget to include information that served as the purpose for the letter in the first place. Schmidt's first letter to Saint didn't arrive for some time, and when it did there was nothing enclosed but a travel expense report and a short note. Already a bit edgy from the wait and now perplexed by the contents of the letter, St. John wrote back, "I note at the bottom your written note to the effect that you evidently forgot to enclose this expense account in your other letter, which leads me to inquire, what 'other letter?!' Up to now I have had no word from you since you left."[49]

The confusion only grew worse when they tried to arrange schedules. Saint wanted to be in Columbus when Schmidt arrived to begin spring football at the end of March, but both men had conflicting commitments that made this impossible. Through letters and telegrams that kept crossing each other, Saint made it clear that this was okay, and Schmidt kept apologizing "like the devil" as he wanted to get off on a good foot. Finally, sorry he ever brought it up, Saint wrote back sternly, "I believe I already wrote to you to the effect that your inability to get here before I had to leave is quite understood and is perfectly satisfactory to me." Dealing with Schmidt's manic personality was going to take some getting used to, especially if Saint refused to spring for a couple of long-distance phone calls.[50]

One thing that *was* resolved in this postal chaos was the assistant coaching situation. Schmidt declared he was "satisfied and pleased" with the current assistant coaches—Godfrey, Larkins, and Stahl—saying, "They are as nice a bunch of men as I have ever met." Even if they were nice, it was rare for a newly hired head coach to accept in its entirety the remaining staff of the former regime. But Schmidt never seemed overly concerned about the makeup of his staff. He accepted five head coaching positions in his career, and in all those transitions he brought an assistant with him just one time. We'll discuss later why Schmidt wasn't too concerned about who his assistants were or weren't.[51]

Although Saint hadn't bargained for the craziness that accompanied Schmidt, he was certain that the new coach's obsession for offensive football would be of great value. Willaman's record had been very strong, but his brand of football was less than thrilling, which, when combined with the effects of the Depression, had led to declining attendance for Ohio State football. St. John figured if Schmidt could at least post the same record as Willaman but do it in an interesting fashion, both attendance and revenue would climb once again.

And if Schmidt really was an offensive genius, his services had never been more in demand. Since World War I scoring in college football games had continually dropped. During the 1933 season, teams averaged a measly 12 points per game. This was almost a full point less than the previous year's average and a full touchdown less than the average in 1922. Defense had achieved the upper hand as it continually faced the same tired offensive schemes, many of which had remained virtually unchanged since 1906. Recent rule changes attempted to open things up, but after decades of ultra-conservative strategizing, coaches were fearful of embracing the new rules, let alone exploring their possibilities. The risk of looking foolish outweighed the desire to run headlong down an uncharted path. The game of football needed men of imagination and daring to capitalize on these changes, and Francis Schmidt was the perfect man at the perfect time. The next phase in modern football was at hand, and it had been a long time coming.[52]

Four. The Open-Game Movement

In 1893 after witnessing a football game, one Ohio newspaper reporter described what he'd seen as "a kind of battle, in which the chief purpose of each side is to disable, wound, and knock out its opponents as quickly and severely as it can be done without using knives, revolvers, or slingshots. Less attention is paid to the real science of the game than to kicking, slugging, wrenching, tripping down, and crushing the undermost man. Arms and legs are knocked out of joint or broken; hips and shoulders are dislocated; noses are mashed and eyes are blacked; contests are won, not by skill in playing, but by wounding and placing the opponents hors de combat."[1]

Such was the condition of American football in the 1890s, some twenty years after its birth. What had started out as a wide-open rugby-like game had, through a series of rule changes and resulting strategies, turned into a closed, violent game wherein spectators hardly saw the ball except during punts. Forward passing was still illegal, meaning that every play was a running play. The offensive linemen locked arms and legs, and ball carriers were pushed and pulled into the line as part of standard strategy. The starting eleven generally played the entire game, and the physical abuse they exchanged was a black-and-blue badge of courage.

Yet even as the game had devolved into a writhing slugfest, the hoopla surrounding the contests had continually grown. The handful of battles waged by each school during the fall was spectacular, and the investment on the part of the players—the willingness to surrender their bodies for school pride—was the purest, most honest of all sporting endeavors. These titanic struggles had created an air of drama, and the anticipation of each contest had created pomp and a certain amount of delirium that other sports just couldn't match. The celebration had outgrown the student population and was attracting growing numbers of local citizens and newspapermen. Where there is such interest there is profit, and where there is profit there is ethical compromise—in this case, recruiting and eligibility abuse. While school administrators were pleased with the growing revenue stream, they were beginning to understand that a monster had been unleashed. Besides the internal, academically related abuse was the outside fanaticism—a concoction of violence, drinking, betting, hysteria, and moral turpitude. Football had turned fall weekends on campus into veritable Roman holidays—not exactly in line with the school officials' desire for decorous academic pursuit. All of this bacchanalian turbulence left them struggling to find a safe stance on intercollegiate football. But even more troubling for the administrators was one particular aspect of this sport gone awry: the increasing number of serious injuries and deaths. Dozens of players across the country were being killed each year while playing this "game." Most of them involved high school or unorganized sandlot games, but universities were the creators and caretakers of the sport, and the public began to look to them for answers. A few college administrators and disappointed newspapermen spoke loudly regarding the evils of football, using as a lightning rod this issue of physical danger. Some talked seriously about abolishing football on campus or of making it illegal. Legislation in Nebraska and Indiana sought to ban the game. The game's playing rules were revised again and again by national rulemakers, each time opening the game up slightly, but not enough to make a real impact. The physical tragedies continued unabated. By the end of the 1905 season some had had enough. Columbia and Northwestern dropped their football programs altogether. California and Stanford switched to rugby. President Teddy Roosevelt—a lover of football—intervened, imploring the colleges to satisfy the public before the game was outlawed on a large scale. In answer to his plea, a precursor to the NCAA was formed for the sole purpose of making the game safer. Most of the members agreed it was time to take drastic action with regard to the rules. The game needed to move back toward its roots by encouraging a more open, flowing style of play as opposed to its current boxed-in state, where all the action was crowded in the middle of the field and ground was gained one brutal thrust at a time. What resulted was a radical revision of the game, a revision that would take several decades to reach its potential. But, for the time being, it was enough to salvage the sport.[2]

This all-important revision involved a series of core rule changes between 1906 and 1912 that separated antique football from modern football. Players' safety was the impetus for most of the overhaul, but not all the changes were embraced by the old guard, who only begrudgingly compromised so that football could live on. Forward passing was allowed for the first time ever, albeit with constantly changing restrictions. Downs and yardage requirements changed so that instead of a team's needing 3 downs to make 5 yards, they now needed 4 downs to make 10 yards. The game was shortened from 70 minutes to 60 minutes and was divided into quarters. The value of a field goal was dropped from 5 points to 4 and finally to 3, while a touchdown was increased from 5 points to 6. On offense a team was now required to have at least seven men on the line of scrimmage when the ball was snapped in order to curb mass-momentum plays. An offensive lineman could no longer pull or shove his ball-carrying teammate through the line nor lock arms with his linemates. A player who had been replaced by a substitute could now return to action the following quarter, whereas before he was prohibited from reentering the game. The short axis, or roundness of the ball, was reduced from 27 inches to 23 inches, making it a skinnier "watermelon" although still too fat for proper gripping. The size of the field was finalized at 100-by-53 yards, and end zones were added.[3]

This period of rule changes represents the final layer of bedrock for American football. The first modern period had begun. With touchdowns now being twice as valuable as field goals (more if you included the point after the touchdown) the indisputable objective of a team was now to cross the goal line. To get to that goal line, a team needed to gain twice as much yardage per set of downs, but now they could use a forward pass to aid in this expanded quest. These core elements now constitute the very soul of American football.

Strategically, even after all of these changes, the initial modern period (approximately 1906–40) still looked very different from today's game (the neo-modern period? Some might say today is the third modern period. "Modern" is a term easily applied but rarely questioned or revoked). At that time substitution was still not truly "free," meaning there was no distinction between offensive and defensive players. The same guys played both sides of the ball, sometimes throughout an entire game. Also, the ball itself was still too round, making it difficult to throw with accuracy. These factors, along with the game's historical mindset, combined to keep football under the thumb of a Victorian philosophy that guided strategy until after World War II. This philosophy held that football was a game of defense and risk-aversion. A team sought victory by allowing the opponent to score less. One played not so much to win, but rather not to lose, and a game's ending in a tie was wholly accept-able. Field position and ball protection were the paramount con-cerns on offense, and scoring merely a bonus residual.

Turnovers were the ultimate taboo, and even though teams did all they could to avoid them, many factors from this period con-tributed to their inevitable occurrence. Fields were not nearly as pristine as they are today. Any sort of bad weather would create sloppy conditions unsuitable for safe ballhandling. On top of that, the long-sleeved woolen jerseys worn at the time were notorious for becoming bulky and slippery as they sopped up the muck. And of course teams primitively used the same ball throughout the entire game if possible, bad weather or not.

The cautious attitude literally started with the coin toss. The win-ner nearly always chose to kick off, thus giving their opponent poor field position to start the game. If there was a healthy wind blow-ing that day, a team might choose to receive with the wind, hoping to continually pin their foe early, force a turnover, and get that al-mighty first score. With so little scoring and so much hesitation on the part of the offense, the first points were hugely significant. And this hesitancy extended beyond the opening kickoff. Many coaches, utilizing an old option left in the rulebook, chose to kick off rather than receive after being scored upon. They were more concerned with the opponent's field position than with obtaining possession of the ball. Fielding Yost, one of football's patriarchs, held firm on this idea deep into the 1930s, mocking those who disregarded the religion of field position. "If a football team wants to rub its pants against its own goal posts all afternoon, it should receive the kick-off—receive, receive, receive." The occurrence of a long, sustained drive from the offense was so rare that it was disregarded as a real threat. Instead, teams often punted, each side waiting for its oppo-nent to make a mistake.[4]

Because of this preoccupation with caution, punting on the

second or third down was not only common, it was standard practice, especially if a team held weak field position or would need to pass in order to achieve the yardage necessary for a first down. Teams trapped inside their own 10-yard line usually punted on first down rather than risking a turnover. The player chosen to punt was usually a backfield man (there were no special teams) and he was expected to punt long and out of bounds where the ball couldn't be returned. Today, punting is regarded as a bit of a nuisance, but for decades it was a prized skill that garnered players fame and decided the outcome of games. A newspaper's game recap often began with a synopsis of how one team's punter had terrorized the other squad. "When in doubt, punt" was the overriding order given to quarterbacks.

Within this code of caution, forward passing was discouraged and was used only as an occasional surprise or as a move of desperation when a team was trailing late in the game. The few passes that teams actually threw were most often based off the sweep (today's rarely seen halfback option). As a matter of fact, pass blocking (as we know it today) wasn't really taught, meaning that linemen didn't use the controlled retreat they do now when forming a pocket for the quarterback. Passing was considered a bit of disguised trickery solely intended to free up the running game. Why was this? After its legalization in 1906, wouldn't teams jump at the chance to exploit such a radical new weapon?

Conventional wisdom says that forward passing would have immediately changed football strategy. After all, the defensive team had always played all its men near the line of scrimmage, knowing that a run was coming (the exception being a solitary safety playing deep for the punt that could come at any time). The newly legal forward pass meant that defenses would now have to guard against more options and cover much more open space, all at the cost of a fortified line. Sort of a damned-if-you-do-and-damned-if-you-don't quandary that would leave defensives tentative and offenses rubbing their hands together in evil anticipation of the horror they might now induce. But it didn't work out that way. For one thing, the game's reigning aristocracy, led by Walter Camp, may have grudgingly allowed legalization of the forward pass, but they made sure it came with some harsh restrictions, such as loss of possession following an incompletion or out-of-bounds throw. And even if there had been no legislative boundaries, there was still a problem with the size of the football. Even reduced from its original near-roundness, the ball still measured 23 inches around the middle: too fat for a man's hand to properly grip for hard, accurate throwing.[5]

The throws resembled something that a shot-putter might heave. Because of these lobs, sophisticated timing between receiver and thrower was nearly impossible, and route running never developed. Most "patterns" consisted of an end or wingback's releasing from the line, running to a point, turning around, and playing jump ball with the defenders who began to gather as the ball slowly arced toward earth. If the pass was caught, the ball generally advanced no further as the receiver could easily be downed upon the ball's reentry through the atmosphere. Pass interference was generously interpreted in favor of the defense and was rarely called. Throughout the first modern period, passing did evolve, but only relatively. Even near the end of this period, pass completion hovered around 35 percent, and passing resulted in far more interceptions than touchdowns. In this environment of over-cautious strategy, coaches almost never allowed their teams to rely on a play that could lead to so many negatives: turnover, incompletion, and loss of yardage due to sack or penalty. Additionally, teams faced the problem of stamina. With players' staying in the game to play both offense and defense, they had to pace themselves to a certain extent. A signal-caller was doing his ends a great disservice if he required them to run consecutive "routes." He would gas them, making them less effective for the more important acts of blocking and tackling. Sammy Baugh operated on the cutting edge of forward passing philosophy but still recalls the strategic compromises that were required in the 1930s:[6]

> Wide receivers are just wide receivers [today] and they only play half the game. When we played and the fourth quarter came around, everybody, and I mean everybody on the field, was dog-tired. We paced ourselves and we had gimmicks to help us in that. For example, if I knew on a play that I was going to throw to the right, I might shorten the pattern for the men on the left so that they didn't have to run so far. . . . I would never send a man deep unless it was absolutely necessary. You had to protect your players.[7]

One can see why this new form of "attack" was not readily embraced as anything more than a gimmick or an act of last resort. The risk (turnover, sack) and cost (stamina) were too great, while the benefits were sporadic at best. Moreover, the occasional pass was considered acceptable, but passing too often earned a team the reputation of being a little less than manly. The play was legal, but it skirted some of the ruggedness that separated football from the genteel sports. Some detractors even mockingly compared football tossing to the game of basketball, where boys and girls played in little shorts and avoided physical contact, per the rules. "Pop" Warner called the forward pass "a bastard offspring of real football" and "always believed that the legalizing of forward passing was a mistake." Even though passing was barely used by most coaches, Warner was already horrified by its legitimate place at the table. "Within a few years the rules committee will have to curb its use by further rules to prevent it from dominating the game at the expense of rushing and kicking the ball and to keep the game from being considered 'passball' instead of football."[8]

Some of Warner's famous contemporaries actually liked the pass, but they were just as reluctant to use the maneuver. John Heisman, the renowned coach and trophy namesake, was one of the strongest proponents for legalizing the forward pass in 1906, yet twenty years later his timidity for throwing was perfectly in line with the rest of the cautious coaching community. "Don't disclose that you are going to pass," was his number one axiom for throwing. Without sophisticated routes and timing, a team had to hide their intention to pass, or the defense would easily defend it. Taking it a step further, Heisman declared, "A forward pass should never be attempted inside your own 30-yard line; should it be intercepted you will, in all probability, lose a perfectly good game of football right then and there." Knute Rockne was even more cautious when referencing his rules for throwing at Notre Dame: "He [the passer] will never take unnecessary chances. He is told that at the start of the game when the score is even and in his own territory, he must not forward pass. He must not forward pass in the second half when he is ahead. He must not forward pass when near the other team's goal line nor must he forward pass when his running game is working well." This was the essence of Victorian football—field position, ball security, and caution, caution, caution. Giving up just one touchdown was critical when teams played not to lose.[9]

That is not to say the forward pass didn't have its day in the sun. When Knute Rockne was still playing for Notre Dame in 1913, he and teammate Gus Dorais broke out a passing attack in a big game against Army that was so unexpected and so successful that many fans still wrongly believe the forward pass originated on that day. During the 1920 Rose Bowl, California shocked Ohio State with passes (completing 11 of 13), including one monster off the hand of Brick Mueller that traveled an estimated 57 yards through the air.

Swede Oberlander of Dartmouth threw for 6 touchdowns against rival Cornell in 1925. These were tremendous performances, and many want to believe these examples of passing had some effect in changing the game, but the reality is that these were just glimmers, freaks, and exceptions. Teams threw very little before these isolated episodes, and they threw very little after them as well. Even years later, in 1939, a typical major college team only completed 5 passes per game for an average of 66 yards. Passing was not truly embraced for many decades following its legalization.[10]

Coaches who were successful or manly—and most often both—confined their base strategy to the much-safer running game that had worked in various forms since the game's beginning. Rather than tinker with the legalized but unwieldy passing game, football strategists of this first modern period used their imaginations to devise a better running game. Dr. Henry Williams, coach at the University of Minnesota, introduced a system based on multiple players'—often the entire backfield—shifting almost simultaneously with the snap of the ball. The shifting confused opponents and allowed his offense to generate some physical momentum early. This quasi-legal theory made its way to Notre Dame where eventually Knute Rockne perfected it. Those who played for Rockne and later became coaches—and there were scores of them—almost always imported the Notre Dame system to be used as their new team's offense. This system featured a box formation and well-designed wide runs using an end split 2 yards off the line.

But the biggest innovation of this first modern period was a run-based scheme developed by Pop Warner while he was coaching at the Carlisle Indian Institute in Pennsylvania. There he developed a series of plays run from his "A-Formation," later called the "Single Wing." Fully deployed in 1912, this arrangement focused on power running. Its strengths were pulling linemen, double team blocks, and an unbalanced line (both guards on one side of center). The idea was to mobilize the team's power to one side of the ball and puncture a hole in the bunched-up defensive line. Warner added enough sweeps and reverses along with the occasional pass to significantly thwart the defense from overbuilding to the strong side. The Single Wing quickly became the foremost look of offensive football for three decades; until the early 1940s few schools ran anything other than the Warner System, the Notre Dame System, or a slightly modified version of either. Both packages were run from one or two base formations and, depending on the coach, usually consisted of about two dozen standard plays plus a handful of gimmicks. By today's standards these schemes would be considered incredibly simple. They were so simple, in fact, that soon after World War I, their effectiveness began showing signs of exhaustion.[11]

The very popularity of these two systems began dooming them. The players who ran them were the same players defending them, and they had seen almost nothing but the same football strategy since they had learned to play the game. Predictability was giving defense the upper hand, and scoring was dropping. Still nearly every coach continued to use the same basic methods of offense because offense was not about eating up large chunks of yardage; it was still about safety and field position. Football's Victorian philosophy soldiered on, ignoring the modernizing world around it. Not everyone, however, was content with sleep-inducing offense.

Even as postwar scoring was declining under the weight of tired, common football, an open-game movement had begun. As with most movements, its start was slow, its proponents were isolated, and its acceptance was reluctant. Those involved had no higher goal than to better their teams through contrarian strategy. The timing was good in the sense that American society was caught up in a transition from brawn to brains. A handful of coaches simply tried to apply the lesson to football. But considering that football had always been defined by its brawn, the open-game movement would be a tough sell.

Robert Zuppke of the University of Illinois was the most well known of the postwar experimenters. He'd actually been fooling with gadget plays many years earlier and had proven himself unafraid to try new things. This fit his personality. The little German with the thick accent was not your typical coach. An artist, philosopher, and intellectual amongst roughnecks, he was considered an iconic figure in football circles because of his persona alone. As for his coaching record, his teams were up and down, but when they were up they were great, winning or sharing in four national championships during a stretch lasting from 1914 to 1927. He's most remembered for coaching Red Grange, for introducing the huddle as a standard element of offense, and for concocting a series of zany plays with equally zany names. Today, whenever a team uses a gadget play of any sort there is a good chance it will be called a "flea flicker," a term derived from a single play created by Zuppke and named for the play's quick backfield pitches and the way they were tossed with fingers flung like a man trying to flick a flea. A handful of Zuppke's other equally fun plays were nicknamed the "Flying Trapeze," "Razzle-dazzle," and "Whirligig." These tricky plays were not part of the standard offense that Zuppke ran from his old-fashioned T-Formation, but their rare deployment could be effective, especially during this period when play calling was so pedestrian. Zuppke included a relatively large amount of passing and open play for the era, but it was the gimmick plays with the whimsical names that really stood out. Because Zuppke's crazy plays were so highly engineered and well publicized, because he won games in an elite conference, and because he was so beloved by his contemporaries, his reputation for daring was celebrated while others with the same whimsy might have been dismissed as ostentatious. So, if nothing else, Zuppke lent the open game some credibility.[12]

Zuppke may have been the big name connected to the open-game movement, but its headquarters were really in the Southwest. Some claimed the region's warm weather was conducive to experimenting with ballhandling. Others thought the open game gave the region's ragtag outfits a better chance to compete with deeper teams from more established parts of the country. Then again, it might have boiled down to that maverick independence that's always been the basis of pride for Southwest folks, particularly in Texas—the *Lone* Star state—where even the cattle walk with a swagger. Anything unanimously accepted on the nation's coasts has always been viewed with suspicion down where cactus and oil derricks grow side by side. Whatever the reason, there was no denying that an advanced state of experimentation was taking place on the prairie.

Take, for example, Frank Bridges of Baylor University. Bridges's specialty was exploiting loopholes in the rules, which he did with all the aplomb of a mob lawyer. He proudly claimed twenty or more rule changes to be the result of his strategies and experiments. He rigged up a chest harness to aid his linemen in their blocking (now outlawed), created a hidden ball play were the ball was snapped to the guard who hid it under his generous stomach (now outlawed), used an overinflated ball to frustrate his opponents (now outlawed), and often had his kick returners punt the ball upon receiving it (the ultimate quick kick—now outlawed). But Bridges was no freak show act. He also used his imagination to create a series of running plays for his tackles (Russell Blailock scored 8 touchdowns in 1922 from his tackle position), a clever wedge-blocking scheme for his linemen, and a great delayed blitz package on defense.[13]

Even more successful in spreading the word of openness was Ray Morrison at smu. He specialized in using the forward pass as an integral part of the offense. The former Vanderbilt quarterback had been impressed by the success of the passing game when employed

by teams trailing and desperate in the fourth quarter. He wondered
why it wouldn't work just as well, or even better, when it *wasn't* expected. "I found that our opponents' knowing we might pass on
any down from anywhere improved our opportunity to gain on running plays." Again, the running game came first, but Morrison's
Mustangs had learned to disregard some of the dangers of forward
passing. The number and variety of passes employed by Morrison
and his boys in a typical game was nothing like today, but this attack was bold in relative terms, and on occasion it was spectacular. Of particular note was a trip SMU made to New York in 1928, a
game that would cement the reputations of Morrison and the SWC
forever.[14]

The opponent was a powerful Army team who, because of their
independent status and generous definition of eligibility, had trouble scheduling top-notch eastern foes. This made them open to interregional opponents, and both sides benefited. Army was able to
play exotic teams, and the visitors got a chance to put on a show for
the godlike Gotham press. Notre Dame had been the first to exploit
the opportunity, wisely saving their forward passing show for the famous Army visit in 1913. SMU was just as smart, saving the indus-
trial-strength version of their passing game for the Cadets in 1928.
Although SMU lost 14–13 on a failed extra-point attempt, the ultra-
conservative eastern football establishment was dumbfounded as
the Mustangs attempted a staggering 36 passes from every part of
the field. This was an unheard-of barrage of passes, obscene even
by Southwest standards. As if that wasn't enough, SMU's brightly at-
tired jazz band and a raucous cheering section that had traveled
from Texas augmented the outrageousness of the whole spectacle. The Southwest visitors and their brand of football went beyond
what was advertised. The easterners were not ready to grant the
SWC major-league status on this game alone, but Morrison's Mustangs had earned their region a spot on the football landscape—a

spot where football carried its pistols in plain sight and didn't apologize for drinking before lunch. Texan football was still viewed as a novelty, but now it was viewed as a dangerous novelty.[15]

At the forefront of this stirring on the prairie was Francis Schmidt. He was not just one of the original contributing members of the open-game movement—he was its most obsessed member. Schmidt built his system not only by contributing original thought, but by adapting, plagiarizing, studying, and contemplating offensive football like no man before him or after him. He absorbed everything he saw and heard, then filled in the blank spots with his notorious imagination. Schmidt's tireless interest in football strategy meant that his system was continually growing at a rate previously unknown to the sport even if his fame wasn't.

During this period simplicity was the goal, and this was reflected in skinny playbooks. Because less was safer, and safety was the paramount concern of offensive football, giving a team too many plays was considered foolhardy. Pop Warner, whose namesake system reigned supreme within the sport, thought that "about twenty, or no more than twenty-five plays, are all any team should have." Other successful coaches of the era advised likewise. Howard Jones (USC) gave his quarterback "twenty to thirty-five plays," and Lou Little (Columbia) felt that "two formations and eight or ten basic plays from each are ample for any team." Most coaches agreed with the philosophy of former Army coach Charles Daly who explained his use of twelve standard plays by saying, "More than this number would probably prove burdensome and lead to mistakes and errors. Simplicity is the key to a successful attack. A small number of simple plays yields the best results." John Heisman offered this assessment: "No team should have more than twenty offensive plays or forty signals. . . . All plays should proceed and develop from as few differing formations as possible." It was within this prevailing environment that Schmidt achieved his maniacal reputation. The new

Ohio State coach ran his offense from seven formations, and this offense included over *three hundred* plays, or ten times the amount other coaches taught their teams. It was damn near ridiculous, and it only got worse. At nearly every practice, plays were introduced, added, tweaked, or sent to the corner. His bulging playbook was forever shifting and growing. During his time at Ohio State, Schmidt added over two hundred more plays to the main playbook. From a theoretical standpoint, Schmidt believed that more plays and more formations and more movement created more confusion for the defense, more matchup problems, more field to cover, and therefore less aggression, which is the hallmark of defense. When executed perfectly an offensive attack was a dizzying exhibition of shovel passes, sweeps, power thrusts, long passes, traps, laterals, power, and quick passes over the middle. This idea of ultraversatility—of making the defense defend innumerable possibilities—was in direct contrast to the prevailing system of pounding the defensive line until they were too punch-drunk to defend the knockout play.[16]

Schmidt had supreme confidence in what he had jokingly referred to as his "touchdown system." He held that a strong offense was the best defense—that by constantly moving the ball you dictated how the game would unfold. If your offense was good enough you didn't worry about the other team. They would make enough mistakes just trying to keep up. "I know this conference is tough," he said about the upcoming Big 10 season, "but we know what most of the other teams will do. They'll have to worry about us." At TCU the previous year he'd had one returning starter, but undaunted, he had declared they would win another championship simply on the basis of his system: "We haven't made any changes in our coaching staff or system. . . . We will take the same system that won last year's championship—a system that calls for a variety of plays ranging from passes to direct line plunges." In essence Schmidt believed that *good* players could be made *great* through the use of limitless strategy. This too was a twist on prevailing thought, which held that material was perfected through fundamentals such as blocking, tackling, and stamina. The bottom line to Schmidt's thinking was that you should score as often as you could by any means necessary while the other guy tried to keep up. Schmidt spent an inordinate 80 percent of practice time on offense and made no apologies. But, while his wayward view of football was admirable both in conviction and scope, it still left other football instructors dubious, and for good reason.[17]

Too much was too much, they argued. This had been the prevailing wisdom since the game was developed. A coach had to choose between quality and quantity, and quality would always triumph when it involved the time-consuming task of training young men to execute orders in flawless unison. Too many plays and formations watered down practice and taxed the minds of young men. Any advantage gained by confusing an opponent with so many variations would be lost in the certain failure to execute such an unwieldy array. In other words, you end up confusing your own offense as much as—if not more than—the opponent's defense. Nobody had ever achieved consistent success with quantity. Then again, nobody had ever explored the theory of excess like Schmidt had. His belief was that overengineered football wasn't impractical, it simply wasn't overengineered enough. Today some teams have playbooks with over one thousand plays run from dozens of formations. Complexity is the new standard. But before something can become the standard, it has to be the exception, and in 1934 Schmidt's system was that exception.[18]

While no one was willing to concede that Schmidt's approach to offense was the right path, there was no denying that offensive football had reached a fork in the road. Major college teams averaged a scant 12 points per game in 1933. This was a full touchdown less than was averaged in 1922. The game was in the midst of a national scoring drought, and everyone was looking for someone to blame.[19]

Some thought scheduling was the culprit, and they had a point. The Depression had caused a chain reaction. Some of the heavyweight schools were still paying off loans on mammoth stadiums built during the overexpansive 1920s, and almost all of the larger schools had become dependent on football gate receipts. Now, with tough times and declining attendance, the big programs were ditching lowly warm-up opponents that no one cared to see in favor of other big-name programs that drew crowds. Having been bumped from the grown-ups' table, the smaller schools were now playing each other more. Thus, with teams playing like-sized opponents more often there were fewer blowouts to skew scoring averages upward.

Others thought it was the aforementioned overuse of the Warner and Notre Dame systems of football that had led offense to become stale and predictable. The systems' theories were rather cautious to begin with, and by now they had shown all their cards. Apparently, it wasn't much of a hand.

Others thought the game's rules had grown stale. Too many restrictions still retarded the possible development of forward passing. Maybe there should be fewer men per team or rules that handicapped defenses. Those in the know—coaches and rules committee members—were pretty unanimous in their belief that something should be done, but they were equally worried about the degree to which football should be changed. One overreaching misstep might lead to all sorts of unintended consequences, so they continued to approach the situation with caution.

Thankfully, the collegiate football establishment had a poor, blue-collar cousin whose desperate financial state didn't have time for overcautiousness. During this worst part of the Depression, only one spot in the football universe needed money worse than the big colleges and that was the adolescent National Football League. So far the professional league was surviving thanks to a slightly more open game and a density of talent, but without a built-in base of alumni to count on for attendance, they needed their brand of football to entertain first and foremost. So it was that pros, for the first time, began to adjust a few of the sport's rules for their own use. The timing was perfect, just as the collegiate game was beginning to change things up as well. They ignored some of the NFL's ideas, copied a few, and inspired others. Even though the two cousins were not in alliance (collegiate football found the pro game coarse and distasteful), they began pushing each other to legislate a more interesting game. In 1933 the roundness of the ball was reduced another inch to its present-day dimensions, and tighter specifications regarding air pressure and the use of pebble-grained leather were put into effect. This made for a sphere that was much more conducive to gripping and throwing. Hash marks were also introduced; teams could now run plays toward the sidelines without getting trapped. Prior to this, the ball was snapped from wherever it had been whistled dead on the previous play even if it was a few inches from the sidelines. For plays that had finished out-of-bounds, the team in possession had to waste a down calling for its placement back on the field of play. Now with hash marks running lengthwise down the field, 10 yards in from the sideline, no plays had to be started so near the boundaries. And recently, just days before Ohio State contacted Francis Schmidt, the 1934 National Rules Committee had eased restrictions on forward passing. A team could now throw multiple incompletions per set of downs without incurring a 5-yard penalty, a previously unreasonable double jeopardy. Additionally, a team was now permitted to throw an incompletion into the end zone without losing possession. Obviously, up to this point, risk-averse teams would not chance a throw over the goal line as part of their strategy if there was a strong chance of losing possession due to an interception or a rules violation. Even after these changes, forward passing was still somewhat restrictive, but this was a big step, giving coaches much more latitude to open up the game with fewer consequences.[20]

These rules were absolutely crucial for allowing the open game to escape from its box, but years of caution were not easy to overcome, and the new legislation had only a small overall effect on the game. Scoring barely increased over the next few years. Many of the austere coaches still had no real desire to engage in sissy ball no matter what the rulemakers wished. Major Robert Neyland, the successful coach at the University of Tennessee, was the perfect spokesman for status-quo football: "They (fans) want their team to win every game and they don't want to see it gamble away its chances with a lot of long-shot plays." And who could argue with his success? Using military-style play, brute strength, and caution, Neyland (61-2-5 from 1926 to 1932) and a few of his like-minded contemporaries were engineering the winningest teams in America.[21]

The leaders of the pack, the ones consistently at the top of the rankings like the Vols, were highly unlikely to change their methods. Thus, logic dictated that if those teams continued to be elite by using cautious football, why take a chance employing open football? In this cycle there just wasn't room for the open game—scoring and thrills be damned. Legislation helped, but the motivation for an open game had to be built, the new methods proven. Some like Schmidt and Zuppke had already begun the movement, but if it was to continue growing and possibly change the face of the game, it would require some high-profile examples of success earned by means of blatant disregard for traditional football. The first modern period seemed poised to give way to the next, but without a designated leader. If only it had someone willing to take the big leap. Someone like Schmidt.

If there was one coach who seemed to be the unofficial leader of this transition it was Francis Schmidt. He was one of the early pioneers of the open-game movement, and his system was still growing to the point that it was now considered extreme. Ohio State made for a perfect proving ground. The head-coaching job in Columbus was one of the most high-profile positions in all of football. As far as the open-game movement was concerned, Schmidt was the right coach in the right place at the right time. He was ready for the challenge. If anything, he had scaled back his attack at TCU because of personnel issues, but now he had resources equal to any program in America, and he intended to come out swinging.

The open-game movement had no name or agenda; it was just a trend, but Schmidt sure as hell considered himself the authority. All those years of studying, tinkering, and experimenting had secured him the job at Ohio State—a spot of national prominence. He intended to step up his strategy to meet the new stakes. And the new stakes were huge. Not only was Schmidt charged with the task of improving the fortunes of Buckeye football, he was also responsible for improving the reputation of Southwest football and proving the viability of a behemoth playbook. The outcome of Francis Schmidt's tenure at Ohio State was sure to have a resonating impact on the game of football, and everybody was watching for the first hint of what the future would hold.

Five. Razzle-Dazzle

In the summer of 1934, Francis and Evelyn Schmidt left the Southwest behind and settled in Columbus, Ohio. They moved into a tall, narrow house at 120 Fifteenth Avenue. The house sat on a rise, off the street; it had a small front yard and a driveway running along the side to a garage located behind. The house had two floors, each with a porch facing the street. On the first floor were the kitchen, dining room, and living room, while the second floor contained the bedrooms. Above the bedrooms was an attic along with a single room whose window stuck out of the roof. This was Francis's office. In a neighborhood of nice family homes, student housing, fraternities, and sororities, the Schmidts lived just a few houses down from High Street and the original entrance to the Ohio State campus. Evelyn made a point of living very close to the campus in order to minimize Francis's commute.

Francis tended to get lost in thought, so driving a shorter distance meant less risk. And while it was true that Francis could "space out" while driving, that was only a part of the truth. He was actually more dangerous on the road because of his incredibly aggressive driving tendencies. He raced through town like a bat out of hell, exhibiting no patience and a hostility that was often disproportionate to the conditions. He would weave in and out of traffic in his powerful Cadillac, dodging trolleys and pedestrians, all the while loudly offering a profanity-laced soliloquy, punctuated with outbursts directed at especially slow drivers. Evelyn was worried that somebody was going to die one day—either Francis or a jaywalker frozen in stride—so she made sure to reduce the odds when she could. Of course, the short distance between work and home could only minimize the danger, not eliminate it. That fall, Schmidt brought Harold Olsen, the school's basketball coach, home for lunch, and while "flailing his arms about, trying to describe a football play," Schmidt found himself close to driving on the sidewalk. As Evelyn recalled, "On the return trip Mr. Olsen insisted upon driving and asked Mr. Schmidt to sit in the rear seat and do his football explaining from there. I guess I might have to do the same thing when we go riding." Whether the story of the trip is accurate or simply Schmidt mythology, it's interesting to note that even his wife found it hard to tell the difference at times.[1]

Schmidt's arrival in Columbus felt strange to the local Buckeye football fans, like an arranged marriage to someone they hardly knew. Ohio State fans were rabid about their football and proud of their school, so much so that it felt awkward to have a complete stranger suddenly holding the most important, intimate position within the family. Sam Willaman was an OSU graduate, and, before him, John Wilce had earned his medical degree at OSU and, at the time, was the director of student health services for the university. Those two men had covered the head-coaching position for twenty-one years between them. But here was Schmidt: not only did he have no Buckeye ties, he had no Big 10 ties and no Midwest connection whatsoever. He was—depending on where one gathered the information—either a Texan, a Nebraskan, or a Kansan. To most Ohioans, the distinction was trivial: together those plains states were all one giant, dusty whistle-stop on the way to California. Suffice it to say that Schmidt was from the outskirts of nowhere, and to those who took their Buckeye football seriously, this "marriage" was a mixture of vulnerability, hope, and wariness.

Lynn St. John had been very judicious in his role as matchmaker. He knew from his time with Schmidt on the national basketball rules committee that his new hire was colorful—at times a bit too colorful. A little charisma can make for great press and generate additional interest in a football program, but too much can generate controversy. Hiring an unknown from Texas was controversial enough for St. John, and he had tried to make it clear to the outspoken Schmidt that it was crucial for him to be on his best behavior. So far the new coach had been nothing short of oddly charming. Schmidt taught summer courses and had proven himself a capable educator, although one who talked too fast for proper note taking. He had also spoken to various alumni groups around the state as chosen by St. John and had shown himself to be verbose and educated, not some unshaven, gun-totin' ruffian who had been plucked from a cattle trail. Schmidt proved to be a clever speaker who knew how to captivate his audience; with the Michigan-putting-on-their-pants quote he had used just the right amount of flair to entertain rather than offend. Even so, many school officials and sportswriters were discovering Schmidt to be nothing short of eccentric.

Part of it was his look, with the big hawk-like nose and the intense eyes. And often he let slip a trace of a smile as though he knew a secret or had x-ray vision. His suits, while not traveling-salesman loud, were a bit enthusiastic and were almost always adorned with one of his trademark colorful bow ties, an accessory rarely worn by football coaches. He was big and tall, and when he was "on," his presence dominated the room. He talked loudly and quickly—always getting straight to the heart of the matter—with no patience for preamble. Everything about him was intense, offering the smallest hint of maniacal possibilities. His blusterous confidence and caustic humor always seemed out of proportion to his surroundings, and he was a relentless contrarian. The whole effect was odd but enchant-ing, like a man born to an obscure throne who assumed author-ity and whose knowledge was implicitly greater than others. All in all, he radiated a folksy, tumbleweed pomposity with enough slang and humor to make him likable and enough swearing to deem him unforgettable.

But underneath all that was the Schmidt who preferred to keep to himself, sharing his strange charisma only when necessary. He also possessed a certain childlike vulnerability and was genuinely hurt when he felt someone didn't believe in him. Completely at odds with his public bombast, when he perceived the slightest bit of doubt from someone he was quick to verbalize his self-pity. He was a study in contrasts: on the one hand he was a hell-bent leader who ordered on the fly, but on the other hand he would cave eas-ily under pressure from his underlings. His love of counterlogic made him a trailblazer, but this love overpowered reality at all the wrong times.

His racing mind usually kept him far from the maddening crowd. And what a strange mind it was, unable to relax, rarely permitting Schmidt more than a few hours' sleep. But that was all the sleep he needed. All part of his mental makeup, today it would most likely be diagnosed as something called "hypomania."

Usually this condition is associated with bipolar disorder, an ill-ness wherein the patient experiences wide swings between heavy depression and an overblown, energetic happiness. This second part—the high—is the hypomania. Some people live only in this state, never really succumbing to the low swings. Schmidt was one of these people: a hypomanic. According the American Psychiatric Association's manual (DSM-IV-TR), hypomanic behavior includes, among other things: pressured speech (rapid talking), inflated self-esteem or grandiosity, decreased need for sleep, and a flight of ideas—all things for which Schmidt was well known. He was also known for more unofficial traits like risk-taking (manifested in his football philosophy and his driving) and having little fear or doubt, especially in social situations where others might experience such emotions. This condition was Schmidt's strength and his weakness. In his book, *The Hypomanic Edge*, author John Gartner describes how hypomania makes "the urgency of action irresistible" while making its consequences questionable: "This pressure to act creates overachievers, but it also leads to impulsive behavior and confident leaders who glibly take their followers over a cliff." Schmidt had already overachieved, thereby garnering followers, but the question remained as to whether or not he would lead them over a cliff.[2]

Nobody was familiar with hypomania in 1934, and the public was just beginning to learn that mental conditions could be classified as something other than "normal." But they didn't need a term to classify Schmidt. The sidelong glances shared by sportswriters said all that needed to be said. They hoped the eccentricity was a by-product of genius, something that could help the Buckeyes like it had apparently helped the Horned Frogs of TCU.

Schmidt's incessant diagramming of football plays provided some raw proof of the connection between outlandish and out-standing. "It seems as if Schmidt has been diagramming ever since he first hit town," said Jim Renick, local sportswriter turned OSU public relations man. Every football coach was known to fiddle with diagramming—it was part of the job—but Schmidt seemed to at-tend to this business like it was a matter of life and death. He based his diagrams on his huge collection of notes gathered from attend-ing hundreds upon hundreds of games, clinics, and classes. The diagrams had taken on mythical proportions; one former player claimed he had gone to the movies with Schmidt and had been forced to sit through four showings so that Schmidt could make notes "of all the blocking assignments" he'd seen on some partic-ular plays on the newsreels. Building on this obscene amount of information, Schmidt worked on creating new plays every waking hour of the day. Scraps of paper covered in Xs and Os could be found all over his desk, in his pockets, at home, and sticking out of the seat cushions in his Cadillac. If one wished to talk to Schmidt in his office, it was with the understanding that he would be working on diagrams while only half listening to the conversation. His mind was not only fascinated with the possibilities of football strategy but was rather compelled to explore them.[3]

Evelyn Schmidt had long ago accepted this obsession that kept Francis in another world. That's why she lobbied for a shorter, safer commute for him. That's why she could laugh about the pad and pencil he kept on his nightstand. True, it wasn't so amusing to her when his obsession held up bridge play or interrupted conversations, but his obsession was as much a part of him as was his need for food.

This insatiable interest in football strategy led to his reputation as a comical figure as he strode about the Ohio State campus. With a large portfolio tucked under one arm, he studied his notebooks so earnestly that he lost track of his surroundings, often walking through flowerbeds and, on at least one occasion, into the side of a building. Once, when asked about the huge briefcase he carried, Schmidt admitted it contained nothing but a couple of ten-cent notebooks and some pencils for his diagramming. The briefcase was an attempt to keep the prodigious output in one place, and he figured it was easier to keep track of one large portfolio than a bunch of small notebooks.[4]

After months of watching this obsessive behavior, Buckeye fans were fascinated to see what their odd Mr. Schmidt had in store for the team. Schmidt was just as fascinated. He had already decided this Ohio State job would be the defining phase in his life, and he was going to hold nothing back. The offensive system he installed during fall practice was his most ambitious yet. Relative to the offenses being used elsewhere, this one was a wide-open jugger-naut, and soon enough writers would name the spell-binding show, "razzle-dazzle"—a term forever synonymous with Francis Schmidt.

Three weeks of fall practice (the amount allotted by the Big 10) did not allow much time for a new coach to teach a complex system to a new group of players. Additionally, Schmidt had just four of eleven starters returning, and only one of them was a lineman. To make matters worse, the regular-season schedule, which had been put together by St John, called for a brutal beginning. Instead of the usual warm-up contest against a lightly regarded school, the Buck-eyes jumped directly into the fray, starting with conference foes Indiana and Illinois, followed by a much-anticipated battle with Colgate, an Eastern power who had given up just 12 total points during the past two seasons.[5]

The Big 10 couldn't stop coaches from plotting ahead of time, and two weeks before fall practice officially opened Schmidt and his assistants huddled to discuss personnel. For one thing, it had to be determined when players would be available for camp. Line-man Charley Hamrick, for example, would be several days late re-porting as he had to finish his summer job. With the Depression raging and the almost complete lack of athletic scholarships, the coaches couldn't argue the boy's priorities. Much of the coaches' time, however, was spent discussing possible lineups and combina-tions—standard conversation amongst all staffs during the era of limited substitution, but as with everything Schmidt did, this ele-ment was taken to extremes. In spring practice Schmidt had jug-gled his lineup so much that one observer lamented, "One mo-ment he will have an end playing center and a halfback at end or maybe fullback up in the line." Part of this constant tinkering was based on his experience, but much of it was rooted in the restless-ness of his frantic mind, which tended to dwell more on football than was practical. Constantly fooling with the lineup was his nervous habit.[6]

Finally, at 9:30 on the morning of September 15, 1934, fall practice officially commenced. The players, wearing newly styled uniforms, took to the practice field adjacent to Ohio Stadium and anxiously gathered around Schmidt for his opening address. Too impatient for superfluous rhetoric, Schmidt simply said, "Let's get going." There was no talk of the upcoming season, sacrifices, relying on teammates, or any of the other traditional motivators. Unlike so many mentors who were renowned for instilling passion through opening-day keynote addresses, Schmidt had neither the time nor the social wherewithal to dabble in emotions or psychology. He felt his furious pace spoke more loudly than words. But without details or structure as ballast, his frenzied activity often resembled a madly spinning propeller only half submerged in the water: awesome to behold but wholly inefficient. This had always been the weakest link in Schmidt's system, and it would play a major role in his downfall years later. But on this crisp fall morning all was well, and hope was palpable. After his three-word speech, the players were turned over to the media for some goodwill publicity. Schmidt remarked "We'll get all this picture taking out of the way early, and then when we get started we won't be bothered by too much outside stuff."[7]

The sixty-odd players who answered the invitation to fall practice were wearing their new game uniforms in honor of the photographer's presence. The jerseys, unchanged from the last year, were still long sleeved, made of thin wool, and colored a deep scarlet red. The pants that used to be khaki were now grey with scarlet inserts on the back of the legs. These inserts, made of a more flexible jersey material, not only added color but would supposedly give the players more freedom of movement. Black socks and black cleats covered their feet. Schmidt approved of the new look, conceding that the "dash of color seems to please the crowd." The helmets were still completely black (logos being a decade away), but their composition had been tweaked. Schmidt had personally worked on engineering a new design during the spring, and the result was a leather-and-rubber version that was lighter in weight by an average of seven ounces.[8]

After the boys posed for glory and posterity, Schmidt immediately got down to business directing both blocking and tackling drills. He despised fussing with fundamentals but understood that a certain amount of time had to be spent on them and obliged as long as he could stand it. He also knew that physical contact and aggression needed to be fostered after a summer that included little to none. After all, the mind, body, and spirit have to warm up to the idea of seeking pain. Much to the surprise of the players, Schmidt himself joined in the activities. Sam Willaman had always been a hands-off coach, often conducting practice from the front rows of the stands while talking to others, content to delegate. Schmidt was autocratic, overinvolved, and horrible at delegating. Choosing Johnny Kabealo, the team's large fullback, Schmidt proceeded to demonstrate tackling technique, but demonstrating at full speed without a helmet proved painful for the coach, and he injured his ear. Already impatient to start implementing his precious plays and now angry about having been hurt, Schmidt called an end to the drills and had the boys scrimmage. This was highly unusual for the morning of an initial practice, but Schmidt often made decisions about practice on a whim. Following the two-and-a-half-hour morning session, the team ate lunch, listened to an hour-long lecture from Schmidt, and then finished up with two more hours of drills.[9]

By the next day, Schmidt—his injured ear bandaged—could contain himself no longer and ditched the boring fundamental drills in favor of having the boys running his precious plays. He had hundreds to teach and only so much time during which to teach them. Learning the first few plays was simple enough, but it soon got trickier as Schmidt continually added new ones. On top of that, the plays became increasingly complex, requiring more and more of the players' concentration.

As Schmidt mentioned at a YMCA luncheon that month, "The old system of playing sports with brawn has been so revised that the mental requirements are now equal or above those of strength." Of course, Schmidt had an advantage when it came to mental requirements. His hypomania meant that he slept very little and was never able to quit thinking about football strategy. The game ruled his mind. If his obsession had been cooking, he'd have owned a restaurant featuring a menu as thick as the Bible, and food would have been served twenty-seven hours a day.[10]

The young football players did not have the "advantage" of hypomania. Instead, they had regular minds that thought about girls, schoolwork, food, and . . . girls. Football occupied their minds when it was the proper time, but Schmidt considered every minute of the day to be the proper time. For the young men at Ohio State who were being immersed into Schmidt's system, the vast number of plays and formations was bewildering, and they were struggling to stay afloat. It was far beyond anything they had experienced in their few years playing organized football. Even assistant coach Ernie Godfrey, who had been involved in college football for twenty-two years, was so confused that he had already written off the season. "He [Schmidt] is so far ahead of his team and his assistant coaches this year that this can be considered merely a formative period."[11]

Not only was Godfrey overwhelmed, but his assimilation into the new scheme was being hindered by one of Schmidt's biggest weaknesses: the inability to delegate. Schmidt was untrusting, paranoid, and impatient. Teaching the assistants to teach the players was too

time-consuming, not to mention the fact that the assistants probably wouldn't get it right anyhow. Instead of a practice field full of
small groups receiving specialized training from individual assistants, Schmidt's practices involved a single mass of players and assistant coaches forming a circle around him as he worked with eleven
men at a time. He was brilliant in technique and theory, and the information poured out of him at breakneck speed, but before the
eleven players could fully absorb or learn through repetition what
Schmidt was trying to teach them, he sent them back into the herd,
hollered for a new eleven, and continued to overwhelm them as
well. The assistants were initially given some freedom to pull a boy
aside and work on a technical problem they had seen, but Schmidt
later discouraged even that. He thought it was distracting them
from the information he was giving, which he always felt was more
valuable, so the assistants mostly just watched with the players.

The person who was really on the spot was the quarterback, as
he was in charge of calling all the plays during a game. The rules in
1934 forbade anyone on the sideline from signaling a play. Even a
substitute as he entered the game and joined the huddle was not
allowed to speak a word until the next play. The logic behind this
rule was that a student should direct the proceedings, an original
and important feature of the game designed to promote the spirit
of amateurism and teach self-sufficiency. In Schmidt's system the
quarterback was also responsible for throwing nearly all the forward passes. Today, quarterbacks and passing are synonymous, but
in 1934 quarterbacks were generally signal callers first, blockers
second, runners third, and throwers fourth. Most teams used the
single wing in which the left halfback was the primary thrower; in
the double wing it was the fullback. Schmidt liked the idea of isolat-
ing two eggs in one basket—the throwing and thinking—and then
strategizing so that this important position was exposed to less punishment, thus producing better results. Quarterbacks who spent a

good deal of the time blocking or being tackled had less chance to calmly appraise the next play choice, and the wear on their bodies might adversely affect their thinking.[12]

Schmidt was pleased to discover that he had two men with both excellent brains and arms. His starter was Stan Pincura, a junior from a well-known football family in Lorain, Ohio. His throwing ability was a godsend to Schmidt's scheme. The backup job was not set, but Schmidt had taken an instant liking to a little sophomore named Tippy Dye.

Everyone liked Tippy; it was difficult not to. He was a burst of charisma and raw athletic talent packed into a 5-foot-6-inch, 132-pound package. Tippy was born William Henry Harrison Dye, named after an uncle, who was named after the fourteenth president. William Henry Harrison—the president—had been known by the nickname "Old Tippecanoe," and anyone named after him was sure to be given a similar nickname. In Tippy's case, the nickname was shorter, as was his stature. He grew up in Pomeroy, Ohio, a small coal-mining town across the Ohio River from West Virginia. His parents had separated, and Tippy and his older brother and sister lived with their mother, "Mayme," who ran a tearoom out of a building on Main Street. The tearoom was on the ground floor, and the family lived on the third floor. Operating on Main Street was good for business but not always good for staying dry, as the Ohio River liked to overrun her banks and usually headed straight for Main. Pomeroy wasn't a glamorous town, but, like most children, Tippy didn't know the difference. He was always smaller than others his age, and this caused some standing-up-for-himself fights when he was younger, but when he reached high school he channeled his energy and tenacity into sports and won a staggering fourteen letters. He had been somewhat of a loner until high school, but that changed when he met a bright, beautiful girl named Mary Kennedy

Russell, the youngest daughter of a local attorney. Like her two sisters and brother she was an academic whiz, and, like them, she planned to pursue excellence at Ohio State upon graduation from high school. This presented Tippy with a bit of a problem. He had been recruited to play basketball at the smaller Ohio University in Athens, which was only about twenty-five miles away and was already educating his two older siblings. Having fallen in love with Mary, he felt himself being pulled to follow her to Columbus. It was a tough decision, but Tippy was no fool. One can get an education from and play sports for any college, but finding the perfect girl just doesn't happen that often, so Tippy followed Mary to Columbus.[13]

Tippy's collegiate athletic career would have to start from scratch. He had not really been pursued by recruiters for football—understandable given his size—but Tippy still enjoyed the sport and went out for OSU's freshman team as an unknown walk-on. He wasn't alone. Enough newbies showed up for twelve full teams. Tippy started out on the seventh string. With the help of freshman coach Dick Larkins—his fellow frat brother and future best friend—Tippy worked his way up the depth chart, and by the season's end he was the top-ranked quarterback on the freshman team. Now entering his sophomore year Tippy still faced challenges. He had been small compared to the freshmen, but amongst a mature varsity squad his relative smallness was exaggerated, and now he was forced to learn the new, complex system being installed by Schmidt. But Tippy was a fearless player, a quick thinker, and a natural leader. Before fall camp was over he had greatly impressed Schmidt, and by the time the season started, Tippy was practically splitting the quarterback job with Pincura.[14]

The learning curve was most severe for incoming freshmen. Schmidt understood that his system was light-years away from the rudimentary strategy taught on high school gridirons; therefore, he revamped the way osu's freshman squads conducted business. Because Big 10 rules forbade freshmen from playing on the varsity or against other schools' freshmen teams, the youngsters had always been used primarily as training partners, learning the plays of upcoming opponents and then scrimmaging with the varsity. The 1934 freshman squad, which numbered over two hundred, was now broken into groups, each being assigned a main task. Four groups were to learn the Schmidt system of offense, one group was to practice Michigan plays, and the rest were to learn other Big 10 teams' schemes.[15]

For most of fall practice, assistant coach Dick Larkins and his freshmen worked apart on another field away from the varsity, but on October 3, three days before the season's first game, the freshmen reported to the main practice field for what was supposed to be a dramatic, inspirational talk from Schmidt. Even though this had been prearranged, Schmidt was predictably unpredictable. He was caught up in the job of preparing for Indiana University, and the freshmen politely watched as he ignored them. After some time this began to get awkward, and Larkins inquired as to what Schmidt's plans were. Schmidt explained that he had no time for such nonsense, and Larkins was left with the embarrassing task of leading his neglected young charges back to their own field. It was difficult to grasp just exactly what made Schmidt tick, and it was best that the freshmen learned this early on.[16]

As fall practice progressed, Schmidt's style of coaching provided distinct topics of discussion among observers. Much of the talk centered on the sheer number of plays being practiced as well as on the level of imagination they involved. An observer at one practice claimed, "Don't be surprised if the umpire suddenly turns into a ball carrier, or if the pigskin disappears when the Buckeyes start their drive." This was the sort of thing that sportswriters loved, and they excitedly told readers to expect a good deal of hocus-pocus from their Buckeyes in 1934.[17]

Another topic amongst insiders was one they did not share with the general public as it involved Schmidt's relentless use of profanity during practices. An occasional swearword was not unusual when testosterone and training were combined, but Schmidt, a man who wore bow ties and held an advanced degree, cussed like a Teamster when he was on the practice field. The reckless fervor of his swearing stunned witnesses in its veracity and in its setting—amongst students and educators. "His normal language was cussing," remembered Tippy. "It wasn't that he was mad or anything, it was just the language he spoke." Schmidt didn't even seem to realize how much he cursed, but nearly every sentence he uttered during practice was laced with some piece of sarcastic blasphemy. And it was loud. His voice was as big as his frame. Off the field he managed to restrain himself to some extent but still slipped often enough to shock women and school officials who had never endured such language—certainly not from a college man. After a few weeks of practice, the players were growing used to the cussing and even finding it hilarious. Schmidt was like an angry W. C. Fields act gone blue. When he was coaching football, he was at his most sardonic, and he punctuated his angry satire with profanity. During one practice at Ohio State he impatiently told his right tackle to spread out a little from the right guard. The right tackle obeyed and moved a foot away. "Sonofabitch," Schmidt cried, "I didn't say to scoot a goddamned mile. Now move back this way where you should be, damnit." This manner of speech was all too typical for some, but for St. John, the man who had discovered Schmidt and had received warnings about his rough talk, it was worse than had been imagined. St. John could only pray that the team's record would speak more loudly than did the coach.[18]

During the last weekend of fall practice, Schmidt actually skipped practice and shot over to Bloomington, Indiana, to scout his opening-day opponent. The Indiana Hoosiers were starting their season a week earlier than the Buckeyes, and this presented a golden opportunity for Schmidt to scout their strengths and weaknesses. They had a new coach, Bo McMillin, who boasted some prairie roots of his own, having grown up in Texas and having recently coached at Kansas State. Interestingly, the Indiana job had opened up at about the same time as the Ohio State job, and though McMillin had never applied to coach at Indiana, the Hoosiers pursued and signed him a week after Ohio State had signed Schmidt. Apparently, Schmidt's hiring had made dipping into the prairie for coaching en vogue. Now there were two outsiders where there had been none, and a third would be added the next year.

Finally, on October 6, Schmidt's regular-season debut at Ohio State took place in front of a home crowd of 47,736—the largest opening day attendance in the stadium's history and the largest overall crowd for the past three seasons. Part of the reason for this turnout was the competition. Instead of the usual sacrificing of some small school like Wittenberg (OH), the Buckeyes were opening up against a Big 10 team for the first time in a decade. Another factor drawing so many spectators was the anticipation of Schmidt's razzle-dazzle, which for weeks had been rumored as something to behold. Fans didn't have to wait long to be delighted and never really questioned the outcome of the game. Racing to an early lead, the Buckeyes manhandled Indiana 33–0—the worst beating they had inflicted on the Hoosiers in eighteen years. Schmidt's boys rolled up 343 yards of total offense to the Hoosiers' 111. These numbers are more impressive when you consider that during the early 1930s the average team gained about 200 yards per game in total offense from scrimmage (with less than 70 yards of it being achieved by passing). The game's score might have been even more lopsided, but the Buckeyes, still getting used to the intricate ballhandling of Schmidt's offense, fumbled the ball a staggering 11 times, losing 7. Despite their turnovers and their only having a tenuous grasp on Schmidt's system, the Buckeyes gave their hometown fans a taste of what to expect. Not only did the offense line up in several different formations, but they managed to spring one of Schmidt's more entertaining plays, a fake reverse that sent Frank Boucher on a wild 78-yard touchdown run. Ohio State had performed much better than was expected, but the real test would come in the next two games, the first of which was a road game against conference foe Illinois.[19]

Traveling to Champaign to meet the Fighting Illini meant facing a team coached by the shrewd Bob Zuppke. The little German had been the Illinois head football coach for twenty-two years, during which time his squads had won all or part of 7 conference titles. He was now on the downside of his career but had developed a habit for plotting—and often succeeding in—one big upset each year. There were rumblings that this year's target was Ohio State and Francis Schmidt, and for good reason. It would be a battle of reputations.

When it came to football strategy, Zuppke had long enjoyed his notoriety as the Big 10's resident trickster. As was mentioned earlier, his gadget plays with their outrageous names had aptly expressed the artistic showman in his personality and had helped to build his renown. It seemed only natural that Schmidt, with a system of innumerable clever plays at its very core, might be perceived as a threat to Zuppke's renown as the most imaginative strategist. Much like the now-forgotten automobile inventor who watched Henry Ford hog the spotlight, Zuppke didn't wish to be left in Schmidt's meteoric wake. Schmidt's full repertoire dwarfed Zuppke's, but his Buckeyes were still loosening the training wheels. The changing of the laureates was inevitable, but would it take place during their first skirmish?

At 8:30 Thursday night, October 11, the Buckeyes boarded their train headed ultimately for Champaign, Illinois. Except for the shortest of trips, which involved buses, all teams during this era traveled by train, usually in a special car. Each football coach had his own ideas on traveling, but leaving at nighttime, as the Buckeyes did, was a common strategy. Besides the fact that traveling overnight minimized interference with classes, many, like Schmidt, felt the best way to maintain discipline amongst energetic young men on a road trip was to spend most of it while they were asleep. Big 10 rules did their part in controlling the chaos by limiting the traveling party to forty individuals, including coaches and trainers. For the Illinois trip, Schmidt brought along thirteen backfield men, which was more than usual. The Illini had a solid passing game, and Schmidt wanted backs for patrolling the air, plus he was still trying to sort out which backs were the best fit for various offensive situations.[20]

After traveling through the night, the Buckeyes arrived in Danville, Illinois, thirty-eight miles outside of Champaign, where they would spend the day before the game. By stopping just short of the final destination, a football squad could enjoy fresh air and activities while avoiding the revelry and distraction of the actual college town. In the morning the team worked out at a local field, and that evening they attended the Danville vs. Decatur High School game. Afterward, before going to sleep on the train, Schmidt led them in a "skull session," discussing strategy and going over the game plan one more time. Zuppke was on his mind, and he warned them once again to look out for his inevitable trick plays. Late the following morning, near game time, they arrived in Champaign.[21]

The University of Illinois was celebrating Red Grange Day, and among the over 35,000 in attendance was the honorary legend himself. Grange's relationship with the university was damaged when he went pro mid-semester in 1925, but the two parties eventually mended fences, and it was now time to celebrate the ten-year anniversary of his jaw-dropping performance against Michigan where he scored 4 touchdowns on long runs in the first ten minutes of the game, establishing himself as football's first national superstar. Having retired from the Chicago Bears and pro football after the previous season, Grange was now ready to enjoy football without absorbing any punishment. With their golden child in attendance and the prospect of an entertaining battle between conference foes, fans at the stadium were buzzing with excitement as the Buckeyes arrived.

Still uncomfortable with their new offense, Ohio State continued their fumbling ways early, but many thought the officials were partly to blame. Midway through the first quarter, Johnny Kabealo busted off a 10-yard run up the middle before losing the ball while "sliding along on his neck and ears for 3 yards." Referee Milt Ghee called it a fumble, and Illinois recovered near midfield. Three plays later the Illini scored on a high-arching, wobbly 16-yard scoring pass that safety Stan Pincura mistimed. The officiating only got stranger when Illinois missed the kick for the extra point while Ohio State was offsides. This meant a re-kick was in order, but Ghee, who had been a star player two decades earlier, declared the extra point to be good by virtue of the offsides, an outdated and now-inaccurate ruling. Pincura pointed this out to the confused Ghee, who finally ruled that Illinois must re-kick, which they did, this time converting to take a 7–0 lead. Midway through the second quarter, the Buckeyes looked like they would tie the score, having strung together some nice plays and marched to the Illinois 1-yard line where it was second down and goal-to-go. Schmidt's big play offense had enjoyed the open field, but now they sputtered when things got tight. The next two running attempts yielded nothing, and the Buckeyes decided to go for it on fourth down, but disaster struck. The ball was snapped while signals were still being called, and nobody was ready. It shot past fullback Johnny Kabealo, who chased it down and jumped on it after it had rolled 16 yards. The Buckeyes' best scoring chance of the first half had resulted in yet another fumble, and they entered halftime being shut out.[22]

Just after the intermission, Zuppke, with his flair for the dramatic, decided to surprise the crowd almost as soon as the curtain opened for the second half. The Illini brought the fans to their feet, scoring their second touchdown from 31 yards out using the Flying Trapeze, a wild play that involved three laterals in the backfield before a deep pass. It was quite possibly the most convoluted play Zuppke had ever put together, and he'd delivered it just for Schmidt as a welcome-to-the-conference gift. Now trailing 14–0, the Buckeyes continued to struggle. They were on the road against a good team and still seeking their own identity on offense. The Ohio players had spent their entire youth learning standard football but only a few weeks learning Schmidt's aggressive version. Like a housecat given its freedom, the Buckeyes seemed to be reluctantly inching from the porch, torn between a history of caution and a new world of possibilities. Not until the final play of the third quarter, with defeat looming, did they finally leap to freedom. Opening up Schmidt's bag of tricks, Pincura called for a quick pitch to a reverse rollout followed by a long pass for a 26-yard gain that put the Buckeyes deep in Illini territory. On the same drive, facing fourth-and-five, they went for it and sprung Buzz Wetzel for a 15-yard touchdown run behind a pulling center.[23]

It was an important moment for Schmidt's "touchdown system." The players now had proof that his system of complex deception could work against top competition. However, the joy of Wetzel's epiphanous touchdown was short lived. Regis Monahan—the team's captain, starting guard, and regular place-kicker—missed the extra point, pushing it just wide left and leaving Ohio State trailing 6–14. Still the Buckeyes seemed to be gaining confidence in their new offense, and later in the fourth quarter, after another spirited drive, Dick Heekin rushed for Ohio State's second touchdown. This time Monahan converted the point after, leaving the Buckeyes down 14–13. But their comeback was running out of time. The Buckeyes had one more drive, and they moved the ball to the Illinois 39-yard line where they were forced to attempt a field goal with only seconds left in the game. Attempting a field goal from this distance was practically unheard of in this era, and, as expected, the kick was wide and short, and the Ohioans lost 14–13. Zuppke had beaten Schmidt in round one of their annual meeting. The victory and the Flying Trapeze awarded Illinois the headlines, but Schmidt's squad ran up 312 yards from scrimmage to Illinois's 275. In addition, they completed more passes and achieved more first downs, but an early bad snap and a barely missed extra point had doomed them. At practice the next week Schmidt, using some of his aggressive humor, told his boys, "Don't be surprised if Illinois votes a couple of you guys an honorary 'I' at the end of the season for your work in that game." Zuppke, pleased to emerge with his reputation intact, was still gloating two weeks later when he called Ohio State the "kind of team that will beat teams that might beat Illinois." Ultimately, however, Zuppke's fears of being surpassed by Schmidt were realized. He and Schmidt met six more times, and Ohio State won them all by a combined score of 105–20.[24]

Schmidt was pleased to see bold playcalling late in the Illini game but was disappointed with the relentless fumbling. Even more distressing was the number of injuries his team accumulated during the game. So many of them had occurred in the Buckeyes' backfield that, heading into their game with Colgate, an entirely new backfield crew would be starting. This was the worst possible scenario for a team trying to grasp a complex system. Something else was puzzling Schmidt: the unexpected disappearance of Johnny Kabealo's punting skills. As a sophomore he'd been the best punter in the conference—one of the best in years—but now instead of making 50-yard kicks out of bounds, he was sending pigeons 30 yards down the middle.

Punting was still a huge part of the game in the 1930s when field position and waiting for turnovers continued to dominate offensive strategy. A good punter was a highly valued weapon. Schmidt also believed in the value of a good punter because, like everything else, he liked to use punting as yet another weapon for confusing the defense. He liked to feature the quick kick, an unexpected punt on an unexpected down from regular formation. If done properly, the opponent would be caught without a man deep enough to return the kick. Most teams telegraphed their intention to punt by switching from their base formation to the short-punt formation, but one of Schmidt's preferred base formations *was* the short punt, which helped to disguise forward passes as well as quick kicks. He encouraged quick kicks when they were least expected, whether it be on first down, fourth-and-one, or against the wind. This was all part of the larger scheme of keeping the opponent's defense in a constant state of uncertainty. With so many injuries to the backfield, Kabealo would continue to do the punting for now.

Ohio State's chance at a national championship was squashed with their 1-point loss to Illinois, but the team they were hosting in the next game, Colgate University, still had national championship aspirations of their own. The Red Raiders had given up just 1 touchdown in their last 19 games and had lost only a single game since 1931. They were widely considered the preeminent team in the eastern region for 1934. While the East no longer monopolized football as it had throughout the nineteenth century, there were still occasional squads good enough to compete for the title of best team in America, and this year Colgate was one of them. And even though their defense was beyond outstanding, they were better known for their flash. They wore maroon and white uniforms with pants finished in satin and white helmets that were polished until they shone. They also played an entertaining brand of football, having no qualms about using the lateral pass. As a matter of fact, Colgate's coach, Andy Kerr, along with Schmidt, was the nation's leading exponent of the lateral. Both had preached the daring play at a summer football clinic they cochaired.

Although Kerr's overall scheme was not nearly as large and complex as Ohio State's—none were—it had kept the East entertained for some time and was drawing large crowds who wanted to see wide-open football. For the second week in a row Schmidt was opposing a coach who was recognized for his colorful approach to football, and for the second week in a row he was entering the fight with a team struggling to find rhythm.

The Buckeyes were slowly catching on, however, and for three quarters the game was a beautiful but frustrating extravaganza. They were able to move the ball up and down the field all day, but Colgate's proud defense stuffed each threat, and the Red Raiders held a slim 7–3 lead through three quarters.

Late in the fourth quarter a terrible Colgate punt gave Ohio State possession on the Raiders' 35-yard line. Schmidt had been saving some risky personnel moves for just such an opportunity. He reinserted Tippy Dye, a sophomore, to run the offense and added halfback Jack Smith, who had not played all day due to an injured knee. After Dye's creative playcalling helped Ohio State move the ball to the 9-yard line, Schmidt sent his two best sophomore linemen into the game. Behind quick, fresh blocking, Jack Smith carried the ball for the first time all game and moved it to the 1-yard line. Here, Tippy surprised even his own teammates by calling for a play they had never used and one Colgate had never seen. All 132 pounds of Dye took a spot on the line next to the tackle, and from there he barked out the play, a direct snap to Smith who scored without being touched. Colgate's defensive fullback, who would have had the best shot at Smith, was so confused by the play that he merely watched it develop, frozen with indecision. The final two minutes passed without incident, and the Buckeyes held on to win 10–7. It would be Colgate's only loss of the season. Although the score was low, the action was fast and furious. Ohio State held the advantage in total yards 353–225, with 214 of them coming by way of the forward pass. The two teams delivered on the promise of excitement, and "so intense was the struggle that the 29,130 fans who witnessed it were completely worn out when the final whistle ended the hostilities."[25]

Through three weeks, the Buckeyes were averaging a terrific 322 yards of offense per game while still learning Schmidt's system. Seemingly, the offense could only get better, and it didn't hurt that their next opponent, Northwestern, was having an off year defensively.

During the week Schmidt called one of his ex-players, Phil Handler, a guard for the NFL Chicago Cardinals. Schmidt knew Handler had seen the local Northwestern team in action and was looking for some inside information. Handler found the call to be an oddly endearing reminder of his coach's personality: "I said, 'Hello, coach.' He didn't even say 'hello' before asking, 'Say, Phil, has Northwestern got any spreads or pass plays?' He never stops thinking football."[26]

The Wildcats' hope for an upset was strengthened at the outset, thanks to a 92-yard opening kickoff return for a touchdown, but hope was fleeting. Ohio State dominated the rest of the way and, despite failing to convert several scoring opportunities, still coasted to a 28–7 victory. Offensively it was no contest; the Buckeyes rolled up 317 yards of offense while Northwestern could barely move. The Wildcats were a perfect example of cautious, Victorian football. Even though they were unable to run (39 yards rushing for the game) and they trailed big, Northwestern rarely attempted a forward pass. Even as time slipped away they stuck to the tenet that a team should not pass when pinned deep—a problem, considering their bad field position throughout the fourth quarter. In all, the Wildcats completed just one single pass for 8 yards. It was Northwestern's severest defeat at the hands of Ohio State since 1917.[27]

Despite their difficult opponents, injuries, and inexperience with a new system, Ohio State's 3-1 first half of the season was a success. Buckeye supporters were more than pleased with Schmidt and were still holding out hope for the conference title that had eluded them since 1920. Unfortunately, this was the year that conference foe Minnesota fielded one of its all-time great squads, and the odds of their losing even once seemed slim. Schmidt certainly would have enjoyed delivering a championship in his first season, but he was still concerned with proving himself and his methods. He was encouraged that his team's offense was continuing to open up more each week as the boys became more comfortable, and even though they had fumbled 27 times (the work of twelve different backs) at least the rate of fumbles was decreasing. The remaining schedule was favorable, and Schmidt thought the Buckeyes were about ready to surpass expectations.[28]

Up next was Ohio State's partner in collusion, Western Reserve. Despite being cast off by OSU, Sam Willaman was still a fine coach and had proven so at Western Reserve, where his team entered the game undefeated. As a smaller school they were decided underdogs to the behemoth Buckeye program, but there was no way they weren't going to give it their all against the coach's former employer.

Football protocol says that the coach of a vastly superior team must preach to his team the dangers of underestimating the hapless opponent. Naturally, Schmidt did not. Practically dismissing Western Reserve, Schmidt announced they would begin practicing some new plays to be used against the University of Chicago the following week. He also decided that a goodly portion of the traveling squad for the Western Reserve game would be made up of reserves and lower stringers, this being the last road game of the year and thus their final chance to be part of a road trip. The first stringers who weren't too injured would start, but the other boys would get most of the playing time. Besides blatantly dismissing Willaman's boys, Schmidt had recently confided to a friend in regard to the Buckeye players he had inherited from Willaman that he had never seen so many good players so badly spoiled by incorrect teaching. It was an obvious slam on his predecessor, and, to make matters worse, it made the newspapers. If Schmidt was deliberately trying to jinx his advantage, he was doing all the right things.[29]

Those who showed up at League Park in Cleveland hoping to see an upset were left wanting; what they witnessed instead was a mauling. Ohio State beat Western Reserve 76–0, "exhibiting almost every spectacular play known to football." According to plan, the backups played the entire second half, but this only augmented the abuse. Hungry for action, the backups relentlessly razzle-dazzled, scoring 21 points in the third quarter and another 27 in the last quarter. Fascinated by the execution of his dreamed-up plays and not wanting to dim the enthusiasm of his substitutes, Schmidt did nothing to rein things in. Just before the game ended the Buckeyes executed a flashy shovel pass to halfback John Bettridge who scored from 20 yards out in one final act of mayhem. The Buckeyes had seemed bent on trying every play in their arsenal, and the results were 4 touchdowns from forward passes and 25 separate plays involving laterals. Western Reserve did not achieve a first down until the middle of the third quarter, and even then it was only the result of two straight offsides penalties against the Ohio State defense.[30]

Afterward, the Ohio State Alumni Association of Cleveland provided a "gala dinner" in the Carter Hotel's Rainbow room. Some four hundred guests celebrated the triumphant return of Buckeye football to Northern Ohio, enjoying toast after toast in honor of touchdown after touchdown.[31]

Schmidt might have been a hero to the alumni, but his lack of compassion for Western Reserve did not please others. Although "Schmitty had everyone who made the trip get into the game except Ernie Godfrey, trainer Tuck Smith, and himself," he was skewered by some in the press for running up the score on a helpless victim. Causing particular distress were the 4 touchdowns in the fourth quarter when the game had long before been decided.[32]

If anyone had a right to be upset about the Western Reserve massacre—other than Western Reserve—it was the scouts in attendance. Game films were still in their infancy, and the home team that shot them did not make them available to other teams. Thus, it was the job of each school's scouts to personally attend games and gather information on upcoming opponents. This was a difficult job—trying to describe a team on paper by noting the tendencies and movements of eleven men at once. There were no scoreboards with instant replays. You captured what you could in a single take and then scribbled like mad. Fortunately for these scouts nearly every team used the same formation and only a few plays, meaning they could concentrate more on studying individual players, noting their strengths and weaknesses. This was not the case with Schmidt's Scarlet Scourge. Sportswriter Oscar Ruhl spent the entire Western Reserve game sitting next to Kyle Anderson, lead scout for the University of Chicago, and found much amusement in watching the scout try to keep up with Ohio State's trailblazing offense. Anderson "gave up his note-taking job in disgust after seeing the Buckeyes ramble through the Reservites for one quarter," and later he turned to Ruhl and confessed, "I'm in a helluva fix. I've seen the Ohio State team three times this season. I'm beginning to wonder if it ever works the same play twice. I don't believe any scout can recommend a defense that is surefire against Ohio's offense." His only recommendation to the Chicago Maroon was going to be: "Look out for anything." Good advice considering Ohio State had already spent one week adding new plays for the Maroon and now had another week to add even more.[33]

Another head scout in attendance at the game was the University of Pittsburgh's Bill Kern. He viewed several Ohio State games before turning in a final report to head coach Jock Sutherland: "Undoubtedly, the most versatile and dangerous offensive team I have ever seen. They combine sheer power with tricky and dangerous forward passes, shovel passes, and laterals. Their main offensive formation is the short punt . . . next comes their double wing . . . often inside the 15, they like to use their goal-line formations consisting of one, two, or three shifts into a spread, oftentimes there being only three men in the backfield . . . they'll throw laterals anywhere—off intercepted passes, shovel passes, runs, forward passes." Attached to the report were 112 of the plays that Kern was able to capture on paper. Included in the collection were the "single-wing pass, goal-line pass, delayed pass, backs to weak-side pass, reverse and backward delayed pass, sideline pass to left halfback, reverse pass with ends crossing, and many others. End runs, delayed buck, deceptive plays like fake reverses, Statue of Liberty, fake-punt end run, sucker on guard, sequence to sucker on guard, etc." Even by today's standards it was a rather interesting assortment, but at the time it was positively groundbreaking, science-fictional stuff. Nobody had ever witnessed such an eclectic and bewildering assortment of plays—the foundation on which today's football is built—and Chicago was about to receive a painful vision of the future.[34]

November 10 was "Dads' Day" in Columbus, meaning the players' fathers were allowed to sit on the sidelines throughout the game. After being introduced to the spectators, the fathers sat on a row of folding chairs, away from the actual team, wearing placards that hung over the backs of their suit jackets displaying the jersey number of their individual sons. This always provided an extra source of motivation for the boys, but today it wasn't necessary. Chicago's program, already faltering, was missing its star player due to injury. Jay Berwanger, who would win the first-ever Heisman Trophy the next year, had a badly bruised thigh. The Buckeyes, gaining command of Schmidt's playbook, used all their formations to propel themselves to another lopsided victory. After receiving the opening kickoff, the Buckeyes threw 6 consecutive passes, completing them all and storming to the Chicago 6. A mistake squandered that scoring opportunity, but before the first quarter was over they had scored 2 touchdowns on breathtaking plays that started as Tippy Dye–Sam Busich shovel passes and concluded with Busich lateraling to teammates for touchdowns. The fun never stopped for the Buckeyes as they pursued a 33–0 win. The final touchdown, a 39-yard Frank Fisch–John McAfee pass, came with one minute left. It was the worst beating Ohio State had ever handed Chicago, and had it not been for some dropped Buckeye passes in the open field it might have been much worse. On defense the Buckeyes intercepted more passes (3) than the visitors completed (2). Johnny Kabealo even regained his punting touch, pinning the Maroon deep on several occasions. Schmidt substituted continuously throughout the second half, giving every dad a chance to see his son participate in the frenzied Maroon bashing. Chicago coach Clark Shaughnessy, in absolute awe, declared: "Ohio has the greatest ballteam in the world today."[35]

This game marked the second straight contest in which Ohio State had destroyed its opponent, and it was the second straight time she had added insult to injury by scoring a touchdown with a minute left in the game. A derisive nickname that would forever be associated with Schmidt was about to be born. AP writer William Weekes declared that Schmidt had "adopted[ed] 'show 'em no mercy' as his slogan." Three days later, Harry Kipke, the Michigan

Wolverines' head coach, wrote a syndicated column wherein he stated that "Francis Schmidt has announced a 'shut the gates of mercy' platform." That actual phrase had been given to Kipke by a Michigan alumnus, who almost certainly was inspired by Weekes's earlier wire service article. Whatever the inspiration, the alumnus had definitely borrowed the exact phrase from Thomas Gray's famous eighteenth-century poem, "Elegy in a Country Churchyard." To this day, Schmidt still bears the nickname of "Shut the Gates of Mercy," a tribute to his overwhelming offense as well as to his lack of compassion for the vanquished. For now, Schmidt didn't bother to defend himself, probably a bit pleased with the controversy as it focused on his offense's playing *too* well. Schmidt was an extremist, barely understood social morays, and loved offensive football more than anything else in the world. Wasn't scoring an obscene amount of points the whole ambition behind football? In all likelihood he viewed the venom as jealous praise. If so, he undoubtedly enjoyed that writers were also using the nickname "Scarlet Scourge" to refer to his team.[36]

One of the typical traits of a Schmidt team was the spreading of wealth amongst the backfield members. Although his offense featured the occasional star, Schmidt constantly rotated his backs throughout the game. Also, his theory on playcalling was that many different backs should be featured so as to increase deception and create advantageous individual matchups. Schmidt also liked to keep his guys involved in the game's flow and flavor. Twelve backs who were used as veritable starters meant twelve guys who knew they had a chance to make contributions on each possession. Furthermore, this meant a backfield deep in playing experience, which was handy when dealing with inevitable injuries. Jack Smith and Dick Heekin, the team's two best runners, hadn't been healthy all season, and yet the Buckeyes were still scoring, with many different players' tasting the end zone. So far Schmidt had been blessed with excellent work from young backs like Dick Beltz, John Bettridge, and the three Franks: Fisch, Boucher, and Antenucci.

More important, Schmidt had been blessed by the steady play of Damon "Buzz" Wetzel, the pile-driving fullback who was nearly impossible to bring down on first contact. He'd earned tough inside yards throughout the season, and without that constant threat of power running, teams might have spread out more to counter the razzle-dazzle. All of the backs were to be congratulated for their fine play, but now was no time for taking bows. The Michigan Wolverines were coming to town, and for one week nothing else would merit discussion in Columbus.

If Schmidt had any doubt as to the importance of the Michigan game, its stakes were clearly outlined by sportswriter Fritz Howell: "To the Ohio fans the season starts and ends with tomorrow's game. If the Buckeyes win, the season is a huge success. If the score is heavy, it's a stupendous season. If Ohio loses, nothing can assuage the grief of the thousands." The Wolverines had won 6 of the 7 meetings held at Ohio Stadium and 24 of 31 contests overall. They had cost Sam Willaman his job; they were not merely a rival, they were *the enemy*.[37]

Although Michigan had, by consensus, been named national champions the previous year, the 1934 squad had suffered a steep decline in material, resulting in several tough losses. Even their team MVP, Gerald Ford, would not be named to the all–Big 10 team, his future reign as the nation's president being of no value at the time. Some in Columbus were worried that Schmidt might awaken a sleeping giant with his usual loose talk, but he wisely chose a political stance. "I think this will be our hardest game," he lied. "I'll be mighty glad to win by one touchdown." Not even bothering to admit that his team might actually lose was backhanded humility at its finest. But it sounded humble, and Buckeye rooters breathed a sigh of relief. The fanfare was always excessive for this intense rivalry, and with Michigan's having a down year and Ohio State's pulverizing opponents of late, folks in Ohio were more excited than usual, certain they would receive satisfaction this year. To top it all off, this was homecoming week. By Thursday morning the Columbus hotels were full, as were the sorority and fraternity houses. Temporary stands capable of holding an additional 1,500 fans were erected at the Horseshoe for the first time since the Depression had descended four years prior.[38]

The first practice of the week was intense, devoted to plays that hadn't worked against Chicago. "Some of the boys didn't carry out their assignments," lamented Schmidt. "Some of them missed passes that should have been caught. They'll have to carry out these assignments if we are to beat Michigan, and they'll have to learn that a forward pass won't stick to a thumb." The three-headed, forward-passing monster (Stan Pincura, Tippy Dye, and Frank Fisch) had been accurate all season, but receiving passes had proved problematic. Undaunted, or just plain neurotic, Schmidt added 6 more pass plays to the team's repertoire.[39]

On Friday night the Buckeye team made their traditional move to the Columbus country club, which, due to its location on the outskirts of town, meant the team would be safely harbored, far from the pregame revelry. Michigan, meanwhile, tried to sleep at a downtown hotel, surrounded by a noisy throng of Columbus celebrants. The next day the Wolverines remained in their hotel until noon before absorbing waves of jeers on the way to the stadium for a two-o'clock kickoff. The Buckeyes were rested and waiting, having been escorted earlier from the country club by a team of motorcycle cops while thousands of roadside fans cheered on their conquerors.

By two thirty some of the Wolverines probably wished they had stayed in the hotel. The United Press summarized the carnage thusly: "Ohio used everything from everywhere and had the

Wolverines guessing all the time. They opened up with passes on the second play of the game and never let up. They kicked on first down and fourth down and passed the same way. Michigan never knew who was to kick or pass, which helped Ohio's running attack. . . . Coach Schmidt used every man on his squad, and the third- and fourth-stringers seemed as effective as the regulars." True to form, the Scarlet Scourge continued throwing forward passes late, including two touchdown throws in the final quarter. Ohio State won the game convincingly, 34–0. Since their first meeting in 1897, the Buckeyes had never scored more than 20 points in a game against Michigan. They had never beaten the Wolverines by more than 2 touchdowns. And the final score was the least humiliating of the statistics. First downs were 24–3 in favor of Ohio State. Net rushing yardage favored OSU 319–5, and total yardage (including punt/kick returns) was a jaw-dropping 638 yards to 86. It was easily the worst loss suffered by Michigan in the 31-game history of the rivalry.[40]

Michigan head coach Harry Kipke, like many coaches before him, was awestruck by the imagination of the offense and recalled a play early in the game. It "started out with a shovel pass and ended up with a couple of laterals," recalled Kipke. "I turned to one of our coaches on the bench with me and wholeheartedly announced, 'That was a whale of a play and perfectly executed'—and that was about the first time, during the heat of a game, that I ever made such a remark." The play he spoke of was number 84 in the Buckeye playbook. Left end Sam Busich ran parallel and close behind the line at the snap, took a shovel pass from Tippy Dye, and, just before the hole inside right tackle closed, he pitched the ball to the trailing left halfback Frank Boucher. After a couple of strides that drew the remainder of the Wolverine pursuers, Boucher then pitched the ball back to Tippy Dye, the quarterback who had started the play and would now finish it for a 16-yard gain. It was razzle-dazzle at its best, and even a badly beaten coach couldn't help but admire it. As further proof that Schmidt's system was bigger than its parts, a different player scored each of the 5 touchdowns.[41]

The only thing that went wrong for the Buckeyes all day was an incident involving Tippy Dye and Schmidt's absurd playbook. "There were so many plays that we [quarterbacks] had cards with the plays written on them that we stuck underneath our helmets. During timeouts we took them out and looked at them. Pincura, the other quarterback, also had them. During a punt return, I got cocked pretty good. It knocked me out a little. My helmet flew off, and the plays scattered all over the field. I was still a little out of it, but I made sure and picked 'em up."[42]

For the mob that filled Ohio Stadium to the brim, the opportunity to indulge in spiteful joy had been decades in the making. At the final whistle, the attendees' unleashing of pent-up enthusiasm was almost as spectacular as the game. Writers in the press box sat transfixed as "the crowd went wild after the game, tore the goal posts from the ground, snake-danced across the gridiron, and were still milling about the field—their voices getting hoarse from shouting—an hour after the game." For the first time ever, Ohio State had not only beaten her bitter rival but had done so in a most humiliating fashion. Schmidt and the boys had taken unofficial ownership of Columbus, and razzle-dazzle was beginning to grip a football-mad nation.[43]

The totality of the win was of great relief to Schmidt. His beloved offense had reigned supreme when it counted most, and the game that had been hanging over his head since he was hired was now a triumphant memory. Wanting to savor the victory in solitude—his favorite state of being—Schmidt left the house Monday morning for some rabbit and pheasant hunting. There amongst the quiet of the trees he spent a perfect morning internalizing his success. Still feeling satisfied when he returned at noon, he stopped by the locker room and posted a sign that read "No Practice Today." Not once in his time at Ohio State had he canceled a practice. It was a profound statement from a man with boundless energy and an insatiable desire to tinker with football. The burden of the Michigan game had been so great—and its relief so sweet—that even Schmidt's obsessive mind was freed to relax for one day.[44]

The players had their own response. Still keyed up from the win, the boys wanted to savor it with some action. With no practice scheduled, the freshman and sophomore team members decided this was the perfect afternoon to engage in the annual scrimmage between the two classes. Nothing unites a team like a big win, and many of the team's upperclassmen used their free afternoon to cheer the youngsters on. To nobody's surprise Coach Schmidt was unable to resist a game of football, and he soon joined the onlookers, no doubt enjoying the view from the top of the world.

As the week wore on, Schmidt refocused on unfinished business. The season-ending game with Iowa remained to be played, and the Hawkeyes had not played a game for two weeks, instead practicing exclusively with Ohio State in mind. Reporters still wanted to talk about the huge Michigan win, but Schmidt deflected all those questions, choosing instead to talk about the Iowa game. He reminded reporters, "Their coach Ossie Solem saw us beat Michigan and will have a pretty good line on our offense. Guess we might have to change things around a bit for Saturday's game." Considering the variety of plays used against Michigan, it's hard to believe Solem had a better idea of what was coming than any other coach. Instead, it sounds like Schmidt—the mad scientist—was trying to justify giving his subjects a new series of experimental drugs. Regardless, this game was still important. If the Buckeyes won—and they were heavily favored—they could still share the Big 10 crown providing, of course, that Minnesota somehow lost to an inferior Wisconsin squad. There were also some strong rumors that if both Minnesota and Ohio State won they might meet in a special Western

Conference championship game. This was baseless talk, spurred on by delusional hope. The Big 10 forbade postseason games, and besides, why would Minnesota jeopardize their clear-cut title? As a result of the rumors, however, some folks who might have purchased tickets to the Iowa game held out for the bigger game that never came to pass.[45]

Schmidt and his squad were not worried about titles and rumors as much as they were worried about a post-Michigan letdown. The Iowa team they were preparing for was not particularly talented, but it had two advantages: the aforementioned two weeks of uninterrupted practice and a black halfback named Ozzie Simmons.

While pro baseball and pro football were adhering to unwritten codes of discrimination, blacks could still occasionally be found on the squad of a major college football program. The Big 10 enjoyed the talents of several during the 1930s, including Bill Bell and Charley Anderson, who played for Ohio State. Of them all, Ozzie Simmons was the most dynamic. Simmons had grown up in Fort Worth and attended Terrell High School. There he had won 11 letters and ran the 100-yard dash in a record 9.8 seconds. Schmidt had scouted him and was highly impressed but felt like his hands were tied when it came time to recruit Simmons for college. At this time, Southwest schools were not encouraging the pursuit of black athletes thanks to the widespread discrimination that shaped athletic policy. Simmons had heard that Iowa might be the place to go. During the war Iowa's head coach, Ossie Solem, had been the commander of a black regiment, and the University of Iowa was where the famous black lineman Duke Slater (first-team All-American and three-time all–Big 10) had attended school. With just a bedroll, Oze (Simmons's nickname) had jumped a freight train to Iowa City. He easily made the freshman team, and talk of his brilliant play spread quickly. Now a sophomore, Simmons had commenced his varsity career with fireworks. In his first conference game, he had played so breathtakingly against Northwestern that one writer nearly lost his head, claiming, "This slithery, rubbery, oozy flier with his gyrating brilliance, cool, masterful mental poise, sleek, smooth, fluid, weaving hips, and the most perfect open-field pivot probably in the game today can make his lithe legs talk more languages than even Grange's could when he was a sophomore." Others celebrated Simmons with nicknames like "the ebony eel," the sort of compliment-by-compromise nicknames reserved for any successful black player of the era. Simmons had a flamboyant style of running with the ball, dodging runners while he held the ball in his outstretched hand, seemingly taunting his opponents as he left them grasping air. But then the season had run out of fun. His performances had slowed; some claimed he wouldn't play hurt and that he was surly. Others pointed out that Simmons was being singled out for malicious tackling (the Minnesota game had been particularly ugly) and that he was trying to run behind a line that had been decimated with injuries. There was just no room to run. When he was at his best—healthy and with room to maneuver—Simmons was elite. Schmidt knew from years of watching Simmons that he had better prepare for the dangerous version.[46]

The Buckeye squad, still on a high after decimating Michigan, put in a spirited week of practice. The seniors on the team were preparing for their last game of college football, and they wanted to savor every dwindling moment of fun. On Friday afternoon after Ohio State's final practice the fun turned to melancholy. Schmidt upheld a Buckeye tradition in honor of the senior players called the "Last Tackle." Leading his ten seniors over to the practice field next to the stadium, he called out their names and watched as each made their "last tackle," slamming into the tackling dummy one last time.

Anyone who questioned how serious Schmidt was taking this final game got an answer early on. On the opening kickoff of the Iowa game some questioned whether the Hawkeyes' return man fumbled, and when the ruling went against Ohio State, Schmidt stalked onto the field and engaged the officials in a zestful, animated conversation. The ruling stood, giving Iowa one of its few breaks of the day, but the Buckeyes were determined to finish the season in style. Even with extra practice the Hawkeyes were powerless to stop the crushing momentum Ohio State had been cultivating all season long. On their way to a 40–7 victory, Schmidt and his boys put on a masterful exhibition of offensive variety, and for the second straight week each touchdown was scored by a different player. The mix of power and deception was never more evident than in the second quarter when Ohio State used a lateral off of a Statue of Liberty play to get to Iowa's 11-yard line, followed by 4 straight punishing runs up the middle for a touchdown. With everything clicking, it opened up Ohio State's passing game, which struck for 230 yards and 3 touchdowns while Iowa's passing game never materialized, going 0 for 10 with 2 interceptions. The Hawkeyes' running game never materialized either; Simmons and his talented backfield mate Dick Crayne were repeatedly trapped behind the line of scrimmage. Simmons did, however, score the Hawkeyes' only touchdown on a scintillating 85-yard interception return behind some beautiful blocking. Simmons also picked off another pass in the fourth quarter and returned it 43 yards, deep into Buckeye territory. But that final Iowa threat was killed before it ever started when Schmidt sent eight of his first stringers back into the game. By sending his best players into a blowout that late, Schmidt was either shutting the gates of mercy or giving his seniors one last thrill. Either way, Schmidt could probably cross out the name of another conference coach from a list of potential friends. For the third straight week Ohio State had beaten a conference opponent by the largest margin in the history of that series between the two teams. Nearly flawless in the second half of the season, Ohio State had won all 4 games by an aggregate total of 183–7.[47]

One unusual occurrence in the Iowa game—only slightly noteworthy at the time—was the substituting for Gomer Jones. Early in the game, the Buckeyes' starting center was hurt and had to be replaced. It so happened that the injury occurred near the Ohio bench, and the boys on the field, seeing that Schmidt was going to send in what they considered to be an inferior replacement, began pleading for George Kabealo, Johnny's brother. Schmidt agreed and gave the players what they wanted. One reporter who witnessed it swore he had never known a Big 10 coach to allow a substitution based on the will of his players. It seemed like a small thing in 1934, but it was a harbinger of Schmidt's downfall.[48]

Meanwhile, Minnesota won their game with ease, not only crowning them Big 10 champs but consensus national champions as well. The Buckeyes' amazing season had yielded only a second-place conference finish.

At the football banquet four days later, Schmidt, flush with success and seeking to maximize its resultant leverage, asked for the media to start referring to the Buckeyes as the "Bucks." The news media had often used the nickname "Bucks" as a change-of-pace truncation, but only sparingly and without meaning. Schmidt, on the other hand, was advocating its full-time use and with a completely different purpose. He apparently thought the team *needed* a nickname that referenced a fearful beast rather than one that referenced the nuts of an indigenous tree. "I want everyone to picture the team as a ripsnorting one with fire flying out of its nostrils, and they won't do it if you call 'em 'Buckeyes.' Let's call 'em 'Bucks,'" he pleaded. It was a completely audacious request that had no relationship with reality. Nobody, no matter how successful he is, can spontaneously change a team's identity. Those gathered quietly nodded their heads, hoping Schmidt would come to his senses by the next fall. The coach finished his banquet speech with some typical sarcasm, telling his team, "You fellows learned quite a bit this season. Next year we should be able to open up a little bit." The players were glad to wait. They'd had enough football for one year. Schmidt, on the other hand, could never get enough. Three days later, he was in Pittsburgh watching the Pitt–Carnegie Tech game, and three days after that he was in Philadelphia watching the Army–Navy game.[49]

Although Ohio State had barely missed a share of the Big 10 title, they ranked in the top five nationally according to most of the unofficial year-end polls for 1934. Their wins over Chicago, Iowa, and Michigan had been the most lopsided in the series' history, and the victories over Indiana and Northwestern the most complete in nearly twenty years. Just as important to cash-strapped OSU was the windfall produced by Schmidt's exciting style of play. Gross receipts from ticket sales had nearly doubled from the previous season, expanding from $137,000 to a quarter million. Including road attendance, the exciting Buckeyes had played to more fans than any school in the Big 10. It was Ohio State's most profitable year since 1928 when the economy was still roaring.[50]

Ohio State's final statistics bear witness to what a dramatic year it had been. Their 33.4 points per game made them the highest scoring team in school history. In forward passing Ohio State had completed 62 of 136 (46 percent) for 1,188 yards with 16 touchdowns and 11 interceptions. Opponents were 32 of 105 (31 percent) for 418 yards, 2 touchdowns, and 21 interceptions. In rushing yardage the spread was 1,455 yards to 432. There were 110 Buckeye first downs to their opponents' 34, and—in the category that counted most—they scored 39 touchdowns to 5.[51]

Two rather insignificant statistics are interesting for how they highlight the way the game in 1934 was different as compared to today. In the category of field goals, *the Buckeyes and their opponents combined to convert only one field goal the entire season.* Place kicking had not yet evolved in technique, and the chances of an accurate kick were such that teams almost always chose to "go for it" on fourth down inside the opponent's 30-yard line. Even extra-point kicks were an adventure with teams' converting just over half the time.

The other enlightening category was that of penalties. Ohio State received 21 on the season, while their competitors received 23. At less than 3 infractions a game per team, it's obvious that officials were more lenient during this era.[52]

Oddities aside, it was nearly impossible to speak too highly of Schmidt and the Buckeyes. In the *Ohio State University Monthly*, Larry Snyder was nearly beside himself as he tried to capture the glory of the 1934 season, writing, "We have the fightingest football team, the greatest coach, and such high morale as a group that Ohio State University in all its branches and departments has moved on to a higher plane in the hearts of all who love her, or casually know her." Even more important was the praise from Schmidt's bosses. At Ohio State's annual meeting, J. L. Morrill's report from the athletic board left no doubt as to their euphoria: "Praise has been heaped on him until it is difficult to find new words and phrases with which to describe our happiness in having Francis Schmidt in charge of football."[53]

Adulation for Schmidt was not reserved for Ohio. His brand of football was building a national fan base. The *Saturday Evening Post* contacted Schmidt about writing a feature regarding this new style of pigskin. The article, which would appear the following autumn, was entitled "The New Open Game." In it Schmidt decried the predictability of the traditional game and discussed the movement that was changing the future of football. "Ground-gaining will probably follow more diversified lines," he wrote. "Teams will pass more frequently on first down, and they will sock a few serious throws when they are clear back in their own territory. . . . The field will be opened, and, with the use of laterals beyond the line of scrimmage, the game will produce more unexpected excitement. More short passes will be thrown, and there will be more quick kicks. Defenses will need the same speed and agility as the offenses, for against every action there must be an equal and opposite reaction." Schmidt's belief in this open-game movement was strong enough that instead of begrudging what other coaches had added to the mix, he applauded them. There was room in the laboratory for many scientists, and he praised Andy Kerr (Colgate) for using laterals and Bo McMillin (Indiana) for pushing the envelope with a controversial five-man backfield. He even praised Ozzie Simmons as the most exciting player in the game, an example of the immense talent that could be maximized with an open game that created space and momentum. So excited was Schmidt about the future that he even saw this openness spreading to the defense. He gleefully related the possibilities of defenders' using laterals after interceptions and related that he had given Ohio State his blessing in trying this maneuver—a maneuver that would be considered high-level sacrilege by standard coaches, for one did not fool with the precious gift of a turnover received.[54]

Whether Schmidt and the open-game movement were merely a fad or were indicative of the future of football was anyone's guess, but after watching the 1934 Ohio State Buckeyes anything seemed possible. Buckeye fans were already tingling with anticipation for 1935. Most of the Buckeye starters were returning a year wiser and experienced with the intricacies of Schmidt's system. And if that weren't enough, next season's schedule, for the first time ever, included Notre Dame. The excitement and anticipation were unprecedented.

Six. The Game

Since his days at Arkansas City High, Francis Schmidt had always jumped directly into his basketball coaching duties as soon as the football season ended. There was never a full week between the two sports. This was inconvenient for the athletes who played both sports and wanted to enjoy a few afternoons without practice, but it suited Schmidt just fine. The demon that caused so much restlessness in his brain did not disappear with the end of football. It demanded action: a project, a puzzle, something to occupy a portion of his mind at all times. Basketball held less strategic possibilities than football, yet it required enough thinking to keep the hungry furnace fed. But now Schmidt was at Ohio State—the big time—and in the big time each sport had a separate coach. Harold Olsen had been coaching the Buckeye hoopsters since 1923, and, although he hadn't been overly successful, he seemed to be entrenched.

Without basketball coaching to occupy him, Schmidt's obsession with football began to take on new dimensions. Unable to contain himself, he sat down in late January and wrote up a letter for his thirty-some returning lettermen, declaring that winter football practice would start the first week of February. This practice overkill was to last for a month and take place indoors away from inclement weather. They players were to report in tennis shoes to the physical education building where mats copped from the wrestling team had been strategically placed. Indoor winter practice had been used in degrees by coaches in the past, but never so early and for such a lengthy period. "We have several new ideas including plays, formations, shifts, etc., that we want to try out, and this looks like a fine time," explained Schmidt. "Two months is long enough to lay off from football, anyway. I want to get all the preliminary stuff out of the way so that when spring practice rolls around, and we can get out, we will be ready to start mapping out our attack. We will spend most of the time on lateral and forward passes and we'll spend a whole month at it." Not only was winter practice unusual, but so was the emphasis on flinging the football rather than on fundamentals. February practice had its pros and cons. It was nice to run around after being cooped up because of the cold, but then again, February was prime time for the remediation of one's academic record after posting first-quarter grades that had suffered because of football. Thanks to Schmidt's relentlessly demanding football program, students were having a difficult time focusing on their studies. This was not without consequence. Five lettermen, including Stan Pincura and Joe Williams, would need to attend summer school in an effort to regain football eligibility. Five other potential lettermen would be joining them. Schmidt didn't believe any of the cases were "serious," but then again, worrying about grades was not on his radar.[1]

In the meantime, spring football demanded their attention. During this session, Schmidt surrendered to the practicing of some basic foundational football, but he did so with the attitude of a kid who eats vegetables only so he can get down to the serious pursuit of dessert. "The boys will be worked pretty hard so that by next fall we'll be able to start on plays and formations and lose no time on things all football players should know." Despite understanding their importance, Schmidt hated fundamentals, hated the mundanity of blocking and tackling drills with their monotonous repetition, but he begrudgingly recognized their place. Just not often enough.[2]

After devoting winter and spring to football, Schmidt stayed the course through summer. He began by conducting a grueling six-week coaching course at Ohio State that involved three two-hour classes every day but Sunday. As had been the case the previous summer, Schmidt was an amusing sight, striding about campus with his usual impatience, his head bent down, either studying one of his notebooks full of plays or just lost in thought, oblivious to things around him. One exception was the big pair of feet he noticed one day. Looking up and not recognizing the face, Schmidt asked, "Big boy, why aren't you out for football?" The prospect of fresh talent was the one thing that always garnered Schmidt's attention.[3]

Following his Ohio State summer duty, Schmidt returned to Fort Worth where at the request of former assistant Dutch Meyer, he headlined a football clinic sponsored by TCU. Schmidt was also to be the featured basketball instructor at a Texas Tech coaching school soon thereafter. Even though he no longer coached hoops, his reputation had not diminished. After the Texas tour Schmidt returned north and helped run a clinic at Northwestern with the Wildcats' new coach, Lynn "Pappy" Waldorf, a friend of Schmidt's from their days of coaching on the prairie.[4]

Schmidt had earned his usual late-summer vacation, but he wasn't really built to relax, and vacations were often hard for him to reconcile. "Well, I'm glad that's over," he announced upon returning from three weeks at a secluded fishing camp in Canada. "Now maybe we can get something done. Oh, we fished and swam a little, and played a little golf. And I mapped out a lot of new football plays, spent a lot of time worrying about Pittsburgh, Notre Dame, and some of the other teams we meet this year and wound up by watching the All-Star professional football game in Chicago last night." Finally, having endured the pains of relaxing, Schmidt was ready for the traditional football season.[5]

When fall practice opened Schmidt had a squad of forty-nine men to work with. It was, not accidentally, the smallest number in the conference. Schmidt had too many plays to experiment with and didn't want to waste his time teaching them to players who he didn't expect to be part of the core rotation. And since he didn't delegate much, he could only single-handedly manage a smaller mob. Furthermore, no coach was more steadfast in the belief that players either had value or they didn't. Those he did choose, he played. No coach in the conference substituted more players during games than did Schmidt. To arrive at this core group Schmidt typically invited about one hundred men to spring practice with another two or three dozen boys wildcatting. At the end of practice he was judicious in deciding which players were legitimately potential regulars. This distilled group would be invited to fall practice along with a handful from the just-missed layer in case he needed replacements for those who would become injured or ineligible. The screening process was hard-line compared to that of Ohio State's opponents. In contrast to Schmidt's forty-nine invitees for the 1935 season, Notre Dame opened camp with just under one hundred, Purdue had eighty-seven, and Zuppke had seventy-five at Illinois.[6]

Schmidt's opening speech was a little longer than his three-word opus from the previous fall and included this bit of verbal algebra: "We have a lot of new men who'll have to learn the plays; we'll have a lot of new plays for both the new and old men, and I suppose half of you have forgotten all you learned last season—so we're practically starting from scratch." He also warned them not to believe the hype that Ohio State was favored to win the national title. "You guys can forget all about that championship baloney. I want you to get out there and hustle and keep so busy you won't have time to think of it." The advice was intended for himself as well. Schmidt hated pressure, and the pressure to meet expectations plagued him day and night.[7]

The team had a lot of experience along with some players who had excellent personalities. Creating a stable team atmosphere wasn't really Schmidt's forte, and more often than not it fell to the players to properly organize and motivate themselves. The 1935 squad was blessed to have dynamic quarterbacks like Tippy Dye and Stan Pincura, but its real strength could be traced to the amiable, steadfast nature of Gomer Jones. As the team captain, All-American center, and leader of the linemen, Gomer needed to keep his teammates grounded and ambitious at the same time.

Gomer was good natured and well loved by his teammates. They hadn't considered anyone else when electing their captain for 1935. Physically, Gomer was the quintessential "bowling ball," short and round at 5 feet 8 inches and 200 pounds, with most of the bulk residing in his midsection. Playing center in this era was an incredibly important job. Like other teams, Ohio State's offense called for airborne (shotgun-like) snaps on nearly every single play. This is tricky enough, but in Schmidt's system, with its multiple formations and hundreds of plays, the length and direction of the snap changed frequently. With accuracy and timing being so crucial to the success of each play, Gomer had to be perfect with his touch each time. It was practically a carnival stunt, but Gomer had mastered it. On defense he was just as good, possessing the uncanny knack for getting through the line. Schmidt couldn't have been happier with his center, and he wasn't even the most naturally gifted of the Buckeye linemen.

Merle Wendt had been quick enough to be a star left halfback in high school. Schmidt had moved him to the end position where he was making a big name for himself. Even faster was sophomore guard Inwood Smith. At 6 feet and 198 pounds he would be 100 pounds too light to play today, but in 1935 he was an average-sized lineman. His foot speed, however, was above average, and Smith wreaked havoc when pulling and leading interference from his guard position. Then there was Charley Hamrick. The huge tackle was poised for an All-American season, but he'd hurt his knee during the summer while pushing a lawnmower, and he wasn't moving so well. Though he played the entire season, he never exhibited the level of play expected from him. (Had it been available, modern medicine with its computer-aided assessments would undoubtedly have revealed the cause and extent of the problem and have allowed doctors to prescribe a proper recovery regimen—one more example of the difficulty in making intergenerational player comparisons). All four linemen were naturally devastating defenders, which was a good thing seeing as what little time Schmidt spent on defense. With Gomer in charge, this part of the team gave Schmidt little to worry about.

Fall practice unfolded just as expected. Schmidt had the team practicing on the first day, "plays that some of the boys know and some don't." For three weeks they concentrated on offense, and only during the last week of fall practice did Schmidt begin working on defense. As fall practice drew to a close, it was obvious to all that the 1935 Ohio State Buckeyes were as good as had been advertised.[8]

Just as he had the year before, Schmidt took advantage of the fact that Ohio State's opening-game opponent started their season early. Kentucky had already played two games, and Schmidt personally scouted both, with road trips to Lexington and Cincinnati. For Schmidt, scouting the Kentucky Wildcats wasn't just a chance to gain some information about the season-opening opponent, it was a chance to prepare for Notre Dame as well. Chet Wynne, Kentucky's head coach, was a former "Domer" and one of many loyal Knute Rockne disciples who continued to use Rockne's

Notre Dame system of offense. All told, there were some thirty ex-Irish players now coaching at colleges throughout the nation, and most of them had retained the "Notre Dame Box" formation with its quasi-legal shifting and precise blocking schemes. Yet despite the number of coaches propagating this system, Schmidt had not faced many. Rice University, under "Jack" Meagher, had used Rockne's system, and Texas Christian, under Schmidt, had easily beaten the Owls each season, but that was just one version. Schmidt, of course, had spent so many hours studying football strategy that the Notre Dame system was no mystery to him, but he wanted to see more of it in person to get a better feel for its rhythm and quirks. Kentucky had proven very helpful in this respect.[9]

So why was Schmidt so interested in preparing for a game with the Fighting Irish that wouldn't be played until November? Simply put, it was a dream matchup between two of the most fervently followed football programs in America. Despite their regional proximity the two schools had never met on the gridiron, and the excitement for this heavyweight fight had been building since the 1934 season had ended.

Since just after World War I, and continuing to this day, Notre Dame has had the largest national following of any college football program in the country. Without compare, Notre Dame's football has been feted in all forms of media, and its followers are thick from coast to coast. This phenomena transcends the normal regional and alumni loyalty that other teams enjoy, largely because Notre Dame has always trod a separate path from other schools.

Ironically, the school with the nickname "Fighting Irish" was born of a French Catholic order, the Congregatio a Sancta Cruse. The school was established in 1860, and its football program was technically born in 1897, but it struggled to find footing for several years, playing a large percentage of its games against clubs, high schools, and medical schools through the turn of the century. Notre Dame joined the ranks of big-time football late—around 1910—and had some advantages that allowed it to quickly make up for lost time. It was a remote school, totally comprised of male students (until 1972) and not burdened by stringent admission standards. Its open-door policy, which accepted any student willing to trade labor for tuition, was a magnet for boys traveling a less-than-traditional academic path. The school didn't seem to fit anybody's mold. Compared to other mainstream schools it overemphasized the molding of manly character (mostly through religious study) and underemphasized a standard academic curriculum. And yet amongst Catholic schools it was rather progressive in providing instruction toward professional degrees from which some shied away. Notre Dame also embraced and encouraged a physical, athletic culture that other longstanding institutions only tolerated. With its testosterone-fueled campus and somewhat divergent educational goals, Notre Dame was not unlike West Point or the Naval Academy, where even intramural sports rivaled the importance of intercollegiate endeavors and manly men could be found around every corner. For these reasons Notre Dame excelled at all sports. And it was through sports—particularly football, the most popular of all intercollegiate games—that Notre Dame emerged as an anomaly: a school that was the flagship for an entire religion rather than just a region or academic specialty. How it got there was the result of happenstance, timing, and shrewdness.[10]

Part of the equation involved a new segment of the American population with a need to be filled. Thanks to a massive second wave of immigration, nearly 20 percent of the U.S. population in 1920 was Catholic, making it the largest single religious denomination represented in America. And of that new minority, it was estimated that 75 percent had been born outside of the United States. It was a group whose regional pride was in transition, and they latched onto certain things to keep them culturally afloat. Among those things was sports, the most popular of which was college football. In this environment a Catholic school that played exceptional football would surely endear itself.[11]

By virtue of their culture Notre Dame had developed a great football program. And because they were so good, so Catholic, and still a bit unusual academically, other large Midwest schools were using these reasons not to schedule them. The Big 10 had repeatedly denied their application for membership. Needing money and needing good competition to get it, Notre Dame ended up with a far-flung schedule including stops in the East, wherein lay the greatest concentration of Catholics, the original ivy-covered football powers, and a press that ruled American brain waves—the perfect launching pad for the Notre Dame mystique. Notre Dame invaded West Point in 1913, stunning Army and the eastern establishment with a 35–14 win that set their fame in motion. The next year they added Yale and Syracuse to the schedule. After Notre Dame won the unofficial national championship in 1924 and began playing games at large venues in Catholic strongholds, the love affair between Catholics and Notre Dame was sealed. When playing in New York, Baltimore, Cleveland, and Chicago they would regularly draw capacity crowds, many over 70,000 strong. Yet Notre Dame Stadium, which had opened in 1930 with a seating capacity of 54,000, had sold out just one time in its five-and-a-half-season history. As a matter of fact, during that period, the Irish had averaged only 23,342 fans per home game, just about half capacity. Notre Dame was a one-of-a-kind national sort of team, waving the banner for Catholic football fans all over America who needed to latch onto a new source of pride in a new home country.[12]

So it was that this game between Notre Dame and Ohio State had generated so much advanced excitement. They were two skilled teams with rabid followings that had never collided. If by chance the two teams also happened to be undefeated when they met, it would be a huge national spectacle.

For Ohio State, this march to the big game started on October 5 when Kentucky came to Columbus. While this was Ohio State's season opener, the Wildcats had already played two games, winning both. Floyd Stahl, who had scouted Kentucky along with Schmidt, thought they were already in midseason form. Not only that, but the Wildcats had two excellent halfbacks in Bert Johnson and Bob Davis.

Any worry that the underdog Wildcats might cause trouble was forgotten early when the Buckeyes scored on the first series of the game, swiftly chalking up 5 first downs while moving 80 yards for a quick touchdown. But Kentucky wasn't going to be easy. The Wildcats were a much lighter team, but they held their own on the defensive line, allowing Johnson and Davis to run free in support. The two backs seemed to be everywhere, and their great tackling kept the game close. The Buckeyes held a slim 12–6 lead entering the fourth quarter when Jumpin' Joe Williams emerged. The little sophomore halfback began breaking big runs. First an 18-yarder that was called back on penalty, immediately followed by a 20-yard burst around right end, which was then followed by 24 more yards around left end. Kentucky knew it was over even before Williams finished the job by scoring the final touchdown in a 19–6 win. Despite the team's 331 total yards, and Jumpin' Joe's thrilling heroics, the Buckeyes had looked less than elite. The opening-game record crowd of 56,686 was glad for the win but had expected something a little more decisive. Apparently Schmidt felt the same way.[13]

Disappointed with the Kentucky game, Schmidt cussed and prodded more than ever at practice the next week. The Ohio linemen had been outclassed by a smaller Kentucky line, and too many of his backs were earning membership in "that damned fumbling society." Seeing as how the next opponent, Drake (Iowa), was a small hapless school without a prayer of being victorious over Ohio State, many coaches might have saved their ire for the following week, but Schmidt was too impatient and too organically bombastic to finesse personalities in this way. Instead, he threatened to bench starters if they didn't put forth maximum effort during a nasty week of long, hard practices. The result was to be expected.[14]

Ohio State humiliated Drake 85–7—the biggest point total for the Buckeyes since 1916 and their second highest ever. The starters for the visiting Bulldogs gave everything they had, and midway through the first quarter they had achieved a 7–7 tie, but Ohio State, after a hellish week of practice, was not about to get complacent. In the second quarter the Bucks scored 5 touchdowns, and it was all over but the usual insult from Schmidt's hungry reserves. The final statistics were not suitable for children; Ohio State had overpowered the little Des Moines school in every way possible including first downs (39 to 3) and net yards (646 yards to 21). Five touchdowns came on forward passes and another 4 came from halfback Jumpin' Joe Williams who also gained 107 yards on 8 carries. It was a rare occurrence in Schmidt's system for a single player to score so much in a game, but the disparity in the teams' abilities made for the unusual. Schmidt employed all forty-seven men on the varsity squad except for the two who were injured. The backups, as usual, were ruthless, scoring 26 points in the fourth quarter.[15]

Schmidt had received the effort he had demanded but was still not fully satisfied. In the locker room following the game, Schmidt spoke to several of the players personally, discussing their mistakes by referencing the notes he had jotted down during the game. The reporters watching this were shocked and were left wondering how to defend Schmidt after he allowed his team to savage a helpless opponent. Schmidt wasn't remorseful. In response to the sticky question of whether he had unfairly run up the score, Schmidt issued a dismissive question of his own: "The idea of the game is to score touchdowns, isn't it?" Shut-the-Gates-of-Mercy Schmidt was back in the media's crosshairs.[16]

The reporters turned to Joe Magidsohn, referee for the game, who gave his interpretation of the proceedings: "Their plays just clicked, that's all. Ohio State players were not bearing down at any time in the game after the first five minutes. They were working easily."[17]

That didn't really answer the question of why the Buckeyes had been so merciless, and for the next couple weeks the press pestered Schmidt for an explanation. Finally, he decided to give them what they wanted and described how the Drake game had spun out of control:

> It's like this. My first team was obviously too good for Drake, but I started the varsity anyway. If I didn't, it would amount to an insult. They scored 2 touchdowns so rapidly that I could hardly call out the names of the replacements I wanted to send in. Well, I pulled out the first stringers.
>
> I instructed the second-string quarterback to play safe and go along on a 12–0 score—unless a touchdown stared him in the face—until the end of the half. But I know what he thought as he ran out there to report to the official. "Here's where I make the first team," he probably growled through gritted teeth, "watch me make the coach smile at the way I run the team." A couple more touchdowns there, of course, and I hauled the second string signal caller out.
>
> The third-string quarterback nearly dropped dead when I told him to go into the game. He acted as if he was inspired, playing his head off as a third-string team ran wild in the sharing of his enthusiasm. I pulled out the third team and sent in

whatever substitutes and unknowns that were around. They blocked, tackled, smashed, passed, lateraled, and all the while I am sitting there, dejected as a Siberian prisoner and just as cold in the thought that they'd call me a murderer. And they have. There was nothing I could do about it.[18]

As far as explanations go, this one was classic Schmidt. He mixed humor, paranoia, and blame in such equal amounts that one was left to wonder whether he was a comedian or a jerk—the quandary shared by all who knew him. Was he genius or insane? Was he affable or sarcastic? Was he jocular or cruel? Was he myopic or just plain indifferent? Trying to label his particular brand of odd was difficult, and, to make it worse, he didn't seem to take seriously the importance of one's reputation.

Legends like Rockne and Stagg had on occasion allowed their teams to run up outrageous scores, but it occurred rarely, and when it did they understood how to minimize these indiscretions by taking responsibility, not by making light of them like Schmidt had. Even John Heisman, who allowed his team to beat Cumberland 222–0, had emerged with his reputation intact. That game is now remembered as a wacky fable, and Heisman's name adorns college football's most iconic trophy. Schmidt did not understand the importance of currying favor with the press. Perhaps he figured that if his teams kept winning titles then he could run up scores and laugh at sportswriters without any lasting repercussions. It was a lot easier being hounded to explain lopsided wins than it was explaining even the slightest of losses. Because of Schmidt's attitude, writers were left to wonder if he actively encouraged the running up of scores, something that did not endear him to those in charge of his legacy.

John Whitaker, editor of the *Hammond (Indiana) Times*, didn't give a damn whether Schmidt was consciously cruel or not. "Schmidt's practice is not creating new or keeping old friends. Football fans in general will be awaiting that afternoon when the worm turns and Ohio State winds up on the small end of the score. Other teams may win conference or national championships, but the squad who knocks off Ohio State in its own backyard will be credited with the greatest achievement of the season." Writing for a paper located seventy miles from South Bend, Whitaker may have been hinting that Notre Dame was just the team to settle the ethics imbalance in Columbus. The fanfare for The Game was building toward a deafening crescendo.[19]

Despite all the fallout from the Drake debacle, there was some good news in Columbus—the emergence of a bona fide backfield star in Jumpin' Joe Williams. Even though Buckeye fans were satisfied that their team was powerful, they still longed for a star player with star statistics; that's just human nature. But Schmidt's system of offense wasn't always the perfect vehicle for creating heroes even though it achieved immense yardage and scoring. It was built to utilize many players' performing many tasks well. Still, a star or two were bound to emerge occasionally. Cy Leland had emerged at TCU, and now here was Jumpin' Joe. Schmidt called him "Little Joe"—probably because he forgot his last name—but the name fit as Joe was listed at 5 feet 5 inches and 163 pounds. The sophomore from Barberton, Ohio, had been a prep dynamo, scoring a staggering 60 touchdowns for his small high school. The "Jumpin'" sobriquet resulted from tributary comparisons to "Jumpin'" Joe Savoldi, Notre Dame's star halfback at the time. The nickname was even more fitting because Williams was an Irish-Catholic interested in playing for Notre Dame. After graduating in 1934 Williams took a job with a car dealer delivering autos from South Bend to Akron. This gave him the opportunity to see Notre Dame up close, and his affinity for the school grew stronger. No one was surprised when he offered his playing services to the Irish that fall, but the football program only responded with halfhearted interest to the little guy from a little school, making no real effort to secure him a job. A disappointed Williams then turned to his high school coach, Jimmy Price, for advice and was told that something might be arranged at Ohio State. After all, Price had played for the Buckeyes' line coach, Ernie Godfrey, when both were at little Wittenberg College. So Jumpin' Joe enrolled at Ohio State, starring on the Buckeyes' freshman team, holding a job at a Columbus meat-packing plant, and living at the Sigma Nu house. During spring practice in 1935 Jumpin' Joe had earned a top spot on the varsity team with his spectacular play, but by fall practice he found himself back on the bench thanks to poor defense, fumbles, and uninspired blocking. He was very low key, and when things were going well he was perceived as being "laid-back," but when things went badly he was considered nothing better than apathetic. When it was time for real game action, Jumpin' Joe had come off the bench and run circles around Kentucky. Because he was smaller, because he was a sophomore, and because his defense was weak, Schmidt would continue to bring him off the bench, using him as a designated scorer when the Buckeyes moved into enemy territory. Used properly, Williams was a nice weapon in Schmidt's arsenal, and Buckeye fans roared with excitement every time No. 13 entered the game. Supporting a winning team that scores plenty of points is great, but there's just something special about having a star player to call one's own.[20]

After the Drake game, Ohio State began their Big 10 schedule. Playing their third straight home game, the Buckeyes knocked off Northwestern, winning 28–7. Three of the touchdowns came on forward passes (2 from Tippy Dye) and the other on a 25-yard run by Jumpin' Joe Williams. Even though it was a Big 10 game and Northwestern was not to be underestimated, Schmidt pulled most of his starters early after Ohio State scored 3 touchdowns with just 13 offensive plays. Either he was smarting from the criticism over the Drake debacle or he had been encouraged by Saint to ease up. Or maybe he was just being predictably unpredictable. Later the Wildcats put themselves in position to score on several occasions but were unable to close the deal due to penalties, fumbles, or OSU's defense.[21]

Bob Zuppke, whose team had the weekend off, was in attendance, scouting both teams the Illini would play later in the season. When it was over, he told syndicated sportswriter Harry Grayson that he had never seen anything like Ohio State's offense and that it left him "awed" and "overwhelmed." This reaction of astonishment was particularly satisfying coming from the early leader of the open-game movement—one whose reputation was being eclipsed.[22]

OSU now had only one more game before Notre Dame. It was a conference game, it was on the road, and it was Indiana's homecoming. Ohio State was a 10–1 favorite, but if players' minds were preoccupied with Notre Dame, it was the perfect scenario for an upset. The Hoosiers were tired of hearing about Ohio State and Notre Dame, the neighborhood bullies. This was evident on the Buckeyes' first possession when Indiana unleashed a furious attack, boring through the line and making tackles in the backfield. Then, less than five minutes into the game, the Hoosiers offense scored on a 57-yard pass play, sending their homecoming crowd into a frenzy. The Buckeyes were stunned by Indiana's aggression, which didn't let up. With nothing to lose, the Hoosiers' defense switched to a five-man line (seven men was still the standard in this era of power football). Indiana was determined to stop any passing or outside runs, two of Schmidt's most successful strategies. Seemingly, their defensive front would now be vulnerable to power, but Ohio State's offensive linemen were now matching up against men out of normal position, creating angles and assignments they hadn't practiced. Even with a smaller line, Indiana was thus able to continue getting pressure into Ohio State's backfield. The Buckeyes got just one break the entire first half, and they jumped on it. After recovering a bad snap, Tippy Dye hit Jumpin' Joe Williams on a 13-yard screen pass for a touchdown and a 7–6 halftime lead. As might be guessed, the adrenaline and the gimmick strategy that kept Indiana on the verge of an upset died at the hands of that great momentum killer: halftime. Following a joint sermon on strategy from Schmidt and Godfrey during the break, the Buckeyes opened the second half with trap blocks and shovel passes for big gains. Immediately the Hoosiers sent in a substitute with instructions for returning to the seven-man line. How quickly aggression can turn to caution in football. And just as quickly that synergetic vibe that dared to believe in something special vaporizes, leaving nothing but despondency to fill the vacuum. The Buckeyes had survived apathy and shock, and now they were the aggressors. With their foot placed securely on Indiana's throat, Ohio State used 22 forward passes en route to a 28–6 victory.[23]

Looking at that score the next day, a stranger might have thought Ohio State had won with ease, but the Buckeyes knew differently. Jumpin' Joe Williams felt like he had survived a street brawl. After the game he had his jaw and foot x-rayed for breaks, but there were none. "They played me dirty as heck. They all do. They twist my legs—try to get me out of the ball game," he complained afterward. Through 4 games he had scored 8 touchdowns to lead the nation. As a team, his Buckeyes also led the nation in scoring. Despite a tough game with Indiana, everyone was ready for Notre Dame. Jumpin' Joe, who had once loved Notre Dame only to be rejected by them, was thinking about the game more than most.[24]

If it had been hard for the players to concentrate on the Indiana game, most Buckeye fans were sympathetic. They too had been growing restless, ready to get on with the Notre Dame game. The contest had been highly anticipated since it had been announced the previous year, and since the beginning of the 1935 football season that enthusiasm had grown exponentially with each passing week. At first the hoopla had centered around the fact that it was the first meeting of two iconic football schools, but as the season unfolded and both teams kept winning it was obvious that this game was headed for fantastic heights. For the first time since Knute Rockne's death, the Irish were contending for a national championship, having started the season 5-0 and coming off a huge win over powerhouse Pittsburgh. This was the triumphant rebirth of the nation's most popular team, and here they were, headed to Columbus to play OSU, whom many thought was "perhaps the greatest team in the land." Suddenly this battle had the potential for deciding who was the best college football team in America.[25]

Besides the Rose Bowl game, only occasionally did other contests warrant such attention that the New York sportswriting aristocracy would mobilize and head west. The 1935 Ohio State–Notre Dame game was one of those instances. On Monday the newspaper royalty began boarding trains. Anybody who was anybody would be at this one. Besides having national-title implications it involved storylines that appealed to their rum-soaked hearts. For one thing, the Irish were favorites of the Gotham scribes, due in part to Notre Dame's many eastern visits and in larger part to the beloved and charismatic Knute Rockne. Rockne's untimely death in 1930 had only bonded this relationship, and the writers had taken a protective position toward the orphaned program. Now that unfortunate golden child from South Bend, with the aid of Rockne disciples, had emerged from mourning to the thrill of its media benefactors.

As for Ohio State, they represented something of a dark curiosity, the home of Shut-the-Gates-of-Mercy Schmidt and his Scarlet Scourge. In the national theater of college football, they played the roll of the greedy family, given to excess in everything. They employed more strategy than anyone, scored more points than anyone, and played before more fans than anyone. Yet the Buckeyes weren't exactly villains. It was fun to watch them execute their tome of plays, and their coach was a fascinating, odd man. The spirit of their fans was awesome to behold, and, frankly, it seemed like they deserved one perfect season. Other Big 10 teams like Michigan, Minnesota, and Illinois had won mythical championships, but Ohio State had never quite grasped the crown. In the past three decades they had won just as many games as those teams but never bunched their wins in the right place at the right time. The extremism of the Buckeye faithful had never been repaid in kind. They had earned their fairy tale, and 1935 looked like they year they just might receive their reward. The New York sports media wasn't often breathless about doings out west, but this one had seized their full attention.

Publicly, Francis Schmidt had not made special mention of the Notre Dame game. He was worried enough about all the championship talk adversely affecting his team and he wanted desperately to keep each game in context. He still understood that beating Michigan was the priority where his job security was concerned, and winning the Big 10 conference for the first time since 1920 was his primary goal, but he also knew that beating Notre Dame would go a long way toward making his program and his system of football famous. When asked for an early prediction, Schmidt wisely chose not to betray his emotions or put pressure on his team, saying, "Looks like we'll have a pretty fair crowd, doesn't it?" But don't be fooled, he had spent his entire adult life waiting for a game like this.[26]

On Monday afternoon with classes finished for the day, one by one the Buckeye players trotted out to the practice field for the start of Notre Dame week. The sky was gray and cold, and a drizzling rain only added to the seriousness of the mood. Besides the players and coaches, there were only a handful of sportswriters in attendance. If the weather hadn't chased most observers away, then Schmidt finished the job. His paranoia always increased with his stress, and for this stressful week "the practice field was locked up as tight as a bank vault." In an unusual move for Schmidt—and one that laid bare the gravity of the coming game—he began practice by having the boys work on defense. In particular, he wanted to emphasize the stopping of the forward pass. Although this element had not been savagely exposed during games so far, it had not been strong either. He considered it Ohio State's Achilles' heel and had a sick feeling that Notre Dame did too. Schmidt was more worried about his own team's vulnerability than he was about Notre Dame's passing "attack." Through 4 games, The Irish were only averaging 8 attempts, 3 completions, and 52 yards per game, less-than-robust numbers even by 1935 standards. As practice wore on and darkness fell, the floodlights were engaged, illuminating the swirling mist. The freshman scout team ran Notre Dame plays as instructed by the coaches who had studied the Irish. While the freshmen went through the action of the plays, the varsity players were instructed to stand still at their defensive positions and absorb the feel of the plays, concentrating on the direction of the blockers and increasing their intuitive powers. Finally, soaked and exhausted, the players were allowed to trudge off the field to the locker room, but Schmidt wasn't finished with them yet. After they had all dressed he made them watch "motion pictures" from the Pittsburgh–Notre Dame game. As this was Notre Dame's toughest game to date, Schmidt felt the largest portion of Notre Dame's repertoire was probably exposed in that particular contest as they fought for their lives.[27]

It was a long practice—perhaps too long. Because Schmidt did not delegate and he was an obsessive, unorganized worker, his practices had always lasted longer than those of most other coaches. Counterparts like Jock Sutherland at Pittsburgh felt that time must be used efficiently in practice. More could be learned in less time if done properly, and then the boys would still have zest for game time. Schmidt's lengthy, arduous practices were a common complaint among the players, and this week's were sure to be worse yet.

The Irish players could empathize, at least for a day. On Monday in South Bend, Notre Dame head coach Elmer Layden ran a three-hour practice focused exclusively on defending Schmidt's system. It was a disaster. The varsity, particularly the backs, were continually fooled by scrubs running Ohio State plays and gave up far too many long gainers. Layden was also worried about Ohio State's line, which was heavier and more accomplished than his. He had assistant coach Joe Borland busy trying to decipher Schmidt's offensive-line schemes so they could map out a defensive-line plan. They were not panicked, however; Notre Dame was used to playing against tough competition, and they even received some good news: Mike Layden, Elmer's much younger brother, was returning from injury to fill the right halfback spot.[28]

The next day Notre Dame continued working on defense. Spending so much time trying to solve Schmidt's system was creating a quandary for Layden that was familiar to Buckeye opponents. "We won't have a chance to work on our own offense this week," admitted Layden. "We could spend all season setting up a defense for the numerous plays Ohio State runs from its many formations. Ohio has more formations than any other team on our schedule, and we'll just have to concentrate on holding the score down." Fortunately for Layden, his own Irish offense was relatively simple and didn't need a lot of work. They hadn't had to learn "more than a half dozen new plays all season."[29]

What Layden's offense needed was not more repetitions, but more threats. It wasn't that they were unable to score, it's just that they were having to grind for everything, and defenses were getting more aggressive, not fearing big plays. Notre Dame needed a couple of Jumpin' Joe types of their own—guys who scared the defense and took the pressure off teammates to be perfect. In fact, Notre Dame did have one player who had that kind of potential, and Layden was really hoping that his emergence the previous week had not been a tease.

Like Jumpin' Joe Williams, Andy Pilney had also been a high school legend. When he graduated from Chicago's Harrison Tech High School, the young halfback was being touted as the next Red Grange. He had led his team to a mythical prep national title, and when he enrolled at Notre Dame he was considered the jewel of the team's post-Rockne future—the most talented player at the most famous football school in America. Then, nothing happened. He occasionally showed off his electric running skills, but it didn't happen often, and he wasn't a starter. No one could conclusively pinpoint the problem. Some speculated that he was conceited or that he just wasn't willing to learn. It didn't help that he fumbled the ball a little too often, leading to questions about his toughness. Coach Layden knew Pilney was dangerous in the open field, but the problem was getting him past the line of scrimmage. He was too quick for his own good and seemingly unable to exercise patience, continually hitting gaps in the line before they became holes. Pilney was also impatient with his lead blockers, running away from them before they could help him. Assistant coach Chet Grant had worked hard with Pilney, and in the game against Navy the previous week something had seemed to click. Perhaps Pilney saw his football career slipping away as it was his last year to play, or maybe he felt a tinge of senior pride, or maybe Grant's intense coaching had conjured up an epiphany. Whatever the reason, Pilney had come off the bench and saved the Irish with some brilliant running and passing in the second half. It was the Pilney they had dreamed about, but none of the Irish coaches were getting too

excited. Pilney had shown flashes of greatness before, only to disappoint anew. Not wanting to take any chances on a Pilney psycho-
logical letdown before the OSU game, Layden resorted to a little
gimmick created by Rockne: an occasional article in the *South Bend
(Indiana) Tribune* under the byline of "Bearskin." The head coach
used these anonymous editorials to play mind games and "deflate
any egos that he felt needed deflating." Pilney was featured in this
week's Bearskin article, and his desire was questioned in ink. It was
a ploy not without some risk as one never knew how a young man
would respond to public criticism, but Layden felt he needed to
gamble—just like Schmidt—for this was one of those games that
could alter a program's fortunes or a coach's reputation.[30]

Joe Williams, *Syracuse (New York) Herald-Journal* sports editor, told
his readers that this clash of behemoths was all about the coaches.
"In the matter of material there isn't or shouldn't be much difference," he claimed. "Year after year Notre Dame attracts fine material and in great numbers. This has also been true of Ohio State.
The issue then, should concern the coaches. To come right out
and make a choice between the two teams is to indicate you think
Layden is a better coach than Schmidt, or vice versa, because this
seems to be strictly a coaches' game."[31]

Among professional odds makers, Ohio State opened the week
as a 5–3 favorite. Aside from the huge chunks of cash being bet
on the game, it was also being estimated that $1 million would be
spent by those attending the game on tickets, hotels, taxi rides, and
the like. Already, Columbus taxi operators had sought permission
to double their rates from fifty cents to a dollar per passenger, but
Columbus Mayor Henry Worley refused to allow it.[32]

Tickets to the sold-out game were nearly impossible to find; even
some big-shot boosters who had earned favors were unable to get
seats. For those who were desperate enough, tickets were available through scalpers, but the markup was ugly—$20–$25 (a small

fortune during the Depression for a ticket with a face-value price of $3.30. Considering inflation, a ticket scalped for $25 in 1935 would equal a $388 ticket in 2008). Adding to the confusion and to the circus atmosphere that strained state and local resources, a group out of Philadelphia printed two thousand counterfeit tickets; four detectives were assigned the task of breaking the ring. Another 105 special-duty policemen were assigned to crowd control, and the Ohio Highway Patrol had reassigned forty-five motorcycle officers and nineteen patrol cars to the Columbus region to "keep traffic at a lively but safe and sane pace." For the nearly 10,000 folks coming from other regions, there were no fewer than twenty-four special trains scheduled to carry them to Union Station in Columbus. The regular trains were adding dozens of special cars just for the game. Unfortunately, it was impossible to add more tracks.[33]

Not only did this mayhem test resources, but it tested loyalties as well. Regional and religious prides were colliding to the discomfort of some Ohioans. Father Jim Kirwin of Circleville, Ohio, had always followed both teams. He had attended the game Notre Dame won over Pitt the previous weekend and would be in attendance for OSU–ND game. Now, for the first time, Kirwin was feeling pressure to choose a side. A faithful priest couldn't very well cheer against Notre Dame, but a good Ohioan couldn't turn his back on the state team either. His own brother was the editor of Ohio State's school newspaper, for goodness sake. He was finding it difficult to declare a final allegiance.[34]

While some were divided, some outsiders were united in dislike for both of the big-shot teams. Said John Whitaker of the *Hammond (Indiana) Times*: "Wouldn't it be a classic joke if these two stupendous, colossal, unbeatable, super, point-a-minute, powerhouse aggregations played a scoreless tie in which neither 20-yard line was violated?"[35]

Friday, a train carrying forty-seven Notre Dame players along with coaches and staff arrived in Columbus around ten o'clock in the morning. They had been delayed nearly two hours by the wreck of a freight train near Bradford, Ohio. Since Notre Dame's train had no dining car, the boys were plenty hungry. Upon arriving, they headed directly to their temporary headquarters, the St. Charles Borromeo Seminary on the outskirts of town. The seminary was a departure from the raucous downtown digs used by other visiting teams, and, as Layden pointed out, this favorable retreat was also "reasonable in cost"—another lesson on how to travel from the original nomads of the football scene. Upon reaching the seminary, the grateful players were only too happy to fill their stomachs and stretch their legs. Layden, meanwhile, was immediately whisked away to a ceremony in Columbus where Mayor Worley presented the coach with a key to the city. After the presentation had been photographed, Worley took the key back, explaining that it was the only one they had. Later, after Layden had rejoined his team, they traveled over to Ohio Stadium for a light workout. Normally such a workout would go unnoticed, but not this time. "We got used to playing before big crowds wherever Notre Dame went," recalled Irish fullback Steve Miller. "That part of it never bothered us, because a lot of the people in the stands were Irish fans. But when we got to Ohio Stadium that day, the noise was incredible. Those people were wild, and they never stopped yelling at us." One observer guessed there were 15,000 on hand, their favorite jeer being "Go home, Catholics" or a version thereof.[36]

At eight thirty that evening, Elmer Layden joined Francis Schmidt in Columbus as guests on the national radio broadcast on NBC's *College Prom* show. As the show concluded the two men wished each other luck, but afterward they refused to shake hands for the cameramen. It had been a long week. Meanwhile, the Ohio State students were conducting a furious pep rally on campus. And around town certain farsighted Columbus businessmen were preparing for the following night, moving furniture and breakables in anticipation of possible postvictory mayhem.[37]

Finally, on November 2, the wait was over. Well before game time the noise at the stadium was already thick as marching bands from both teams were engaged in a premeditated "battle" that would continue at halftime. Huge temporary bleachers had been built at the open end of the horseshoe, and close to 10,000 wooden folding chairs covered the track and the area surrounding the field. Four major newsreel teams were on hand, positioning their cameras on top of the press box. Inside the press box, 275 reporters fought for elbow room. Amongst those given a little extra space were Grantland Rice, Henry McLemore, Damon Runyon, and the rest of the New York sportswriting elite. The game was being carried live on national radio by all three of the major networks: Columbia, Mutual, and National Broadcasting.[38]

As each team entered the field 81,018 overexcited fans roared. Ohio State won the coin toss and elected to kick off. The two teams exchanged punts after gaining little, and, as expected, Notre Dame's advantage in this area was evident as they gained net field position. On their second drive the Irish moved into Buckeye territory, reaching the 30-yard line. In this third of the field, forward passing was acceptable according to the unwritten rules that dictated football strategy in the era. The Irish were anxious to make something happen and called for a pass. Mike Layden, the coach's little brother, rolled out to the left side and was immediately under pressure, forced to retreat. He made a terrible decision, throwing against his body and off his back foot as he was being pulled to the ground. The overthrown pass was intercepted by Ohio State's Frank Antenucci, a fullback/linebacker starting the game because of his prowess in pass defense. Almost simultaneously with his landing, Antenucci lateraled the ball to his much quicker teammate, Frank Boucher. Ohio State quickly formed interference and made two brilliant cutback blocks to free Boucher down the sidelines. Only Wally Fromhart, the Irish quarterback, seemed to have a chance at making the tackle. At the Irish 15 Fromhart dove wildly, but Boucher, a track man, was gone, completing a 72-yard run untouched. The horseshoe was bedlam as the game was off to a start even the Buckeye fans hadn't dared dream about. Schmidt was elated on two accounts. Not only was his team leading early, but his sermons on risk-taking had borne fruit. A month ago in his *Saturday Evening Post* article, he had mentioned how he would love to see more laterals used when returning a turnover and had worked with the defense to take more risks in making big plays. Dick Beltz was substituted into the game to kick the extra point, which he promptly did to give Ohio State a quick 7–0 lead.[39]

Another exchange of punts and a Boucher fumble gave the Irish their next big opportunity at the osu 25. Again they attempted to pass deep in enemy territory, and again the Buckeyes' pass defense rose to the occasion. This time they knocked down a throw from Shakespeare at the goal line. It looked like all that work in practice was paying off. On the next play, Shakespeare was tackled behind the line as he drifted right, attempting a pass off an option, ending Notre Dame's threat. Another exchange of punts followed before Pincura picked off a Shakespeare pass with a "shoestring catch" near midfield. Schmidt had been waiting for this moment. He replaced Pincura at quarterback with Tippy Dye, the aggressive signal-calling sophomore. On his very first play Dye called a double lateral that worked for 10 yards. Sensing an important scoring opportunity, Schmidt sent Jumpin' Joe Williams into the game. Dye now mixed in running plays to all three of his backs using misdirection, sweeps, and power. The Buckeyes were 17 yards away from the end zone when the first quarter ended. Schmidt sent Pincura back into the game. The Buckeyes didn't lose any momentum, finishing the drive when Jumpin' Joe Williams ran through a gaping hole at right tackle and scored easily. This time Sam Busich came into the game for the extra kick, but his attempt was wide. The Buckeyes now led 13–0 early in the second and were looking dominant. Layden knew the next drive was crucial; the Irish had to stop the Buckeyes' momentum now. He replaced Shakespeare with the enigmatic Andy Pilney. His best punter was done for the quarter and was being replaced by unstable dynamite. It was an aggressive decision.[40]

Pilney instantly changed the momentum. Much like he did during the Navy game, Pilney brought energy and elusiveness that forced the defense back on their heels. The Irish were now unstoppable, and they motored down to the Buckeye 13-yard line, but two wide running plays spelled disaster, combining to lose 10 yards. Without a reliable kicker, Notre Dame went for it on fourth down, throwing a long pass into the end zone. It was incomplete, giving the Bucks possession and negating Pilney's good work.

The Buckeyes didn't take advantage, and neither did the Irish afterward. The half ended with Ohio State up 13–0. The fans needed a break to catch their collective breath.[41]

It had been a great half for osu but a frustrating one for Notre Dame. Schmidt had worked hard to improve his team's pass defense, and the first-half stats reflected his success. The Irish completed just 2 of 9 passes and were intercepted 3 times. Grantland Rice recalled his thoughts on Ohio State as halftime began: "Here was a big, fast, smartly coached team we had all heard about. 'One of the greatest teams I ever saw' was a common comment from the towering press stand, as speed and deception were mixed with laterals which involved as many as four men on one play. Not only that, but the Scarlet line was out charging and splitting Notre Dame's forward wall wide open. Ohio was doing all the high-class blocking." Most everyone in the press box agreed that the Buckeyes were even better than had been advertised.[42]

While the band blasted away and the home fans buzzed, Elmer Layden was calmly talking to his team in the visitors' locker room. Turnovers had been their main problem. They were just as good a team as Ohio State, he reminded them, but they had to avoid self-inflicted wounds. As for his linemen's getting pushed around, Layden responded with action instead of pleas. Just before returning to the field he surprised everyone in the locker room by announcing that the second-string linemen would be starting the second half. It was a shrewd ploy that Layden had been saving for the right moment during the right game. If it worked, the back-ups would fight like the devil to honor the coach's faith while at the same time the ire of the starters would be aroused, and hopefully they'd take it out on Ohio State when they got back in the game. If it didn't work, a group of inferior linemen were about to dig a deeper hole while the starters groused over being blamed for the first-half woes.[43]

Over in the home-team locker room, the Buckeyes were getting their usual double dose. Schmidt offered some technical advice, and Godfrey gave a restrained plea for passion.

Although Schmidt was emotionally invested in each game, he wasn't one to translate that emotion into inspiration, and he rarely tried. Instead, he usually stuck to strategy and some sarcastic reviews of what went wrong in the first half. Godfrey took care of the emotion—he had been known to cry—but because of his malapropos delivery and unusual speech patterns, his performances could come off as slightly comical. Halftime was not a strength of the Schmidt administration. In a profession where dramatic midgame speeches are legend, Schmidt did nothing to make himself legendary.

The third quarter began with a punting duel, and as expected, Shakespeare's skills could not be matched. He kept burying the Buckeyes deep on the field. Leading 13–0 but with bad field position, Ohio State's heart began to falter a bit. Their play choices were less aggressive than usual. An inspired group of Irish backup linemen was not helping. The Ohio attack lost momentum, and two punt exchanges netted the Irish great field position on Ohio's 41. On the next play, fullback Steve Miller found room inside right tackle and ran for 30 yards before being brought down at the 11-yard line. Rather than risk another turnover, Notre Dame chose to run inside. Three rugged smashes gained 7 yards, leaving a fourth down at the 4-yard line. It was a tough angle for a field goal, even if they had a reliable kicker. Four yards was too much for straight power, so the Irish decided to play Schmidt at his own game and called a shovel pass, but Vic Wojiehovski fumbled it. Teammate Steve Miller recovered the loose ball, but Ohio took possession on downs.

Again the Buckeyes failed to move the ball. The wide-open play-calling that had been so effective in the second quarter was now being replaced with caution. They had a 2-touchdown lead; they were beating the famous Notre Dame Irish; they were moving ever closer to being crowned national champions. Again the teams exchanged punts, and again Notre Dame won the field-position battle. Shakespeare pinned them deep with a beautiful punt that landed out-of-bounds at the Buckeyes' 8-yard line. His job done, he was then replaced by Pilney—another moment when Layden felt his team had to take a chance. Just a few plays after reporting, Pilney fielded a terrible line-drive punt by the Buckeyes. Catching it on the run, Pilney avoided tacklers with some great moves, and returned the ball 27 yards to Ohio State's 12-yard line. With the Irish yet again standing in the shadows of the Buckeye goalpost, the third quarter ran out of time. How many more threats could Ohio State withstand?

The answer came two plays into the fourth quarter. After Pilney passed for 11 yards, fullback Steve Miller rammed it over the goal line, running behind center. The Irish fans in attendance could finally let loose. Tilley, a tackle, was sent in for the important extra point. His kick was a low one, hitting the cross bar and bouncing up into the air where it seemed to hang forever before dropping in front of the goal. The missed kick meant Ohio State now led 13–6. If anything, Notre Dame would only be able to salvage a tie game. For Buckeye followers, that would be better than a loss, and in all likelihood the national title would still be a real possibility. Hopefully, Schmidt's offense had been reawakened and the ramifications of a tie wouldn't become an issue.

Then again, even a tie wasn't a sure thing. After another failed offensive series by Ohio State, the Irish swept their way down the field and appeared to have tied the game on another Steve Miller plunge, but he fumbled just before crossing the goal line, and Jim Karcher recovered for the Buckeyes. Schmidt and his boys had dodged a bullet, but momentum and confidence were most definitely owned by Notre Dame.

Jumpin' Joe Williams managed to fly around right end for 24 yards on the next OSU possession, but that was as far as the drive would go. The Buckeyes were still playing offense with the goal of not losing—a passive, frightened mindset that ran completely counter to the aggressive kick-'em-while-they're-down offense that Schmidt preached.

After they punted to Notre Dame, Schmidt decided this would be Ohio's most crucial defensive series of the game as he sent Jumpin' Joe's suspect pass-defensive skills to the bench. Upon reaching the sideline, Williams angrily threw his headgear into the helmet pile. It had been a frustrating half. "I was sore, but I was sorry a minute later and apologized," he remembered. Schmidt had always substituted more than other coaches, and with Notre Dame's seemingly controlling the second half, Schmidt had been forced to maintain his aggressive ways. Between trying to stop Pilney and the newly inspired Irish linemen as well as jump-start his own offense, Schmidt had worked himself into a corner. Based on the rules of the era, anyone who was removed from the game in the fourth quarter was ineligible to return for the duration of the contest. The most important game of Schmidt's career was now being decided with several backups on the field.[44]

There were less than four minutes left in the game, and Notre Dame needed to move 79 yards for a touchdown and then convert the extra point just to salvage a tie. It all came down to Andy Pilney and a forward-passing scheme that had done little all season and nothing in the first half of this game. The Buckeyes were prepared; they had worked all week on pass defense. Knowing the Buckeyes were guarding against anything deep, Notre Dame called for a quick little pass from Wally Fromhart to Pilney. It worked perfectly. Pilney found plenty of space and scampered for 37 yards to the Ohio 38. Some of the Buckeye backs would later claim that the Boucher interference call from the previous series had curbed their aggressiveness, but it's just as likely that the Buckeye defense was being overcautious simply because they were trying to hang on to a lead. Regardless, Notre Dame couldn't be stopped. Three more pass attempts connected. The final completion went to Mike Layden—a 15-yarder he caught between two Buckeyes before stumbling into the end zone. It had been thrown by the omnipresent Andy Pilney. Ohio State's lead had been slashed to 13–12, and there were less than two minutes to play. The importance of the upcoming extra point could not be overstated. The stadium was gripped in tension, all eyes on Wally Fromhart as he positioned himself for the attempt. Those who knew Notre Dame football knew that Fromhart had struggled all season with his kicking. The team's coaches had given him extra attention all week in practice hoping to cure his ills. But whether he would have been accurate on this historic kick will never be known. The snap was poor, and the timing was thrown out of synch. The Buckeyes' Stan Pincura and Fred Crow broke through the line and combined to resoundingly block the kick. Ohio State had risen up when it counted and held a 13–12 lead with just over a minute and a half remaining.[45]

Everyone across the nation listening on radio, and every nerve-racked fan who was jammed into Ohio Stadium, knew Notre Dame would try an onside kick. It was their only chance. It failed. The Buckeyes recovered near midfield with ninety seconds remaining. Ohio State's dream season had survived its greatest test. The Buckeyes' offense still had to run a couple plays. They huddled to discuss their next move. What happened next is open to debate. Schmidt says he instructed them to "freeze" the ball, meaning they were to secure the ball and forget about gaining ground. Others claimed there was dissension in the huddle as to what should be done. The play that Ohio State finally chose was a sweep right out of the Single Wing Formation. Halfback Dick Beltz took the direct snap, angled right, and exploded past the right end. He found some room and had 5 yards when he was met by none other than Andy Pilney, who hit Beltz and knocked the ball loose. The ball actually ricocheted forward, and it began skipping toward the sideline. Two Irish players seemed to have a slim chance at the ball, but neither could recover it as it finally rolled out of bounds. However, just before it did, Notre Dame backup center Hank Pojman had been able to barely touch the ball. Today the rules state that a fumbled ball rolling out of bounds goes to the team who last possessed it, but in 1935 it belonged to the last team to have touched it. Improbably, Notre Dame now had possession of the ball on their own 45-yard line. There was just over a minute left.[46]

Now it was Elmer Layden's turn to strategize. A loophole in the substitution rules allowed that a quarterback entering the game could speak in the huddle, so Layden gave his play call to substitute quarterback Frank Gaul and sent him into the game.

Pilney, who had just forced the fumble, was the passer on the

play. He took the deep snap and drifted back, looking for his receiver. He was immediately under pressure from one of the Buckeyes and barely sidestepped before deciding to run. With the clock
ticking and a frenzied Ohio State crowd imploring their defense to
save the game, Pilney found no one in the middle of the field and
ripped off several yards. He dodged a defender and moved toward
the left sideline. Another tackler had him by the waist, but Pilney
spun free and continued running down the sideline. As he reached
Ohio's 19-yard line, two Buckeyes jumped on his back just as Pincura hit him square in the knees. Pilney's mad dash ended with his
lying in a heap on the chalk next to Notre Dame's bench. The fe-
rocity of the gang tackle caused Layden to race up, yelling at the
officials, "Keep your eyes open! They used everything but stilet-
tos on him! What the devil do you fellows have whistles for?" The
clock stopped with fifty seconds remaining in the game. Pilney was
not getting up. The vicious tackle had torn up his knee. Eventually
Pilney was placed on a stretcher, and even though he was in great
pain, he asked to remain lying near the sideline where he could witness the dramatic finish. This long time-out augmented the drama
to an agonizing level. The Buckeye defenders were glad to catch
their breath and hoped this would stall momentum, as often happens in such cases.[47]

Andy Puplis, the Irish's third-string quarterback, was sent into
the game with the next play. Bill Shakespeare took over Pilney's
spot as the triggerman at left halfback. To no one's surprise Notre
Dame ran another pass play. Shakespeare took the direct snap and
faded straight back. He seemed to stand forever, looking downfield, before finally launching a pass to the front of the end zone,
but the only player there was a Buckeye. It was Dick Beltz; the same
back who had put them in this predicament by fumbling was now
making the redeeming interception. The ball floated right into his
arms, but as he tried to hold on to it, it escaped his cradle and fell

to the ground. The crowd swallowed their roar and offered a collective moan instead. Beltz, a truly nice guy as all goats seem to be, had been all alone, as if the pass were intended for him. What seemed to be a certain interception was now just an incomplete pass. It was now second and 10 from the Ohio State 19-yard line with forty seconds left on the clock.

The next play Layden had in mind was a crossing route involving the two ends, but he had no way to send the play in. He was out of quarterbacks. The two teams on the field were standing in loose huddles. Andy Puplis, the third-string quarterback playing the biggest game of his life, pondered his play choice. Shadows were long, uniforms were dirty, and throats were hoarse from shouting. The heavyweight battle everyone had expected only held time for a few more tired punches.[48]

Assistant coach Chet Grant appeared at Layden's side with a player in his grasp. The graspee was Dick McKenna, fourth-string quarterback. He had not been part of Notre Dame's traveling squad but had made his own way to the game and had been allowed to suit up before sitting buried on the bench. In he went, stopping only to report to the referee. Off the field trudged Puplis.[49]

The reverse pass, as the Irish referred to it, was called at the line of scrimmage by McKenna. The two ends were the only receivers in the pattern. The Irish shifted to the left before the long snap went to the fullback, who spun and handed it to Shakespeare. It took time for the receivers to run their long diagonal routes. Finally Shakespeare launched a high arching ball toward the goalpost. It was intended for Wayne Millner, the team's best receiver, who looked to be well covered by Stan Pincura. The Buckeye safety jumped, but he jumped early, and the ball floated past his outstretched hands. Behind him, Millner executed perfect timing and pulled the football out of the air. As he fell to the ground, he instinctively tightened his grip on the ball. Time froze, and as Millner returned to earth his eyes happened to fall on Andy Pilney, still lying on a stretcher near the sideline. Buckeye fans held their breath, waiting for Millner to drop the ball. He never did. There were twelve seconds left when Millner's cleats hit the end zone to score the winning touchdown. "The Notre Dame team, screaming and waving their headgear in the air, swarmed down upon him. For a full minute they hugged and patted him."[50]

Henry McLemore, one of the New York sportswriting elite, couldn't believe his eyes. "In the press box, men who had seen them all went just as wild as the 80,000 spectators."[51]

Notre Dame missed yet another extra point, but it didn't matter. After the kickoff and one failed pass attempt by Pincura, the game was over. Notre Dame had stunned Schmidt and the Buckeyes by scoring two touchdowns in the last two minutes to win 18–13.

Because Dick Beltz had fumbled and dropped a sure interception that allowed Notre Dame to win, he would forever be infamously associated with this game. What he remembered most were the shocked fans: "I've never seen the place so silent after a game in all the years since." The only noise came from the Notre Dame fans who had traveled to the game, many of whom stormed the field in celebration, trying to tear down the goalposts. Columbus policemen, in no mood for conversation, used nightsticks to beat the young fans back. Layden was in disbelief at the outcome and was just as shocked by Schmidt's reaction. "Francis Schmidt raced across the field and shook my hand as if he had won rather than us," recalled Layden. "I admit I was rather numb from those last two minutes, but I will never forget his graciousness."[52]

Notre Dame, its passing game useless in the first half, completed 8 of 12 for 128 yards and 2 touchdowns in the second half, nearly all of it in the fourth quarter. The Buckeyes attempted only 3 passes after the intermission, a shocking departure from their usual strategy. After dominating the first half and holding an advantage in total yardage (111–58) and first downs (9–2), the Buckeyes had tightened on offense and panicked on defense, while the experienced big-game veterans of Notre Dame had overcome a slew of mistakes and persevered.[53]

That night, back at the seminary, an emotionally spent Layden plopped down in a chair and looked over some of the many telegrams he'd received. Near the top was a telegram of congratulations from Vee Green, coach of the Drake football team that had endured Ohio's 85–7 beating three weeks earlier.[54]

The next day newspapers were deeming it the game of the century. Henry McLemore, writing for the UP wire service, called Notre Dame's comeback "the most glorious and heart-stopping rally in the history of football."[55]

Schmidt was still in shock. It was the defining game of his career. He watched and rewatched film of the game.

> My heart is broken. We made a couple of mistakes in the last period. With less than a minute to go, and Ohio holding a 1-point lead, I sent in a substitute to have the team receive the kickoff and freeze the ball. I knew that all the remaining time could be used up in running a few harmless line plays. Then came that fumble, Notre Dame recovered, tossed a couple of passes, and it was over. The boy that fumbled can't be blamed. Every back fumbles at some time or other, and this one just happened at the wrong time. Pilney should have been stopped behind the line, instead of making his long run, but he fooled us. That touchdown pass which beat us was long enough to give our boys time to knock it down, but they just didn't get there. It was probably the greatest football show I ever saw, and it was just our misfortune to be on the losing end.[56]

Everyone had a theory by Monday. The Buckeyes were coasting in the second half. Notre Dame was in better shape and/or had better spirit. The ghost of Knute Rockne was somehow involved. Others were a little more specific. The scoreboard clock had been too slow. Schmidt shouldn't have replaced his backs in the fourth quarter, particularly Boucher and Heekin. Some scouts questioned Schmidt for sticking with a seven-man line on defense instead of dropping men back when it was obvious the Irish needed to throw. The Buckeyes didn't do any of their usual quick kicking, and their punt-return strategy of looking for laterals instead of blocking was a mess. Punt-return yardage had been 117–3 in favor of Notre Dame.[57]

The real sign of a game's fame is not in its emotional toll, however, but in its physical toll. Of course there were injured players, and none more tragic than Andy Pilney, who lay in a hospital bed in South Bend, his mother at his side. It was a forgone conclusion that his knee injury would cause him to miss the rest of the season. But the true sign of a game's fame lies in the injuries to fans. David Kirk Jr., a prominent Findlay, Ohio, banker, suffered the ultimate injury, dying on Monday after a heart attack he sustained during the game. In Potsdam, New York, Helen Duffy was also making preparations for a funeral. Her husband, Christopher Duffy, had died of a heart attack at age fifty-five while listening to the game on the radio. Born in Ireland, and with a daughter in a nunnery, he was Irish to the end, cheering for his team with his final breaths. Wyoming's state treasurer, J. Kirk Baldwin, got off easy. In a fit of excitement while listening to the game he had jumped in the air only to land on a rug that shot out from under his feet, causing him to fall and fracture a wrist.[58]

Thirty years later Elmer Layden summed it up thusly: "I still like to think that this was the most exciting football game ever played. When sportswriters were polled in 1951 to pick the most thrilling football game of the first half of the twentieth century, they chose the 1935 Ohio State–Notre Dame game. This was the game that taught Hollywood writers how to put a thrilling finish to the rash of 1930s movies about football. It was a game that most of the Hollywood scriptwriters would not have dared to dream up. It was too unbelievable to be true."[59]

While Hollywood was busy turning inspiration into scripts, the real thing was showing in theaters the following week. A one-reel special showing highlights of the game was being shown as a feature lead-in for films at various theaters across the country.

And as the rest of the nation celebrated a game for the ages, the Buckeyes turned their attention to the job at hand. Ohio State still had three football games to play, all against conference foes. The national title might have been snatched away by Wayne Millner, but the Big 10 title was still within reach. The Buckeyes were worthy, but would they be able to recover from the emotional devastation of losing the game of the century? "Just what effect it has on the attitude of the team remains to be seen," admitted left guard Inwood Smith. "Naturally, I hated like everything to lose, but that game brought out a lot of the team's faults. It may do us a heck of a lot of good in the long run, and I think we have a good chance of going through the rest of the season undefeated." Even the weather was melancholy, making practices gray and wet as the Buckeyes prepared to play Chicago. Usually Schmidt had his team practice in a workout space underneath the stadium during inclement weather, but this week he had them working in the rain. Perhaps he wanted them to be prepared in case the rain continued into game day, or maybe he hoped the rain would wash away any remnants of the Notre Dame debacle.[60]

As it turned out, the weather in Chicago was terrible. Freezing rain fell throughout the contest. Amazingly, some 15,000 hardy souls showed up at Stagg Field to watch a mediocre Maroon team. Most of them probably anticipated the opportunity to see Jay Berwanger, Chicago's amazing senior halfback who was at the top of everyone's All-American list. He was big and fast, a perfect combination of power and mobility. The last thing this hungover Buckeye team needed was to hit the road and face a giant underdog with an elite ball carrier.

Despite the weather, Ohio State was able to move the football during the first half, but they continually shot themselves in the foot. On three separate occasions they gambled on fourth down and short inside Chicago's 15, misfiring each time. Meanwhile, the Maroon were gaining confidence, and late in the second quarter they blocked an Ohio State punt, setting up a short 12-yard scoring drive and a 7–0 halftime lead. Word began to spread around Chicago's campus that their team was working on an upset, and throughout halftime the crowd slowly grew. On Chicago's first offensive play of the second half Berwanger added to the fervor with a spectacular run. With the ball on Chicago's own 15-yard line, Berwanger took the ball and swept right. Just before he reached end, a hole opened up inside the tackle, and Berwanger cut back, found some space, and broke into the open. He angled across the field toward the left sideline before cutting upfield, "dodging some, outrunning others, and straight-arming some more." Two men in the Buckeye secondary seemed to have him bracketed, but he gave them a devastating fake at full speed and was gone, finishing an 85-yard touchdown with a "long line of would-be tacklers strewn after him." It was one of those rare runs people talk about for decades, spectacular for having all the desired elements of vision, speed, power, and escapability. More important, at that moment, it gave the Maroon a shocking 13–0 lead over a floundering Buckeye team. The drenched crowd delighted in the possibility of an upset, emboldened by the way their star had left the mighty visitors impotent and scattered on the turf. Ironically, Berwanger's run was *too* fantastic. The sudden glee of the upstart fans and the disgrace of one man's putting eleven to shame seemed to arouse the Buckeyes from their

Notre Dame–induced lethargy. On their next possession, the Buckeyes mixed a couple passes into a steady, pounding march that went 90 yards for a touchdown. Then, on the following possession, Ohio State covered 44 yards on 3 straight pass completions for another touchdown, tying the game at 13–13. That score had come with a cost, however, as quarterback Stan Pincura (9 of 11 for 162 yards passing) was knocked out of the game with a bad shoulder injury after braving a pass rush. For now it didn't matter. Ohio State had rediscovered their pride, and on their third possession since the Berwanger run, they scored again. This time they used Jumpin' Joe Williams and a sideline-to-sideline running attack to move 70 yards and take a 20–13 lead with four minutes remaining in the game. The Maroon mounted one last assault, but Tippy Dye intercepted a pass on the Buckeye 25-yard line, effectively ending the game and keeping Ohio State from suffering a humiliating upset.[61]

After the final whistle, the relieved Buckeye players—muddy and grass stained—gathered around Berwanger, congratulating him on his unbelievable run and a tremendous college career. The accolades would continue all the way to New York where exactly one month later the Downtown Athletic Club would present him with their first-ever trophy for outstanding player of the year, later to be known simply as "The Heisman."[62]

Though some might have shaken their heads at osu's escape, Gomer Jones would later count this victory as his "greatest thrill" as a player. He was particularly proud of the perfect blocking that led to the final touchdown. For the team, the win had been a unifying moment even if it had taken a scare to bring it about.[63]

The emotional toll of the Ohio–Notre Dame game had left both the Irish and the Buckeyes disoriented. Ohio State was able to recover in time, but Notre Dame wasn't so lucky. After pulling off one of the great comebacks in the history of football, the Irish had returned to South Bend where they were upset 14–7 by Northwestern the following Saturday.

For their Homecoming game the next Saturday, Ohio State hosted Illinois. The Buckeyes played without Stan Pincura because of his shoulder injury, meaning Schmidt would be without the quarterback he called "one of the smartest field generals I've seen in my nineteen years of coaching." But Schmidt still had Tippy Dye and felt confident that Dye was just as good. He would need to be because it rained and rained, making the field sloppy, saturating the ball, and forcing both teams to play defensively. The most exciting moment of the game happened midway through the first quarter when Tippy Dye fielded a punt over his shoulder at the Ohio State 37, spun, and broke toward his left sideline. The Illinois coverage followed him en masse, and Dye, realizing he would be hemmed in, threw on the brakes, back pedaled a few steps, and broke toward the right sideline. Suddenly the Illini coverage was trapped, fighting to gain traction as the action reversed field. With more blockers than he needed, Tippy raced down the far sideline, untouched, for a score. The Buckeyes missed the extra point, but the 6 points were enough. Illinois didn't even cross midfield till the fourth quarter, and even then they almost immediately threw an interception. The Buckeyes continued to battle through the slop, driving inside the Illini 7-yard line on three occasions during the final period, but couldn't add to their total, settling for a 6–0 win. The game was not as close as the score indicated, the Buckeyes amassing 376 total yards to Illinois' 129. Zuppke made no attempt to play Schmidt's game, using only 13 men and attempting just 3 passes, completing none.[64]

The Buckeyes, who had once been national-champs-in-waiting, were now doing just enough to win. Schmidt continued to work hard, and he implored his boys to recapture the swagger that had earned them the Scarlet Scourge nickname, but it was a tough sell; the players just couldn't shake the stigma from the Notre Dame game. Elmer Layden could empathize. Since stunning Ohio State, his Irish had lost at home and then had tied Army 7–7 in New York. Both teams desperately needed a big game with some meaning to recapture their enthusiasm, and that's just what they got. Notre Dame ended its season by hosting west coast nemesis USC (winning 20–13) while the Buckeyes finished up with Michigan.

Beating Michigan senseless in 1934 had been satisfying for Buckeye fans, but the possibility for fun was heightened in 1935 as the game was being played in Ann Arbor and a conference title was on the line. Michigan, at 4-3, was having another tough season, and they entered the week as decided underdogs.

During the spring Michigan coach Harry Kipke had declared some interest in opening his offense up a bit, possibly inspired by Schmidt's offense, which had annihilated the Wolverines the previous fall. "I plan no radical changes for next fall. But I plan to have a more open attack if I can find capable ball handlers. I'd like to do more forward and lateral passing, but until I know whether I have the boys who can do it, my program will have to wait." Neither the talent nor the commitment for an open game had emerged, and the Wolverines entered the week having been shutout in consecutive games. Kipke would not be the last coach to learn painfully that an open game takes full commitment.[65]

On Friday evening, at the end of practice, Schmidt led his seniors in that bittersweet, private moment: the Last Tackle. Most notable of those hitting the bag one final time was Gomer Jones. The affable bowling ball had been a perfect captain and almost as good a player. Although Jones was graduating, he would be reunited with Schmidt down the road.

In one of his last moves as team captain, Gomer asked Tippy Dye if Stan Pincura could start the Michigan game. Tippy was slated to be the starting quarterback, but Gomer and Stan were close friends, and this was Stan's last college game. Tippy agreed, and when the idea was presented to Schmidt he allowed the change. The way that Tippy and Stan had remained friends while gracefully sharing the same position played a huge part in the success of Schmidt's offense during his first two years as Ohio State's coach.[66]

Those Buckeye followers who made the trip to Ann Arbor had to feel a twinge of dread when their boys fumbled on the first possession of the game, giving the ball to Michigan 19 yards from the end zone. Sadly, for the Wolverines, this was the high point of their game. A few plays later they missed on a field goal attempt and then only managed to enter Ohio State territory one more time during the entire game. For the second straight year, Ohio State ran roughshod over their bitter rivals, rolling up 447 total yards while five different players scored touchdowns in a 38–0 blowout. And it could have been much worse. The Buckeyes failed to convert several other chances, had 2 touchdowns called back because of penalties, and lost another when an easy pass was dropped in the end zone. They also missed on 5 extra-point attempts. Still, there were plenty of thrills. Tippy Dye returned another punt for a score, this time on an electrifying 73-yarder full of twists and turns, plus traffic direction, as he pointed out blocking opportunities while slithering down the field. And possibly because it had so fascinated Kipke the year before, Ohio broke out play no. 84, the shovel-pass-to-triple-lateral piece of insanity where the guy who carried the ball across the goal line had been the original passer. That one scored the Buckeyes' fourth touchdown. Emerging from two weeks of emotional lethargy, Ohio State cavorted like schoolboys right up to the finish. The final scoring drive involved a forward pass, two backward passes, an end run, a triple lateral, and three brutal line thrusts that gained the final 8 yards and a touchdown—a humiliating experience not only for the Wolverine players but for the Ann Arbor fans who were unaccustomed to hosting such ugliness. By game's end their frustration had turned to rage.[67]

Determined to tear down the goalposts, Ohio State fans poured onto the field. The Michigan faithful fought back. Some estimates place the number of Buckeye fans present at 20,000, but it's unlikely that so many left the stands. Still, there were plenty who did, and the field quickly evolved into a teeming mass of emotion. Fistfights began to crop up all over the field. Eventually, the south endpost was toppled, but the home crowd fought back with all their pent-up pride to preserve the other. An hour after the game, with twilight descending and most of the players already having changed into street clothes, disconnected pockets of fighting continued to dot the field.[68]

Ohio State finished the season 7-1, the single loss a blot so dark it somewhat overshadowed the good news: the Buckeyes had won a share of the Big 10 title, matching Minnesota with a 5-0 conference record. It was Ohio State's first conference title in fifteen years.

Once again, fans talked of the Buckeyes' and Gophers' meeting in a special postseason title bout, but it was mostly wishful thinking. After fifteen fruitless years, Ohio was too pleased to have a piece of the crown to risk it now, and Minnesota with its staggering depth and brute strength was the undefeated, consensus national champion. The Buckeyes had everything to lose. The two schools had not met since 1931, and with their programs' fortunes rising to new heights and postseason play being impossible, clamor erupted for a regular-season meeting in the near future. Unfortunately, the two universities were booked to play others through 1938, meaning supporters would have to wait through three more seasons before their wish was granted. When it finally happened, there was no shortage of curious spectators.

Even though the worst of the Depression had passed, the economy was still struggling, and disposable income had not yet returned to what it had been a decade earlier. Despite fans' economic hardships, however, the razzle-dazzle Buckeyes had played in front of 353,314 spectators, the most in the history of the Big 10.[69]

Ohio State may have set attendance records, outscored its opponents 237–57, and won a share of the conference title, but Schmidt still had to defend himself at the football banquet two days after the Michigan game. "This team had an uphill fight from the very day it started practice. It was put squarely on the spot when nominated as a sure thing for the national championship. . . . You know the result. Every team we met pointed for us, and as a consequence we had to be better on our off days than the opposition was on its 'on' days. We faltered once along the road, but I don't think that detracts in any way from the accomplishments of this team."[70]

Unfortunately, that one falter against Notre Dame *did* detract from the overall feeling about the season. The Big 10 title was nice—really nice—but the national championship and Notre Dame had been theirs for the taking. This was a squad who possessed the talent and the scheme to be forever remembered in Columbus, but all had been lost in the blink of an eye. It was the kind of blow that wouldn't go away, the chain of mistakes played over and over in the minds of those who loved the program. Something had changed that November day. The honeymoon had ended. Ohio and Schmidt began looking at each other a little differently. Could Schmidt, the eccentric outsider with the reckless streak, really be trusted? Schmidt's first two seasons had missed perfection by the thinnest of margins, leaving Buckeye followers more frustrated than ever. Maybe 1936 would be the year when everything fell into place. Then again, some wondered if the school would even still be operating in 1936.

The governor had cut even more of the university's operating money from the state budget, and as 1936 dawned, Ohio State simply didn't have enough to pay its bills. There were no funds for fuel, water, or phone services; janitorial supplies; or library books. The administration scrambled to get coal on credit. On top of all this, the freshman class was again 10 percent bigger than it had been the previous year. It seemed like everybody was enrolling—34 freshmen between the ages of 15–16 and another 143 freshmen over 25 years of age. Female students enrolled to study in departments like medicine, law, and engineering, which for many years were frequented mostly by male students. With the exception of history and geology, classes were "jammed beyond capacity." The newest division—commerce (aka "business")—was the most popular, as students who had little money sought training on ways to earn big money. Meantime, the school providing this training was surviving by playing shell games with its dollars and begging for time. As it turned out, the university did scrape by in 1936. Schmidt was hoping to do much better than that on the football field.[71]

Seven. The Immovable Object

At the press gathering following his hiring, Francis Schmidt told reporters he didn't believe coaching at Ohio State would be any more stressful than performing the same task at other schools. Now, two years later, he was feeling the enormous weight of which he'd been warned, summing up the gravity of his job with the declaration that "the state of Ohio is judged largely on what Ohio State does on the football field." And though this might have been an overreaching belief, the intensity of the Buckeye fan base made it feel all too believable. In the two years under his guidance the Buckeyes had won 14 of 16 games by a combined score of 504–91. They'd won a share of the conference championship for the first time in fifteen years, and twice they had beaten senseless the hated Wolverines. Yet, as Schmidt entered the last year of his contract he had begun to understand that his definition of success was not necessarily shared by Buckeye fans.[1]

Their standards had been set high from the beginning. Ohio State had entered the Big 10 in 1912, and even though they had arrived late to the party, they had won 3 conference crowns in 9 seasons. Of their first 4 Big 10 games against Michigan, the Buckeyes won 3. This was the sort of success Ohio expected from its talent-rich state. But things leveled off after 1920, and the Buckeyes hadn't even had consecutive seasons with more than 6 wins before Schmidt arrived. He had returned the program to that level considered acceptable by the fan base, but now they wanted more. They wanted an undefeated season, they wanted another unshared conference title, and they wanted to be revered as national champions. Conference counterparts Illinois, Michigan, and Minnesota had enjoyed all these spoils within the last few years, and Ohio was seething with jealousy. Schmidt's first season might have been *the* year except for that failed extra-point attempt. His second season would have been *the* year except for the questionable tactics he employed against Notre Dame. Now it was up to the 1936 team to give Ohio its rightful reward.

Schmidt wanted a national championship as much as the fans did, but he also understood the reality of the situation. Due to graduation, the 1936 team was slated to be a little younger and a little thinner than were Schmidt's first two squads. Aggravating the situation even further was a regular-season schedule that wasn't exactly friendly.

Lynn St. John would have liked to make Schmidt's path a little smoother, but he had problems of his own. The athletic director was caught in a web of diverse challenges, trying to please his employer, his coach, and his conference. St. John's boss, the athletic board, needed money for their department. They had already tightened their belts as far as they were able without resorting to the outright elimination of minor sports, and there was no use turning to the school for help, as it didn't even have enough cash for gasoline and library books when winter session opened. Football was the only sport within the department even remotely capable of generating enough cash to keep Ohio State's athletics intact. Adding more games to the schedule might have solved the problem, but Big 10 guidelines limited the timeframe during which conference schools could play their games. Generally speaking they could start playing games three weeks after school started and continue until Thanksgiving. It was part of the Big 10's effort to place itself on a higher plane than other conferences by keeping football and academics in a reasonable balance. The conference's football timetable was designed in part to befit schools like Ohio State that worked on the quarter system, meaning that finals started after the Thanksgiving break. With football finished—and postseason games outlawed—the players could properly concentrate on their big week of academic testing. St. John advocated students' being properly educated, but having one, two, or even four fewer regular season games than teams from other conferences was a difficult stance to enjoy in the midst of the Depression. So, by what means could he increase profits?

In 1936 television was still in its experimental stage—a decade away from real commercial viability—and there were no network television contracts—the cash cows that keep today's collegiate football programs fat and happy. Some radio stations bought broadcast rights, but they were mostly regional, and at $100–$250 per game per station, they didn't produce much revenue for Ohio State. Instead, almost all football income was generated through ticket sales. Big 10 opponents split the gate fifty-fifty between host and visitor, subtracting expenses like officials' salaries and discounted tickets for approved groups. Nonconference visitors usually received a guaranteed portion depending on their notoriety, skill, or ability to draw fans. Ohio State might keep a larger portion when scheduling teams like Muskingum because the mismatch drew smaller crowds, but smaller crowds meant a smaller pie from which to slice. As St. John saw it, attendance could be increased in three ways: having a winning team, having an exciting team, and playing top-notch opponents. The hiring of Schmidt and his breathtaking razzle-dazzle football had taken care of the winning and excitement, so it came down to scheduling if St. John wanted to improve finances, and this meant re-examining the way he'd lined up opponents in the past.[2]

All told, Ohio State had eight games to schedule. A minimum of five of those were required to be Big 10 contests in order for them to stay in good standing with the conference as well as qualify for the conference title. That left three slots. For years St. John had been using his extra slots to schedule the Lilliputian teams that dotted Ohio—small schools like Wooster, Oberlin, Wittenberg, and Muskingum—which were realistically incapable of defeating the Buckeyes. One of these guaranteed victories—and often two of them—were scheduled for the start of the season so the Buckeyes could work out their kinks in safety and christen each season with some warm, fuzzy debauchery. Another small-school snack was usually served near the end of the season. This one gave the Buckeyes time to recover from injuries and allowed the younger players some game experience without the threat of mistakes that might actually lead to a loss.

This mode of scheduling was not unique to Ohio State. In fact, other schools were bolder and more creative with their scheduling tactics. When Schmidt coached at TCU they had three or four sacrificial schools lined up to start each season—a season that covered eleven or twelve games. For a few years Michigan had satisfied form and function by splitting her team up and playing two different lightweight opponents on the *same* season-opening Saturday. But the Depression was affecting schedule making, especially in the Big 10 with its limited number of games. Those little schools that had provided warm-up contests had no star power, provided few thrills, and consequently drew fewer fans. When it was obvious the Depression was to be taken seriously, St. John began upgrading the Buckeye schedule by swapping the annual cupcake matches for some that were meatier. Because games were usually lined up three years ahead of time, St. John's new tactic was now bearing fruit, much to the chagrin of Schmidt. For 1936 the three nonconference games were played against teams that had been highly successful the previous season: New York University (7-1), Pittsburgh (7-1-2), and Notre Dame (7-1-1, and the only team to beat Pittsburgh). These were on top of the contests already mandated by the country's toughest conference.

If you asked Francis Schmidt, he would tell you the whole thing was getting to be damn brutal. When he wasn't thinking about formations he was thinking about the schedule. "I'm still trying to figure out how Saint missed getting Minnesota on the schedule," quipped Schmidt in January, referring to the 1935 national champions. "This is an awful tough conference," he told reporters in the spring, "and there is no telling what'll happen. Ohio State will be good alright, but we may lose 8 straight games." He'd already begun spring practice with this lament: "When I watch the boys practice, I feel pretty good, then I think of that schedule and begin to feel blue." Certain elements of Schmidt's personality came into play here. First, he foresaw a drop-off in talent among his upper classmen for 1936, and realizing the potential for a drop-off in wins as well, he was already laying the groundwork for excuses. Nothing could ever be *completely* his fault. Second, the same mind that was obsessive about diagramming plays was obsessive about anything that seemed important. *Not losing* is, obviously, very important to a professional coach. Playing more quality teams means an increased chance for losses, which in turn leads to a tenuous hold on one's coaching position. Add to that a zealous fan base, and it was becoming clear to Schmidt that the Ohio State job might be more difficult than he imagined.[3]

Upon returning from his annual preseason vacation, Schmidt sent out invitations to the players he had chosen for fall practice. Naturally, he mentioned the schedule. "We have probably the toughest schedule in the country. Can we and will we measure up to expectations? Nothing but fine spirit, hard work, and your being in good condition when you report can help make a winning team."[4]

This year's fall invitation had gone out to sixty men, which was a large number for Schmidt. Because of the uncertainty heading into the 1936 season he had added some extra bodies as insurance. With his usual lack of tact, Schmidt told a sportswriter, "We know that some of them will be of no value, but we hope to uncover a few good boys to take the place of some of the fine ones we lost." These sentiments probably didn't help lift the spirits of those deep reserves who read in the paper the next day that they had "no value," but it was important for them to get used to Schmidt's rambunctious ways.[5]

On September 9, 1936, just three weeks before the Buckeyes' opening game with New York University, Schmidt and his coaching staff met to finalize plans for fall practice, which was to start the next day. Along with holdover assistants Godfrey, Mackey, and Stahl, two new coaches were added to the mix. Schmidt didn't seek out the additions as he already had too many coaches to suit his style. Rather, Saint decided to hire "Red" Blair and "Cookie" Cunningham, both ex-Buckeye star players. St. John had been able to uncover a few extra coins in the athletic budget for the sake of a couple of unemployed legends in need of steady work. He was either being noble in tough times or simply thought that if he threw enough assistants at Schmidt, the autocratic whirlwind might begin to feel obligated to use them. Everyone was growing a little concerned about Schmidt's apathy toward delegating.

Blair and Cunningham had been popular athletes at OSU in the 1920s. Blair—now an ends coach—had recently resigned from the position of athletic director and head football coach at the University of Akron after fighting battles with school alumni. He'd spent the summer enrolled in Schmidt's intense coaching course, hoping

to get a head start on learning the vast Schmidt system. Cunningham had been bouncing around Ohio playing pro basketball (this
was before the NBA) with teams like the Cleveland Rosenblums, Akron Firestones, and Columbus Athletic Supplies. Of the two, Blair
had the better football mind, but Schmidt continued to under-
utilize him and everyone else that St. John added to the staff.[6]

Still cursing the Notre Dame catastrophe, some Buckeye fans
hoped a larger coaching staff would allow for more training of fundamentals, the backbone of all great teams. Their wish was not
granted. Schmidt emerged from his meeting with the coaches and
declared, "The opening game with New York University is only
three weeks away, and we can't dillydally around teaching the boys
things they should know already, or get them into condition."[7]

True to his word, when fall practice began Schmidt had his squad
practicing plays almost immediately. Over the next five hours, with
breakneck fervency, Schmidt engaged two full squads at a time.
They scrimmaged, passed, and punted, "shunning all thoughts of
preliminary exercises and other accepted early-season fundamentals." Schmidt's stress over the season's schedule had him working
like a demon, but the overall efficiency of his methods was worsening. Coaches still stood around without work, and players were still
trying to practice reams of plays at a pace prohibitive to suitable
mental absorption.[8]

Those players who weren't in shape picked the wrong season
to pay for their sins. Besides trying to work at Schmidt's absurd
pace, they had to contend with the heat. The Midwest usually remains hot and humid well into September, but this year was worse
than usual. Two-a-days had been scheduled for nearly the entire three weeks of fall practice, but when temperatures got high
enough, even Schmidt realized he risked pushing the players too
hard. When temperatures reached the mid-90s on September 15,
Schmidt eased back on the afternoon's practice plans and had the

players take part in a sprinting contest. Grouped by position, the players were timed as they completed 30-yard dashes. Naturally, the backs were quickest; John Bettridge, Paul Burkholtz, and Johnny Rabb ran the dash in 4 seconds flat.[9]

Rabb's run was particularly impressive given his size: 6 feet 2 inches and 210 pounds. No one was surprised though. He had always been known for his freakish combination of size and speed. Rabb had actually played freshman ball at Fordham University in New York before transferring to Ohio State, where he was received with high hopes. He had the speed of a halfback, the power of a fullback, and a style of running that fit both. For now, the path to starting fullback was blocked by Jim McDonald, a player Schmidt trusted enough to occasionally call signals. But Rabb looked like he was ready for stardom after some depth-chart gridlock had buried him as a sophomore the previous season.[10]

It was easy to get a little lost among the masses. Depth charts could get pretty deep. All players in this era fell into 7 basic positions that covered offense, defense, and special teams. In 1936 at fall practice Ohio State had 5 fullbacks, 6 quarterbacks, 12 halfbacks, 11 ends, 9 tackles, 11 guards, and 6 centers. This meant there were 5 full squads on the varsity plus most of a sixth string, not to mention the handful of uninvited go-getters who showed up without fail, determined to make the team no matter how loosely. Those clinging to the bottom of the chart could not rest. A freshman squad comprised of over 200 eager young men was already eyeing those spots. Considering the lack of athletic scholarships and the fact that all these players were volunteers, one's status on the depth ladder was of utmost importance because of the increased playing time that accompanied each successive rung. A talented guy like Johnny Rabb may have taken his skill for granted when he was a sophomore and ended up stuck behind others with less skill. The same thing had nearly happened to Jumpin' Joe Williams, who

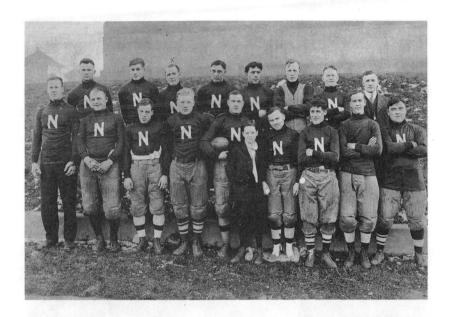

1. The 1906 Nebraska Cornhuskers football team. Ironically, as a collegiate player Schmidt (back row, fourth from left) was better known for his defensive play. (Courtesy of author)

2. Schmidt with Sam McBirney, circa 1916. McBirney was responsible for Schmidt's hiring and ascension at Henry Kendall College, later renamed the University of Tulsa. (Courtesy of the University of Tulsa)

3. Slingin' Sammy Baugh shows his throwing form while at TCU, circa 1937. (Courtesy of TCU Photo Collection, Special Collections, Mary Couts Library, Texas Christian University)

4. Francis and Evelyn Schmidt, Columbus, Ohio, 1934. (Courtesy of University Archives, The Ohio State University)

5. "The Game of the Century," Notre Dame at Ohio State, November 2, 1935. (Courtesy of University Archives, The Ohio State University)

6. Schmidt in practice gear on the Ohio State main practice field, which was located just outside the open end of Ohio Stadium. It was the site for much of Schmidt's legendary swearing. (Courtesy of University Archives, The Ohio State University)

7. Schmidt rising from the sideline bench at an Ohio State game. The bow tie, handful of notes, and level of intensity were Schmidt's trademarks. (Courtesy of University Archives, The Ohio State University)

8. Ohio Stadium, nicknamed "the Horseshoe," circa 1936. In the foreground is Buckeye Grove, where a buckeye tree is planted for every Ohio State all-American player. (Courtesy of University Archives, The Ohio State University)

9. Schmidt with former assistant "Babe" Brown at the University of Idaho, 1944. Already looking thinner, the soon-to-be-unemployed Schmidt died just a few months later. (Courtesy of Special Collections & Archives, University of Idaho Library, Moscow, Idaho)

10. Sid Gillman—the greatest of
Schmidt's protégées—coaching the
San Diego Chargers, November
1962. Gillman's game-day bow ties
were a tribute to his mentor.
(Courtesy of the San Diego Chargers)

got a second chance due to injuries among the starting squad and capitalized on the opportunity. Another talented back in training camp faced the same crossroad. Bill Booth, a 177-pound dynamo, had been captain of the freshman team at Illinois, where he was favorably compared by the coaches to Red Grange. A native of Liverpool, Ohio, he had transferred back to his home state and was now trying to crack the Buckeyes' starting lineup as a sophomore, just as Williams and Rabb had done with opposing degrees of success. Booth's skills were outstanding, but he was young and new to Schmidt's complex system. If he didn't bear down, he would be forced to travel the long road to glory like Rabb, but if he worked hard he might make the most of a break like Williams had. Schmidt didn't like to start sophomores but was pleased to make an exception when he witnessed a youngster's exceptional play.

If any of the talented backs failed, it was unlikely that a poor line would be to blame. Although Gomer Jones had graduated, three other excellent linemen remained. Merle Wendt—now the team captain—and Inwood Smith were models of consistency. And huge Charley Hamrick seemed to be back in fine form, a year removed from his knee injury.

Stan Pincura had also graduated, meaning Tippy Dye would receive the majority of snaps at quarterback, with another little guy, Nick Wasylik, serving as his backup. Schmidt called the diminutive quarterbacks his "E-flat boys." Their size didn't cause any trouble on offense, but it did present problems on defense. This dilemma perfectly illustrates the personnel struggles that confronted a football coach before free substitution was permitted.[11]

For Schmidt, the problem was his defensive backfield, and it started with Jumpin' Joe Williams. Part of the reason Williams was a designated "scorer" on offense was because he was a terrible defender. Typically, a guy who played halfback on offense would play halfback on defense (i.e., cornerback). Williams, however, was unable to properly execute on defense and had to be shifted to the deep safety position. Because teams threw so few passes in this era, it was a far less demanding position. The deep safety (generally the *only* safety) was responsible for stopping big plays and running back punts. Because of this, Schmidt found that having Jumpin' Joe and Tippy on defense at the same time was a problem. Hiding Williams's defensive deficiencies at safety meant that Tippy would have to be moved to halfback—much closer to the line where the players and the action were exponentially larger. Too bad Tippy wasn't. Playing near the line at less than 150 pounds when teams were running the ball 90 percent of the time was a far-from-ideal scenario. Tippy was plucky, and he never backed down from a tackle, but the reality was a compromised defense. Moreover, Tippy was the team's best punt returner. The only remedy was to pull Williams from the game when Ohio State was on defense. However, if you did that too early in the quarter he would not be available for offense until the *following* quarter because of the substitution rules during the era. But what if you suddenly had a scoring opportunity only to realize your best runner was trapped on the bench? Such was the dilemma for Schmidt, who had to find a way to use his biggest offensive threat without sinking his defense. (Can you imagine what football would look like today if free substitution was still illegal? What would a coach do with throwing specialists like Peyton Manning or Dan Marino on defense? Can you picture such slow, unathletic men trying to defend a receiver or return a punt?) For Schmidt, it was better to have a versatile, undersized guy like Tippy Dye on the field most of the time than to have a one-trick pony like Williams playing weak link all too often.

During their time together, Schmidt had become protective of Tippy because he was small (he'd "bulked up" to 142 pounds as a senior) and because of his brains and courage. The Schmidts had no children and never would, so occasionally Schmidt felt a fatherly connection to one of his players. "I thought he was a great, great coach and a fine individual," remembered Tippy. "He treated me like a son—both he and Evelyn did—and I loved both of them. They had me to dinner sometimes, and I don't think they ever had anyone to dinner. He was a very unusual person. And he was so funny. Anytime he'd put me in the game, as we talked on the sideline he'd say, 'Put your weight to 'em, Tippy.'"[12]

Schmidt would probably have loved to spend every day talking about football with Tippy, but the occasional dinner with the Schmidts was just one of many things that filled Tippy's busy schedule. He was all-conference in basketball and a starting middle infielder on the baseball team. For three years he had lived at the Phi Delta Theta house and paid for his meals by washing the house dishes. He earned the rest of his money doing odd and seasonal jobs. He sold Pontiacs long enough to earn one for himself. Along with teammate Charlie Ream he worked at F&R Lazarus, a popular department store. He even worked at the State House of Representatives as a page, earning $3 a day. (It was here that he became friends with another page, a young black man named Jessie Owens, who achieved permanent fame with his otherworldly track and field performance at the 1936 Olympics). Whatever free time Tippy had left after work and sports was devoted to Mary and his studies, usually both at the same time. After dinner he would go over to Mary's sorority, Pi Beta Phi, where she was the president. They would go the library and study together until ten o'clock, when he would drop her off back at the Pi Phi nest. Now in his senior year, Tippy was stretched enough from all his activities that he declared he wasn't going to play baseball in his final spring. That decision lasted until Nick Wasylik, the team captain and third baseman, ended up hurt, and Tippy answered the plea to replace him. He'd played third base in high school, and a return to the hot corner sounded fun, so return he did.[13]

Despite the heat and Schmidt's less-than-perfect training methods, everything seemed to be clicking during fall practice. On September 19 the varsity destroyed the reserves 36–0 during a full-length scrimmage filled with big plays and laterals. Schmidt delighted in watching his imagination come to life but afterward was horrified to discover one of his notebooks full of plays was missing. After a frantic search involving all available players and personnel, the prodigal book was discovered underneath a locker. Either Schmidt had been careless, or the boys had grown tired of learning new plays and hoped he wouldn't miss one of his many notebooks full of diagrams.[14]

On the last weekend of September, Schmidt mercifully gave his players the weekend off, as he was off to scout some football. Although he could never fully redeem himself for the spectacular loss to Notre Dame in 1935, another opportunity to prove his worth in a big game presented itself early in 1936. The University of Pittsburgh would visit Columbus during the second week of the season, and Schmidt wanted to see them play before he hosted them.

With the exception of Minnesota, Pittsburgh was the best team in college football during the 1930s. Not only did they win continuously, they did it playing strong schedules. And that's the way they liked it. The Panthers had mastered cold-blooded, methodical football. They won with exacting power, designed to crush their opponent in body, mind, and soul. They ran all their plays from the single-wing formation, and their play selection consisted almost entirely of rushing. During one season, the Panthers used a total of eighteen different plays. Most involved hard, brutal runs that targeted the manhood of the defensive lineman. They took pride in pounding the opposition's strongest link until his wobbly legs could defend no more. It was the same violent mindset of football played in the 1890s and one that had been subsequently legislated into submission because of the public outcry over the mayhem it created.[15]

Pittsburgh's head coach, Jock Sutherland, was the driving force behind this machine. The transplanted Scotsman adored Victorian football, and his team's success while using the brutally cautious approach to the sport was a booming argument against the open-game movement and razzle-dazzle. Taciturn and immensely organized, Jock Sutherland was the antithesis of Schmidt in almost every way imaginable.

Sutherland's practices were centered almost entirely on fundamentals; everything was executed with precision and efficiency both on and off the field. His practices were "limited in number and duration" with an "allotted time to absorb" the fundamental nuances. This system of precise teaching would be copied by Paul Brown and others who achieved longer-lasting fame than Jock. He never swore, nor did he give impassioned speeches. It was all business when his perfectly conditioned players coolly walked out of the tunnel each Saturday.[16]

On September 26, Schmidt and two of his coaches, Godfrey and Mackey, attended the Pitt–Ohio Wesleyan game to size up the Panthers. They came away duly impressed. After the game Schmidt told sportswriter Bill Snypp that it was the best Pitt team he had ever seen and that he was amazed at their condition so early in the season. (Whereas Schmidt *hoped* his players would get in shape and stay that way, Sutherland was fanatical about conditioning and saw to it that his players were in top shape throughout the season.) The Panthers' backfield, perhaps the best in the nation, clicked with ease. Especially outstanding was a sophomore named Marshall Goldberg who exploded for 208 yards and 2 touchdowns on just 15 carries. Schmidt had already spent a year worrying about the Panthers, and watching them only intensified his dread. "I don't see how we can get by Pitt on such short notice," he lamented. Not only was Ohio

State's schedule tougher than ever, but St. John was scheduling a tremendous opponent in just the second week of the season, a time when teams were still trying to find their groove. Schmidt considered this practice nothing short of heresy, but there was no turning back now. Enough tickets to the Ohio–Pitt skirmish had already been purchased that temporary bleachers were being added to the Horseshoe more than two weeks prior to the game.[17]

Before the Buckeyes hosted Pittsburgh, they had to open the season by hosting New York University. The Violet had been a minor player in the eastern football scene for decades, but recently they had been on the rise, upgrading both their talent and opponents. They were in that middle-ground stage where they could beat up other minor programs on a regular basis but were only strong enough to *hang* with the big boys, not *beat* them. A trip to the Midwest to play an upper-tier, Big 10 squad was a huge gamble that could make or break the school's momentum.

For the second year in a row, the Horseshoe was filled on opening day thanks in part to a wave of high schoolers. Ohio State had initiated a program where students from the state's 1,440 high schools were invited for a Saturday campus tour. After being herded around campus where they witnessed lab experiments and the like, they were brought to the stadium where they purchased heavily discounted twenty-five-cent tickets to the football game. The myriad of school buses that were required to make this happen made it seem as though Columbus were under attack by a swarm of yellow locusts. All told, approximately 30,000 high schoolers had migrated to Columbus, and most of them bought the cheap tickets, thereby inflating the attendance to 72,948 spectators, the biggest opening-day crowd in Ohio State history. What they witnessed was a lopsided blowout. On the very first play from scrimmage, Ohio's Jim McDonald intercepted a New York pass and returned it 32 yards for a touchdown. Like a matching bookend, on one of the game's final plays, Nick Wasylik ran back an interception 26 yards for another score. In between, the Buckeyes scored 7 more touchdowns, making the final score 60–0. It wasn't until the fourth quarter, when Ohio State was deep into its bench, that the Violet finally crossed midfield. Led by Tippy Dye, the Buckeyes attempted 23 passes, completing 11 for 227 yards, or over 20 yards per catch—an astounding passing display both in its success and cruelty, with most of the damage being done while OSU held a big, unthreatened lead. Schmidt substituted 40 different players into the game. Any of the visiting students who were waiting for a sign before choosing Ohio State as the place to further their education had received as much.[18]

"New York was much weaker than I expected," said Schmidt the diplomat, "but I thought my boys did very well." He was especially pleased with their downfield blocking. When asked why his team revealed so much of their passing repertoire with Pittsburgh next on the docket and their scouts in the stands, Schmidt shrugged and got pragmatic. "What's the use of wasting any kind of running attack when you can score by passing? A pass is the easiest way to get a touchdown, so that's what we did."[19]

Now that OSU had polished off that surprisingly light fare from New York, it was time for the game everyone was anticipating. Because Pittsburgh and Ohio State played every few years, this game wasn't girded with insanity the way the 1935 Notre Dame contest had been, but it was still a celebrated conflict. Pittsburgh is less than two hundred miles from Columbus, closer than any of the Buckeyes' Big 10 rivals, so a multitude of fans from both of the highly ranked schools usually attended the big game. But this year the curiosity factor served to increase the promise of something unique. It was Sutherland versus Schmidt. The extreme practitioner of status-quo football versus the ringleader of the open-game movement. The Inquisition versus the Maypole. Simplicity versus complexity. The brutal versus the beautiful. Even standing room in the stadium was completely unavailable, and tickets were being scalped at ten dollars apiece. Republican presidential candidate Alf Landon was planning on attending, conveniently fitting Columbus into his four-day Ohio campaign on just the right day. After the game he was scheduled to visit the Phi Gamma Delta house and reminisce about his own college experiences, which included hell-week and everything it entailed.[20]

Schmidt had already gone on record as saying that his team didn't stand a chance at victory, but when Sutherland was asked for his opinion, he echoed the doomsday sentiment. "Pitt never has had such a stern early test. This is an experimental game for us. We are trying to move faster, but I doubt if we will be ready in time." If the dour fears of both coaches could somehow be realized, then the sellout crowd was going to see history in the making as two teams would both lose the same game.[21]

Although some 3,000 ticket buyers may have been scared off by the cold, cloudy day, there were 71,714 fans anxious to witness the battle. They were rewarded with a tight contest, but the great experiment of brute strength versus deception never really unfolded as planned, mostly because of Pitt's front wall. Although Ohio State's line fought all day, they were no match for the Pitt linemen who dominated with their quickness from the outset. Afterward, Schmidt declared it the fastest line he had ever witnessed. On defense the Panther linemen plagued the Ohio State backfield early and often, sacking the quarterback and knocking down passes. On offense Pitt "hammered relentlessly and dynamically at guard, tackle, and end with a wide run attempted only a time or two." Not only did Pittsburgh pound the ball inside all day, but as a coincidental ode to nineteenth-century football they did not throw a single pass—forward or lateral—the entire game. Even in Ohio State territory, they were content to punt over and over on fourth down no matter the field position or the yardage needed, and every punt but one went out of bounds, thus preventing Ohio State any chance for a return. One writer thought "the game would have seemed more appropriate if the scene had been old Ohio Field, if carriages had been hitched just outside, and if horse cars had been passing up and down High Street."[22]

Harassed by the Panthers' penetration from the outset, the Ohio State offense immediately went into a shell and began playing at Pittsburgh's pace, only attempting the occasional screen or shovel pass out of habit. The two teams settled into a grueling game of watch and wait. Knowing that one break would turn the game around they clutched the ball tightly, determined not to fumble, which neither team did throughout the proceedings. Another by-product of old-fashioned, philistine football is illegal fighting, and this game included plenty. The two squads engaged in lots of slugging, but the officials were mesmerized with the game's personality, letting the boys scrap and calling few penalties, including a host of offsides that went unchecked. At the midpoint of the fourth quarter the game remained tied 0–0. The Buckeyes—their offensive confidence shattered—had only crossed into Pittsburgh territory once. Pittsburgh, on the other hand, spent most of the afternoon in OSU territory, where the homeboys fought with all their hearts, absorbing line plunge after line plunge. When the game's big play finally arrived, its swiftness left everyone stunned. The Panthers were lined up at OSU's 32-yard line with but a few minutes left in the game when the clouds parted for the first time all day, sunlight washing over the field as signals were called. It seemed like an unearthly sign of sorts. Seconds later, Pittsburgh's right half, "Curley" Stebbins, took the handoff, broke off a sweep, and darted inside the right end. He veered back toward the right sideline until he hit the secondary before shooting left and dashing untouched into the end zone to score the game's only touchdown. Oddly, he crossed the finish line engulfed in silence. After two hours of savage football wherein the greatest movements had been measured in inches, nobody was prepared for the powerful simplicity of this sudden run. Finally, a collective groan swept the stadium, followed by cheers from the outnumbered Pittsburgh faithful. After the kickoff, the Buckeyes' stunned offense stalled and punted yet again, never to regain possession. In pure Panther fashion, Pitt had broken Ohio State's will, and now they were using up the last five minutes of the game by slowly and methodically pushing the exhausted Ohio defense down the field, slamming run after run into the line. Pitt was 4 yards from the end zone when the clock ran out.[23]

Russ Needham, sportswriter for the *Columbus (Ohio) Citizen* summed it this way: "Pitt forced the play and dictated the terms. Ohio accepted, not ingloriously, but fatally. Pitt had the better power team, one of the greatest, but Ohio may be just as good an open team. We'll never know." The Panthers had knocked Ohio State backward early, forced them into playing possum, and then shoved them around when the game was on the line. Pittsburgh won the total yardage war 251–77, and the fact that they didn't attempt a single pass made the discrepancy even more convincing. The national press played this up as proof that razzle-dazzle was no match for *real* football. Said Schmidt, "There were two good teams out there playing for a break, and Pitt got it. Aside from that, Pitt is the most powerful team I have seen."[24]

As it turns out, Schmidt's scouting trip may have been more harmful than it was helpful because it left him in awe of Pittsburgh. As soon as the Panthers punched his razzle-dazzle in the nose, he let his guys play for the "break"—a stunning reversal of philosophy coming from the country's most aggressive offensive mind. Everyone knew that Schmidt was a man of many personalities—a man who had perfected unpredictability—but no one dreamed there was a part of him that was fearfully cautious or that had the capacity to become starstruck by a team that was seemingly superior to his own.

By the next day, Schmidt had returned to his standard operational mode of blame, nonsense, and defiance. "We were put in a hole before we even started when we failed to win the toss. If we had won the toss we probably would have won the ballgame for then we could have opened up our offense immediately. If we played them again tomorrow we might lick them." The following day at practice Schmidt had the boys spend almost the entire time working on pass offense. Later he declared that his position as head of the open-game movement would not be swayed by one loss:[25]

> The experts have been putting us—or rather our razzle-dazzle offense—on the pan since Pitt beat us. The boys seem to think power is the only thing in the world to win ball games with. It is a good thing—power—but listen, I've seen horses pulling fine automobiles . . . when some little thing went wrong with the engine . . . but you won't find anyone saying that horses are better than automobiles just because a car goes bad every once in a while. Well, the other boys can stick with their 'horse and buggy' football . . . but we believe automobile football is here to stay . . . and we'll play it that way.[26]

The osu-Pitt game was not the only ammunition used by those who claimed razzle-dazzle was an ultra-liberal fad that would never replace simplistic, cautious power football. On the very same day in New York, the Mustangs of Southern Methodist had visited Fordham University and had attempted 48 forward passes—an insane amount of throwing for this era, an amount that smu had saved for the New York writers and the resulting nationwide publicity. The problem was that smu lost 7–0. Fordham only managed one first down the entire game but somehow intercepted one of those Mustang throws and returned it for a touchdown. Fordham—a team whose love of hardnosed football closely mirrored Pittsburgh's—had played for the break, and wide-open football had provided it. Weekends like this slowed the development of the open game. Even though Schmidt may have sounded like a man in denial, it was important to the movement that he refused to compromise the party line—his faith in the open game, the game of the future.[27]

One final aspect of this debate between "horse and buggy" football and "automobile" football intrigued sports fans in the 1930s and is definitely worth mentioning here. Those two examples of ultra-conservative football—Pittsburgh and Fordham—actually played each other for three consecutive seasons between 1935 and 1937, and all three games ended in a 0–0 tie! Some of the players and many observers claim those matchups illustrated football at its finest, and they may have been right. There is something to be said for the taut emotions that are stretched with every aching minute of a game in which one play can decide everything. Every detail is magnified. The game becomes an art form of its own, and as with all art, beauty is in the eye of the beholder. One of Fordham's linemen, Vince Lombardi, gained notoriety as head coach of the Packers twenty-five years later by utilizing power football even as it was slipping out of vogue.

Coming off their complete sacking at the hands of Pitt, the last thing the Buckeyes needed was a road game against a tough conference opponent like Northwestern, but that's just what St. John's schedule called for. This particular Northwestern squad appeared to be one of the most talented in school history. In their two games so far, the Wildcats had given up a *total* of 4 yards rushing.

The Wildcats were in their second year under Pappy Waldorf, a gentle but shrewd coach who always found a way to maximize his talent. Pappy and Schmidt knew each other well. During the exact years that Schmidt had coached at TCU, Waldorf had been the head coach at Oklahoma A&M (now Oklahoma State). The two of them had often run into each other on the scouting/recruiting trail during this period, and Waldorf still recalled one of his earliest Schmidt memories: "I remember one time down in Oklahoma, he [Schmidt] was a spectator at a high school game, and before it was over he had a whole notebook full of plays." In Waldorf's first summer at Northwestern, he had invited Schmidt to co-chair his football clinic; the pair of Southwest expatriates unified in a strange land.[28]

Acting as though the Pitt disaster had never really happened, Ohio State opened their game up against Northwestern. Wasylik and Tippy each threw for a touchdown, giving the Buckeyes a tenuous 13–7 lead as the game entered the fourth quarter. The Buckeyes were actually playing better than the score indicated, but two mistakes hurt them. They had missed an extra-point attempt, and Bill Booth had fumbled, awarding Northwestern possession on the Buckeyes' 5-yard line. The time and the place of the fumble exposed one of those nagging compromises that Schmidt hated. With both Tippy Dye and the defensively deficient Jumpin' Joe Williams in the game, Tippy was forced to play near the line as a defensive halfback. Northwestern alertly ran a sweep at Tippy on the first play. Don Geyer was the ballcarrier, and Tippy met him near the line, but Geyer was 40 pounds heavier, and he ran over Tippy, practically dragging him into the end zone for a score. Two mistakes had kept the score close, and now two plays would decide the game.[29]

The first came as Ohio State's offense was moving down the field midway into the final quarter. Jumpin' Joe Williams was on his way to a gain of no less than 10 yards when his trailing teammate, Jim McDonald, decided to attempt a block on the Wildcat who was approaching Williams from the side. "I'm cutting," yelled McDonald to let his teammate know he was no longer available for a lateral. Jumpin' Joe mistakenly thought his teammate was *asking* for a lateral. Williams briefly looked back, saw McDonald, who was a split second away from cutting to the blocker, and tossed the ball. As the ball hung in the air, both men assumed the other had the ball, and each was busy pursuing a block in support of the other. The ball hit the ground and rolled around for a bit before Northwestern jumped on it, claiming possession. Schmidt's wide-open offense often died from wounds inflicted by their own swords. A team playing status-quo football would never think about attempting such a stunt while in the lead, no matter the size, field position, or opportunity.[30]

The second game-altering play came with just a few minutes left on the clock. After an exchange of punts gave the Wildcats possession of the ball on their own 45, they decided it was time to try some open football of their own. This was considered acceptable since they trailed, since they were at midfield, and since the game was winding down. Don Heap, Northwestern's all-conference left half, took a toss in the backfield and waited for his receiver to get down field. It was to be a long pass play, requiring time to develop, time that Heap was struggling to buy as a heavy Buckeye pass rush forced him to drift more deeply into the pocket. Finally he launched a massive rainbow that seemed to take forever to travel its 50 yards, attracting defensive backs all the while. The Buckeyes should have easily defended it, but instead John Kovatch, Northwestern's left end, snagged it at the 13. Three plays later the Wildcats scored the game-tying touchdown on a 10-yard rocket pass from Bernard Jefferson (one of that handful of black players in the Big 10) to none other than Don Heap. Northwestern converted the extra point to secure a 14–13 lead. With time running out, Schmidt and the boys emptied out their bag of tricks and put a scare into the Dyche Stadium crowd. Using a "dazzling array of laterals, fakes, and tricks" the Buckeyes "ripped and soared" their way close to the end zone. But with less than three minutes remaining, Jumpin' Joe Williams threw a pass off the halfback option that was intercepted at the 8-yard line by the omnipresent Don Heap. The pass had been attempted well within field-goal range, leaving many Buckeye faithful to again question whether Schmidt had encouraged too much reckless abandon amongst his boys. After running some time off the clock, the Wildcats' Steve Toth then nailed a monstrous punt that soared over Joe Williams's head and rolled out of bounds after traveling 71 yards from Toth's toe. Game over.[31]

It was Schmidt's second-ever Big 10 loss, and, just like the Illinois defeat in 1934, his team had lost by the margin of a single extra point. It was also the first time in six seasons that a Schmidt team had lost consecutive games. Even worse, it reminded many of the Notre Dame game when Schmidt had sacrificed a lead at the hand of his aggressive philosophy. Now only three weeks into the season, any sort of title seemed completely out of reach, and the Buckeyes still had to play Notre Dame in South Bend.

But before the rematch with Notre Dame, Schmidt needed to rally his troops for a game with lowly Indiana. He knew this was the perfect game for a letdown and he worked the players hard in practice all week as a result. He also added new plays, his panacea for all things football-related.

On game day, Schmidt tried to inspire his troops with another gimmick: he had them don their new all-white uniforms for the first time ever. As the team poured out of the tunnel and onto the field in their brand-new gear, the Columbus crowd went wild. It felt like a fresh start to the season. Then came . . . nothing. Tippy Dye had perhaps the worst passing game of his career, never establishing a rhythm and contributing heavily to the 7 interceptions thrown between the two teams. He did, however, throw a touchdown pass to Merle Wendt—a beautifully timed play that would be described today as a tight end seam route—the ball hitting Wendt on the hands as he split two zone defenders near the goal line. Tippy was finally pulled as Ohio nursed a 7–0 lead. The Buckeyes then tried to run the ball more, but their ground game wasn't clicking either. Then, in the fourth quarter, Schmidt inserted sophomore Johnny Rabb, and the young beast took care of business. He "ripped the Indiana middle wall to shreds," eating clock and preserving an ugly 7–0 Buckeye victory. It hadn't been pretty to watch, but sandwiched between two top-ranked opponents like Northwestern and Notre Dame, this win gave Ohio State a much-needed boost.[32]

Still, many fans felt alarmed. Few expected Ohio State's 1936 squad to be as lethal as Schmidt's previous two, and everyone understood their boys faced a difficult schedule, but who among them thought Schmidt's "touchdown system" would score a paltry 20 points over a 3-game period. It seemed as though the razzle-dazzle had lost its bearings. And when it did start to work, some sort of error would kill the momentum. When the negative side effects outweigh the cure, people tend to grumble and question the necessity of being cured in the first place.

Time had finally arrived for the Notre Dame rematch. On Halloween eve the Buckeyes boarded a train to Elkhart, Indiana, where they practiced at the local high school before spending the night in a hotel. The next day they traveled by bus the final fifteen miles to South Bend, arriving just before game time. This "official" trip, which was paid for by the school and met conference requirements, included 34 players. By game time, however, some 50 Buckeye players would be suited up on the sideline. A provision in Big 10 law allowed any number of players to participate in a road game, but those not included in the official traveling party had to make their own way to the game at their own expense. In this case Schmidt "named" extra players to show up. Eleven of them, led by coach Cookie Cunningham, spent two days making the trip by automobile, and a few others would join fans on the Saturday morning special trains. And there would be plenty of Buckeye fans to mingle with. According to the Ohio State ticket office, approximately 14,000 tickets had been purchased on their end, accounting for nearly 30 percent of the tickets that were issued for a home game at Notre Dame. All together 50,017 fans attended the game, only the third time in 29 contests that Notre Dame Stadium had hosted 40,000 or more fans.[33]

The sequel to the game-of-the-century could never match expectations. Mother Nature made sure of this, unleashing a cold Halloween rain that left the crowd shivering and the field mucky. Both teams executed some exciting plays and were determined to attempt some forward passing, albeit in vain. They combined to attempt 24 passes, but even more telling was their combined 23 punts.[34]

The Buckeyes scored first on a safety when Charley Hamrick blocked a Notre Dame punt in the end zone. The Irish countered with a second-quarter touchdown following a steady 75-yard march down the field. It was the only time Notre Dame entered Ohio's territory the entire game, but they had made it count, and their 7–2 lead held deep into the fourth quarter.

As if playing on the road against a stout defense on a wet field wasn't bad enough, Ohio State had the additional handicap of an injured starting quarterback. It happened when Tippy Dye fielded a punt. "Just as I caught the punt, two guys—one on each side—hit me just right, giving me a slight concussion, but nobody knew it. So I stayed in the game. But I started calling plays we'd never had, and Schmidt decided he'd better take me out. Mary had come down to see the game, and Schmidt let her ride back on our train with me, and she took care of me all the way."[35]

Unlike the previous year when Notre Dame had staged one of the great reversals of fortune, this time Ohio State was trying to make a furious comeback. Wet and exhausted but with one more burst of desire left in them, the Buckeyes went for broke and turned on the razzle-dazzle. With substitute Nick Wasylik doing the quarterbacking, the Buckeyes advanced 58 yards to the Irish 13-yard line. The last two plays had been pass completions to halfbacks totaling 33 yards, leaving the Irish defense staggering. Earlier in the game Wasylik had thrown an interception when Ohio was 3 yards from scoring, and this was his big chance to make up for it. With less than a minute remaining, Wasylik called for a pass into the end zone, which fell incomplete. Players debated in the ensuing huddle. Wasylik wanted to throw another pass over the goal line, but that was risky. According to the rules of the period, two incompletes thrown into the end zone during a series of downs resulted in a touchback. Wasylik decided time dictated that they go for it, but the second pass was also incomplete, and Notre Dame took possession and ran out the clock. Ohio State's heart-stopping revenge would have to wait. If the game's outcome had been decided like a boxing match with judges, Ohio might have won based on consistency and style, but football is judged solely by the scoreboard, and Notre Dame had made their one big punch count. The Irish seemed to find ways to win, while the Buckeyes found only ways to lose. For Ohio State fans, an opportunity for revenge would have to wait until the two teams met again, fifty-nine years later, at which time Ohio State finally got the upper hand with a decisive 45–26 victory.[36]

The just-concluded two-game series had filled both stadiums and had produced one of the most exciting games ever. Why wouldn't they play one another again until 1995? Lynn St. John, who had been OSU's athletic director since 1912 and held the position until 1947, considered it a matter of preserving college football as a unifying event for the region. He explained his position in a confidential letter to an OSU booster and fellow Shriner, claiming the problem lay in the attitude of "Catholics who attend such a game and who very obviously look upon it as a contest between the Catholic

Church and other people." Referring to the game held in Columbus, he wrote:[37]

> All of the Catholics who attended this football game were ra-
> bid partisans and rooters for Notre Dame. The distressing part
> about this was the fact that the Catholic members of our uni-
> versity faculty and the Catholic members of our student body
> . . . were vigorously rooting for Notre Dame on that particular
> day and date and not for Ohio State. It would be perfectly ob-
> vious to you, I think, that this condition brought about a good
> deal of bad spirit among our students and faculty, a most un-
> desirable product of any intercollegiate contest. This condi-
> tion was general—not just a sporadic case here and there. In
> place of football being a rallying ground for the spirit of an
> institution and of a community, a football game under these
> conditions becomes a great producer of dissension. Intercol-
> legiate football under these conditions becomes a liability and
> not an asset.[38]

Saint went on to describe local Catholic churches that had conducted prayers on behalf of Notre Dame football, and parochial
schools that forced children to be a party to the same thing: "The
difficulty no doubt goes too deeply for any satisfactory correction
or remedy to be applied. It is to be found in the fact that Notre
Dame as an institution represents the Catholics of America, people
who put their religion above everything else." In Ohio putting anything above Buckeye football is almost unthinkable, so Saint probably thought he was performing his civic duty. Still, one wonders if
he might have been more understanding had Ohio State won both
games.[39]

Although St. John stated his case for breaking off football relations with Notre Dame due to issues concerning school spirit versus
religion, it was obvious that other hard feelings were influencing

his decision. Notre Dame's success on the field was surely a factor, and St. John tried hard to justify his ill will there, as well. A couple years later, Griffith would query St. John as to why Notre Dame had gone 36-4-3 against the Big 10 over the last two decades. Saint's confidential response was a mishmash of reasons that had been espoused by others before him.

> Any team in the Western Conference playing Notre Dame does so with the very slight chance of winning. The competition is very unequal, due to the fact that Notre Dame draws outstanding football players from all parts of the country, owing to the fact that they are the outstanding Catholic institution. Their large number of high-class players, living in what amounts to a big training club, having no interference on account of studies with their daily football work, never having anybody ineligible on account of scholastic difficulties, are among the chief factors explaining their football superiority and answer the question why our best teams in the conference are not able to win a fair share of games from Notre Dame. I think any good football player can attend Notre Dame at practically no expense to himself.

The first accusations Saint leveled were accurate enough, but the claims about ineligibility were incorrect, and the final claim hinting that Notre Dame was essentially a professional team was just plain petty. Indeed, emotions still ran deep, even though Saint claimed the Buckeyes' two losses didn't color his view. The two teams continued to compete in other sports, but apparently these less popular sports didn't significantly endanger a man's soul.[40]

The Notre Dame issue notwithstanding, the 1936 Buckeyes were piling up some ugly numbers. Over the last 4 games they had lost 3, scored a mere 22 points, and averaged just over 160 yards of offense per game. Schmidt—the miracle worker—had been granted an exemption for the stunning Notre Dame loss in 1935, but this stretch of poor play was fair game for second-guessers. It seemed as though the team's offensive psyche had been damaged during the Pitt game and had never been able to recover. The defense had never been better, but the paralysis on offense was an unwelcome trend. The Scarlet Scourge that battled for a national title in 1934 and 1935 had lost a total of 2 games in those two years. The 1936 squad had now lost 3 times in twenty-two days.

Many were looking for answers and alibis. Schmidt had warned that this schedule was inhumane and that expectations should have been tempered. And really, Ohio had lost all 3 games by a total of just 12 points. One more extra point and a couple of accurate passes might have resulted in an undefeated season for the Buckeyes. But others didn't want explanations. After all, good teams beat other good teams all the time, so why was Ohio State suddenly unable to beat the good teams it faced? Maybe Schmidt spent too much time on strategy. Maybe he needed to spend more time inspiring the boys instead of just working them. Maybe the open-game movement had simply stopped moving.

This season was a mess, but there was still a chance to salvage it. Ohio State's schedule now concluded with their three biggest annual rivals: Chicago, Illinois, and Michigan. Schmidt's contract was up for renewal next spring, and though it was unlikely that one bad season on the heels of two beauties would sink him, it was almost certain that running the table to end 1936 would keep him in Columbus and temper the wolves for awhile.

The first of the three rivalries seemed to be the easiest. Despite a near upset over Ohio in 1935 when the Buckeyes were despondent over the Notre Dame mess, Chicago's football program was a wreck. The University of Chicago had at one time been the largest and most prestigious school in the conference, her football program a fitting jewel in the athletic crown. Under the guidance of Amos Alonzo Stagg, Chicago had won several Western Conference titles between 1892 and 1924. After that, Maroon football had slowly died. Part of the problem was the sixty-something Stagg, who clung to old strategies and, more important, old politics. In the post–World War I sports world of frenzied media coverage and huge stadiums, the stakes had soared. A coach needed to recruit players, coddle rich alumni, and be creative in "helping" players pay tuition. In short, they needed to be aggressive, with a healthy disregard for the spirit of the law. Stagg's program wasn't as pure as a nunnery, as most football followers wanted to believe, but it certainly wasn't playing loosely enough with ethics to keep up with the rest of the conference sinners. Like Zuppke, Stagg had too much pride to beg kids to play for him, and the quality of his material showed it. Another problem plaguing Chicago's football program was an increasingly education-minded administration that was no longer offering an easy path of learning for the athletes. Frivolous classes and physical education courses, a traditional boon for athletes, were offered in short supply on Chicago's campus.

Robert Hutchins, who in 1929 became the school's president at the sprightly age of thirty, was responsible for increasing the difficulty level of the curriculum being offered. Hutchins was an educational extremist who believed that "The object of the educational system, taken as a whole, is not to produce hands for industry or to teach the young how to make a living. It is to produce responsible citizens." If learning a career was not a worthy pursuit, then intercollegiate football was a pox. Hutchins would have been thrilled to see Chicago's football program disappear altogether, but he didn't have the guts to finish it off. Instead he was starving it, biding his time until disheartened onlookers cried for its merciful euthanasia. Then he would pounce.[41]

Ohio State's razzle-dazzle needed a lift, and the scheduled arrival of the defenseless Maroon couldn't have come at a better time.

Tippy Dye, having recovered from his concussion, connected with Frank Antenucci for a pair of touchdowns in the first quarter, each pass play covering over 50 yards. The rest was bedlam. Schmidt used 43 players—including 19 sophomores—and the youngsters barely controlled themselves, scoring 30 more points to finalize the score at 44–0. Three additional Buckeye touchdowns were called back because of offsides penalties, and the Scarlet Scourge only punted twice during the entire game. To understand just how lopsided it had been, one need only look at the game's passing numbers. The Buckeyes completed 9 of 10 forward passes and all 6 lateral passes while the Maroon completed just 3 forwards while having 5 intercepted.[42]

Clark Shaughnessy was growing weary of his education and was probably wishing he had accepted the offer to leave Chicago when he had the chance. "We couldn't hope to cope with Ohio's fine team. They had hundreds of men to smother us."[43]

The Buckeyes had an easy time at the Illinois game as well, but by different means. A gale-like wind affected strategy, forcing them to call running plays almost exclusively. They kept the game tight by losing 4 fumbles, but a crop of sophomore backs with fresh legs made sure Ohio State was victorious 13–0. Johnny Rabb, Howard Wedebrook, and Bill Booth wore down the Illinois defense throughout the second half, with Booth dealing the final blow. From the Illinois 8, Tippy Dye faded back to pass, looking at the corner of the end zone, his arm extended and ready to fire, when Bill Booth swept behind his quarterback and snatched the ball out of his hand—the Statue of Liberty play. But the misdirection play wasn't quite as deceptive as had been hoped. Several back-side Illini had stayed home, forcing Booth to improvise. "Without a blocker in front of him, Booth hammered his way past seven Illinois tacklers and over the goal." If this game is to be remembered, however, it should be remembered as a game belonging to Johnny Rabb.

The sophomore who had emerged during the Indiana game was virtually unstoppable in Champaign. Inflicting most of his damage between the tackles, Rabb carried the ball 19 times for 147 yards; Illinois did everything they could to stop him.[44]

It was the Johnny Rabb everyone had been anticipating. "Jarrin' Johnny" or "Ol' Jawn" was a big hit with the fans because of his fast, powerful runs, but his trademark was returning to the huddle after the run. Slowly climbing to his feet, Rabb looked as though he wouldn't make it through another play. Once his big frame was finally upright, he would begin a bedraggled saunter back to his waiting teammates. At the next snap of the ball Jarrin' Johnny would explode from his stance, laying waste to opponents until the whistle was blown, when the whole melodramatic process would begin anew. Because of Rabb's power and Bill Booth's talent for avoiding defenders, Buckeye fans were ecstatic about the future of both sophomore backs.[45]

With just one game left, Ohio State had a winning record for the first time all season. At this point things should have been at their rosiest between Schmidt and the press corps, but something had changed during the rough campaign. They had each discovered something about the other that diluted future enchantment. Schmidt had warned the writers that this was a cruel schedule, yet they had continually second-guessed him during the losing patch. For two seasons he had provided them with colorful quotes and some of the most exciting football in sports history, but at the first sign of trouble they had played the part of executioner rather than friend. These reporters, for their part, were just doing their job. They were still fascinated with Schmidt, but the public wanted to know why his squads always managed to lose the big game, and if you want to sell papers you give the public what they want. What bothered the scribes the most, however, was Schmidt's unpredictability: "Schmidt, relatively easy to approach in the middle of the campaign when the Buck fortunes were at a low ebb, exhibited an icy exterior and answered questions with clipped phrases after the Illinois triumph." His attitude was backward from that exhibited by most coaches, or even by most people, for that matter. For instance, when he had run across the field to gleefully shake hands with Layden after the devastating loss to Notre Dame the previous season, had he feigned joy in losing as a defense mechanism? Was his apparent coldness in victory just calculated retribution? Writers were beginning to learn that the caustic, confident Schmidt could be hurt easily, and though he was loyal to no one but his wife, he expected loyalty from everyone. Such unrealistic expectations are a common trait of hypomania.[46]

Though Schmidt and the press were not holding hands, they were both focused on the season's final game. Ohio State had beaten Michigan in three consecutive games from 1919 to 1921, but had never turned the trick since. The Buckeyes' seniors may have had a rough year, but they had a chance to graduate having gone undefeated against Michigan as members of the varsity. At dusk on Friday night, Schmidt led those seniors through their Final Tackle. Among that group were Merle Wendt, Inwood Smith, Charley Hamrick, Frank Cumiskey, Frank Antenucci, Bob Miller, Augie George, and Tippy Dye—Schmidt's favorite son.

Ohio was heavily favored to defeat the Wolverine squad that entered the game at 1-6, having scored a measly 36 points all season. But anyone who follows football appreciates the fact that records don't count for much when a rivalry of deep passion is involved. Such was the case early in this affair; the intensity kept the game scoreless through the first quarter. But Ohio State was too good, and the Wolverines could only operate on adrenaline for so long. Soon the Buckeyes were doing what they did best, masterfully mixing power and deception, playing the entire field and keeping the opponent guessing as to what would come next. Tippy Dye—in his final game—was brilliant. On the Buckeyes' first scoring drive he completed 4 of 5 passes for 57 yards, finishing it off with a 14-yarder to Frank Cumiskey over the middle. He also unleashed two magnificent punt returns, one for a touchdown and the other all the way to the 4-yard line. Jarrin' Johnny Rabb added to his growing notoriety by doing most of the work on the second scoring drive, including rushing the final 26 yards off a shovel pass from Tippy. The only thing that didn't go well was the kicking. Bill Booth completed a 26-yard field goal but missed two other attempts, and all three of his extra-point tries were blocked. A heavy rain came pouring down in the final period, slowing the action and sending many fans off to begin celebrating early. The final score was 21–0 in favor of Ohio State. Even in victory the reporters found something to grouse about: "The Ohioans had players coming and going practically all the time, and there was little chance for anyone to shine with any consistency." Schmidt's system spread the glory awfully thin, much to the disappointment of those who wanted heroes. If there was a star it was Tippy Dye, who walked off the Horseshoe's turf having defeated Michigan during all three of his seasons as a Buckeye, a feat that would go unmatched by another Buckeye quarterback until Troy Smith seventy years later.[47]

The win over Michigan gave the Buckeyes a tie for second place in the Big 10, despite a disappointing overall record of 5-3. Closer examination of the record gave Buckeye backers a small sense of consolation. The 3 losses had come at the hands of three of the top-ranked teams in the nation: Pittsburgh (No. 3), Northwestern (No. 7) and Notre Dame (No. 8). All three teams had figured prominently in the race for a mythical national championship. Northwestern had halted Minnesota's 21-game winning streak and was the No. 1 ranked team in the AP poll before being pounded 26–6 by Notre Dame in their final game of the season.

Losing to such quality teams was nothing to be ashamed of, but

Schmidt would have loved to have won at least one of those games, and his growing reputation was damaged as a result of losing the big matchups. St. John would have preferred more victories as well, but he did accomplish his goal of pulling in more revenue. A total of 391,375 spectators had watched OSU, a number that led the Big 10 and broke the school's all-time attendance record set in 1929. Coinciding with the start of Schmidt's tenure, it was the third straight year of increase and the third straight year that the Buckeyes led the conference.[48]

At the football banquet two days later, George Trautman—toastmaster, OSU athletic board member, and overall program big shot—made an announcement regarding Schmidt's expiring contract, telling the audience that Schmidt had been invited to "continue on a gentleman's agreement for another three-year period." Some thought the decision to keep Schmidt might have been strained, but aside from some eccentricities, a lot of profanity, and a few big losses, Schmidt really had done a great job.[49]

A possible factor influencing the university's decision to offer an extension four months before the initial agreement ran out may have been that other schools were interested in Schmidt, most notably the University of Texas. A rumor had surfaced in Columbus the previous week that the Longhorns were interested in bringing Schmidt back to the Southwest. Only Schmidt knows whether he was being savvy or just his usually candid self, but his statement about the rumor was extremely well played. Yes, he admitted, he had been "approached by influential alumni of the University of Texas at Austin." No, he didn't give them a "great deal of encouragement," but he didn't decline them outright either. And in case anyone was curious, Schmidt added that the Longhorn job was "the best in the Southwest," and that "Texas is a rich school, and it would be a great spot if anyone wanted to go back there." No formal offer had been made by the school itself, he added. The next day,

Schmidt coyly told reporters the whole Texas situation was "much ado about nothing," even though he was partly responsible for creating the "ado." Whether Schmidt had plotted to create the anxiety or was simply speaking his mind, it worked. Later that winter, after Schmidt had accepted the gentleman's agreement from Ohio State, the Nebraska Cornhuskers inquired as to his availability. Schmidt would have loved to coach at his old college, but by then he had committed to returning to the Buckeye fold.[50]

Four days after the Buckeyes' season had finished, Schmidt hit the rails in search of more football. Non–Big 10 schools played longer schedules that often carried into December, and he couldn't ignore the siren's call. Schmidt stopped in Dallas to watch TCU play on November 28 before continuing on to Los Angeles to view the USC–Notre Dame game on December 5, followed by a hop up the coast to watch TCU battle Santa Clara on December 12. For expense account purposes, Schmidt justified his long-distance tour as a scouting expedition since Ohio State would be playing both TCU and USC the following season, but, truth be told, Schmidt was the quintessential football fan and would have headed west to watch those games regardless of OSU's schedule, just as he had done for years.[51]

He returned from his pigskin tour on December 19 but only stayed in Columbus long enough for a bit of holiday cheer. On Christmas Day he was on the train again, this time headed for the East Coast and the NCAA meeting. Of prime importance to Schmidt was the rules committee debate. He was concerned about the interpretation of "pass interference." He felt that "two men going after the same ball have the same rights . . . and contact on the play does not always constitute interference." Also of concern to him was the poor treatment of the shovel pass. Current rules called for loss of possession on a shovel pass that struck an ineligible man. Schmidt felt that the penalty was too harsh when one considered how bunched up the players were behind the line of scrimmage. If there was ever a champion of the shovel pass, it was Francis Schmidt, and he intended to defend the pass during the debate.[52]

His mad dash from coast to coast finally ended during the first week of January when he returned to Columbus for good. At this point most people would have been tired of traveling, tired of football, and ready to relax and enjoy the winter weather inside while sitting in a comfortable chair near the fire. Schmidt, of course, was not like most people. He was a hypomanic whose obsessions never yawned. There was always something he could be doing, especially following a bad season. The season that had just ended was his worst since he had coached at Arkansas in 1926, and unlike his days with the Razorbacks, this current "failure" was on a national stage. The same football nation that was curious about his unique offense was also forming the opinion that Schmidt's teams couldn't win big games against big teams. In other words, Schmidt's success had a ceiling. If Schmidt's system was as wonderful as he thought it was, he needed to prove it, and the only theory of improvement that Schmidt understood was the theory of more—more of everything—starting with winter practice. Instead of starting in early February, which was already bordering on the ridiculous, he tacked on an extra session for freshman and deep subs that began the second week of January. Invitations were sent out the very week Schmidt returned from his travels. He would hold practices three days a week for the next month until "regular" winter practices began.[53]

Besides inviting the young and the inexperienced, Schmidt also included all of his centers among the invitees. He was hoping to move a few of them to the end position, which was looking thin for 1937. The worst part about being a college coach is being powerless to control personnel turnover. No thanks to those pesky graduations, spots always needed to be filled. Last winter Schmidt had dreaded trying to fill Gomer Jones's cleats at center, but his successor, Ralph Wolf, had been surprisingly good and nothing if not durable, playing 438 of a possible 480 minutes. He'd been named the team's MVP for 1936 and had been rewarded with co-captaincy for 1937 along with Jim McDonald. Wolf's tenacity allowed Schmidt to deplete depth at center in favor of throwing bodies at the threadbare end spots. And so it went, the never-ending talent treadmill. Sometimes things lined up well, but sometimes availability and necessity just didn't overlap at all. Unfortunately, there is no waiver wire, and trades are not permissible in college football.[54]

A lot of talented players graduated later that spring, but for personal reasons Schmidt was especially sad to see Tippy Dye go. Schmidt was genuinely fond of the little quarterback and proud of everything he had accomplished. Tippy was graduating with a fine academic record that he had earned while working multiple jobs, and he had *nine* varsity letters to show for his athletic prowess— tying an all-time school record. But of everything Tippy could boast, the greatest came two days before graduation exercises when he married his sweetheart, Mary, in a double ceremony, shared with Mary's sister Dorothy and Ray Farnham, Tippy's high school coach. Francis and Evelyn Schmidt proudly attended. Two days later, after returning from a quick honeymoon in Cincinnati, Tippy finished his Ohio State career, receiving a diploma in the depths of the stadium, where graduation was held due to rain. Mary graduated magna cum laude.[55]

Schmidt wasn't the only head coach mourning the loss of an exceptional athlete he cared about. Down in Texas Dutch Meyer was lamenting the departure of Slingin' Sammy Baugh. Their fates had been intertwined for several years. Meyer had worked hard to land a third baseman for his baseball team, only to discover a tremendous quarterback just in time for his shift to varsity football coach. Meyer possessed a great love for football and had received outstanding

training from Schmidt, but Baugh had made his job that much easier. The two of them had combined to create the best forward-passing team in the nation. Entering his senior season Baugh had been
described in the *Illustrated Football Annual* as "the nation's outstanding leather slinger, feeding them long and short into the hands of
his mates with an uncanny accuracy that smacked of witchcraft." Injuries and bad weather had slowed Baugh and the Horned Frogs in
1936, but nothing could shake his label as the country's best passer.
Official statistics were not available, but Baugh's career touchdown
passes (39) and passing yardage (3,384) were certainly higher than
any player before him.[56]

During TCU's football clinic that summer, Schmidt and Meyer
would have a chance to reminisce about Baugh and commiserate
over the loss of their best passers, but the solidarity could only go
so far. The Buckeyes and the Horned Frogs were scheduled to meet
each other at the beginning of the 1937 season.

Eight. Slingin' for Dollars

In December of 1936 Sammy Baugh, then a senior at TCU, received a curious message from the Washington Redskins informing him that he was the team's first selection in the NFL draft. Baugh recalled his confusion at being so honored. "I didn't know what they were talking about because, frankly, I had never heard of either the draft or the Washington Redskins," he said. "Down here in Texas, no one knew anything about pro football. Hell, they didn't know what it was."[1]

It wasn't just Texas that knew little or nothing about pro football; a good portion of the country was completely oblivious. In 1937 only six of the nation's forty-eight states even fielded an NFL team, and none of them were west of Green Bay or south of Washington DC. Those in the remaining forty-two states who knew much about the NFL were hit and miss. Some areas—mostly large cities with tropical climates like Miami and Los Angeles—were popular barnstorming destinations during the winter, where an NFL team would play a temporary collection of local players, usually misnamed "All-Stars," who offered only slight resistance on the field. There were also smaller locales within the NFL belt such as Fredrick, Maryland, or Trenton, New Jersey, that hosted exhibitions just before or during the season. If, however, an NFL team did not visit your neck of the woods for an exhibition, there was a good chance you were completely unaware of the league's existence. National radio networks might broadcast six or more college games on a Saturday during football season, but they covered zero professional games on Sundays. Newsreels shown in the theaters devoted huge chunks of footage to college football but almost none to the professional ranks. Thus, with the sights and sounds of the NFL accessible only to certain regions, the rest of the country was dependent on newspapers for enlightenment, and it wasn't receiving much. Large to mid-sized papers across the country received pro scores, standings, and tidbits as part of their AP and UP wire service subscriptions, but most ignored the information. Some printed the scores and standings in small type and stuck them in the bottom corners with bicycle race results and local bowling scores. Hundreds of little papers without wire service subscriptions might have guessed the NFL was some New Deal organization created by President Roosevelt.

The 1937 draft, in which Baugh had been selected, was only the second annual version for the NFL. The process had been started the year before at the behest of certain owners whose teams were having trouble competing. Chief among the supporters was Bert Bell, owner of the hapless Philadelphia Eagles (the Eagles had just finished a two-year stretch where they went a combined 3-20 and were outscored 111–385). Unable to run the ball (2.79 yards per carry) and usually trailing early, the Eagles had relied on a desperate passing "attack" whose numbers would make a hardened coroner avert his eyes: 25 percent completion percentage, 9 touchdown passes, and 66 interceptions. Bell was suffering the effects of a vicious circle that prohibited the second-division clubs from fairly competing. Because the Chicago Bears, New York Giants, and Green Bay Packers were older and had more well-established programs, they won more games, which attracted more fans, which brought in more money. With this additional money they were able to buy choicer talent, perpetuating the cycle while the have-nots were powerless to do anything but stand and watch. Between 1927 and 1935 (the last season before the draft) the big three had won 7 of 9 league titles and had winning records in 26 out of the possible 27 instances during that period. Obviously, status quo was fine with them, but their representatives ascertained diminishing acceptance for this trend among fans and cooperated with the newly formed draft. They understood that competition was good for the box office. Hopefully in late November, when the temperatures plunged, the division races would be heated enough to lure fans from their snug homes.[2]

Not long after receiving the news that he'd been drafted by the Redskins, Baugh was contacted by the team's owner, George Preston Marshall, and was offered $4,000 annually to play in Washington—a substantial offer by NFL standards. Baugh declined the bid, however, mentioning his inclination to accept a job offer from Dutch Meyer to serve as head coach of freshman athletics at TCU. What Baugh didn't mention was his lack of knowledge regarding professional football and his fear that he wouldn't measure up to the necessary skill level.[3]

While initially discouraged, Marshall did not despair. This was only the first offer, and several months remained until the season started (the draft had been held in December *before* bowl games were even played). Besides, a collegiate All-American who decided against going pro was the rule moreso than the exception in those days. Even those graduating heroes in the Midwest and East who knew about the NFL usually opted for another line of work, basing their decisions on salary and social pressure.

Relative to positions available for college graduates in the real world, NFL football offered competitive remuneration. At a time when a male college graduate earned an average of $1,314 in his first year out of school, a pedestrian NFL player might earn between

$100 and $150 dollars per game, including exhibitions, which meant a rookie could make as much in a few months as the rest were making in a year. There were, however, hidden costs to playing professional ball. The player paid his own travel expenses to get to camp and almost always paid for equipment like shoulder pads and shoes. Also, these per-game deals were not usually guaranteed, meaning a player could be subject to an instant unpaid dismissal. A team was under no obligation to pay an injured player for time missed, nor pay for his medical bills. But besides the side-by-side comparison, young athletes had to consider the big picture upon graduation. A nice little wad of cash for playing a seasonal game was certainly enticing (and he would still have the off-season for a second job), but after a few years, the footballer would inevitably be forced to retire due to injury or declining skills, and when he did he would need to select a long-term "real" career. With a sketchy résumé and little to no experience, his new career would lag behind that of other men his age. The promise of riches and a leisurely retirement would now be more intangible than ever. Already, at eight years after having graduated from college, the typical male was making $2,383, or 181 percent more than he did during his first year. An ex-player might have to play catch up for the rest of his working life. And even NFL money was not guaranteed, with many a player collecting his paycheck and running straight to the bank, where the first checks cashed stood the best chance of clearing. After seventeen years of existence, the league was still on shaky financial footing; teams lost money more often than they made it. And another economic concern to consider was the Depression. With unemployment rates so high, it was harder to pass up a stable, lucrative career for the chance to indulge in football awhile longer.[4]

Baugh's decision was more difficult. He was one of those special players who had made a big name for himself in college and offered large entertainment value to any team who signed him. He had a chance to land the one big contact that each team saved for a player who had the capacity to draw crowds. These rare megadeals could be worth as much as $10,000 annually and might include a small guaranteed cut of the gate receipts—enough to live on year-round and often better than any other offer awaiting a player upon graduation. Still, many of the elite players passed on the NFL. For one thing, premium opportunities could be had in the business world. The collegiate fame that had the potential to earn a player a generous offer from the NFL was the same fame that translated into big bucks in commerce, especially when selling things like stocks, where a well-known name practically guaranteed success. Coaching was another option. High school and collegiate positions were always available for famous ex-players, a respectable career opportunity that would not be so readily available after their reputations had been stained while playing pro ball. While professional baseball was considered an acceptable extension of one's career, professional football was still demonized by most sportswriters and coaches.

Famous college coaches like Amos Alonzo Stagg and Fielding Yost were adamant in their disdain for professional football, regretting even having to acknowledge its existence. Stagg believed that the NFL was "purely a parasitical growth on intercollegiate football," and that any collegiate letter winner should be "ashamed to sell his athletic skill." For a long time the Big 10 banned the hiring of coaches who had "played for hire." Thus, during his university days, a young player was likely to hear many unflattering depictions of the NFL. Professionals, they were told, were men who idled off the field like cheap pool hall loiterers. They put forth mediocre effort on the field as they were more concerned with their health and its accompanying payday than with winning a game for the small group of uninspired spectators who bothered to watch. Players had no fire, felt no emotion, and did not desperately need to beat a half-century-old rival on homecoming day. These were men who reeked of cigarettes and beer, taking the path of least resistance toward a sad and unimportant future. To leave college and go pro was tantamount to picking up a prostitute at the gates of the cemetery where they had just laid your mother to rest.[5]

Along with the coaches, many influential sportswriters were opposed to professional football, and they constantly railed against it. They saw it as a threat to the amateur college version they held so dear. Those writers, sports editors, and coaches who were most venomous toward the pro game were generally older men who had been raised on the Victorian tenets of decency, selflessness, and hard, honest toil. And nowhere in the sporting world did these attributes find greater manifestation than in college football, where virtuous young men sacrificed body and soul for something as simple and pure as pride in one's school. In a world where women smoked in public and jazz bands ran amok, college football was not so much a refuge but rather the last stand of Victorian America itself, a reminder of a better time and a better country. Here, eleven boys huddled in unity agreed on a singular strategy and then carried out their individual—often unheralded—piece of the plan. One player's failure was capable of destroying the good work of ten others, and nearly every play demanded full effort from *all* involved. To do this, the young men suffered great physical pain and exhaustion, leaving the field only when injured to be replaced by yet another noble young warrior. College football represented virility in its purest form with no weapons or misguided motivations, a game of rare standards played by brave, alert young men within the nurturing walls of academia. These lads, after giving everything to their school and receiving equal in return, would accept diplomas and take their lessons of hard work and ambition out into the workforce, helping keep America on top of the world. For the most romantic of sporting enthusiasts, seeing a boy play the game for monetary reward was adulterous.

Their greatest fear was that football would go the way of major league baseball, where men seemingly cared more about money than the game, where boys straight out of high school were signed and shipped to some remote burg to learn baseball and nothing but. After years of cheap living and minimal moral guidance, most of these youngsters would be kicked to the curb when their baseball skills failed to blossom as expected, common young men with a common lack of education and a common future. Not every college football player was a scholastic whiz, but there was no way they would end up illiterate and naïve like Shoeless Joe Jackson. Football was too pure a game to be cheapened by professionalism.

Without the overemphasis on college athletics, Sammy Baugh would never have received a college education and its accompanying opportunities. Then again, Baugh wasn't overly impressed with his new degree. He didn't even bother to attend his own college graduation. Instead, he signed with a semipro baseball team as soon as he could, just like he'd done every summer since high school. And what better way was there to contemplate the future than to enjoy a summer getting paid to do what he loved. A "real" job could wait. In addition to the coaching job at TCU, Baugh had been offered and reoffered a coaching job with a high school in Phoenix, Arizona. He continued to vaguely consider pro football, but, for the moment, baseball was all that mattered. And before the summer was over, his baseball skills had captured someone else's attention, further complicating his career dilemma.[6]

Baugh's summer baseball team, an outfit called the Pampa Roadrunners, was playing a baseball tournament in Denver when he caught the eye of baseball legend-turned-scout Rogers Hornsby. Hornsby was canned shortly thereafter by his employer, the St.

Louis Browns, but upon resurfacing as a scout with the crosstown rival Cardinals, Hornsby mentioned Baugh to his new general manager, Branch Rickey, and the recommendation led to the offer of a contract. Baseball was Baugh's first love, and he jumped at the chance, but as it was late August and the season was nearly over, Baugh was told his chance at a professional baseball career would have to wait until spring training the following year. Baugh figured he could do some coaching during the fall and winter to prepare for his big baseball opportunity in the spring. As for playing football, he had one final commitment to fulfill the following week before ending his career in that sport forever.[7]

Earlier in the summer, Slingin' Sammy had agreed to play in the All-Star game, so he headed up to Chicago for his last game of organized football. The All-Star game was an annual charity exhibition pitting the reigning champion of the NFL against a squad of elite, newly graduated college players. The idea for the contest, which started in 1934, belonged to legendary *Chicago Tribune* sports editor Arch Ward. Profits went to an unemployed workers' relief fund. Played at Soldier Field, the game was very popular, requiring temporary seating to accommodate the sea of curious spectators. It was a partisans' delight, and Chicago was the perfect spot for the battle. The drama when the professionals faced the collegiate players on the gridiron was exceedingly relevant in the city that boasted the Bears and Cardinals of the NFL as well as several neighborhood collegiate teams including Northwestern, Illinois, Chicago, and Notre Dame. The participating players derived their own satisfaction from the exhibition by sharing a slice of the gate receipts. In 1937 each Green Bay Packer (the NFL team participating that year) received about $900 for playing, and each collegiate All-Star was enriched by $150 plus expenses.[8]

Now it's true that Baugh loved baseball first, and as a football player he wasn't the rough and tumble sort looking to trade bruises, but he really did enjoy the action and the matching of skills. When fall rolled around each year, Baugh invariably felt that familiar twinge of pigskin yearning. That autumnal longing led him from the University of Texas to TCU, and now that same latent passion welled up inside him as he practiced with his new teammates. In this vulnerable state of emotion Baugh had a revelation that would impact football for years to come. "I talked with the rest of the boys on the All-Star squad and found that a bunch of them were going to play pro football," he recalled. "I found that most of them were just like me, that they hadn't been out of the country too often themselves, and that I could play ball better than 99 percent of them. So I became a little more confident about whether I could or couldn't play pro football." For the first time Baugh began to seriously imagine himself playing professional football.[9]

On September 1, 1937, an estimated crowd of 84,000 fans attended the charity game between the All-Stars and the Green Bay Packers. The large attendance was no doubt inspired by the ongoing debate as to whether college or pro ball was better, but football does not offer simple answers without first having taken into account a multiplicity of factors. In this case, half the participants were young college graduates who had never played together, nor had they even played football in the past nine months. The Packers had also gone months without playing football, and many were concerned that the pros were a little slower to shake off the emotional lethargy of the off-season. So much rust meant that the offenses—dependent on timing and practice—would invariably suffer the most. Not surprisingly, in light of these circumstances, the three previous games in the series, when combined, had produced a total of 19 points. This is not to say the annual contests didn't provide any thrills, it just meant that one had to temper expectations when using this annual contest as a gauge for which version of football was superior. The three previous games had been tight, with two ending in a tie. So far the collegians had never won.

On this night, behind Baugh, the youngsters were finally victorious. The final score was an innocent 6–0, but the crowd had enjoyed a fast-paced game full of forward passing and great tackling. The All-Stars and the Packers managed to finally bring some offensive fireworks to the game, combining for 25 first downs and 508 yards of total offense—strong numbers for the era. Most remarkable—and most appreciated by the audience—were the 317 yards gained by forward passes. The lone score came on a pass play in the first period when Slingin' Sammy connected on a 48-yard pass to Gaynell "Gus" Tinsley, an All-American from Louisiana State. By general consent Sammy Baugh was the star of the game, not only for throwing the game's lone touchdown pass but for playing solid defense (two interceptions) and outpunting all others in the game. Considering he suffered a seriously bruised sternum in the match, his was a tremendous overall performance worthy of the praise. It was the first time that many reporters, coaches, and scouts had ever seen Baugh play, and what really struck them was the visual spectacle of his throwing.[10]

"He's all I've heard about him and more," said Bill Hargiss, a noted Big 6 scout who had attended the game. "Notice how quickly and how unerringly he rifles that ball." That last sentence is only ten words long, but with it, Hargiss captured the three elements that marked Baugh as a forward passing freak unlike any before him: quick release, bullet trajectory, and unusual accuracy. For better or worse, the next modern period of football had arrived, a period that in part resulted from an abstract recipe featuring Slingin' Sammy with sprinkles of Francis Schmidt, Dutch Meyer, a slim football, and the Southwest Conference. The age of the forward pass as a viable, respected weapon was unfolding, and Baugh was the prototype passer. Only one small problem remained: Sammy Baugh, the ball chucker for a new world, had not made up his mind to continue with football. His renewed thirst for the game had been abated by the sternum injury, plus he already had a baseball contract and two substantial coaching offers on the table.

While Baugh wrestled with his future, George Preston Marshall was more certain than ever that the kid's career should involve football. Impressed by Baugh's showing at the All-Star game, Marshall upped his offer to $5,000 per year—an attractive offer for a boy from small-town America. Still, he already had some pretty solid offers on the table for coaching jobs at high schools in Phoenix, Arizona, and Hobbs, New Mexico, among others. None of them paid $5,000 annually, but they were a sure thing and would be a lot easier on the body. The widespread use of agents still being decades away, Baugh turned to the man who was "like a father" to him—Dutch Meyer—and asked for advice. Meyer figured that as long as the high school coaching job was a firm offer and paid more, Baugh was playing with house money in his NFL negotiations. The Redskins had already upped their offer to $5,000. "If they're willing to pay that," Meyer advised, "ask for $8,000 and see what they say."[11]

With nothing to lose, Baugh followed his mentor's recommendation and was surprised when Marshall agreed to the counteroffer. Once again, Baugh's life had taken another last-minute turn. Now he could make big NFL money and still be free to play baseball for the Cardinals during spring training. Baugh joined the Redskins just in time for the season to open. His elation upon receiving an annual contract for $8,000 would be dimmed somewhat later that season when he discovered that the next level of pay on the team to be *substantially less* at $2,700 per year and that its recipients included three successful teammates with tenure. Even more disturbing to Baugh was that other hardworking veterans were playing on a per-game basis at $150 to $200 per contest.[12]

"It scared the livin' hell out of me, because I was afraid they might find out how much I was making and kill me," said Baugh. "It made me feel really strange to know I was so overpaid when we had guys doing their job just as well as I was and making less than $200 a game." Needless to say, current NFL rookies have managed to bravely overcome this guilt.[13]

Besides the pressure of being a highly touted draft pick and earning a load of money, Baugh also entered the 1937 season with the additional pressure of pleasing the Redskins' new hometown, Washington DC.

From 1932 to 1936, the Redskins had called Boston home, but they'd never received the support expected from a large city known for its rabid love of sport. George Marshall blamed it on the newspapers, and he probably had just cause. Directly across the river was Harvard University—the birthplace of America's rugby-like version of football—and not too far away were other long-standing college programs. Perhaps some of the local press weren't looking for a second act, especially a professional one. Regardless of the reason, attendance never reached levels that satisfied Marshall, and he began considering a move for his team. At season's end in 1936, things reached a breaking point. The Redskins won their first-ever division title, and Marshall figured an important championship game deserved important pricing, and by this he did not mean *discounting*. The Boston papers hammered the owner for price-gouging, and he responded by moving the title game to the Polo Grounds in New York, thus depriving Boston fans of a home playoff game. Those who believe in karma would be interested to know that the Redskins lost the championship game to Green Bay. At the owners' meeting in February, Marshall's request to permanently move the Skins to the District of Columbia was approved. The team's main office was set up on Ninth Street within walking distance of the Palace Cleaners headquarters, bringing the whole wayward affair to

a nice, tidy finish for the savvy Mr. Marshall, who had built his fortune through the Palace Cleaners. He'd inherited a two-store operation and built it into a beast, consisting of more than fifty outlets, riding the wings of the company slogan: "Long Live Linen."
Marshall was equipped with all the traits necessary for success: a
love of self, an unwavering confidence, and a forceful imagination.
He dressed boldly (his full-length raccoon coat was well known),
spoke brazenly, and moved about town like he owned the place.
He was relentlessly social, a mainstay on the theater and nightclub
scene. Marshall even attempted theatrics as a sidelight, both as ac-
tor and producer, but enjoyed only marginal success. Always one to
blur the line between acting and living, Marshall was married twice
to actresses, first to a Ziegfeld Follies girl and second to Corrine
Griffith, the former silent-screen legend. Those who knew Marshall
could laugh at his over-the-top vanity, charisma, and capriciousness,
but they could also tell tales of cheapness, racism, and a robust temper that couldn't be bothered with facts.[14]

Baugh and the Redskins started off brilliantly in their new home.
On September 16, with 24,942 fans in attendance at Griffith Park
for the opening game of the season, the Skins knocked off the New
York Giants 13–3. Although teammate Riley Smith scored all the
Redskins' points on 2 field goals and a long interception return, it
was Baugh who had everyone talking as he headlined "an aerial circus that handed the near-capacity crowd thrill after thrill." None
of Baugh's throws resulted in a touchdown, but the sportswriters
in attendance raved about the sharpness of his passes and noted
the lanky rookie's willingness to run with the ball. This Texan was
no myth.[15]

Slingin' Sammy's statistics for the night were equally impressive.
He had completed 11 of 16 attempts for 116 yards with no interceptions, and 3 of the incompletions had come on drops by the receivers. These might be considered below-average passing numbers

today, but they were strong for the NFL of the late 1930s. During the previous season, the league's teams averaged 83 passing yards per game and completed just 37 percent of their attempts. Interceptions occurred at the staggering rate of once every 8 throws and outnumbered touchdown passes by a 3:1 ratio.[16]

Baugh's arm had given the DC crowd the entertainment it was expecting, but George Marshall had left nothing to chance; he added some musical entertainment as well. While Baugh and the boys battled on the field, a "jazz and rhumba" band played on the sidelines. Stationed on a 40-by-50-foot sheet of mahogany at the 50-yard line, the band played upbeat nightclub music with great fervor, lost in their sound and oblivious to the oddly juxtaposed violence unfolding behind them. During timeouts the band added vocals as a "handsome young man . . . stepped to the microphone and rendered such fine old gridiron tunes as 'When Irish Eyes Are Smiling' and 'It Looks Like Rain in Cherry Blossom Lane.'" The many fans who were attending their first professional game must have been amazed at the whimsical proceedings (imagine a Super Bowl with the musical headliner performing on the sidelines throughout the game instead of just during halftime). To Marshall football was theater for the masses, and theater was best when accompanied with music. Although the rhumba experiment never found a foothold, Marshall was determined to have in-game music, so he eventually copied the collegiate tradition of having a small pep band play from the stands. It's still a part of the DC football experience today.[17]

Later that evening a train departed Washington's Union Station headed back home to Manhattan. Near the back of the train, the New York Giants, along with guests and visitors, rode in a "special" car. The atmosphere inside was subdued after the season-opening setback, but for one particular guest, the workday was not over.

As their train sped northward, Henry McLemore was busy trying

to capture the reaction from Baugh's recently vanquished opponents. McLemore was the sports editor for the *Syracuse (New York)*
Herald-Journal, a syndicated sports columnist, nationally influential,
and just a peg or two below Grantland Rice.

Steadying himself against the slight sway of the train, McLemore
made his way to a seat next to "Red" Corzine, reserve fullback/line-
backer for the Giants. Corzine was a league veteran, entering his
fifth season, and he was known for his colorful persona. In full hy-
perbolic mode, he offered testimony as to Baugh's toughness: "He's
as tough as a steer," Corzine enthused. "Early in the game I put a flying block on him that knocked him 10 yards. It was my Grade-A, all-
I-got block. I hit him so hard I damn near stunned myself. And all
he says as he jumps up is 'Say, fellow, you keep on blocking that way
and they'll give you your varsity letter.' Then he just grins at me."[18]

It was a reminder that for all his notoriety as a passer and punter,
Baugh was also required to be an active runner and a defender. Undersized offensive specialists like Baugh had to prove their toughness early and often if they wanted lots of playing time.

But it was Baugh's forward passing that had everyone abuzz, and
McLemore wanted to hear more about that. He made his way to
Steve Owen, the Giants' head coach. "Stout Steve" was known as
a defensive tactician and old-school fundamentalist who taught
football in the traditional no-nonsense manner. Some might have
thought Owen was too cautious to properly appreciate Baugh, but
Owen was really more of a moderate than most gave him credit for.
He was skeptical of modern football and swore allegiance to the
off-tackle run, but Owen just thought that's what the odds dictated
and played it close to the vest as a result. He was pragmatic enough,
however, to understand the utilitarian benefits of an efficient passing threat, and though his Giants didn't throw often, they were usually among the leaders in touchdown-to-passes ratios as well as fewest passes intercepted. Owen, who not only coached against the

great Benny Friedman but was a former teammate of his, had this
to say about Baugh:

> He's the greatest passer the game ever saw. Friedman never
> saw the day he could throw strikes with Sammy. And Benny
> was nobody's monkey with the ball. We were all set for him in
> that game with Washington, but he completed 12 of 18 [ac-
> tually 11 of 16] and the 6 failures weren't his fault. You see,
> Sammy throws the ball so fast and so accurately that there's
> little or no chance of knocking it down. And his anticipation
> and timing is perfect. Even when he's being rushed by two or
> three men he seems to know just the moment when the re-
> ceiver is going to get that extra step on the defender and make
> a cut. Then he lets fly, and just the split second the receiver
> cuts and turns there's the ball right in front of him."[19]

The greatest passer the game ever saw? This is proof that conver-
sational exaggeration was a popular art during the period, and Red
Corzine's claim of knocking Baugh 10 yards surely didn't give readers pause, but Steve Owen wasn't normally one to join in this practice. Anointing Slingin' Sammy as the game's all-time preeminent
passer after one professional game and 116 yards passing was undeniably stunning, but it had less to do with numbers as it did with
possibilities. Owen had been around the league for twelve years,
yet he had never seen such a combination of throwing ability and
understanding of the passing game. Owen's reference point had
been altered, and the idea of forward passing took on a frightening
new dimension. What would the NFL look like if there were several
Baughs? When Owen called Baugh "the greatest passer the game
ever saw," he was not only talking about the talent before his eyes
but also the skill set that would forever change football strategy if
replicated. He was talking from the future, a place he had been
briefly transported while watching Baugh in his first NFL game.

Because of financial restraints, it had seemed like the NFL was always one step from folding since its inception in 1920, but the league was actually growing and becoming steadier despite the Depression. In terms of attendance, money, and publicity the NFL was still the poor cousin to college football, but in terms of the level of play, it was on top, just as it should be. Its players were bigger, stronger, and faster. They were more experienced, had more finely honed instincts, and were better equipped to absorb strategy. Red Grange, the most famous football player in America, had seen the best of both sides, and there was no doubt in his mind where things stood: "I say that a football player, after three years in college, doesn't know anything about football. Pro football is the difference between the New York Giants baseball team and an amateur nine. College players not only don't know how to play football, but they don't take as much interest in the game as the pros. In college, you have studies to make up, lectures to attend, scholastic requirements to satisfy. In pro ball you're free from all this. You have nothing to do but eat, drink, and sleep football, and that is just what the boys do." Grange's version of the NFL was much more accurate than the biased version given by many important college coaches. Francis Schmidt, for example, still refused to give the NFL legitimate credit: "The pros don't like to block and tackle," he declared. "Then too, their schedules often require them to play three games a week [exhibitions included], and this demands there be less body contact among players." The "less contact" angle wasn't really true, nor were most of the other claims made by college coaches. Unlike Grange, they hadn't been immersed into pro football and could not make accurate comparisons. They were simply trying to protect their amateur game, facts be damned. The truth was, the NFL was a superior brand of football, and those with any instinct knew it would one day outpace the college game in importance. Hopefully, though, it wouldn't kill the college game in the process, as had already happened with baseball.[20]

Despite the hand-wringing claims of football puritans, the NFL was never intended to steal customers from the intercollegiate version but rather to supplement it. Not only did the NFL's pioneer executives know that direct confrontation would be financial suicide, they had no desire to harm the university game. From the beginning, the pros had agreed to leave collegians untouched until their football eligibility had ended and to leave Saturdays off their NFL schedules. The league believed that many postgraduate football players still loved playing the game, and players' abilities were still peaking, meaning that if they continued playing, theirs would be the highest level of play in America. And who wouldn't want to watch that? The college game had its rabid alumni, energetic students, and enormous regional implications, while the NFL had talent and the makings of concentrated big-city followings. Because they weren't competing with college ball, the pros marketed their brand of pigskin to a supposedly forgotten segment, commonly known as blue collar or working class—the type that didn't attend college and never developed a school loyalty. Ned Irish, a New York athletic impresario and promoter, speaking on behalf of his client, the NFL, explained that,

> We draw only a comparatively small percentage of college addicts. For the most part our crowds are made up of people who have never seen college teams play. They are the Sunday-off crowd and, being sports-minded, they come to the pro games. Most of 'em like it and keep on coming. You'd be surprised at the number of season books we sell around the circuit. If anything, we're making new customers for the colleges. We're bringing out people who never were interested in college competition, the so-called middle-class guy and his family,

and it is safe to assume that as the years go on this interest will
broaden and the colleges will benefit by it.

Charles Bidwill echoed the marketing credo after taking ownership
of the Chicago Cardinals in 1933: "We hope to attract letter carriers, streetcar conductors, clerks, and—above all—kids. In brief,
the success of professional football depends in no small measure
upon its ability to draw the workaday sport fans who either have
been ignored by the colleges or who can't get away to attend Saturday games." The pro game was courting nonprofessionals. An ostracized business and an ostracized demographic came together as a
perfect match to fill a void without harming the college game.[21]

So what does Sammy Baugh have to do with the demographics of
an NFL crowd? Well, these supposedly new converts to football, with
no preexisting expectations and no indoctrination into the finer
points of conservative football as taught on campus, wanted to be
entertained first and foremost. Strategy and team loyalty would follow. The college crowd was willing to settle for less entertainment
on the field in exchange for victory and all the maniacal expressions of school loyalty surrounding the games. NFL attendees either
developed a loyalty from scratch or needed to be fully entertained.
If not, they would find something else to do on a Sunday afternoon,
especially in November and December when cold winds whistled
through a sparsely filled stadium. For the NFL, the surest way to
make this fragile new connection was to give the blue-collar crowd
what it wanted. And what it wanted was adrenaline.

The NFL understood this, and they had already begun to mod-
ify the game accordingly. Concerned that tie games were not satisfying ticket buyers' desires for a final verdict, the NFL returned goal
posts to the front of the end zone in 1933, hoping that with field
goals' now being more attainable, deadlocks would diminish. They
were correct. There had been 30 tie games in the four years prior

to the rule but only 11 in the same length of time after the rule. Also, in 1933, the professional owners voted to make deception and passing easier by doing away with an archaic rule requiring forward passes to be attempted from at least 5 yards behind the line of scrimmage. Until these two rules were passed, the league had always followed a set of national rules shaped exclusively by the collegians. The 1933 break from this shadowing had been made in order to foster a more entertaining game. It wasn't exactly a declaration of independence, but it served notice that they foresaw the mechanics of football going in a slightly different direction as mandated by their fans. The next year they added another dimension to separate themselves from the collegiate version: they established a playoff system that crowned a single indisputable team champion each season. The fans seemed to like this very much, indeed.[22]

It might be argued that drawing and maintaining a loyal following was as simple as fielding a winning team. There is no doubt that winning helps, but the league's short history was littered with cities that had once hosted successful teams: Frankford, Providence, Pottsville, Kansas City, Boston, Duluth, and Portsmouth. An NFL team needed to woo new fans through any type of streak and every type of economic condition, and the best way to keep them was to entertain them.

The NFL owners understood this. One of them, Art Rooney, owner of the Pittsburgh Pirates (the pre-Steelers), had attended Baugh's first game and was now riding back to Manhattan as a guest of the New York Giants. Born to Irish immigrants in a poor section of Pittsburgh known as the First Ward, Rooney knew blue collar all too well. He'd worked hard in everything and had tried a lot of things along the way. Whatever he did, he usually did well. As a young man he had played minor league baseball, had started and played on a semipro football team, and had won amateur titles as a boxer. Later, his money had come through a batch of endeavors, including playing the stock market and promoting fights, but it was his prowess in betting on the ponies that won him both wealth and national notoriety. During the summer that had just concluded, Rooney was rumored to have parlayed $1,000 into a quarter million by picking a string of winners over the course of the racing season.

Henry McLemore couldn't pass on the opportunity to interview the best-known man in the car, and, after getting quotes for his Baugh story, he made his way to Rooney. The writer inquired directly as to the actual size of the rumored summer winnings. Rooney studied some notes in his pocket-sized red notebook and, after some deliberate mental calculating (and no doubt hesitancy with regard to baring one's financial matters to the press), went so far as to declare his net take was near $200,000.[23]

A sincere and humble man, Rooney was quick to follow up his exploits with a bit of self deprecation. "I had a bad day at Aqueduct the other day. Lost $40,000 on one race. Went overboard on a 3–5 shot." It was a staggering amount. In one race he'd lost an amount equal to the yearly salary of thirty-three average Americans working in the manufacturing industry. McLemore was curious to know the name of the offending horse that had cost him, but Rooney, "for the life of him, couldn't remember." That was probably more impressive than the monetary loss itself.[24]

Art Rooney's making a living at betting on horses was unusual and would be disparaged by the league today, if it were tolerated at all. In 1937, however, Rooney wasn't the only owner with strong gambling ties. Besides running a coal company, Tim Mara, owner of the New York Giants, was a legitimate bookmaker and a fight promoter. He wasn't even a football fan when he bought the team on a whim in 1925. And Charlie Bidwill, a former corporate lawyer and current owner of the Chicago Cardinals, was now running a printing business but was heavily involved in sports promoting and horse racing, even owning a racing stable. Dick Richards, owner of the

Detroit Lions, not only bet on his own team but "would get some of the players to go in with him." All four men counted among their contacts individuals ranging from the famous to the dubious to the shady.[25]

Reputations like these helped assure college football apologists they were right when decrying the pros as money-hungry, soulless men. Football was just one more thing for the owners to manipulate for cash. But in order for the NFL to thrive, it needed gamblers, hustlers, and promoters at the top—guys with flair and an appreciation for entertainment. And the owners, as a collective lot, had a strong promoting streak. Mara and Bidwill were involved in promotion as a profession. George Preston Marshall engaged in the art of selling himself as a routine exercise, and his business ventures went along for the ride. Dick Richards, owner of radio stations, bought the Lions *as* a promotion.

A long-held axiom among promoters has been "give 'em what they want." When it came to football, the paying fans wanted star players, thrilling finishes, and, according to NFL commissioner Joe Carr, "fans like to see the ball at all times and don't want it hidden under masses of players." Sammy Baugh was capable of giving the NFL exactly what it needed for years to come. Steve Owen had seen it flash before his eyes. The league was already opening up the rules to facilitate excitement, and the owners were already promoting the excitement. Baugh was the final piece to the puzzle. His talent for passing and his advanced understanding of the open-game movement were just what the NFL needed. If the NFL could find more players like him, they had a chance to alter the future of football and secure its place as the most popular spectator sport in America.[26]

What remained—and this was crucial—was for Baugh to prove that his unique skill set was not only entertaining but also capable of creating victories for his team. This caveat was settled for good by nightfall on December 13, 1937. Just over three months after Baugh had decided to play pro football, he and the Redskins defeated the Chicago Bears to win the NFL championship. Baugh was brilliant, throwing for 335 yards and 3 touchdowns—futuristic numbers from a futuristic passer. His 2 clutch touchdown tosses in the fourth quarter proved to be the difference in the Redskins' 28–21 victory. His was an astounding performance at the perfect time.[27]

"People say I changed football," recalled Baugh, "and I guess I did because passing is what I did best. I didn't invent the modern passing game. Hell, I don't know who did. But I was ahead of people in the pro league because I had played under Dutch Meyer at TCU. At TCU our offense was pretty similar to the West Coast offense. TCU's offense at the time was more sophisticated than anything they had in pro ball—and I just started putting those plays into the Washington offense."[28]

The Francis Schmidt effect, by way of Dutch Meyer, by way of Sammy Baugh, had opened a professional branch.

Nine. On the Edge

Throughout his coaching career Francis Schmidt generally took two extended vacations during the year: one after spring football practice and one during August, just before fall practice started. These trips ranged in duration from ten days to a month. But Schmidt didn't take vacations to relax or forget about football. Instead, he took them because he occasionally liked to pursue other activities with vigor, namely hunting and fishing. Jim Renick, Ohio State's athletic publicity man, claimed that Schmidt, "fishes with a pole in each hand." He didn't relax; he just switched obsessions for a couple weeks. And while he worked feverishly at having fun, his mind continued to dwell on football. He still carried his notebooks and pencil stubs for recording ideas. He still worried about the schedules that Lynn St. John had devilishly concocted. He was just not built to relax; because of his hypomania, it was almost mentally impossible for him to do so. Many worried that this wasn't normal, so they did what they could to help. In 1937, for the second year in a row, St. John and Ernie Godfrey joined Schmidt for an August fishing trip to Canada. For ten days it would just be the boys, away from it all. They figured some company would keep Schmidt from slipping into his private world of overthought. But this year's attempt had nearly failed before it even started, and the result added one more story to Schmidt's legend.[1]

The boys took St. John's sedan; St. John and Godfrey alternated as drivers. This made perfect sense since the trip was supposed to be relaxing, and Schmidt, as a driver, was a raving lunatic. Thus the trip began with Schmidt in the back seat surrounded by fishing gear and all the accoutrements of travel. He fell into his favorite obsession: diagramming plays. Out came the ubiquitous notebooks, and he was soon lost in his own world, adding nothing to the conversation as they drove from Columbus into Michigan. Eventually they needed gasoline, and after St. John pulled into a rural service station, he and Godfrey got out to stretch their legs and watch the attendant check the oil and gas, leaving Schmidt to his first love. That's when things started to go wrong. Schmidt, after some time, noticed they were stopped and decided he'd stretch his legs as well. He climbed out of the back seat and began walking in a circle around the station's lot, still studying his notebook. Unfortunately, the other two didn't notice his exit nor did they note the lack of his presence among the fishing gear when they got back in the car. While Schmidt wandered behind the main building, his ride took off, bound for Canada. A few minutes later he discovered he'd been left and, employing his infamous impatience, quickly hired a local and his dilapidated auto to give chase. Schmidt and the local had gone seven miles when St. John's auto screamed past them on the way back to the filling station. It seems that twenty miles out, Godfrey had turned to talk to Schmidt and had received a shock, prompting St. John to hastily retrace their route. Eventually they all met up at the gas station where they were able to laugh—after some finger pointing, that is. They resumed their trip, but not before the hired local demanded and received $5 from Schmidt for putting his jalopy through the paces. Once again, Schmidt's preoccupation with football had complicated things, and his traveling companions took steps to ensure that their next journey would not suffer the same fate. Before their fishing trip in 1938 Saint and Godfrey insisted that Schmidt should at all times occupy the passenger seat as well as announce his departure from the car. More important, as this was to be a social outing to some degree, they declared that Schmidt "must lay aside his football notebooks for the nonce and take part in the general conversation, the two companions making the concession that most of the talk should center around gridiron activities."[2]

This story happens to be true, but Schmidt's unique combination of intensity and absentmindedness catalyzed a whole series of hard-to-believe tales. The most famous of these supposedly occurred off the field, at a gas station garage where he had gone to have his car's oil changed. He had been allowed to remain inside the car where he fell into a deep study of football strategy—so deep that he forgot his car had been lifted into the air by the garage's giant hoist where it hovered over the grease pit. Excited about a play he created, he stepped out of his car to celebrate, only to plunge five feet to the concrete floor where some say he was knocked out cold.[3]

Another famous story had him pulling Red Oliver from the game and having the halfback sit on the bench next to him when they were both at TCU. As the two of them watched, Oliver's substitute then busted a play on the field, causing Schmidt to loudly belittle *Oliver* for not being able to do anything right. "But coach," pleaded Oliver, "that wasn't me. I'm right here." After turning and looking at Oliver for a moment, Schmidt replied, "What difference does that make. If you were in there you would have made the same mistake."[4]

The thing about Schmidt is that any of the tales told about him could possibly be true. Many other coaches were oblivious, bombastic, or unpredictable, but none practiced *all* of these traits to the degree that Schmidt did. With him, anything seemed possible, no matter how outlandish.

The common thread running throughout Schmidt mythology is his addiction for football. By this point, Buckeye followers were convinced that Francis Schmidt loved football like no other. That another human could spend more time thinking about football was inconceivable. His absurd focus during the fishing trip with St. John and Godfrey was merely the latest example. What the followers were now beginning to wonder was why this fantastic effort was getting diminishing returns. True, his teams had been great—often breathtakingly great—and granted, his 5 losses in three years had only been by a total of 17 points, but something was definitely not quite right—something they just couldn't put their finger on. Conference foes had adjusted to combat his futuristic offense, but that was to be expected. Two of the losses had been the result of missed extra points, but that was just bad luck and not really Schmidt's fault. Maybe they were imagining the problem. Talented players were still enrolling each fall, and the board had just signed Schmidt for three more years, and really, statistically speaking, the teams in 1934 and 1935 were two of the best in school history. In addition, the 1936 schedule had been nothing short of brutal, all 3 losses having come against teams ranked in the top 8 in the nation. So nobody was giving up on Schmidt—yet. He was dynamic, hardworking, and an unparalleled offensive genius. That combination of skills would surely be enough to create an outstanding long-term football program at Ohio State.

But many fans were not aware of Schmidt's weaknesses, including his poor delegating skills and helter-skelter approach to organization. Most had no idea as to the extent that he used profanity and acidic humor, and even fewer fans were able to identify another trait that was slowly eroding Schmidt's future: a lack of personal mentoring.

College football coaches are more than just game planners. They are surrogate fathers, counselors, and disciplinarians. They ask for so much from the student player—his time, body, and heart—that they hold an implicit obligation to give back, to mold these young athletes into fine adults by giving them the special attention that other students might not get from a mentor. The cynic might claim that the coach's true obligation is to himself and that by keeping his kids focused, healthy, and academically eligible he is really looking out for himself. The romantic will tell you that the coach does these things because ultimately that's what counts long after the games have been played. The coach creates better players during practices, but he creates better men for a better society when he interacts with them off the field. The cynic and the romantic are both right as long as they subscribe to the ends-justifying-the-means line of ethics. Take the case of academic guidance. It's true that many a football player opts for the academic path of least resistance, but without football he might never have trod the path of higher education at all. At most, a football coach takes great pride in turning boys into honorable men. At the very least, he's saving himself by badgering them to keep their grades high enough to ensure their athletic eligibility. Either way, the players benefit from the coach's mentoring, which forces them to make something of their educational opportunities. The trouble with Schmidt was that he was unequipped to fulfill this aspect of his job partly due to his hypomania. He was so caught up in his own thoughts that he didn't consider things and people around him, even when those things and people were necessary to the success of the project he was relentlessly thinking about. And maybe, in addition to his hypomania, he was just foolish or selfish. He undoubtedly struggled to empathize, being the type of self-motivator who earned a law degree in just three years in college. As is the case with most behaviors, the explanation probably involves a complex combination of genetics and social shaping—the age-old debate of nature versus nurture. Whatever the reason, Schmidt was not your typical mentoring coach.

He had his favorite players like Johnny Vaught and Tippy Dye—clever, hard workers—but guys like these didn't need much help navigating life. Many of the rest of the players needed more—more than Schmidt was able to offer. He was famous for referring to his boys as "hey you" or addressing them by saying, "listen, son." As for worrying about their grades, boosting them emotionally, and helping solve their life problems, those occupied the same category as football fundamentals and physical conditioning: things a boy should be taking care of himself. Schmidt's view of a football coach's job was to gather the best talent available; provide them with a brilliant system of football; and then rant, rave, and rail on the practice field until the players and the system melded. Everything else was the player's responsibility. It wasn't that he fancied himself a detached leader who was above the detailed fray, he just didn't have the patience or the understanding required to be a mentor. He lived within his own blur of thoughts and didn't fully comprehend the subtle needs that his boys looked to him to provide. Having never been a father, he had never been forced even to attempt altering this state. The players were fascinated by Schmidt, and they loved being around him because he injected his odd humor into everything, but they also understood that his was a one-way street. As a result they often gave him back less than he asked for.[5]

In the summer of 1937 this lack of mentoring began to be noticeable, starting with the players' academic problems. First, Jumpin' Joe Williams topped off a lackluster junior year of football by flunking out of school in June. Less than two months later Jim

Strausbaugh had been declared academically ineligible to play football after a fruitless session of summer school. Two of Ohio State's most talented halfbacks were gone, leaving the Buckeyes' backfield thinner and intolerably vulnerable. Was Schmidt responsible for their struggles? Not really. Would greater personal involvement from Schmidt have helped to avoid this situation altogether? Probably. One week before fall practice was set to open, some bad luck made those academic failures even more acute.[6]

Bill Booth had been working a summer job at a steel mill in Weirton, West Virginia, just across the border from his hometown of East Liverpool, Ohio. He was returning home from work on a Saturday evening when his car skidded on wet pavement and slammed into a truck. His skull was instantly fractured, and he was rushed to a hospital, but he never regained consciousness and died seven hours later. It was unbearably sad and shocking, like all deaths involving someone young. In this case it involved an athletically gifted young man who was conceivably but a month away from gaining a certain measure of fame. Booth had been a bolt of electricity that was about to strike in the same way that Jumpin' Joe had before losing his direction.[7]

The collective loss of three top backs left the Buckeyes' backfield rotation in shambles. When fall practice opened just days after Booth's funeral, Schmidt's first order of business was patching and reworking. Mike Kabealo (younger brother of Johnny, the great punter who had graduated) had been set to claim the starting quarterback spot but was now asked to leave this position of playcalling and passing to fill the crucial left halfback spot where elusive running was at a premium but was currently missing. Schmidt even tried sophomore Frank Zadworney at right halfback, a sure sign of desperation as Schmidt hated starting sophomores early in the season. (He actually wasn't keen on starting seniors either, believing their hunger diminished as they neared the finish line. This left only the juniors as a truly acceptable class, and one wonders if Schmidt didn't view them with suspicion as well.) The worst part of this personnel disaster for Schmidt was that he was now forced to simplify the offense—relatively speaking, of course. Even in a state of restraint, the Schmidt system was impossibly multifaceted. And it's not that his system didn't already incorporate a goodly dose of power running, it's just that simple, low-risk running plays weren't his favorite part, a part he would need to temporarily emphasize for survival purposes. "Of course I believe in a strong running attack," he once answered in response to writers' queries about power football. "That's fundamental football. But it's possible with a seven-man line to stop the best power attack ever launched. Only when one team has a pronounced physical advantage and is able to keep hammering until something gives is it possible to depend solely on power. Personally I don't like that kind of football. And, regardless of who is in there, we'll continue to use wide-open offense with some of the so-called 'razzle-dazzle' mixed in. The fans like it, and it's good football." Even with personnel problems, Schmidt could not abstain from his desire for wide-open strategy any more than a drunk could give up alcohol because of the flu. He would just have to make some allowances.[8]

When there were only ten days remaining until the season's start, Ohio State played an intrasquad game including timekeeping and game-like substituting. On the first play from scrimmage, Schmidt's heart sank. Mike Kabealo, the quarterback turned left halfback came limping off the field with an injured ankle. That critical position was beginning to seem cursed. The rest of the game was almost as disappointing. Even with a scaled-back system, the team's play was unrefined and uninspired. It wasn't time to panic, but it wasn't time to relax either. The Buckeyes would just have to work harder. In ten days they would be facing Texas Christian and

Dutch Meyer. Schmidt *the teacher* would do just about anything to avoid being upstaged by Meyer *the student.*

During Meyer's tenure, TCU had become a prolific passing team attempting twice the amount that most other teams did. Meyer had learned from Schmidt and had inherited a system at peak performance, but many observers felt Meyer's offense also owed much of its success to the fact that Sammy Baugh had been the trigger man for the last three years. With the greatest forward passer in the history of collegiate football gone, everyone was watching to see if Meyer's extreme use of forward passing had worked because of strategy, Baugh, or both. The only guy who didn't seem concerned about replacing Baugh was Meyer. He felt confident about his new passer, Davy O'Brien.

Anyone looking at Davy O'Brien had to wonder why Meyer was so sure the junior could replace Baugh. Depending on who one talked to, O'Brien was somewhere between 5 foot 5 inches and 5 foot 7 inches and weighed in the neighborhood of 150 pounds. Not only was O'Brien small, but he'd had very little varsity game experience, starting just one contest in 1936 because Baugh was injured. And that game, played against Mississippi State, hadn't been much of a success. It showcased a horrible combination of pouring rain and mud, and O'Brien wasn't able to display much of anything except his punting, but he had plenty of opportunities to do that. The two teams combined for 44 punts and just 4 first downs during their 0–0 slopfest. Because there was so little tangible evidence that O'Brien had anything special to offer, it was difficult for TCU followers to share Meyer's faith in the diminutive thrower, but Meyer's belief remained strong. "We'll carry on with our passing game just as if Baugh were out there chucking them," declared Meyer. "O'Brien is the gamest little man I ever saw. He'll make a great record, and don't you forget it. He's tough—hard to hurt.

And he's smart." Meyer's belief that his system transcended personnel changes was very Schmidt-like, an important trait for open-game trendsetters.[9]

As for the game against his former boss, Meyer was preparing with his eyes wide open: "I worked with Francis Schmidt . . . for three years . . . here at TCU. You can be sure I have plenty of respect for the kind of opposition we are going to get up in beautiful Ohio."[10]

The two teams met in Columbus on September 25, the first pre-October game in OSU history. A crowd of 68,291 were on hand to witness the much-anticipated offensive fireworks. Equally excited were the major radio networks, all of whom were broadcasting the game nationally. The Buckeye players wore black bands on their left sleeves to honor Bill Booth. They were ready to make him proud while at the same time showing Coach Schmidt's former school a few new tricks. Only poor weather could hinder this matchup of mentor versus student, and of course that's just what they got. The two teams played the first half in a rainstorm.[11]

The Buckeyes, already operating with a patchwork backfield, played conservative ball by their standards, while the Horned Frogs struggled mightily with an inexperienced Davy O'Brien trying to throw a heavy, mud-caked ball and avoiding a relentless pass rush. The visitors from Fort Worth were unable to achieve a first down the entire first half. Not only did the conditions present a problem for TCU, but so did Ohio's left tackle, Alex Schoenbaum, who was playing defense like a man possessed, constantly hauling down Horned Frog runners in the backfield—the sort of effort that would one day make him the successful founder of the Shoney's Big Boy restaurant chain. He was also a blocker on offense when Ohio State scored the only points of the first half. Johnny Rabb ran 3 yards into the end zone, following a Statue of Liberty play and a fake pass that had set them up in prime position.

Early in the second half the Buckeyes added to their lead with a beautifully designed play that began on TCU's 38-yard line. From a double-wing formation, unbalanced to the right, Johnny Rabb took the shotgun snap and handed off to Mike Kabealo before crossing under him and picking up a right end rush. Kabealo dropped back to pass, while the right end Charley Ream ran a crossing route and left end Fred Crow ran a corner route. Gust Zarnas, the right guard, dropped back and picked up the rush on the left side. All of this crisscrossing action slowed TCU's defense, and when the left wingback, Jim Miller, delayed and released straight downfield he easily beat single coverage on the weak side. The Frogs' defensive backs had jumped the first two routes and could only watch as Kabealo's pass hit Miller in stride and he raced the final 20 yards untouched for a score.

Although the rain abated somewhat in the second half, the damage to the field, as well as to pregame strategy, had been done. Neither team was able to execute their open attack, and the game that was supposed to be magical was instead simply bemired. Late in the game O'Brien led the Frogs on a pair of desperate, staggering drives, but the Buckeyes' pass defense squashed both before they got serious. In all, O'Brien completed just 6 passes, and the Buckeyes won 14–0.[12]

The rain had ruined everything, but afterward Meyer refused to make excuses. "They just beat us, that's all. They were just too good. That big left tackle [Schoenbaum] was sure OK on defense."[13]

The fans felt cheated by the rain and its damaging effects. The custom of using the same water-logged, mud-coated football through most of the game delivered a blow to passing teams like Ohio State and TCU. And it wasn't just the ball that suffered. The long-sleeved woolen jerseys of the era absorbed water like a sponge, making throwing and reaching for passes particularly difficult. Coaches like Jock Sutherland, Bernie Bierman, and Bob

Neyland—master practitioners of time-honored, cautious football—would surely have knowingly nodded their heads in agreement. Bad weather favored the traditional closed game and handicapped an open one—just one more reason smart coaches kept their offenses simple while "clever" coaches hurt themselves by building offenses around unnecessary ball movement. After all, isn't football a sport played during fall and winter when weather is known to be cold and sloppy? The unspoken advice from decades of experienced coaches was to just play the odds and avoid creating problems for your team.

Rotating footballs in and out of rainy games was a small glitch that needed to be addressed if forward passing were to fully progress. True, the new rules and the slimmer ball were slowly helping, but it would take time for the improved product to emerge from the pipeline. The first crop of high schoolers who had played with the new ball and new rules were just now becoming upperclassmen in college, and though they were not revolutionizing the game, they were marking advancement. Not surprisingly, those throwers at the top of the learning curve were from the Southwest.

The Big 10's most talented passer was Purdue's Cecil Isbell, a native of Houston, Texas. He had grown up in the Southwest, where forward passing had been practiced at a greater rate than it was in other regions even before the rule changes and the football's slimmer shape. As a matter of fact, the Southwest had actually jumped the gun on the skinnier football, using it before it was even legal. Although Isbell was a senior in high school the year before the final ball size was officially legislated, much of the Southwest was already playing with the slimmer ball. Schmidt, an avid football scout, recalled its liberal use during his final year in the Southwest: "The smaller football—now legal—has been manufactured for several years, and most games [in 1933] were played with it. The new rules merely make it legal." Texas never has had patience for the machinations of bureaucracy. Though Sammy Baugh's class was the first to officially use the slimmer ball throughout varsity and into the pros, Isbell's class in the Southwest had a headstart. Both men had benefited from their region and were talented in their own right. Baugh had already wooed the pros, and Isbell would soon do the same.[14]

For now, Isbell was a college senior doing his best to help a troubled team succeed. In an era when most recruits came from in-state, Purdue had to share the state of Indiana with Big 10 rival Indiana University as well as the monster program at Notre Dame. That didn't leave much room for bad luck, something the Boiler-makers had been slammed with the year before. During fall practice in 1936 two players had been killed and four more injured when a water heater exploded in the locker room after practice. At the time, before its health risks were fully understood, gasoline was used for many things besides fuel, including tricks like washing paint off one's hands. In this case gasoline was being used in the locker room to aid in the removal of adhesive tape from the players' ankles. The gasoline, kept in a bowl, was inadvertently set too close to the flame of the water heater, causing an explosion followed by a wave of flames that swept the floor where the six men were standing. Tom McGannon, the team's star halfback, died of burns, as did senior guard Carl Dahlbeck. Fullback Lowell Decker missed the entire school year recovering from burns to his back and leg. Two of the other burn victims were running backs, leaving a giant hole in the Purdue backfield. With the help of Isbell (who could run as well as throw) the Boilermakers had persevered, but it was hard to forget those conspicuously missing teammates, something the Buckeyes painfully understood. They exited their dressing room through a door over which hung a picture of Bill Booth and his retired No. 9 jersey. On the first Saturday in October the two teams met.[15]

Purdue and Ohio State had not played football against each other for thirteen years. Before that they had met five times, and Ohio State had won them all by the collective score of 104–0. Since their last meeting, Purdue, under the direction of Noble Kizer, had managed to flirt with upper-tier conference status, and now seemed like a good time for them to score their first-ever points against Ohio State, if not beat them outright.

The contest was no beauty. Ohio controlled the action throughout the game but struggled to score. Alex Schoenbaum, star of the previous week's game, missed 2 field-goal attempts, including a 39-yarder that hit an upright. On another occasion the Buckeyes were stopped on a fourth-and-goal attempt at Purdue's 1-yard line. The Buckeyes' defense actually won this game. They shut down Isbell and the passing game, intercepting 6 passes while allowing only 5 completions worth a total of 74 yards. Two of Ohio's thefts set up touchdowns, and the Buckeyes meandered to a 13–0 victory. The Boilermakers would have to wait yet another season to score against Ohio State.[16]

Next up was the event Ohioans had been anticipating for months: a cross-country trip to Los Angeles to play USC. Back in 1933, as part of a Depression-induced plan to upgrade OSU's schedule, St. John had locked up a two-year deal with the famous USC Trojans. This first game would be held in California, and getting there was no minor undertaking. Unlike today when a team can fly coast to coast and play a game all in one weekend, teams in the train era had to block out two weeks for an interregional trip of this distance. In this case, the Buckeyes boarded their train in Columbus at 1:30 p.m. on Monday and arrived at Union Station, Los Angeles, at 8:00 a.m. Thursday. The Buckeyes rode in a special car attached to the Union Pacific's *City of Los Angeles*, a streamlined bullet of silver steel—the line's premier train. As they traveled over two thousand miles of track, the players did their best to keep up with studies, but they found plenty of chances to talk nonsense and play practical jokes on one another as well. Some of them even disappeared into the luggage car where they played craps and cards. The least fortunate members of the squad were the quarterbacks, trapped with an obsessive Francis Schmidt, who never tired of talking strategy and game planning. While these diversions ate up some of the time, the players had hours to look out the windows at the vast, lonely landscape they had only imagined until now. The trip was memorable for them all; most of them were traveling far from home for the first time in their lives.[17]

Like all coaches taking their squad on a lengthy train trip, Schmidt worried about the players' physical conditioning. Whenever the train stopped for any amount of time, Schmidt had the players disembark, stretch their legs, and even run around a bit. Because of scheduling logistics they were only able to arrange a single light drill during the entire trip. This happened at Stagg Field in Chicago while they waited for their special car to be attached to the *City of Los Angeles.* Once the car was attached, the football team had to adhere to the railroad's route schedule, which didn't include any layovers of note. This arrangement wasn't ideal. Chicago came early in the trip, and the weather did not resemble that of Southern California. By contrast, on the way to their semiannual contest at USC, Notre Dame always planned a schedule whereby they had an extended stop in Tucson. Here they practiced at the University of Arizona, where arrangements had been made to use the Wildcats' field ever since the 1924 trip to California for the Rose Bowl. By choosing Arizona they were making sure the players had an extra chance to acclimate themselves, and it was later in the journey when players needed limbering and practice the most—a small matter, but games are often won and lost because of such minutiae. Notre Dame had enough appreciation for their relations with the University of Arizona that they rewarded them with a game on the 1941 schedule even though much more profitable games were available.[18]

Arriving in Los Angeles on Friday morning, Schmidt and his boys were met at the train station by the press, who took some photos and asked some questions. Schmidt fielded nearly all the questions, which was normal for the era. College players were rarely quoted in the papers, partly out of a convoluted respect for their amateur status. Schmidt, as usual, offered little when asked for a game prediction. "We'll do our best. Win, lose, or draw we'll do our best to make it an interesting afternoon." Schmidt's loyalties always seemed to be divided between exciting football and winning football, hoping for both but pleased to accomplish either.[19]

He knew better than to make any serious predictions when preparing for USC. The Trojans had been one of the better programs in the nation from 1927 to 1933, winning 5 conference titles and 2 national championships. Their performance had leveled off since, but they always seemed able to recruit strong players and were always dangerous. Trojan head coach Howard Jones, who had been coaching successfully since 1908, was highly respected for the sound, fundamental strategies that had guided USC to so many victories. That's why it was shocking to hear him talk earlier in the spring about experimenting with some laterals in his system. Not just laterals, but high-speed laterals as were practiced in rugby. He'd even watched the rugby team practice at Santa Ana Junior College to get ideas. As far as Jones knew, Schmidt was the only coach to incorporate this element into his playbook, and the possibilities intrigued him. As it turned out, Jones never did add this element to his system, but it did show how the open game was even capturing the imagination of staunch veterans like himself.[20]

The Buckeyes had left Columbus during the first blush of fall when temperatures were reaching the mid-sixties. They arrived in Los Angeles only to find that out west summer had been cruelly extended into October; temperatures were exceeding ninety de-grees. Tired from the long train trip and ready for a good night's sleep at the Biltmore Hotel, some of the Buckeyes found the heat too uncomfortable for proper slumber. Johnny Rabb, for one, spent the night tossing and turning when he should have been get-ting rest before the big game.[21]

With so many unusual factors in play, it was difficult to know what to expect from this game, but the one thing that had marked Schmidt's time at Ohio State was the spine-tingling finish that seemed to accompany every one of his team's heavyweight bouts. This prize fight was no exception. Despite the heat, a crowd of 65,000 spent most of the game standing to soak up all the action. Johnny Rabb was sensational, running with authority through-out the game. He had been injured the week before and he was still struggling with the heat—even removing his uncomfortable hip pads at halftime—but the Trojans struggled even more trying to stop him. His final numbers included 15 carries for over 160 yards, spectacular for the 1930s. But in an all-too-common sce-nario, the Buckeyes struggled to score points despite being able to move up and down the field all day long. Three times they were in-side the Trojans' 10-yard line during the third quarter and three times they came away empty-handed before finally taking advan-tage of a blocked kick. Following the recovery, Rabb burst off right tackle for 20 yards to the USC 2, and Jim McDonald then went over for the score. Alex Schoenbaum's bad kicking streak continued as he missed the extra point, leaving the game tied 6–6. Early in the fourth, the Buckeyes cashed in on another blocked kick. Recover-ing on USC's 28, Ohio immediately went for the kill. Jim McDonald took the snap and pitched the ball to Kabealo, who faded back and drifted right. When he had drawn enough defenders he threw a pass across the field to the left sideline. It was caught by Dick Nardi, who took the pass in stride at the 10 and scored untouched. It was a dangerous call, vulnerable to an interception that would have been easily returned for a touchdown, but the Trojans were caught off-guard and never had a chance. No longer trusting Schoenbaum's toe, McDonald called on tackle Joe Aleskus to attempt the point after. Aleskus had been the hero, blocking the kick that set up this touchdown, but his star suddenly dimmed when his kick missed, sailing wide. Still, much to the delight of the many Ohioans who had used this game as an excuse for a vacation, their Buckeyes now led 12–6 midway through the fourth quarter.[22]

To this point, USC had managed only 114 yards on offense, but nobody figured the game to be over. Ohio State, under Schmidt's direction, had stumbled on this path before, and USC still had a great player in quarterback Ambrose Schindler—the kind of guy who can arise at any time. After the kickoff following Ohio's go-ahead touchdown, Schindler decided the Trojans would either win or lose on his back. He had already scored USC's only touchdown, and now, when it mattered most, he was more determined than ever to score again. Starting at his own 42, Schindler used speed to run for an 18-yard gain around right end, and then, using power, he carried the ball three straight times into the line, leaving a fourth and two with three minutes left in the game. Schindler again called his own number, and again he pounded into the line, fighting his way to a first down. The crowd roared so loudly that it was hard for USC to hear in the huddle, but not loudly enough to drown out Schindler's thoughts. He'd made a great call: the half-back screen. With a new set of downs and a new chance to halt the drive's momentum, surely Ohio State's defenders would tap into their reserve energy, determined to crash the line and make Schindler eat turf. That's exactly what happened, and Schindler's pass to Mickey Anderson floated over the charging linemen's heads. After securing the ball, Anderson did the rest, weaving through 25 yards of traffic all the way to the end zone, tying the game at 12–12. The crowd roared, but they were still a bit hesitant. There was still the matter of USC's extra-point kick. The Trojans had missed an earlier attempt when the ball had rebounded off the crossbar, meaning the two teams were 0 for 3 on the day. Fatalistic Buckeye fans already knew what was coming, though, and right end Ralph Stanley delivered, converting the kick to give USC a 13–12 lead. With little time remaining, the Buckeyes broke out some desperate razzle-dazzle, but it wasn't enough. Yet again they had lost a big game by the margin of a lousy extra-point kick. Three of Schmidt's 6 losses had been the result of failed extra-point attempts, and none of his wins had ever been owed to the extra kick. A share of the Big 10 championship in both 1934 and 1936 was lost because of extra-point attempts gone bad. And now the 1937 hunt for a national title was in serious jeopardy because of a miss.[23]

Schmidt thought the blame for this game lay in the patchwork backfield. He believed the winning touchdown was caught in a defensive zone that should have been covered by right half Dick Nardi, and Nardi was starting in place of Howard Wedebrook, who had had a miserable opener. Later the next week, a frustrated Schmidt took the rare step of naming a sophomore as starter when he made Frank Zadworney the third different right half within the season's first four games.[24]

The California heat probably didn't help the Buckeyes as the game wound down. Perhaps a day of practice nearer Los Angeles would have acclimated the team as well as ramped up their conditioning closer to gameday.

The loss had been another heartbreaker, but the game was only part of the trip, and the players and coaches had to pull themselves together and enjoy what was left of their big journey to California. Ohio State's West Coast alumni, overjoyed at the prospect of finally hosting their alma mater's football team, had planned a celebration that no loss was going to impede. On Sunday morning the players swam in the Pacific Ocean before enjoying a first-class breakfast and a breathtaking view at the Miramar Hotel. After eating, the assembled alumni and guests chanted for Schmidt to make a speech, and he finally surrendered. After introducing the team members, he turned on his special brand of charisma to the delight and thunderous applause of all those gathered. If ever there were a place that appreciated a humorous, fast-talking, hypomanic, it had to be Los Angeles. Afterward the team was given a tour of the MGM movie studio before catching their train late that afternoon.[25]

On the way home, the Buckeyes' train stopped at the Grand Canyon so that travelers could view one of the world's natural wonders. The Buckeye players wandered and gawked at the crevice, but Schmidt refused to disembark. He seemed to be depressed, perhaps in response to his team's losing yet another big game in the fourth quarter. It is definitely noteworthy that for all of his unpredictability and dark humor, Schmidt was very rarely despondent. He was always too busy, too confident for introspection. He rarely looked behind him, but rather seemed to press on optimistically, always impatient to pursue his next endeavor. For him to be sulking was unusual.[26]

Because of the extensive travel, Ohio State had not scheduled a game for the following Saturday. When the train stopped in Chicago, Schmidt stayed while the rest of the team continued on to Columbus. He wanted to watch the Northwestern game since they were Ohio's next opponent. What Schmidt saw was the defending Big 10 champion Wildcats' winning to improve their record to 3-0, but he was unimpressed. After the game Schmidt committed the double error of being candid and of being so with a reporter. He called the Wildcats "a lucky team," disparaged their star, Don Heap, by calling him "a fair ball player," and claimed that Northwestern had not improved since they had last played OSU. On the list of things a head football coach should not do, the first item listed would be: don't say unkind things about your upcoming opponent to a reporter. The opponent then goes on record as your enemy, and enemies will fight like hell to the bitter end. Schmidt did, however, lustily praise Bernard Jefferson, the Wildcats' halfback. Schmidt had a genuine admiration for those rare, versatile performers who held offenses together—the type that was rarely accorded star treatment while making everyone else look better.[27]

Even without Schmidt's saying too much, this game was already anticipated based on a relatively new idea: in-season national rankings (which currently placed Northwestern as the No. 7 team in the country and Ohio state at No. 13). The AP had introduced a new gimmick the previous season wherein a group of some forty sportswriters from around the country agreed to rank the twenty best teams in the country on a weekly basis and send their results to AP headquarters where they were combined. The result was a consensus top-twenty poll that was published in newspapers around the nation and was designed to stimulate fan interest. Soon, this poll became the final word. Previous to this concept, conference or regional championships ruled the day, and the discussion of a national champion was only debated mildly. It was just too hard to reconcile arguments when teams rarely played interregional contests. Additionally, television was unavailable to provide tangible evidence of a team's merits. These roadblocks still existed, but now the nation's "experts" were combining their wisdom and geographic bird-dogging to create a semi-formal national picture that held just enough value for mainstream acceptance. At season's end there would now be a *de facto* champion since there was no mandate for the two top-ranked teams to play each other. From 1936 until 1992—and the creation of the Bowl Coalition, the precursor to the BCS—the wire services and their polls exclusively decided on the best teams in America, a system that fans and schools begrudgingly but faithfully adhered to.

As it turned out, the build up to the Northwestern–Ohio State game was better than the game itself. Ohio State continued their trend of dominating in total yardage as well as in failed scoring opportunities. Most of the game was played in Northwestern's end, but the final score was a measly 7–0 in favor of the Buckeyes.

This inability to finish off drives was becoming habitual. The Buckeyes' offense was overengineered for the dirty, simple work needed near the end zone. Complicated plays work best with time and space to maneuver, neither of which was in high supply near the goal line. With twenty-two men crammed into a small area, football becomes a game dependent less on strategy and more on fundamentals, execution, and desire. This was Schmidt's weakness and thus his team's weakness as well.

The most interesting play of the day was the game's only extra-point attempt, which was converted in the unlikeliest manner. Jim McDonald, tired of watching his linemen miss opportunities in recent games, called on himself to attempt the kick, only to have it blocked. The rejected ball began bounding toward the right sideline like a drunken rabbit; McDonald and kick holder Mike Kabealo were in hot pursuit. Kabealo finally corralled the ball before lateraling it to McDonald, who ran 13 yards untouched into the end zone. Initially, the officials ruled the point good, but an intense protest from the Wildcats caused the four officials to discuss things further, and soon they had disallowed the point. Then it was Schmidt's turn to howl, and he "stormed onto the field" to give his opinion. After more huddling, the officials made the correct interpretation, declaring the point to be good once and for all. Many considered converting an extra point off a blocked kick to be lucky, but Schmidt was mum where his own team's fortunes were concerned.[28]

The Northwestern rooters who had attended the game at Ohio Stadium were disappointed, but their in-game imbibing probably smoothed some of the painful rough edges of defeat. The B-East section of Ohio Stadium was an area commonly populated by fans of the opposition, and its deck chief, John McEwen, held that visiting fans from Northwestern and Michigan put away the most spirits. During this particular game he thought his "section of the stadium looked something like an outdoor drinking garden." This observation was in direct contrast to those proffered by the Big 10 publicity machine. Since the end of Prohibition, the conference had worked diligently to minimize drinking at games and even harder to minimize its alleged presence. After all, it's tough to justify the necessity of collegiate football as an important part of the academic setting when it's really a thinly veiled Roman holiday where profit, regional bragging rights, and a really good buzz are hotly pursued. A quick conference survey the week before the game made it sound like the boozing hellions of years past were practically imaginary. "There is a minimum of drinking at Iowa games, and we intend to eliminate it entirely," declared an overly optimistic E. G. Schroeder, Iowa athletic director. In Ann Arbor, chief of police Lewis Fohey was heartened that drinking at Michigan games had only reached the point of "four or five court cases." And as for Northwestern, athletic director "Tug" Wilson declared, "We no longer consider drinking a major problem at Northwestern." It's always hard to define when drinking is problematic within a crowd. Does one particularly boisterous drunk make everyone look bad, or is he merely the front man for a stewed section? As in all things college football, there is a thin line between reality and fantasy. That's one of the reasons we like it so much.[29]

The fans with the most justification for getting drunk during games were those few remaining masochists from the University of Chicago. Maroon football had declined steadily each season as the program had been deemphasized and recruiting had subsequently dried up. The student council had recently polled undergraduates as to their feelings on intercollegiate football, and a strong majority

still wanted their team to be Big 10 members, but only if they received enough backing to compete at a respectable level. What the
school would do without proper backing for the football team was
being left unsaid for now. The Maroon had entered a gray area
where neither support from the school officials nor plans for a final demise were entirely clear. Not unlike a couple facing divorce,
the school's administration and football program simply continued to host awkward parties for their uncomfortable friends, one
of whom was Ohio State.

Instead of undergoing the normal preparations for winning a
conference game, Chicago's opponents were now being forced to
plan for how they would deal with the ethical dilemma of competing against a team that was so hapless. This was especially true if the
other team was good and it was coached by Shut-the-Gates-of-Mercy
Schmidt. When asked if he might start his reserves against such an
overmatched team, Schmidt said, "No. The regulars will start. We
intend to win the game. What formerly was considered a commanding lead doesn't stand up long these days. I'll probably use the reserves some, though." His thought that a commanding lead might
not hold up was absurd, considering Chicago's inability to compete. And just to complicate things, Schmidt added that he and the
Buckeyes would be "out to get all we can." Did he intend to run up
the score as he had in the past? Sticking too long with his starters
wouldn't make him any more popular than he already wasn't, and
playing his reserves might prove even more hazardous. In the past,
when given the chance, his reserves had excitedly run around like
freed colts, running up the score with naïve abandon. It would be
up to Schmidt to strike a balance, something he hadn't proven adept at previously.[30]

Perhaps afraid that he couldn't slow his reserves, Schmidt did indeed keep some of his better players on the field throughout much
of the game. Overall, the Buckeyes scored 6 touchdowns on only

5 first downs, thanks to long scoring plays and great field position from turnovers. In the final three minutes Ohio State returned 1 punt 50 yards to set up a short score and then returned another punt 66 yards for a touchdown moments before the clock ran out. Ohio State won 39–0. Shaughnessy, tired of being schooled by Schmidt, had apparently decided his best chance was to emulate him. He'd instructed his Maroon to throw 21 forward passes and plenty of laterals, but his team had still achieved little razzle and even less dazzle.[31]

Having bounced back from the stinging USC defeat with consecutive conference wins, Ohio State's record now stood at 4-1, and they shared first place in the Big 10 with Minnesota—quite an accomplishment considering their backfield losses and the ensuing line-up juggling. Schmidt's continued oddness was becoming an issue, but if his boys could win their final three nobody would really care.

The Buckeyes' next game was against the University of Indiana, long considered the conference's weak sister. The Hoosiers had risen to upper mediocrity for the first time in a couple decades, due in part to head coach Bo McMillin. McMillin, a Southwest expatriate, had been a nationally known superstar when he played halfback at tiny Centre College (Kentucky) in the early 1920s. Centre, whose enrollment was less than 200, built a football squad around McMillin and a handful of other transplanted Texas high schoolers and proceeded to stun the football world by continually beating much larger universities. In 1921 they did the unthinkable—beating Harvard in Cambridge—and by the end of the season many considered Centre to be the mythical national champions. Later, after coaching stints at Centenary and Kansas State, McMillin had taken the Hoosier job in the wake of Schmidt's signing with Ohio State. After three seasons the Hoosiers had achieved respectability, but they still needed to topple a giant or two if they wanted to become a high-stakes player. So far McMillin was 0-3 against fellow prairie expatriate Schmidt.

Saturday, November 6, the Buckeyes immediately launched into their razzle-dazzle routine against McMillin's boys. On their second play from scrimmage, the Buckeyes quick-snapped, catching Indiana off guard and allowing Johnny Rabb to gain 22 yards on a sweep. On the next play, the Buckeyes skipped signals and quick-snapped again. This time "fullback Johnny Rabb took a direct pass from center, and handed the ball to guard Gust Zarnas who pulled out of the line. Zarnas whipped a 32-yard pass to end Fred Crow who ran 18 more yards before being downed" on the 11-yard line. Crow had gotten himself wide open thanks to some trickery. While Indiana was busy recovering from the first quick-snap and scrambling to lineup for the second, Crow had pulled a "sleeper" move, hanging out next to the sideline behind an official rather than returning to the formation. Two plays later, Ohio State was on the Hoosiers' 1-yard line, and the Buckeye faithful prepared to enjoy an easy victory. It didn't happen. On the next play Mike Kabealo lost a fumble as he attempted to score off a little screen pass in the flat. A few minutes later the Buckeyes were back on offense and 12 yards from scoring, but the drive came up empty again. It got worse. In the second quarter Johnny Rabb broke through the line on a perfectly designed misdirection play that soon left him alone in the secondary with only a blocker and the Hoosier safety between him and a touchdown. Rabb stutter-stepped, buying time for his blocker to engage the Hoosier defender. As those two engaged, Rabb cut and prepared to explode for open space and an easy touchdown, but the cut was too much for his knee, and he went down in a heap, untouched. He was carried off the field. The black-shirted Hoosiers now had momentum, and they began to dictate the pace of the game. Their fullback, Corby Davis, pounded the line, eating up the clock, moving the chains, and breaking the

Buckeyes' spirit. Indiana scored twice on long, forceful ground campaigns totaling 145 yards on 18 plays to earn a 10–0 lead. It was a matter of line play, and the Hoosiers' line dominated, playing with their hearts the entire game. On defense, their aggressive ends, Francis Petrick and Bob Kenderdine, were virtually unstoppable, wrecking the timing of Schmidt's razzle-dazzle just as Pitt had done the year before.[32]

McMillin used only eight substitutes, and six of his boys played the full sixty minutes. Meanwhile, the Buckeyes were being beaten to a pulp. Nick Wasylik left the game with an injured leg, joining Johnny Rabb and three others. Suddenly desperate, the Buckeyes began throwing with abandon. This type of furious desperation had worked *against* them, but it wasn't working *for* them. Indiana intercepted twice and ate more clock until not even a crumb remained, and they eventually won 10–0. The Buckeyes were devastated. Losing in Los Angeles by an extra point had been heartbreaking, but this was *soul* breaking. Francis Schmidt's legendary offensive machine had been shut out, at home, by Indiana—the first time Indiana had beaten osu in 13 years. Not only had osu lost the Big 10 title, but their national standing was crushed. Ranked No. 8 in the country before the upset, they fell completely out of the AP top twenty in the aftermath of this catastrophic loss.[33]

Ironically, Indiana had been added to the Buckeyes' schedule gratuitously. Indiana was always fighting to get other conference teams to schedule them. Each year the Big 10 athletic directors held a meeting to hammer out schedules, and each year the Hoosiers were met with excuses. Scheduling a Big 10 home game was especially difficult. Memorial Stadium, where the University of Indiana played its home games, was a small venue with the capacity to hold only 22,000 fans. It had been erected during the stadium-building craze following World War I, but on a much smaller scale than other Big 10 stadiums. Even at that, the donations of 14,000 people had been required just to fund its $250,000 price tag. From 1922 to 1941 the Hoosiers played ninety-four conference games, and only twenty-eight of those were at home. Of those, ten were against in-state rival Purdue, meaning the Indiana Hoosiers averaged about one conference home game per year against the rest of the conference teams. Ohio State was a prime culprit in the imbalance. From 1930 to 1941 the Buckeyes hosted Indiana nine times but played in Bloomington only twice. Things had gotten so bad when planning the 1937 schedule that Zora Clevenger, Indiana's athletic director, was fearful his school wouldn't make the minimum of five conference games. "Clev" appealed to commissioner Griffith, who in turn appealed to the other conference members. "It is not my business to suggest to the directors who they shall play," wrote Griffith in a memorandum to directors. "We are trying to convince the public that our football is not a commercial proposition and that sportsmanship in the conference exists both on and off the field. The press, however, is inclined to call attention to the fact that Indiana cannot persuade the other conference universities to send their teams to Bloomington now and then. Do you think there is anything we can do about this?" St. John couldn't afford the financial hit of playing at Bloomington, but he did surrender one of his sought-after slots to help out old friends. He was rewarded with a punch in the gridiron.[34]

Buckeye followers were not interested in scheduling or in the excuses related therewith. A good team can beat other good teams. They were growing tired of being teased by visions of grandeur every season only to see their boys stumble at the worst moments. The sportswriters echoed this sentiment, and their frustrations were compounded by Schmidt's unpredictable nature. Last season he had clammed up when the Buckeyes won, and now he was clamming up when they lost. Writers were both miffed and amused by the fact that Schmidt, through OSU athletics, had been providing a

two-paragraph postgame statement after conference wins but fur-
nished nothing after the Indiana loss. The next day, when Schmidt
finally did comment, he offered the usual mixed bag full of class
and crass. He made it a point to acknowledge Corby Davis as one of
the best players they had met all season before proclaiming that Indiana was a "good—but not a great—team." Where that left Ohio
State he did not speculate.[35]

He also responded to charges of bad playcalling on the part of
his Buckeye quarterbacks by defending the players and stabbing
them at the same time, as only he was able to do. "It's easy enough
to see what's wrong from the stands or the bench, but out on the
field it's different. The quarterbacks made mistakes, and they cost
us plenty. We'll have to do something about it before the next two
games." That something happened at practice on Monday when
he moved Jim McDonald from starting quarterback to starting fullback, in place of the injured Rabb. Mike Kabealo was switched back
to quarterback where he had been the starter in fall practice. It's
difficult to say whether Schmidt really had a problem with McDonald's playcalling or whether a new injury to the backfield facilitated
a blame game. He had always expressed confidence in McDonald
previously. Some of the players were starting to grumble about the
way Schmidt capriciously shuffled the depth chart.[36]

The press were now openly questioning Schmidt's leadership.
Up to this point they had only hinted at his managerial weaknesses,
but the frustration of losing to Indiana had been the turning point.
The Hoosiers were undeniable underdogs, and Schmidt's boys
had been shut out by them—had been outworked—at home. The
writers began talking about the players' declining attitudes, but it
was easy to see their target was really Schmidt. Said one reporter
who had attended the Tuesday practice, "It was a decidedly listless
squad that Schmidt sent thru its paces yesterday. At least one half
of the players who have held starting berths this season were late in

reporting for the drill. Numerous players 'loafed' in the offices under the stadium or in the training rooms after their more ambitious
mates were already on the field. . . . One prominent backfield man
threatened to quit the squad prior to the encounter with the Hoosiers . . . [and] several sophomores were reported disgruntled over
their failure to see more service this season."[37]

Most teams have disgruntled players. It's a normal condition
where competition for playing time is involved. What makes this
instance noteworthy is that it was becoming widespread and it
was being exposed to the public by reporters who had previously
maintained a sense of loyalty to Schmidt. In a town like Columbus,
you either won titles or you had better be winning over the media. Schmidt and the Buckeyes had just botched a conference title,
and the coach was doing little to garner love from the writers. As a
matter of fact, Oscar Ruhl, the sports editor of the *Mansfield (Ohio)
News* later mentioned in an editorial that "Francis Schmidt is feuding with one of the prominent sportswriters." This bit of gossip, in
and of itself, was a small betrayal. As for the "feuding" sportswriter,
one can only speculate, but a good guess would be Rex Hess or
Paul Hornug, two men who offered the fewest words of praise for
Schmidt during and after his tenure.[38]

Schmidt was colorful enough that he could easily have worked
the press back over to his side, but he was too paranoid about their
motives and he was unwavering in the certainty of his beliefs. He
continued working on plays and running long, loud practices just
as he had from the start. What had saved his reputation each year
was a great run at the end of the schedule, reminding everyone how
dynamic his system had the potential to be. In Schmidt's first three
seasons at Ohio, his lads were 6-0 in the last two weeks of the season, winning by the combined score of 152–7. Except for the Iowa
game in 1934, all of the wins came against Illinois and Michigan.

Two more wins would make people begin to forget Indiana and go a long way toward buying Schmidt job security.

Illinois visited Columbus on homecoming weekend, having scored 6 points or less in their last five games. Against Big 10 foes (not including moribund Chicago) the Illini hadn't scored more than 9 points in a game for *three* years. Zuppke's reputation for wide-open football was now more legend than substance, a fact that made Zuppke a little bitter. After the season he declared, "Francis Schmidt visited two of my coaching schools several years ago, and now they give him credit for razzle-dazzle." Zuppke had indeed played a part in Schmidt's inspiration, but anything more was an overreach for credit. Zuppke was an open-game pioneer for the first modern period, but he had never really expanded his repertoire or experimented with formations in nearly the same capacity that Schmidt had. Rather, sportswriters had cemented Zuppke's reputation for wide-open play. Zuppke was a wonderful, clever, charismatic figure who had good-naturedly been self-promoted to the golly-gee sports press of the 1920s—a sports press that was hellbent on building stars the way Aesop built fables. By the 1930s, however, he was having to defend his reputation against cold, hard statistics. Because Zuppke's pride hindered modern recruiting, his material was diminished, exposing an offensive system whose over-hyped reputation wasn't enough to save him from a string of low scoring disappointments. During the 1930s, Illinois averaged 9.5 points per game. In non-Chicago conference play they averaged 5.1 points per game. Zuppke's pride was taking a beating, and his cattiness toward Schmidt makes sense. Justifiably, he wanted to preserve his place as a pioneer in the open-game movement, a movement he still believed in even if it had passed him by.[39]

Ohio State and Illinois met on November 13 under a dark and threatening sky. In a way, the somber weather was fitting. Before the game, the Ohio State marching band "entered the north entrance and marched to the gridiron at half step, its drums muffled" before going into formation and spelling "Booth" in giant letters to honor Bill Booth. Then with the players' heads bowed, a hush fell over the stadium, and a lone trumpet player played "Taps." It was an amazing, powerful moment for all who remembered the young man who had played at both Illinois and Ohio State.[40]

Five minutes after the kickoff, Ohio was ahead 7–0. Wasylik (the new, old starting quarterback) threw a quick-out screen pass to McDonald, who spun away from his defender, reversed field, than headed for the end zone with Fred Crow escorting him and blocking the last man with a chance at the tackle. Perhaps the Buckeye linemen were still smarting from their whipping by Indiana, or maybe the Booth tribute had inspired them, but they played with vigor, pushing Illinois around and rendering razzle-dazzle unnecessary. Schmidt pulled his starters midway through the first quarter, and for the first time in Schmidt's stint at Ohio State, the Buckeyes did not attempt a single lateral the entire game.

At halftime, in honor of Zuppke's twenty-five years of service at Illinois, Buckeye officials presented him with an "illuminated scroll" that listed some of his accomplishments. The little German was anxious to get back to his team but took a moment to say, "Thanks very much. I'm just a bit of mediocrity trying to make a living." It was classic Zuppke. He was one of the greatest spokesmen for football that ever lived.[41]

In the second half, the Buckeyes' offense added 2 more touchdowns on Dick Nardi plunges, while holding Illinois scoreless. For the game, Zuppke's boys achieved 65 yards total offense and just 3 first downs. The final score of 19–0 could have been much worse.[42]

Harry Kipke, head coach at Michigan, understood how Zuppke was feeling. He knew how little weight one's past accomplishments carried in the hypercompetitive world of big-time college football.

His Wolverines had won 4 straight conference championships to start the 1930s, and the 1933 club had won the national championship. Since then the Wolverines had been less than threatening, winning only the easiest matchups and losing the rest. Their offense had grown as toothless as that of Illinois, averaging 5.8 points per game since the great season of 1933. Worst of all for Kipke, he had lost to Ohio State for three straight seasons. Only the tremendous success of the early decade had saved his head so far. And although the Wolverines had won 4 straight coming into this clash, Kipke's power was so eroded that even beating the Buckeyes would probably not be enough to help him keep his job. His last game as the Wolverines' head coach was in all probability just an exercise in avoiding infamy.

Only 56,766 fans braved the snow and low temperatures in Ann Arbor to watch Ohio State beat Michigan for an unprecedented fourth straight time. The Wolverines only crossed into Ohio territory on two occasions, and in the first instance they were thrown for a 12-yard loss on the next play. Their total offense amounted to a measly 41 yards, and they completed only one more pass (5) than had been intercepted (4). The Buckeyes scored 2 touchdowns on forward passes, another off a plunge, and tacked on a safety for good measure. The touchdown by Dick Nardi was his fifth in a conference game that season, making him the Big 10 scoring champ with 30 points. They were on Michigan's 1-yard line when the clock ran out, leaving the final score at a modest 21–0. Schmidt called it the best Wolverine team he had faced and singled out the progress he'd seen in the "versatility of their attack." This praise, coming on the heels of Michigan's 41-yard game, was typically Schmidt-like in its backhandedness, but aside from that, there was nothing Schmidt respected more than versatility, even if it was only a baby step in that direction. Schmidt also respected the need to eschew inflammatory remarks where Michigan was concerned. You never

*4 STRAIGHT SHUT-OUTS V.
MICHIGAN*

knew when Michigan would be back on top and seeking more revenge than was necessary. For now Schmidt would enjoy the view from the top. No other team had ever shut out the Wolverines for 4 straight years, and the composite score of 114–0 will likely never be surpassed.[43]

For the third time in four seasons, the Buckeyes had finished second in the Big 10 with a single conference loss—more of the same disappointment Buckeye fans had been experiencing for years. Since Ohio State joined the conference in 1913, they had the best record in the Big 10 (70-41-8, .631 percent), just slightly better than Michigan (.629 percent) and Minnesota (.629 percent), but they had only 3 conference titles to show for it. The other two teams had combined for 15 conference titles and several national championships. And of all the tantalizing regimes at Ohio State, Schmidt's was the hardest to swallow with its spellbinding offense but heartbreaking results.

On the upside, the Buckeyes had grandly overcome some key personnel losses. Even with a makeshift backfield, the Buckeyes finished second in conference scoring. Most surprisingly, they led the Big 10 in defense despite that same makeshift backfield and the fact that so little time was being devoted to defense during practices. All 6 of the Buckeyes' victories were shutouts, and in 6 conference games they allowed only 10 points total, all of them to Indiana. And much to the joy of St. John, his ruthless scheduling and Schmidt's exciting offense had not only placed Ohio State's attendance at the top of the Big 10 (again), but had placed it at the top of the national leader board with an average of 54,886 paid witnesses attending each home game. Also, from a national standpoint, the two wins over Illinois and Michigan were enough to convince AP voters that Ohio State was better than the team that had been shut out at home by Indiana. The Buckeyes finished No. 13 in the final poll.[44]

Thirty varsity players were awarded their letters at the football banquet on Monday evening. Sadly for Schmidt, half of them were graduating. Of the returning letter winners, ten were juniors and five were sophomores. As for the freshmen who would potentially be moving up, thirty-nine of them had won "numerals," but that was out of a group that numbered around 250 at fall practice. If 1937 had been frustratingly close to great, then 1938 was shaping up to be just plain frustrating. The pressure on Schmidt was being ratcheted up another notch.[45]

Ten. Spreading the Message

Francis Schmidt and his intricate, open attack had placed him in the center of a growing national debate amongst football coaches. Was this new football simply a fad or a precursor to something great? Every coach had an opinion on strategy, but most had a bias as well. Some were successful with their own style, some were just comfortable, and others felt loyalty in maintaining the strategy they had learned from their mentors. Not many coaches were open-minded enough to consider radical methods, and even fewer were brave enough—or foolhardy enough—to implement risk. There were, however, a few pragmatic moderates, and one of the most respected was Lou Little of Columbia University. He had never subscribed to a particular system but had always been willing to try new things in small doses. Because Little was a leader on the national rules committee and kept a keen eye on developments, his voice carried some weight with the coaching community. For now he was of the belief that open football was good for the sport, but he was not willing to subscribe to it fully until it proved consistently viable. And he pointed to that October weekend in 1936 to explain his fear: "Francis Schmidt at Ohio State has really developed something new," he argued. "He has an intricate, deceptive attack featuring laterals and forward passing. But Pitt beat them without using a pass, and, after all, Fordham, which plays conservative football, did beat Southern Methodist [on that same] Saturday." Little had once believed that laterals might be a futuristic staple but was backing off that claim just as he now backed off the overuse of forward passing. Even though his star player, Sid Luckman, was admittedly the best thrower Little had ever coached, he did not entertain thoughts of unabashed ball chucking. "Just because I happen to have a boy who can throw them, I'm not going to develop a one-sided offense," said Little. "I could probably give 'em [fans] a fancy Broadway show myself if I wanted to let this kid throw the ball all over the field. The crowd would like it for a game or two, but that's about all, because the smart teams would pin our ears back."[1]

It was hard to argue with Little's objectivity. As has been mentioned, the teams that were consistently at the top of the rankings during the 1930s were teams that played football the old-fashioned way. Meanwhile, at Ohio State, Schmidt and his bulging playbook were losing the important games, with risky playcalling being the culprit on at least two very conspicuous occasions. Those big losses notwithstanding, Schmidt had undeniably built an impressive body of work using his aggressive offense. Was it possible that the open-game movement he was leading was the wave of the future and that it simply needed corroborating examples of success in order to become the common method of attack? If so, the season that had just concluded had been an important one.

In the final rankings of the 1937 AP poll, at least four schools among the top twenty showcased offensive strategies that were built around the open game. Besides Schmidt's team, which was ranked No. 13, there was Arkansas (No. 14), Texas Christian (No. 16), and North Carolina (No. 19). That these last three programs were flourishing using new tactics was no coincidence: their head coaches were all former assistants to Francis Schmidt.

What they had learned from Schmidt wasn't a particular thing or a single strategy. Rather, they had learned to consider everything and had been exposed to the full spectrum of offensive football. Sure, there were certain principles—make the defense cover the whole field, keep changing your look with different formations, strategize backward, and involve lots of players on offense—but all of them boiled down to imagination. Lots of imagination. A few simple sequences from the same look cannot prosper indefinitely. Instead, a team needed to find a comfortable core element, come up with a hundred variations of it, and then surround that with a few hundred bits of madness to keep the defense in a constant state of discomfort. If done boldly, this resulted in a myriad of wins as well as waves of grateful spectators, the people who make it possible for players and coaches to make a living off the game. Schmidt's former students had learned this well.

At Arkansas, Fred Thomsen was loading up on forward passing with no apologies. In 1936 the Razorbacks had finished No. 18 in the nation while winning the first swc title in school history. For 1937 they finished at No. 14, the highest final ranking in school history. But beyond the rankings, what the football nation was really noticing was the Razorbacks' obscene propensity for passing on a scale never before seen. In 1936 they had attempted 28 passes per game—more than twice the national average—and still completed 43 percent, which was also better than the typical team. In 1937 they led the nation in pass attempts and completions yet again, this time attempting an unheard-of 31 passes per game. And proving that anything goes, the Hogs had split the passing duties between Jack Robbins and Dwight "Paddlefoot" Sloan, two men with two very different looks. "Jack gripped the ball, Sloan had small hands, and he palmed it," remembered teammate and end Ray Hamilton. "Sloan could throw on a wet day when Robbins couldn't. Jack was better on short passes, Sloan on long ones." Someone had to catch all these passes, and Hamilton did his part, snaring 29 passes, which was second best in the nation. The best? His teammate Jim Benton, who caught 48 passes for 814 yards. This number of grabs stood as an SWC record until 1963! The AP rankings combined with the gaudy passing numbers spoke volumes about the viability of "risky" passing as a legitimate tool. Not as an accoutrement, but as the centerpiece of an offensive philosophy that was being used to consistently win games.[2]

With this extreme strategy, however, came a certain amount of the trouble that plagued Thomsen's reputation and slowed the open-game movement: namely, the tough losses that open football often brought upon itself. Schmidt's problem was that he attempted too much of the offensive spectrum for his own good. Thomsen's problem was that so much forward passing served to atrophy the running game. Former Schmidt player and Thomsen assistant Glen Rose recalled the consequences at Arkansas: "Many a game we'd get ahead with our passing and then lose because we couldn't control the ball. You'd be afraid to pass and you couldn't run. We'd need to make two or three first downs to kill the clock, and we couldn't make them. We couldn't break a plate of glass with our running. I don't know why, because we had running plays. I guess we just didn't practice or use them enough." Such was the price for pushing the limits of an offensive philosophy.[3]

Taking second place nationally for pass attempts and pass completions was none other than Schmidt's former assistant Dutch Meyer and his TCU crew. Using Meyer's philosophy of short throws, the Frogs had attempted 24.4 passes per game in 1937. In addition, Meyer had embraced Schmidt's love for the shovel pass and he believed that the maneuver would become standard in the future. Broadly stated, Meyer's idea was in lockstep with Schmidt's. An offensive attack was just that—an attack. "If we make more points than they do, they can't beat us," said Meyer. "And if we keep the ball most of the time, they can't do their stuff." This philosophy sounds very elementary today, but it ran counter to the prevailing thought in 1937, which involved focusing your resources on defense or stopping the other team. Schmidt's football strategy was to score quickly and score often and then see if the other guys could keep up.[4]

The Horned Frogs had just completed their third straight season among the nation's top twenty. In 1935 with Sammy Baugh at the helm, TCU had gone 11-1 and had won the second-ever Sugar Bowl; their only loss was to an undefeated SMU that many considered the best team in the nation. The 1936 squad had finished at No. 16 and had won the inaugural Cotton Bowl. In 1937 the Horned Frogs had bounced back from a season-opening loss to Schmidt and his Buckeyes to finish ranked at No. 15 nationally. And they had done it with an undersized, inexperienced Davy O'Brien playing on a young team, lending more credence to the idea that an open offensive system not only worked, but occasionally worked miracles.

The SWC had been instrumental in shaping Schmidt, and now his students were shaping the SWC. As 1938 unfolded, Arkansas and TCU, the two "passing-est" teams in the nation, were skewing the conference numbers to the point where true, balanced offense had become a reality. Midway through the 1938 season, the SWC teams had combined to gain 2,973 yards by air and 2,718 by ground. These numbers would be considered quite tame today, but they were nothing short of amazing during a period when college teams ran the ball 75 percent of the time. And if those statistics didn't prove the viability of an open game, one had only to glance at the latest AP poll for 1938. Texas Christian was well on its way to finishing 10-0 and claiming an outright national championship. This would be an important title for the open-game movement, proving to detractors that its methods were capable of securing the biggest prize of them all.[5]

Meanwhile, as planned, the University of North Carolina was

enjoying the fun of cheering for a squad that played open football. The Tar Heel athletic administrators had been determined to join the open-game movement and went about it by targeting ex-Schmidt followers. When the Tar Heels' head coaching job was vacated in 1936, the school had burned up the long-distance phone lines trying to secure Ernie Godfrey, but he rejected their reported $7,000-per-year offer, content to remain an assistant at Ohio State. The North Carolina brain trust then turned to former Schmidt assistant Bear Wolf at TCU. Since Schmidt's departure from Texas Christian, Wolf had maintained his position as the Frogs' line coach but had also ascended to the position of athletic director and varsity baseball coach. It was a tough gig to relinquish, and only after protracted squabbling over a final $500 did they agree on a contract. Almost immediately, Wolf hired John Vaught as his line coach. Wolf and Vaught had both been on Schmidt's short list of confidants, and nobody was surprised when the duo successfully installed a great offense at North Carolina. In 1937 the Tar Heels were second nationally in total offense—averaging 325.9 yards per game—and from Wolf's hiring in 1936 until the end of the decade North Carolina averaged 19.1 points per game while posting a composite record of 29-6-3.[6]

During spring practice in 1938, Sammy Baugh had traveled down to Chapel Hill, where he helped his former TCU friends by doing some quarterback coaching. Even though the reunion of the ex-Schmidt boys was for work purposes, there was something fun about the open game, and Baugh admitted, "We had a blast."[7]

Those forward thinkers who could see Schmidt's legacy developing needed only turn to his current Ohio State coaching staff to identify his next disciples-in-training. Of particular note were two young assistants that Schmidt had officially taken on board in 1938: Gomer Jones and Sid Gillman. The two couldn't have been more

different outwardly: Jones, the rotund muscleman with the infec-
tious laugh and Gillman, the skinny former receiver with the deep
thoughts. Their résumés, however, had much in common. They
were both former Buckeye football captains and had both worked
in various small capacities for Schmidt since having graduated. Additionally, they had both been banned from the NFL for five years
even though they had never played a game in the league.

Although Jones and Gillman went into coaching after they graduated, the NFL kept tabs on them as prospective players. Since they
were both former captains and all-conference performers, the pros
hoped they would eventually be enticed by some quick cash. Gillman's rights were owned by the Boston Redskins and Jones's were
retained by the Chicago Cardinals. In the meantime Buzz Wetzel,
the pile-driving fullback from Schmidt's first Buckeye team, had decided it was his life's mission to build a Cleveland franchise and join
the rival American Football League (AFL). He succeeded in finding
big-name financial backers just before the 1936 season, but there
was a catch: If the sugar daddies were going to invest in something
as speculative as a new franchise in a new league, they wanted assurances that the team would have enough Ohio star power to draw
some fans. Wetzel knew there was nothing bigger in Ohio than a
Buckeye with All-American credentials, and he turned to his old
buddies Gillman and Jones. Since it was their friend Buzz asking,
and since it was a local gig, they agreed. Keeping everything in the
family, Max Padlow, an ex-Buckeye who used to play the end opposite from Gillman, jumped ship and joined the Cleveland franchise,
leaving the NFL's Eagles for more playing time and closer proximity to home. This Ohio State nucleus was enough to give the 1936
Cleveland Rams reasonable success at the gate and in the standings, but, sadly, the rest of the AFL's teams did not fare so well, and
the whole league folded at the end of the season. The NFL, wearing
cash-colored glasses, noted that out of the vanquished rubble of the

AFL there remained one franchise worth embracing. The Rams had solid ownership, the use of Cleveland Stadium, and a rabid group of fans. The NFL invited the Cleveland Rams to become the league's tenth franchise, and the Rams accepted. Not invited were Gillman and Jones, the two men who had previously ignored the fact that the NFL owned their rights. Now the worm had turned, and the boys were banned for their act of treason. It was no great loss to either. They had really been helping out Buzz Wetzel, but now their full attention could return to coaching. Gillman returned to Dennison College in Granville, Ohio, and Jones caught on as freshman football coach at John Carroll University, a Jesuit school in the Cleveland suburb of University Heights.[8]

Throughout this initial postcollege period (Gillman graduated in 1933, Jones in 1936) both men had remained close to Francis Schmidt and had done odd jobs for him such as coaching during the spring, helping with football clinics, and assisting with alumni presentations on the road. Schmidt had great respect for both Gillman and Jones. They both had very inquisitive minds and a passion for football, two traits he could readily identify with. Taking advantage of the athletic department's improving budget, Schmidt indulged in adding a pair of men who wouldn't hesitate to talk football with him for hours on end.

Sid Gillman, in particular, was a unique hire since Schmidt actually requested that he be hired full time. He was the only assistant that Schmidt specifically chose during his time at Ohio State, the others being selected by St. John. Schmidt had long admired Gillman's love of football strategy and thought he was especially talented. Gillman himself thought he had the right stuff to move up the coaching ladder and had dreamed of holding a position in the Big 10, but that option had not been made available to him prior to that point, despite his strong coaching record since graduation. Gillman was sure this had a lot to do with his being Jewish: "Every time a job would open up in the Big 10, I would apply for it. But as soon as they found out I was a Jew, that was the end of it." While Schmidt certainly wasn't a crusader for human rights, he didn't seem to harbor concerns about a person's race or religion. Then again, it's hard to know whether he even noticed Gillman was Jewish in the first place. Gillman was hired with an annual salary of $2,500 and was named the ends' coach, although he would soon learn that, in reality, Schmidt coached every position.

Gillman's partner in crime, Gomer Jones, was well loved by Schmidt and was remembered as a tireless competitor, great leader, and quick learner. For now, Schmidt would fit him in as an assistant line coach under Godfrey, meaning he would have almost nothing to do but watch and learn. Jones started at the meager salary of $850, but Schmidt found opportunities for other football odd jobs to supplement this salary.[9]

If these two guys thought they were going to have a large presence they were wrong. As Schmidt's stress increased each season, so did his counterproductive behavior. His impatience and paranoia—traits that were considered quirks at the outset of his reign—were becoming real liabilities. Schmidt's assistants were allowed to do less than ever at the very same time he had more of them than ever. Practice sessions were becoming embarrassing for the assistants. They had been reduced to standing around, running errands, and chasing errant footballs while Schmidt did all the coaching. Their duties were loosely defined, and they were not given much notice as to what to expect during practices. Most of them didn't even have full access to the master playbook due to Schmidt's paranoia. The players, aware of the assistants' embarrassment, certainly empathized, having been placed in awkward situations by Schmidt many times themselves.

Ernie Godfrey, being Schmidt's top lieutenant, enjoyed a sliver of authority, and Schmidt would occasionally loosen the reins with him. Godfrey was already a respected line coach before Schmidt arrived and had quickly absorbed the intricate requirements for line play in the new system, rendering himself as valuable as was possible in Schmidt's dysfunctional organizational chart. Godfrey had an underutilized talent for teaching technique, but he was unforgettable in his own right. He was the school's ace recruiter and would be for many years to come. He was also a bit excitable and was a master at unintentional malaprops. When given the chance to do some coaching he immediately had the boys smiling with instructions like, "Scatter out in bunches" or "Now, let's pair off in threes."[10]

One place where assistant coaches were always proven valuable—and Ohio State was no exception—was at school-sponsored football clinics. These clinics or classes were usually week-long events held during the spring and summer. Most of the major college programs hosted at least one large clinic, inviting the coaching staff of high schools throughout the region to attend. Using a combination of classroom work and field activities, the high school coaches would learn the latest techniques, strategies, and rules. No matter the format, the assistants at the host college played a big part in efficiently instructing the teeming masses. Ohio State's clinics drew hundreds of coaches, and even the high-energy Schmidt had to concede that he was physically unable to conduct proceedings without great support from his staff.

Francis Schmidt had been involved in many a clinic. When he was younger, he had been a habitual student, soaking in ideas from as many different coaches as possible and committing what he learned to a growing pile of notebooks. His obsession with diagramming and football theory was fed by this catalog of information. As he began to establish a successful coaching career of his own, his role at clinics became that of instructor. At first he was hired to teach the basketball portion. His marvelous string of titles at Arkansas had high school coaches clamoring to learn his secrets. Soon the success of his TCU football teams and their ability to score made Schmidt even more valuable, and he began to be hired more for football lectures. Because he was an expert in two sports and because he was so colorful, he was a popular lecturer. As of 1938 Schmidt figured he had "attended thirty or forty advanced courses by [other] head coaches and conducted thirty or more coaching schools" himself. At OSU he was responsible for hosting a huge football clinic for Ohio's high school coaches that coincided with the end of the Buckeyes' spring practice as well as an intensive summer course for future coaches who were pursuing degrees.[11]

The Ohio State spring football clinic was important to the state's entire football scene. High school coaches from all over Ohio learned new strategies and rules while the university had two full days to endear themselves to these same coaches who would later be involved in helping their best players choose a college.

The final act of the clinic was an intrasquad game involving the Buckeye players. Initially, at the first clinic scrimmage in 1934, Schmidt had split his team into two equally talented squads, but over the years this idea of an evenly contested scrimmage had given way to his desire to show off razzle-dazzle. Now he had his starters play the reserves, and the starters were instructed to put on a show. The games were no longer close in score, but the visiting coaches were treated to a spectacle of wide-open football at its most fantastic.

While the high school coaches were impressed by this show, they weren't always impressed with the clinic as a whole, no doubt owing to the fact that it was conducted in Schmidt fashion. For example, the handouts used in the lectures (churned forth by the technical magic of the ditto machine) were a sloppy combination of typing and free hand. Many of the diagrams appeared to have been composed under severe time constraints. Schmidt had some of his assistants write a couple pages on topics that were germane to the positions they coached, but these neat efforts only made his look worse. Schmidt's lecture itself was delivered with intensity and speed as well as his usual dose of non sequiturs and crazy humor. The audience did not take notes but rather listened with opened mouths and widened eyes. As for the clinic's crowning affair, Schmidt used the scrimmage not as a stop-action training tool but as a fireworks display to amaze visitors with his latest experiments. Some of what was seen would be taken home and implemented at the high school level, but much of it happened too fast and almost completely out of context. Clinic attendees also had to contend with Schmidt's paranoia. He wasn't always forthcoming with details, like a magician who sought to thrill his audience without revealing the secrets behind his tricks. James L. Robinson, head of the Ohio high school football coaches' association, described the typical Schmidt clinic as "haphazard" with a "dearth of helpful suggestions." And he wasn't the only one frustrated by Schmidt's frantic, barely organized style.[12]

Easily, the most distinguished of all the schoolboy mentors was Paul Brown of Washington High School in Massillon, Ohio. His teams were virtually unstoppable during the last half of the 1930s, drawing crowds of nearly 20,000 in a town of 26,000 citizens. The key to his success was an insatiable desire for exacting efficiency both on and off the field. Building on the teachings of legendary organizational masters Percy Haughton and Jock Sutherland, Brown had created a football learning model that would elicit envy from any organization. "Precision Paul," as he would become known, was a guest lecturer at some of the Ohio State clinics, and he was appalled at how things were run by "Frantic Francis." There was no attention to detail, the equipment was second rate, and the strategy was too complex without even taking into account Schmidt's poor teaching methods. Brown and Schmidt had spent time together watching film of Schmidt's Buckeyes and discussing strategy, but the complexity frustrated Brown, who admitted, "I never grasped it, really." To top it all off, Brown found Schmidt's swearing a disturbing contrast to his verbal abstinence. The two men were complete opposites. As far as Brown was concerned, Schmidt's clinics were making Ohio State football look bad. Brown may have been humorless and cruel at times, but he had valid concerns, and his conscience wouldn't allow him to encourage his players to attend Ohio State. He had, however, developed a good rapport with Noble Kizer at Purdue and on at least one occasion went so far as to physically transport recruits to Lafayette. Four of his former players— Jim Miller, Mike Byelene, Red Snyder, and Augie Morningstar—currently played for the Boilermaker football team. This stance, taken by the most esteemed high school coach in the state, did not go unnoticed by other coaches. The clinic, a supposed recruiting tool, had under Schmidt's direction achieved a boomerang effect.[13]

But not everyone was disappointed. Many coaches related to Schmidt's methods and theories, and for them Schmidt's clinics were career-altering. Chuck Mather, a legendary high school coach in Ohio, was one such case. Many years later he recalled how it happened. Mather had just graduated from Ohio Northern University and had accepted a coaching job at Brilliant High (Ohio), a little school that had not fielded a football team for many years. Mather and his new team finished the season at 0-7, and nobody complained when the eighth game was cancelled due to a snowstorm. With one futile season under his belt, Mather fully understood what a massive challenge he had accepted and chose to fight back. "I decided to find out something about football," he recalled. "So I attended the Ohio State clinic and listened to . . . Francis Schmidt. I believe Schmidt was the greatest offensive coach who ever lived. I went back to Brilliant with a notebook full of offense and defense." Armed with Schmidt's system he turned Brilliant into a winner before climbing the high school coaching ladder to its pinnacle: Massillon. In six years as head coach of the Tigers, Mather's teams won 6 state championships and 3 national titles, winning 57 of 60 games. Having no preconceived notions, Mather had been able to absorb more of Schmidt's system than many, and the results were spectacular. For most, however, learning the full spectrum of offensive football as laid out by Schmidt's system required years of exposure. It was complex, it was vast, and it was packaged and delivered by a madman who was autocratic, paranoid, and inefficient at teaching. A student had to connect the dots on his own to see the full picture. Then he had to pare it down to the elements he was comfortable with for his own microsystem—an arduous means of learning. Meyer, Thomson, and Wolf found it worth the effort. Sid Gillman and Gomer Jones's time as students of Schmidt would also yield great things—for themselves and for football. For the rest, learning what Schmidt had to offer was often a baffling, frustrating experience.[14]

Unfortunately for the Ohio State program, Schmidt's haphazard ways were not limited to clinics and classes. A major college football program is like a large business corporation with hundreds of people involved in its running and upkeep. Some of these jobs are highly visible, some clandestine. Some are motivated by pay, others by school loyalty. It was this way in 1938, just as it is today. Gameday at Ohio Stadium is nothing less than the culmination of resources exercised year round throughout the state and at points across the U.S. map. The person hired to recruit high school players uses more resources than any other, and well it should be. Procuring the best playing material increases the odds of producing the best results. But with material spread all over North America (and beyond, today) it takes a small army of school loyalists to round up the best beef and apply their school's brand mark before neighboring ranches make better offers. Because of college football's dogged determination to maintain the appearance of amateurism, roadblocks are set in place to prevent programs from blatantly bidding for a boy's talent. Armed with only a few legitimate enticements, the larger school must persuade the blue-chip lad to choose them over a hundred other schools that offer the same things: a legitimate degree, a pretty quad, conveniently located bars, unencumbered coeds, and a chance to play before the masses. Who then is to sway the youth to choose a particular school? The head coach and assistants play a part, but their roles were limited in the 1930s. This meant much of the proselytizing was left to enthusiastic alumni. Schmidt counted on their help just as much as he feared it. The actions of alumni occasionally led to embarrassing accusations from other schools, but just as often they led to the securing of choice players. A good head coach is adept at stoking this fire without burning himself.

Take, for example, Ed Yeckley. With his multiple chins, Yeckley wasn't one to be immediately connected with athletics, but in the Cleveland area he was well known as an unofficial scout or mentor of football talent. Although not an osu graduate, Yeckley was true to his state and considered himself a prominent part of the Buckeye football machine. He'd certainly done his part to steer talent like Stan Pincura and Regis Monahan to Columbus. He'd even helped Monahan, a Pittsburgh product, establish legal residence in Ohio so he wouldn't have to pay out-of-state fees on top of tuition. Most Buckeye followers would agree that he deserved a nice seat at Ohio Stadium for the sold-out 1935 Ohio–Notre Dame melee, but he was unable to procure even a crummy one. Yeckley had appealed to the leaders of the Ohio State football program with his request for tickets but was told there were none available and that nothing could be done. Admittedly, Yeckley thought he could waltz into town that weekend and withdraw a little love from the football bank, but instead his ego was forced to accept rejection. This slight would have been patched over by someone like Knute Rockne, who was a master at managing a machine, but Francis Schmidt was no Rockne. Schmidt had never corrected Yeckley's affront, and the result was that Yeckley sought affection elsewhere. Now instead of convincing schoolboy standouts Paul Kroner, Jack Meyer, and Ed Czak to become Buckeyes, he helped convince them to attend Michigan and play football for the Wolverines. Meyer had planned on attending Princeton, but Yeckley swayed him into joining himself and some other local players on a car trip to visit Ann Arbor, where they were treated "swell." Consequently, Meyer now wore maize and blue. "I used to feel sort of like an alumnus of Ohio State," a smiling Yeckley said after the 1938 game, "but when I went down in 1935 for the Ohio–Notre Dame game, I found they didn't consider me one. Now I feel sort of like an unofficial alumnus of Michigan. I certainly had a great seat. Michigan treats us alumni fine."[15]

One reason for such glitches in Schmidt's recruiting network was that Schmidt was not a network man. As has already been established, he was a terrible delegator, preferring to handle everything on his own, which is just what he had done at Arkansas and TCU. The SWC, with its homegrown disregard for overbearing ethics, had been a perfect stage for Schmidt. He worked hard at pushing an already lenient code to its breaking point. One of his favorite methods was volunteering to referee high school football games on Fridays. Not only did it give him the ability to judge talent up close, but he could actually sell his school to the best players in between plays. Lon Evans, one of Schmidt's players at TCU, remembered one such scenario: "Once when 'Schmitty' and I went out to officiate a high school play-off game in Breckenridge, he spent so much time recruiting for TCU that he could hardly concentrate on the game! Coach Schmidt recruited everyone who could breathe."[16]

The antics that he got away with in the Southwest were not safely permissible in the Big 10. Among other things, Big 10 code said that members of the athletic department were forbidden from contacting recruits until a recruit had contacted them first. Also, it was "undesirable" for a player to try out for the coaches and for athletic department funds to be used to entertain prospective athletes. Because of Schmidt's reputation as an ultra-aggressive recruiter during his days on the prairie, Saint had admonished him upon his being hired at Ohio State to be on his best behavior. Schmidt had readily agreed in order to facilitate his hiring but would have preferred to remain in charge of stacking his own deck. Instead he was forced to rely on Ed Yeckley, Ernie Godfrey, and others. They too relied on Schmidt, but just as the players had learned, dealing with the hypomanic Schmidt was usually a one-way street.[17]

While Saint may have been determined to keep Schmidt under control, some Buckeye fans expected otherwise. Most schools bent and twisted the spirit of amateur guidelines as far as the media or a snooping, tattletale conference foe would let them, and many just assumed it was Schmidt's job to cheat at least as much as the neighbors.

A perfect example involved Charley Maag from Sandusky, Ohio. The previous year when Maag was a high school senior and one of the best—if not *the* best—schoolboy linemen in the state of Ohio, the good citizens of Sandusky kept waiting for Schmidt to come to town and employ his relentless efforts to recruit Maag. After all, Harry Kipke, the Michigan skipper, had traveled to Sandusky and had pulled Maag right out of his class to spend the afternoon with him. He had invited Maag to visit Ann Arbor the next month, and when the boy accepted, the visit was supposedly paid for. Maag was then "assured that he would not have any difficulty due to finances if he attended Michigan." Maag's father claimed that Purdue had paid for his son to visit Lafayette where, again, finances would not be a problem. It was the kind of hustle that Buckeye followers decried when it involved their rivals but demanded when it involved their own school. Hell, even a couple of bold southerners had invaded Sandusky. Head coaches Josh Cody (Florida) and Major Bob Neyland (Tennessee) had personally visited Maag. While generally disgusted at this Dixie affront, Sandusky had to be impressed with the pursuit, all the while wondering what was detaining Coach Schmidt. The citizens were relieved—and probably a little amazed—that fall when Maag decided to stay in-state and play for Ohio State.[18]

Having been neutered by Saint and the Big 10, Schmidt wisely instituted traditions that might appeal to any talent pushed his way. Traditions made players feel like they were part of something special—something beyond the lectures, hangovers, and graduations that were equally offered by hundreds of other schools. Schmidt fostered three different traditions when he started his first season at OSU. The Gold Pants Club was inspired by his famous dismissing of Michigan. Members of any Buckeye team that beat Michigan were given a small golden charm in the shape of little pants that could be worn on a watch chain. Also, the Captains' Breakfast was held on homecoming weekend when all the Ohio State football captains—past and present—united for eggs and elitism. Schmidt also founded Buckeye Grove near the stadium where a buckeye tree is planted for each of the school's All-Americans. The "Last Tackle" ceremony for seniors (it's now known as the "Senior Tackle" and is anything but an intimate, simple exercise) following the final practice each season was not a Schmidt creation, but he took care to maintain it.

It's true, Ohio State isn't the only school with quirky traditions, but it was to Schmidt's credit that he dramatically increased the breadth of traditions while in Columbus. It was—and still is—a benefit to have as many little brass rings as possible when selling one's school to boys who had options. Who isn't curious about a challenge and a chance at some tiny measure of immortality?

Naturally, the recruiting and the traditions were used to attract the *best* material to Ohio State. As for simply having *enough* players, recruiting was not necessary. In 1938 there were 227 freshmen hopefuls who reported to frosh coach Fritz Mackey in September. At the end of November, 60 of the youngsters earned numerals— signifying a job well done—and of those, 30 won coveted letters as the cream of the crop. These letter winners would usually be invited to join the varsity, but Schmidt offered no guarantees. Among the 1938 freshmen two standouts seemed certain to succeed. Both Jack Graf and Tom Kinkade had lived up to their high school reputations.[19]

The two boys had very different backgrounds. Kinkade came from a small town on the Ohio border and had little money, no car, and no history with Ohio State. Graf was a Columbus local, had some money, and was the son of Campbell "Honus" Graf, captain of the 1914 Buckeye team and confidante of Lynn St. John. A player like Graf had been destined to attend Ohio State since birth. Kinkade was a different story, and it's a story worth retelling because recruits such as he were used to judge the success of a program's "network" from recruiting to retaining.

Thomas Kinkade (no known relation to the present-day "painter of light") grew up in Toronto, Ohio, a factory town with a population of less than 7,000. The Ohio River separated Toronto from that northern prong of West Virginia, which in turn barely separates Ohio and Pennsylvania. Toronto sits on the river across from the Pennsylvania border. Kinkade made himself known at Toronto High School by scoring 52 points in a single basketball game. It was a state record, and before the net had stopped swaying from his last basket, recruiters had begun adding Toronto to their itineraries.

"They came from everywhere," he remembered. "Different people from different colleges would be at my house when I came home. There was Pitt, Carnegie Tech, West Virginia, Indiana, and Notre Dame. You name 'em and they eventually got around to seeing me. That game really got everyone interested, and I guess they found out about my football playing because pretty soon that's what some of them were interested in."[20]

Even though Tom lived in Ohio, he was only about an hour away from Pittsburgh. During high school he used to travel to Pitt football games with a friend and his father. The Panthers were a powerhouse, and they played some great teams. Tom was enthralled with the Panthers, especially the stars who played backfield just like he did. Chickerneo, Stebbins, LaRue, Patrick, and Cassiano were all well-known backs whom Tom would never forget. In particular, Tom followed Harold "Curley" Stebbins, because the bruising right halfback was tall and lanky just like Tom. Thus Tom couldn't have been more excited when Jock Sutherland, master of the Panther program, took notice of him sometime after the 52-point night. "He had some fellow bring me up to the Fort Pitt Hotel, and then Sutherland bought me dinner. I had never really been out socially quite like this and was so conscious about not looking like a bumpkin that I could hardly talk." Sutherland confirmed that he wanted Tom to play at Pitt. Soon afterward, a man from the Pittsburgh firm of Taylor and Thompson contacted Kinkade and mentioned that expenses could be paid but offered no details without commitment from the teenager. Playing for the Panthers and Jock Sutherland was something he had dreamed of, but now he wasn't certain. Something about Pitt just didn't seem to fit his personality.[21]

Later that spring, with graduation nearing, Tom was contacted by Ernie Godfrey, who mentioned that he and Francis Schmidt would soon be traveling together near Toronto on unrelated business (wink, wink). He asked if Tom would like to meet them in nearby Steubenville. Tom agreed, and they all met at a hotel, had lunch, and decided that Tom should visit Ohio State. It was this trip to Columbus that sold Kinkade on playing for the Buckeyes. He met players like Jim McDonald and Jim Daniell, who made him feel comfortable. He felt they were more his "type of people." Pitt's program seemed like a military arrangement, while Ohio's seemed more like a big frat house undertaking. Interestingly, it was a non-Buckeye who sealed Kinkade's decision. Mike Basrak was a Bellaire, Ohio, native who had played at Duquesne, a small Catholic school in Pittsburgh. He had gone on to be an All-American before being selected in the first round of the NFL draft by the Pittsburgh Pirates (one spot ahead of Sammy Baugh). Basrak happened to be hanging out on the Columbus campus the day Kinkade came to town, and besides impressing him with his demeanor, Basrak suggested Tom should attend Ohio State. Because of his two-sport prowess, Ohio State was especially excited to land Kinkade, but before he enrolled, one final issue had to be resolved: money.[22]

Big 10 schools were not supposed to offer any sort of athletic scholarships. This meant that most of the Depression-era players needed a job to pay for tuition, housing, books, and hopefully the occasional social dalliance, time permitting. Few parents had the means to cover these expenses, and the ones who did were fairly likely to send their offspring to a private college. The summer jobs players found back home helped with finances but didn't contribute enough. Without the ability to offer perspective players straight cash or its equivalent, a major college football program needed the ability to offer good jobs, preferably jobs that paid disproportionately to the minimal amount of labor required. Local employers that could facilitate these jobs were a crucial piece of the program's puzzle. Once this network of jobs had been set up, the school could help the player with procuring one of these plum positions, but—according to Big 10 rules—only after the student had enrolled *or* had voluntarily inquired ahead of time. *Everyone* inquired.

Being a premier player recruited by a premier program, Kinkade had nothing to worry about. He was offered an excellent position with a coal company in Columbus. Chester C. Cook was the owner as well as one of Ohio State's biggest boosters. "When I met with Mr. Cook, he said, 'Come in when you can come in,'" recalled Kinkade. "He introduced me to all the heads of the departments and told them that whenever I came in they were to let me work wherever I wanted to in the organization. Most of the work was pretty simple. He gave me a certain amount of money each month, which covered tuition. Cook and I remained close for a long time. He was a great old guy. He wanted a son."[23]

Kinkade spent his first collegiate fall splitting time between freshman football, work, and studies. He joined the Sigma Chi fraternity along with teammate Johnny Hallabrin. On the weekends he traveled back to Toronto to see his girlfriend, Ruth. The former cheerleader had stayed home and had taken a job as a secretary. Tom didn't have a car, so he'd take the streetcar out to a Columbus suburb named Bexley, and from there he hitchhiked. Getting a ride was no problem when he wore his red football letterman's sweater with the giant white "O" on the front. Plenty of motorists were eager to chat about Buckeye football and considered it an honor to transport one of the players. "I could beat the train home," he recalled with a laugh.[24]

Everything was going well for Tom until first-quarter grades came out. They weren't good, and Tom wasn't surprised. "I wasn't much of a student to begin with. I was just there to play ball. After the first grades came out, they told me I could get into real trouble trying to play both sports [football and basketball] because 'you're not that kind of a student.' Which was true, I knew it. I didn't like

that part of it. All I wanted to do was play ball." From Tom's perspective, school work was an annoying pest. All he wanted to do was
pursue his God-given gift of athleticism. He was too young for the
pros, and at his current level of maturity there were no other ade-
quate outlets for the brand of competition necessary for honing his
skills. He was trapped in that part of the football pipeline that demanded academic achievement, albeit completely unrelated to his
athletic achievement. Like thousands before him and tens of thousands afterward, he would have to play the game in order to keep
playing *the* game.[25]

The network had done its job getting Kinkade into school and
providing a job, but now it was Schmidt's responsibility to keep
him there. Since the 1890s when football teams began using paid
coaches instead of team captains, the coaches quickly realized that
their job involved much more than strategy and training. Among
other things, keeping athletes academically eligible had evolved
into an important puzzle piece. If a coach wanted to ensure his
players were maintaining minimum academic standards, he was
wise to stay on top of the player by cajoling him with letters, notes,
and conversations. In dire circumstances it was not unheard of for a
coach to intervene and attempt to exact mercy from a teacher. This
academic babysitting was the worst part of a coach's job but a necessary evil when dealing with a player in Tom Kinkade's position.
Sometimes, a head coach assigned an assistant coach to this duty,
putting the fear of God into a player by threatening football punishment for academic sins.

Schmidt was not inclined to take any of these steps as his time
at Ohio State progressed. He had been more hands-on at TCU, but
he'd had an advantage. "At that time part of the faculty salaries
came from football revenue, and Schmidt knew it," recalled Lon
Evans. "If the professors got rough on his players, he'd tell them
about it." A struggling school in the Southwest had been perfect for

Schmidt. His hypomanic condition, with its unrealistic confidence and larger-than-life ideas, thrived in the rough-and-tumble Texas setting. But at Ohio State, Schmidt's autocratic imagination was restrained by convention. He was unable to coerce teachers any more than he could coerce recruits. He needed a new style that emphasized subtlety, organization, and a measured use of psychology. For Schmidt, such tact wouldn't have been possible had he been given six lifetimes. Hell, he couldn't even properly assign those duties to others. The scholastic failings of Jumpin' Joe and Jimmy Strausbaugh from the previous year were, in part, casualties of this trait. Kinkade, an apathetic student, looked like a prime candidate for floundering. For now it was Floyd Stahl's problem as the freshman coach, but after that, Schmidt would have to find a way to make the most of Kinkade's years at Ohio State.[26]

Schmidt wasn't the type for introspective clarity, but thankfully, the school's athletic administration was kind enough to offer him the occasional observation as to something or other that might be fixed. And because of his delusionary nature, Schmidt interpreted these unsolicited opinions as proof that they did not understand genius, and he generally went about his business as usual. Occasionally, though, a wave of fear would grip him, and he would do what he thought was politically expected of him, even if he never fully grasped the reasons behind the advice.

On September 9, one week before fall practice, Schmidt showed up unannounced on the doorstep of J. L. Morrill, the university's vice president and member of the athletic board. It seems Schmidt had recently been made aware that his program's continued lack of organization was a concern to school officials. Also an issue was Schmidt's use of profanity, which continued unabated. Gripped by one of his rare, sudden doubts, Schmidt impatiently visited Morrill rather than set up a meeting the next day. Upon being invited in,

Schmidt skipped small talk and jumped straight to the point. He would do better, he promised. He presented ideas for cleaning up the program. When he was finished he thanked Morrill for his time and left as suddenly as he had arrived. Morrill was left standing in his doorway, contemplating the tornado that had just interrupted his relaxing evening. The next day Morrill wrote a letter to Schmidt explaining how pleased he was:

> I suppose there is no university enterprise that gets more publicity and is talked about by more people in every conceivable way than football. It *is* important, therefore, that we be shipshape and unassailable in every way and that, so far as our own operations on the inside are concerned, we should be dead sure that they are unimpeachable and would deserve the support and warrant the defense (in case of unjust attack) of every real friend of the university. I just can't say to you how good I feel that you have set out on the course you have described to me . . .[27]

A primary motivation for this self-imposed reformation may have been Schmidt's fear that 1938 was not going to be the best of seasons and that he was going to need all the compassion and support he could get. There were some talented sophomores joining the varsity, but the fifteen returning lettermen were not as strong as usual, leading Schmidt to temper the enthusiasm of the fans: "We've got to start from scratch," he warned. To no one's surprise, Schmidt also declared the 1938 schedule to be the "toughest ever faced by a State team." After his weeding-out process in the spring, Schmidt had only found forty-four players worthy of a fall invitation. It was, as usual, the smallest group in the Big 10—so small, in fact, that Buckeye old-timers couldn't recall a tinier group ever to have started the fall at Ohio State.[28]

The swaggering Schmidt who had dived head-first into Columbus in 1934 was now sounding unsure. At the first fall practice, Schmidt could be heard sighing and then muttering, "It looks bad." With a light rain falling, Schmidt worked the boys hard. He needed the sophomores to surprise him, and as much as he hated the thought, he needed one of the youngsters to fill the vacant quarterback position. Using his trademark blend of slang and acid, he bellowed things like, "Play foxy, don't play dumb," and when the first practice had finally come to a close, Schmidt's last comment was, "Boy, we've got a lot of work to do before we win a game."[29]

Not abating his worries was Johnny Rabb's knee. The great fullback had injured it so badly late in the 1937 season that it had required surgery. Now, on the first day of practice, he tweaked the same knee and limped off the field. It wasn't serious, and he returned for practice the next day, but that knee was a worrisome issue. Even though halfback Jim Strausbaugh had regained eligibility and was set to show off his vast skills, the Buckeyes needed that dynamic inside running that Rabb was capable of providing because there were already too many question marks along the front line. Almost every job on the line was up for grabs. Three or four guys had legitimate shots at some of the different spots. Only 245-pound co-captain Carl Kaplanoff had a lock on his spot at right tackle. Schmidt wanted badly to take his razzle-dazzle to the next level, but personnel questions were dogging him for the second straight year.

One week before the season started, Schmidt reduced practice time to include mornings only. Players needed to register for classes. Plus, he didn't want to burn the players out and wanted to lessen their risk of injuries heading into the regular season. But it was already too late for Johnny Rabb, who had a torn knee ligament. Doctors hoped the knee would respond to rest. For five weeks he walked on crutches, biding his time before finally surrendering to the scalpel once again. His season was finished, and seemingly, so was the unlimited potential that had once defined him.[30]

By the time the season was ready to begin, the Buckeye squad had grown to fifty-six men. Schmidt kept adding players he had previously considered unworthy, a sure sign of his desperation. And of the fifty-six men on the team, a whopping thirty were sophomores. Half the starting lineup would be sophomores by the second game. Such youthfulness was a very bad thing indeed when the offense was built around a monsterfully intricate playbook.[31]

The Buckeyes started the season by playing the two teams that had beaten them last season, Indiana and USC. The Hoosiers were still having trouble getting Big 10 home games but were again grateful to split a huge Ohio Stadium gate. This time, though, the payday didn't include a victory. Schmidt's newly rebuilt Buckeyes barely got revenge, squeezing out a 6–0 win, and the victory looked even less impressive by season's end as the Hoosiers finished 1-6-1 and scored only 21 points the entire year.

Right on the heels of this lackluster victory came the arrival of USC. Ambrose Schindler—the star of the 1937 contest in Los Angeles—was present, but he was too injured to start and was replaced by Grenville Lansdell. After Ohio State stalled on its opening drive they punted to Lansdell, who snaked his way through traffic for an 82-yard touchdown, instantly stunning the sellout crowd. It was the beginning of a frustrating game for the fans. Ohio State ran up 318 yards of total offense and out first-downed the visitors 3:1, but turnovers left the faithful moaning. A Buckeye lineup loaded with sophomores proved the danger of attempting razzle-dazzle where so much youth is involved. In all, the Buckeyes lost the ball a staggering 9 times: 3 times on fumbles and 6 times by interception. USC savored their 14–7 win all the way back to the coast.[32]

Ohio State's first road game of the year was to Northwestern where the Wildcats were fielding one of Pappy Waldorf's weaker prewar teams. The Buckeyes' struggles continued, and the game entered the final minute tied 0–0. Charley Maag, the highly recruited lineman from Sandusky, had not only won the job of starting tackle, he had also proven to be a highly capable place kicker during practice, and now he was lining up for his first game-time varsity attempt. It was a 32-yarder from a tough angle with a cruel cross breeze. Maag ended up being the best kicker Schmidt ever had at OSU, but his start was auspicious: the kick sailed wide, and the game ended scoreless.[33]

Completely out of sync, the Buckeyes needed a break, and they got one: the University of Chicago. The Maroon football program was now in complete free fall. Outmanned but still trying to beat Schmidt at his own game, Chicago coach Clark Shaughnessy had his boys unleash an all-out air attack, filling the air with 30 pass attempts, a huge amount for the era. It didn't work. While 1 of those passes was completed for a 50-yard touchdown, 8 of the others were intercepted by Ohio State. On offense, the Buckeyes opened up the playbook and had a blast sampling Schmidt's creations. Jim Langhurst, the sophomore fullback filling in for Rabb, scored 3 touchdowns as the Buckeyes won their first laugher of the season, 42–7.[34]

For the first time in Schmidt's five seasons at Ohio State, the Buckeyes traveled to a state east of Ohio when they visited New York University. The Greenwich Village school played their games in the famous Polo Grounds. For the second straight week, the Buckeyes cut loose, using a "bewildering assortment of spinners, reverses, plunges, and passes." The Violet were sent back to the Village having lost 32–0.[35]

Despite the dependence on sophomores and Schmidt's dire predictions, Ohio State actually entered November with a legitimate shot at winning the conference title. The scenario was almost identical to that of 1937, and the result was just as bad. Last year it had been a shocking 10–0 loss to Indiana, and this year it was a 12–0 loss to Purdue. The Boilermakers had never beaten Ohio State in 6 contests; in fact, they had never even scored a point. With the game scoreless entering the fourth quarter, it appeared these streaks could go either way. That was before Purdue's Louis Brock decided to take over. The junior from Kansas unleashed a 50-yard run to the 3-yard line, scoring the go-ahead touchdown a play later. Then, as time was getting scarce, he nailed an 80-yard punt from his own end zone and followed that up with an interception that he returned to the Buckeyes' 1-yard line where a teammate scored the final touchdown.

What really had Buckeye fans up in arms were the 2 interceptions thrown by Ohio State early in the fourth quarter when the game was still scoreless. Standard football had little tolerance for forward passing in the later stages of a tie game. Schmidt's open game was breathtaking and futuristic, but losses like this one left people shaking their heads.[36]

Their chances for any sort of title having been shattered once again, the Buckeyes prepared to finish with pomp by beating Illinois and Michigan. It had become a delightful season-ending habit. Not only did Schmidt want to beat these old rivals, but he wanted to see the rest of his playbook in action. He didn't jot these things down in the middle of the night for nothing, and he let his boys know it was time to see his experiments put to the test: "How about all this trick stuff we've been practicing all year? The season ends in another week, and unless you're saving those tricks for a Thanksgiving Day party, we better be using some of them." His quarterbacks listened, and they opened up the offense more than they had all season. Jim Langhurst scored 3 more touchdowns as Ohio State thumped Illinois 32–14, handing Bob Zuppke his worst beating in six seasons.[37]

After the game there was a locker-room fight over the game ball.

At some point, Frank Smith "cracked co-captain Carl Kaplanoff on the nose," which eventually resulted in Francis Schmidt's kicking Smith off the squad. The punishment didn't last long, though. Other players defended Smith by refusing to participate in practice, and soon Schmidt caved, not only reinstating Smith but playing him against Michigan. The players were now complaining against their co-captain and their head coach. It was yet another moment for Schmidt to impose his will, and again he capitulated.[38]

Only the Michigan game remained. An Ohio State victory and a Minnesota loss would mean an improbable share of the conference title for the Buckeyes. It would also be Ohio's fifth straight win over Michigan, something that had never been done to the Wolverines. Beating the maize and blue, however, would not be so easy in 1938. They were now under the direction of Fritz Crisler, and he had turned the program around. Michigan entered with a record of 5-1-1 and were ranked No. 18 nationally. They also had Tom Harmon, a sophomore halfback sporting the No. 98 on his jersey. Harmon had been the original "*highly* recruited" player out of high school, the first to generate foolishness on a grand scale as colleges from all over America tried everything short of kidnapping him or offering him a coterie of virgins. He was only a sophomore but was already looking like the superstar he had been projected to become.

Ohio State's use of sophomores hadn't been quite as fulfilling. Combining them with razzle-dazzle produced volatile results. When it worked it worked beautifully, but too often it resulted in turnovers. Such was the case in the second quarter of this game when sophomore Jim Langhurst tossed a bad lateral. Michigan recovered just 16 yards from the end zone, and Harmon powered it home for a 6–0 lead. In the third period, Ohio State tried a forward pass deep in their own territory and were intercepted by Harmon, who eventually passed for another touchdown, giving Michigan a 12–0 lead.

The desperate Buckeyes began throwing even more, but their best drive was ended by yet another interception, and once again, Michigan turned it into a touchdown, making the final score 18–0.[39]

Ohio State had been bested in every way. Their offense never found much rhythm thanks to the turnovers, batted-down passes, and some clean, fierce tackling by the Wolverines' defense. Michigan's hardy attitude carried over to their offense where they mixed in a little passing with a lot of rugged running between the tackles. One of the stellar performers for Michigan was Paul Kroner, a player who Ed Yeckley had guided to Michigan instead of Ohio State.

It had been a fairly interesting game, but the real excitement occurred on the field when the game was over. Visiting Michigan fans, elated to see the streak of futility end, poured on to Ohio Stadium's turf and headed for the goalposts. They were going to tear the posts down as a final insult and presumably save the pieces as nice trophies. Nothing new there. This pillaging by fans who were intoxicated with excitement had gone on for years and still occurs today. The problem, in this case, was that the Horseshoe's goalposts were not the traditional wood variety but instead were made of steel and set in concrete. The Wolverine mob persisted. They were able to bend the structure out of shape, but no more. All of this labor took time and allowed for a swarm of Buckeye faithful to come to the defense of their turf. Not unlike the 1935 postgame revelry when visiting Buckeye rooters battled in Ann Arbor, a great melee broke out. "The participants suffered scores of black eyes, scratches, and bashed noses," wrote Fritz Howell, the local AP writer. "Several of the gladiators were carried to the sidelines while their mates continued the fight, which lasted forty-five minutes." This would have caused an internet sensation in the twenty-first century, but in 1938 it was just some Depression-era folks letting off steam.[40]

The 18–0 loss was the worst loss suffered by a Schmidt team since

1930, when he was at Texas Christian. It left the Buckeyes' final record at 4-3-1 and their Big 10 placement at No. 6.

Russ Needham, writing for the *Ohio State Monthly*, summed the 1938 season up well: "It was a slow team, on its feet and in its strategy, hesitant as a unit and generally lethargic in its mannerisms. . . . There was little of the so-called razzle-dazzle, and when this sensational type of play was sprung it frequently boomeranged to the advantage of the opposition." The hesitancy in thought and action could be chalked up to youth, and the lack of overall speed was just bad luck, but that lack of fight was something that seemed to be worsening, and the blame was being aimed at Francis Schmidt. His disdain for motivation and a general lack of discipline were eclipsing his brilliant strategy. Schmidt, on the other hand, had his own excuse for the declining results: "Ohio State seems to have a knack of scheduling teams just when they come to the top." While the Buckeyes' losses had come against very good squads, Schmidt was conveniently forgetting that Indiana, Northwestern, Chicago, and New York University had terrible seasons in 1938 and accounted for 4 of Ohio's wins.[41]

Even with the erratic behavior, disorganization, and occasional feuds with reporters, the wolves weren't calling for Schmidt's head the way they had Willaman's. Until the season that had just concluded, Schmidt's Buckeyes had finished first or second in the conference and beaten Michigan all four years. While the High Street judges were a little leery of Schmidt's eccentric behavior, they seemed willing to overlook 1938 as an aberration for a few reasons. For one thing, Schmidt may have been an oddball, but he was a lot of fun. It was almost impossible not to like his intensity, humor, slang, and comedic impatience. And Schmidt made an effort to use his eccentric charm on the downtown pundits a little more often than he did on the press. For example, he had a standing invitation to visit the Quarterback Club, which he did on Wednesdays during the season. At the club, he would "take the witness chair," and provide explanations for his decisions of strategy. "Slow movies" were used to break down plays, and Schmidt would explain everything—good and bad—continually interjecting comical one-liners into the serious proceedings.[42]

Additionally, Schmidt's style of football remained popular. Average home attendance for 1938 had set an all-time school record with 62,978 spectators. Before Schmidt's arrival, Ohio State had averaged over 40,000 fans only once. Since his arrival, they had exceeded that average for all five seasons. And this was during the Depression when discretionary spending on football tickets was more of a luxury than usual.[43]

Generating revenue, beating Michigan, and entertaining the High Street bunch had earned Schmidt the forbearance that Willaman hadn't received. Nothing, however, substituted for wins, and as Schmidt entered the final year of his second contract, he knew all too well that his boys needed an outstanding 1939 to keep the wolves at bay.

Eleven. The Magic Remains

While the scribes and the pundits tried to decide whether Francis Schmidt was the right coach, there was very little debate amongst the students. Anyone who has spent time with college students knows they place a high value on the unusual. Schmidt's nuttiness appealed to the Buckeye students, and they stood firmly behind him. They loved that his football was on the wild side and they loved that he seemed to support all of the school's athletics even though he had little vested interest. Schmidt no longer coached basketball but he still attended all of the Buckeyes' games, keeping notes the whole time. The students thought this intense support was cool, but for Schmidt it was more than that. He really loved all sports, and his delving into the strategy and details provided a relaxing safety valve for his tightly wound mind.

Naturally, the undergraduates found it great sport to try and include the irascible Schmidt in their society. Ohio State is home to an honorary group for juniors called the "Bucket and Dipper Society." The initiation involves running around after midnight and dousing new members with buckets of water. Each year a member of staff or faculty was included, and this year it happened to be Schmidt. Quarterback Jack Graf, who was involved in the society and knew the Schmidts quite well, called Evelyn Schmidt and told her what was happening. "We're coming to initiate Coach Schmidt at midnight," he told her. "When we ring the bell, you get him and have him answer the door." When the late hour arrived, Schmidt answered the door just as planned, and the boys doused him with two buckets of water. "Goddamn!" he hollered. After laughing at his response, the boys told him this was an honor, to which he responded, "An honor, my ass." Evelyn was left with the difficult job of convincing her water-logged husband just exactly how he had been "honored."[1]

In early September of 1939 Schmidt was relaxed just enough from his recently concluded vacation to play host and invite some of the Columbus sportswriters to join him on his front porch where they could talk about the upcoming season while enjoying the shade. It was as laid back as one would ever catch the coach, and the reporters were pleased to listen as Schmidt elaborated on his players and opponents like a normal person. Of course, even when he was relaxed, he opened with some typically Schmidt-like comments: "Yes, this year's squad can be a good one if the boys want it to be, but they'll have to be good to get anywhere with that tough schedule." Thus, in one sentence, Schmidt was able to blame the players' attitudes for the losses in 1938 and the taxing schedule for 1939. And just to make sure the audience understood his plight he added one of his sweeping dramatics: "All our opponents should be stronger than last year," he claimed. The odds suggest that this would be almost an impossible coincidence, but paranoid people expect such difficulties.[2]

As for his playing material, Schmidt was glad Johnny Rabb would be returning after knee operations had cost him the entire previous season. If appetite was any indication of health, then Campbell Graf could vouch for Rabb's recovery. Campbell, a reserve lineman and the older brother of teammate Jack, had invited Rabb to his family's local home for dinner. "He was eating with both hands," laughed Graf. "My mother had never seen anything like it." For now, Schmidt was keeping his expectations tempered and figured on using Rabb as a situational "spurt runner" when fatigue was bogging down the game and a fresh sledgehammer would prove effective.[3]

Of all the players, Schmidt was particularly excited about Don Scott, a junior who blossomed in a big way during spring practice. Schmidt had surprised everyone by naming him starting quarterback after previously having tried him in several different spots. Many questioned whether Scott was aggressive enough for the leadership responsibilities, but no one doubted his athleticism. After two seasons of patchwork at this vital position, Schmidt thought he had found the necessary cog to replace Stan Pincura and Tippy Dye. Hopefully, joining Scott in the backfield would be the supremely talented Jim Strausbaugh. Grade point average was always his biggest obstacle, and his all-important summer-school results were due any day now. As for linemen, Schmidt kept it understated. "Our tackles should be faster and the ends no poorer," he declared. The part about the ends was an understatement as Esco Sarkkinen looked good enough for All-American honors and sophomore Charley Anderson was wowing coaches with his skills. Anderson had played high school ball for Paul Brown, who declared his end to be "just about the greatest football package that has come out of high school." Sarkkinen, the son of Finnish immigrants, was part of the large sophomore bunch from the previous season. His pass-catching skills had sent his stock skyward and garnered him national attention. If any of the linemen were to falter, there waited a new pack of burly sophomores that line coach Ernie Godfrey believed to be the best collection "in the last ten years."[4]

If the seasons of 1937 and 1938 had seemed troubled from the start, then 1939 was full of promise for the Buckeyes. Not only was the material older and deeper, but there was a palpable esprit de corps. Much of this new attitude could be attributed to the team captain, Steve Andrako. The curly headed center from Braddock, Pennsylvania (one of only two non-Ohioans among the squad's top thirty-three) was quiet, but he possessed a rare tenacity. He had been elected captain by his teammates despite not having lettered as a sophomore nor starting a single game his junior season. His leadership was already evidenced in a pledge he had posted on the locker room bulletin board. The pledge was signed by all the members of the team who promised among other things to "keep strict personal training," "work hard—for the good of the team," and "be team players—not rugged individualists." Andrako—along with fullback Jim Langhurst—seemed to have put the squad in the right frame of mind, a job that was usually performed by the head coach.[5]

With everything so nicely aligned, there was little doubt that Schmidt was going to open up the playbook in 1939. Just because circumstances had hurt his recent teams didn't mean he had stopped augmenting his vast supply of diagrams. He was itching to cut loose, and if the annual intrasquad spring game was any indication, it would be an entertaining season. With hundreds of high school coaches watching the scrimmage—the final event of their Ohio State clinic experience—the Buckeyes had unleashed an unbridled "melee" that showed Schmidt's system was more wonderfully impossible than ever.[6]

As fall practice progressed, the news just kept getting better. Jim Strausbaugh had survived the academic wars. He was notified that his summer-school grades were good enough to make him football eligible, and he joined his mates three days into practice. He was just in time for the foot races Schmidt had scheduled that morning, and big Jim promptly ran the quickest time on the team. And as for more general good news, the Big 10 had recently approved of a training table or special eating arrangement for the team. Between school, practice, and work the players often ate on the run or scavenged through leftovers at the frat house. Now they would have a dedicated dining arrangement that provided them a full, warm meal. This way the players saved money, ate well, and properly replenished bodies that had been sacrificed for the good of the school. Instead of merely a sandwich, their typical meal now consisted of vegetable soup, olives, celery, roast beef or steak, baked potato, buttered peas, shrimp salad, rolls with butter, a beverage, and ice cream or wafers.[7]

If there was one troubling portent, it was Schmidt's paranoia. Most football coaches, to varying degrees, worry that opponents will learn their system of plays and playcalling. There is no way to completely stop leaks, but a good coach takes precautions. Some coaches are more suspicious than others, and Schmidt had always ranked near the top of that list. Foster Howell—a tackle under Schmidt at TCU—used to tell the story of Schmidt's "Key Hole Defense":

"It seems that Schmidt thought a rival coach had Dictaphones installed in the hotel rooms where TCU was stopping before a game in Texas, so he went to the clerk and obtained a vacant suite in which to hold a meeting of the squad." Still not comfortable, Schmidt then took the additional step of placing his hat over the key hole in the room's door so that no one would be able to hear his talk."[8]

Part of the problem was that Schmidt not only had the most futuristic offense in football, but he truly believed his system was golden. His was not a just bunch of tweaked plays but rather an *otherworldly* collection of plays built from thousands of hours of study, contemplation, and imagination. He had devoted his adult life to building the perfect offensive strategy, and he was absolutely certain that his system was the ambrosia that every coach in America

dreamed of tasting. He did indeed have reason to fear the covetousness of others, but there was also no denying he was fundamentally
paranoid. Now, six years into his pressure-packed tenure at Ohio
State, his fears were being manifest in counterproductive ways.

Concerned that someone might pilfer some of this gold, he began keeping his master playbooks under lock and key. This would
have been okay, except that he was not inclined to make the books
or the key available to half of the coaching staff. Godfrey and Gillman had access, but they were not to share this privilege with others, which of course added to the internal strife that was building
within the staff. But even worse than the access-to-the-masters issue was the crazy way in which Schmidt doled out individual playbooks to the players. Naturally, each player needed a playbook to
learn what his defined action was on each play, but Schmidt didn't
entrust them with the full picture. So he did the unthinkable. He
issued modified playbooks that revealed *only* the responsibilities
of the player for whom the book was issued. A guard, for example,
would see on the diagram of play B122 that he was supposed to
pull and seal to the right side, but in *his* playbook it would not show
what the other linemen or the ballcarrier were doing. The player
was thus operating in a vacuum when learning and executing plays.
While this method of diagram distribution would indeed minimize
the damage should a playbook fall into enemy hands, it was definitely a roadblock on the road of learning for those players who
dutifully studied their playbooks between practices and wanted
to learn the finer points of plays. Since the quarterbacks were responsible for all the on-field play choices, they were privy to much
more than the others but still had to operate with an eye toward se-
crecy. Schmidt, notorious for flooding his quarterbacks with new
plays and last-minute notes, would constantly add warnings that
the papers were to be returned to him after absorption, as if they
needed more prompting beyond the first couple dozen reminders.

All of this paranoia, combined with his lack of faith in the assistants to properly teach, signaled the beginning of the storm that would eventually sink Schmidt's ship. His lack of focus on fundamentals and his incessant use of profanity had already charted a bad course.[9]

As usual, Schmidt used the last weekend of fall practice to personally scout his opening opponent. This time it was the Missouri Tigers, and Schmidt traveled all the way to Columbia, Missouri, for a peek. He wanted to check out the Tigers' Paul Christman, supposedly one of the better passers in college football. Instead, Schmidt was treated to a lopsided game in which Missouri ran all day as they pummeled Colorado 30–0. But it was still football, and Schmidt undoubtedly saw some things worth adding to one of his notebooks.[10]

When Ohio State and Missouri met at the Horseshoe a week later, the game got off to a rocky start. Jim Strausbaugh returned the opening kickoff 88 yards for a touchdown only to have the play negated by a clipping penalty. Sadly for Missouri, they had been offside, so the game was started anew. The Buckeyes didn't return this one for a score, but on their first drive they moved 71 yards for a touchdown. Don Scott, in his debut as quarterback, finished the drive with a 15-yard forward pass to Frank Clair. It was all they would need as they dominated Missouri for a complete 19–0 victory. Like several other high-profile passers, Paul Christman fared miserably against Schmidt's Buckeyes, passing for only 80 yards and being intercepted 5 times. Total yardage told the story even better: osu 362, Missouri 124. Schmidt rotated a whopping 51 players into the game. No one in the stadium would have guessed that Missouri would win their next 8 games and the Big 8 title before losing in the Orange Bowl. They ended the season being ranked No. 7 nationally.[11]

After shutting out Northwestern 13–0 (the Wildcats, preseason favorites to battle for the conference title, scored only 47 points the entire season and finished a disappointing 3-4-1), the Buckeyes prepared for their first road game of the season, and it was a beauty: a date with the Minnesota Golden Gophers, perhaps the best program in the entire nation during the 1930s. Under head coach Bernie Bierman, Minnesota had not lost a home conference game in *seven* years. They had been Big 10 champions four times in the last five seasons. They had been crowned the national champions in the first-ever AP final poll (1936) and before that, most ranking systems named them national champs in 1934 and 1935. They would win two more national titles in 1940 and 1941, becoming the first team to ever finish No. 1 in consecutive AP polls. They were big, fast, and deep. Big 10 fans had dreamed about an Ohio State–Minnesota matchup ever since Schmidt had arrived. In 1934 and 1935 there had been talk of a postseason meeting, but the rumors were nothing more than that. Only now were their two paths about to cross.

Many aspects of this titanic collision had fans intrigued. In terms of full-time students in residence, these two state schools were among the largest in the nation, Minnesota ranking No. 3 and Ohio State No. 6. During this decade, the two schools had been the pace-setters for the toughest conference in the nation, yet they had not met since 1931. And the type of football they played was vastly different. Since their last meeting, both universities had hired new football coaches with contrasting styles. Ohio had Schmidt with his open game, while Minnesota had Bernie Bierman, whose conservative strategy was often compared to that of the equally renowned Pittsburgh program.[12]

Minnesota, under Bernie Bierman, had much in common with Jock Sutherland and his Pittsburgh Panthers. Both programs were wildly successful and both were a testament to the superiority of traditional, Victorian football. The two schools lived and died with running attacks that had been relentlessly honed during practice. Their playbooks consisted of a small, tight group of plays. Attention to detail and physical fitness were anthems. Neither team embraced the forward pass, which was deemed far too risky. During Bierman's prewar tenure (1933–41) his boys threw on first down only 8.4 percent of the time, and that was the safest time to throw. During those same 72 games, the Gophers threw from inside their own 20 on third down a total of 7 times. And roughly 60 percent of their total offensive plays were rushes between the tackles.[13]

But there was a difference between Sutherland and Bierman when it came to how they used the run. Sutherland wanted to control the pace of the game, eat clock, and break his opponent's spirit via brutal line thrusts. Bierman designed his running plays to break big. Most of the Gophers' run plays were from the Buck series, which in modern terms was a sophisticated play-action run sequence. Down-field blocking was continually preached as the key to making these long runs become *loooong* runs. Unlike Sutherland, Bierman didn't want to disable your line and grind you to dust; he wanted to blow through your line for long jaunts. Instead of victory through sadism, he believed in winning with a practical scheme that balanced safety with explosive possibilities. The hunt for big plays was about the only thing Schmidt and Bierman had in common, but their methods were polar opposites, as were their personalities.

Bernie Bierman was aloof, stoic, and cold. He didn't seek laughter and he didn't offer praise. Some of this had to do with his learned notion of separation between coach and player, and some of it was due to the fact that he simply wasn't a natural-born communicator. Though not verbose, he was far from being disengaged. He was a perfectionist who understood what he wanted out of practice to the nth degree. Bierman was not close to his players, and there were times during his arduous practices that some even hated him, but they all respected him and had complete faith in his brand of football.

Bierman's football strategy was just as practical as he was: "This great college game hasn't changed much throughout a long period of years," he proudly declared. "Look back through history and you'll find that champions of every conference were soundly schooled in the same rudiments." While Bierman was busy perfecting history, Schmidt and his disciples were tinkering with the future. Victorian football and the open-game movement were like surly brothers-in-law. Neither understood—or even really liked—the other, yet every now and then they ended up seated together for some holiday meal, much to the delight of curious onlookers hoping to see some sparks fly. Minnesota versus Ohio State *was* that meal, minus the provocative mother-in-law. After eight years of the two teams' being separated, football followers were ready for a pent-up storm.[14]

The train to Minnesota was scheduled to leave Thursday evening, so Schmidt had the team practice one last time late that afternoon. This was designed to be a fun practice, and the boys spent most of it running around attempting every fancy ball-tossing play they could imagine. Suddenly an urgent message interrupted their romp: the special train to Minnesota was almost ready to leave. Schmidt had lost track of time. The players bolted to the dressing room where a comical flurry of dressing, showering, and packing ensued. They arrived at the station just in time, only to be met by a different brand of chaos. A raucous crowd had gathered for the send-off, and they were already in high spirits, having cheered the 127 members of the marching band as they boarded the train followed by Ohio governor John Bricker and his wife. The frenzied mass now cheered with abandon as the disheveled football team arrived at the last instant and hurriedly boarded the train. As the train slowly moved out of the station to begin its 850-mile trek, a grinning Schmidt whipped the crowd into a final round of hysteria. In an unusual acknowledgement of the need for stopping the ball, Schmidt hollered, "If we've got the defense we think we have, we'll take 'em like we took those other fellows." The crowd roared and waved, hopeful that this trip would result in a breakthrough and that Schmidt and company would finally get that big win they were always missing by the narrowest of margins.[15]

The train eventually stopped in Chicago where they spent the night at the Edgewater Beach Hotel. For some players, it was an opportunity to enjoy a little night life. Tom Kinkade visited one of his favorite Chicago hangouts: The Kitty Davis Cocktail Lounge at Jackson and Wabash. "It was sort of a Big 10 headquarters," said Kinkade. "Kitty had pictures of the Big 10 stars all over her walls. She had a merry-go-round with a band sitting in the middle, and as it rotated the band would play Big 10 fight songs. While you sat at the bar you would sing along; everyone would sing. Different people would holler for their school's songs, and of course there was always someone from Northwestern." One could always catch up on sleep during the train ride from Chicago to Minneapolis.[16]

With their contrasting styles, Minnesota and Ohio State had been neck and neck for the conference scoring title ever since Schmidt had arrived in Columbus, so those who attended the game on October 21 were expecting a goodly amount of points, but the two teams kept fifty-five thousand waiting until the middle of the opening quarter before fulfilling expectations. Jim Strausbaugh fumbled a punt, and Minnesota recovered on the 12-yard line. Two end runs later, Minnesota had stuffed the ball in the end zone and took the lead, 7–0. The Buckeyes answered early in the second quarter with consecutive scoring drives. Both touchdowns came on beautiful passes, a 33-yarder from Langhurst to Sarkkinen and a 28-yarder from Strausbaugh to Langhurst. Like a glorious heavyweight boxing match, Minnesota answered with a big punch of their own, returning the ensuing kick 50 yards. After that, the Gophers needed just two plays to regain the lead, 14–13. One of their trademark long runs—a 38-yarder—had accounted for the touchdown. The final score of the first half came with 48 seconds remaining when Charley Maag, Ohio's 210-pound tackle, hit a 32-yard field goal from a very difficult angle, giving Ohio State a 16–14 lead.[17]

Shocked to be trailing at home and caught up in Ohio's pace, the Gophers strayed a bit from their usual formula and tried to open up in the second half. The results were mixed. On Minnesota's opening drive they tried a rare downfield lateral. It went amiss, and Ohio recovered. This time Don Scott did the throwing, and he unleashed a perfect spiral covering nearly 50 yards that fell into Frank Clair's hands as he crossed the goal line. Ohio State now held a 23–14 lead, with all 3 touchdowns having come on passes from different throwers. The score remained the same into the fourth quarter, putting the Gophers in an unusual position. With nothing to lose, they broke out a couple forward passes, and one of them resulted in a touchdown that cut Ohio's lead to 23–20. A few minutes later Jim Langhurst found a hole in the Gopher line and sprinted 81 yards for a huge score that sealed the victory for Ohio State. Except it didn't count. Much to the dismay of the thousands of fans listening to the game on their radios in Ohio, the play was called back. "Backfield in motion" was the official's call. Two plays later Ohio State fumbled on their *own* 15-yard line, and Minnesota recovered with just over three minutes remaining. Schmidt argued that the runner had been down when the ball came loose, but to no avail. Either way, letting the ball get loose at this time and place was an egregious error that Bierman's and Sutherland's teams simply did not allow to happen. It did happen in Schmidt's offense, however, where they tried to do too much, the 1935 Notre Dame game being the ultimate example. And now it looked like Schmidt's boys were giving away yet another big game. With the winning touchdown only 15 yards away, Minnesota returned to their sane, traditional strategy. Using three straight line plunges, the Gophers moved the ball 9 yards to Ohio's 6-yard line. It was fourth and inches with two minutes to go. With so much faith in their run game and so little faith in kicking, the Gophers decided to go for it. It was another safe inside plunge, this time good for 2 yards and a first down. But there was a penalty. Holding was called on Minnesota, and the ball was moved back 15 yards. The crowd groaned. Now the Gophers had no choice but to go for the field goal. Being a little farther out actually improved the angle of the kick, but 38 yards was stretching the range of accuracy. Joe Mernik was called on to make it a tie game. With the packed stadium on its feet, Mernik hit the ball strongly, but it drifted left. After hanging in the air for what seemed like an eternity, the pigskin hit the left upright, then "struck the center bar of the goalposts, bobbled a split second, and then dropped back," into the field of play. No good. The Buckeyes had dodged a bullet. Overcome with the joy of thanksgiving, the Buckeyes were not about to razzle *or* dazzle. They sat on the ball and punted with less than a minute left in the game. Minnesota had one last chance. Well, actually two chances. The first long pass was intercepted by Jack Graf, but the Buckeyes were guilty of holding on the play. Minnesota took the penalty yardage and cranked up another long pass. This time it was intended for George Franck, a speedy back they had lined up at end, hoping he could blow by everybody, but once again Jack Graf was waiting, and this time his interception counted as he held on, landing at the 5-yard line. Ohio State had won 23–20—the biggest victory in Schmidt's six years, and he had done it his way, with a large assortment of well-executed plays that had kept Minnesota off-balance all day. Especially effective was the Buckeyes' forward passing. They completed 10 of 13 for 168 yards and 3 touchdowns.[18]

The combined 43 points scored by the two teams would be considered tame by today's standards, but it was substantial in 1939. It's even more impressive when placed in microcontext: the 23 points surrendered by Minnesota were the most ever allowed in a single game during Bierman's prewar dynasty (1932–41) and the 20 points surrendered by Ohio State were the most they had ever allowed in the 43 games since Schmidt's hiring.

Afterward, both men were angry about the officiating and pointed to multiple calls that had disrupted their chances, but Schmidt wasn't as angry as he might have been. His Ohio team had finally won a major showdown and had been the first to win at Minneapolis since Michigan beat the Gophers 3–0 in 1932.

For the third time in Schmidt's tenure, the Buckeyes were in a position to compete for the national title. They were ranked No. 4 in the AP poll with only two more substantial hurdles to overcome: Cornell and Michigan. The first of these was coming up the next Saturday when Cornell traveled to Columbus. The Big Red were ranked No. 7 in the nation with one of their best squads ever. Gomer Jones had traveled to Ithaca, New York, to watch Cornell play Syracuse and—two weeks later—Penn State. He thought they were the best in the East. Schmidt was worried about any game that followed an emotional battle like the one they had just waged with Minnesota.[19]

Cornell had also been scouting Ohio State. Their scout, Russ Murphy, had seen all three Buckeye games, and he painted a dark picture for head coach, Carl Snavely—so dark that Snavely was already planning for trouble: "They're not going to ruin my team for the rest of the season. If Ohio runs up an early lead—and I don't see how we hope to harness its power—I am going to use my subs and save our regulars for future Ivy League dates. We have a typical

Ivy League team this year and have no business tangling with a Big 10 power house." It's true that the Ivy League was no longer important in college football—thanks to self-imposed amateurism standards—but this Big Red squad was the real thing. They had finished twelfth in the nation a year ago, and all of their elite players were back. It seemed that Snavely's woe-is-me act was simply for show. Schmidt wasn't buying it. He knew Cornell was the best team they would face all season, and the stress of meeting them on the heels of Minnesota was overwhelming. On Friday he tried to take his mind off the game by going duck hunting.[20]

Winning Big 10 games was hard enough, but St. John's sadistic scheduling of tough nonconference foes was killing Schmidt and aging him prematurely. It seemed like every season was rendered a disappointment by his losing to one of these juggernauts in some heart-breaking fashion. Notre Dame ('35, '36), Pittsburgh ('36), and Southern Cal ('37, '38) had all been losses for Schmidt. Each game had been decided by a touchdown or less, and four of the five had been decided late in the fourth quarter. Once again, an unforgettable season hung in the balance, and once again an elite nonconference game was the deciding factor. If the current Buckeyes had any advantage over previous squads it was that they were Schmidt's most enthusiastic squad to date, full of concern for each other and quick to demonstrate their brotherly camaraderie through laughter and friendly backslapping. If the '34 and '35 teams had been the most talented, then the '39 squad was certainly the most impassioned. They had boundless optimism and rivaled Schmidt in the amount of effort they were willing to put forth.[21]

There was, however, one thing that all Schmidt teams had in common, and it kept fans and writers on edge. "When the fancy stuff is clicking as it did at times against Minnesota," wrote newspaperman Steve Snider, "the Bucks are terrific. When it misfires—it did that against Minnesota, too—anything can happen . . . the danger now is that some alert underdog will snag one of these dipsy-doo shovel passes or laterals the Bucks habitually toss whether they're on your 2-yard line or their own, and another Scarlet Scourge will be just Scarlet." The high risk–high reward offense that Schmidt preached was thrilling to watch, but for Buckeye fans it was also unnerving— like watching a drunken man cross a busy intersection or a woman with a short skirt on a windy day. Ohio State fans barely had time to exhale following the Minnesota game, and it was already time for Cornell, an even better squad.[22]

A freezing wind and snow flurries limited the Ohio Stadium crowd to 49,583, but those who did attend stayed warm with lots of cheering and clapping. The Buckeyes were a precision machine, dominating right from the start. Early in the second period they made it 14–0 on a spectacular run by Don Scott. It was only a 7-yard scamper, but it followed a fumbled snap that left Scott looking trapped and doomed in his backfield. Using every move he had, he avoided the clutches of Cornell's defense, picking his way through disaster and eventually into the end zone. At this point, Snavely either kept his promise to substitute early if things looked bad or he decided new energy was needed. He sent in some backups, and Schmidt, sensing this was a good time to rest his stars, replaced Scott and Langhurst with Jack Graf and Johnny Rabb. On the very first play following the kickoff, Cornell substitute Walter Scholl—a 159-pound jitterbug—took the ball, and proceeded to weave his way through the Buckeyes before finding open field and outrunning everyone for a 79-yard touchdown. Five minutes later, a stunned Buckeye crowd watched Scholl throw a touchdown pass to Jack Bohrman that covered 62 yards. Both plays had gone through Rabb and Graf, and just like that the Ohio lead at halftime had been trimmed to 14–13. In the locker room, the Buckeye players remained confident. Except for the two long plays they had allowed, they were clearly the superior team. Schmidt and the players agreed that they should continue with their wide-open offense.[23]

So, in the second half Ohio State continued to employ razzle-dazzle as they had planned, but they lacked precision. Cornell was starting to gain momentum. The Big Red team's one great attribute was tremendous football intelligence. They understood the game, and their split-second decisions always seemed to be the right ones. This was evidenced in the second half when the Buckeyes quick kicked a few times. Ohio got its desired result as the ball sailed over the safety's head, but each time, Cornell would regroup on the fly, amass impromptu blocking, and turn the problem into a positive with good returns. The Big Red were too tenacious, too fundamentally sound. They slowed the game down and made the most of their breaks in the second half, adding 10 more points while frustrating the Buckeyes' offense. Cornell won the game 23–14 despite having achieved only 8 first downs all day. Sportswriter Henry McLemore wrote afterward, "Ohio State knocked the ivy off Cornell with two quick touchdowns—and then found barbed wire underneath." There wasn't anything wrong with the spirit or aptitude of the 1939 Buckeyes, they had just met a team that knew how to take care of business. Buckeye fans agreed, but they also wondered if Schmidt's razzle-dazzle and insatiable substituting weren't partially responsible once again. The great teams of this era simply did not surrender 2-touchdown leads; they saved their energy for defense and punted and punted, playing the field-position game. Bierman, Sutherland, and Neyland never opened things up when they were in the lead, and they never fooled with a good lineup.[24]

Despite all the grumbling, Schmidt still thought he had an excellent team in a fine position to win the Big 10 title. Their optimistic spirit was on full display the following Saturday when they hosted Indiana. For the last three seasons, Indiana had given the Buckeyes fits, allowing a total of 13 points and pulling off the huge upset in

1937. This time Ohio made sure the game was never in doubt, winning easily 24–0. Don Scott led the offense to nearly 300 total yards, and Jim Langhurst scored twice. Until the very end when Schmidt unleashed a blizzard of low-rung substitutes, Indiana could muster but a single first down and had 2 yards to show for their passing "attack." The win, coupled with a Michigan loss, left the Buckeyes as the only Big 10 team without a conference defeat.[25]

Don Scott was becoming increasingly comfortable at quarterback with every game he played. His dominating performance against Indiana made news within the football establishment. Some were already whispering that Scott might be the best quarterback in the nation for 1940, his senior year. Such talk was hard to imagine just a few months earlier, but Scott had always been a tremendous athlete with the potential for greatness. At Canton McKinley High School (OH) he had been an all-state tackle. Intrigued by his size (215 pounds) and athleticism, Schmidt had tried to make him a left halfback. The experiment progressed well when Scott was a freshman, but his sophomore year had been forgettable. After playing nearly the entire season-opener game in 1938, Scott's playing time diminished steadily throughout the season, culminating in a meager nine minutes on the field versus Michigan in the final game. As part of his routine tinkering, Schmidt had tried Scott at quarterback in the spring, just as he had the year before, but this time with more determination. The switch finally took, and Scott's transformation was amazing. Whether it was due to a little extra maturity or the swagger that comes with being the guy in charge, Scott had risen from flop to fantastic. He was among the nation's leaders in passing and punting and was a genuine threat when running the ball. His blocking continued to be punishing, and during the season he hit 13 of 15 extra-point kicks. Schmidt was impressed, saying, "I can't remember a back as dangerous in so many departments of play. Only comparison I can make is with Ivan Grove."

Scott's next opportunity to shine would probably be a brief one. Ohio State was headed to Chicago, and the starters didn't figure on seeing much playing time.[26]

Chicago's football program was now on its deathbed. Of their last 23 games, they had won but 3, beating Beloit, DePauw, and Wabash. Their last 3 games against Harvard, Michigan, and Virginia had been losses with a combined score of 193–0. The program that Amos Alonzo Stagg had built was now shockingly embarrassing. A growing faction of Chicago's supporters was now calling for a merciful end to the intercollegiate football program. Nurture it or kill it, they begged, but don't let it suffer endless humiliations. Unfortunately, three games remained to be played in 1939—all of them at home—and the worst of the lot was coming up next.

Hosting an Ohio State team that held a 178–20 scoring advantage during the Schmidt era seemed like cruel and unusual punishment for Chicago's death-row program. One writer previewed the game as a "name-your-own-score exhibition" and predicted that Schmidt, "a free-substituter who kept press-box inhabitants dizzy with new Ohio State names . . . likely will surpass his previous efforts." Schmidt's traveling party reflected just how hapless a situation this was. He brought with him just one coach (Godfrey) along with most of the fourth stringers, teammates who rarely played and were almost never part of the concise traveling list.[27]

By no coincidence, the attendance total at Stagg field was as embarrassing as the home team's prospects. A pathetic "crowd" of three thousand showed up for the massacre, and this was on homecoming weekend in Chicago. Though Schmidt claimed he was not interested in abusing Chicago, he did little in the way of reeling his boys in. They seemed to be using this game as an opportunity to practice some of their more interesting plays. The team's stars—Scott, Sarkkinen, and Strausbaugh—all figured in the first-half scoring, which gave osu a 27–0 halftime lead. After that Schmidt began playing the Buckeye substitutes, who had the time of their lives, piling on points with abandon. Even Johnny Rabb returned to the end zone. All told, the pillaging amounted to 473 total yards and included 23 pass attempts. Even with touchdowns called back and fumbles at the goal line, Ohio State enjoyed a 61–0 rout.[28]

Returning to Columbus for their own homecoming weekend, the Buckeyes prepared for another program that had seen better days. Illinois was still competitive, though, and entered the game having won 2 straight conference matches, including a shocking upset of Michigan.

As was becoming a dubious tradition, the game between Illinois and Ohio State was greeted with dreary weather. This time it was a drizzling rain that made things sloppy from the start. The game's first snap from scrimmage got past Strausbaugh and was recovered 8 yards from the end zone by Illinois. It was the first of 7 fumbles lost between the two teams. It was also the best field position Illinois would enjoy all day, and after gambling and losing on fourth down, the Buckeyes took over and marched 93 yards for a touchdown, Strausbaugh hitting Don Scott for 26 yards on his first pass attempt in a regulation game. Early in the second period, Strausbaugh scored on a spectacular 20-yard end run wherein several different Illini had clear shots at the halfback but none could halt him. With a nice lead and increasingly slippery conditions, Schmidt substituted like a man possessed, with thirty-two men coming in and out of the game throughout the second half. Even in bad weather the Buckeyes totaled 336 total yards to Illinois's 139. The final score was 21–0 in favor of Ohio State, but it was a costly victory in that Ohio lost its most powerful runner for the season when Jim Langhurst suffered a knee injury. Still, with this win, the Buckeyes had clinched a share of the conference crown, and only a season-ending victory over Michigan stood between Schmidt and redemption for his much-maligned system.[29]

The 1939 Ohio State–Michigan game was already an oddity before it started. For over three decades, the Big 10 Conference held firmly that no games should be played on Thanksgiving Day or thereafter. Their rationale was that players shouldn't have to practice during the holidays, and for schools such as osu that operated under the quarter system, first-quarter finals were just around the corner. This year, however, President Roosevelt had moved Thanksgiving from the last Thursday in November to the fourth Thursday. Combining this with the Buckeyes' later than usual start in 1939 (October 7) meant that the osu football players and coaches would not be enjoying the four-day weekend as a vacation. Schmidt even had them practice Thanksgiving morning, although he probably needed the vacation more than anyone. The pressure to beat Michigan and the possibility of an outright conference title were making Schmidt even more intense than usual.

On Saturday, when the Buckeyes' train from Dearborn to Ann Arbor was delayed, Schmidt made a spectacle of himself. Having planned it so that the team would arrive close to game time and avoid the Ann Arbor hysteria, Schmidt had not allowed room for things to go wrong. The train's delay was no fault of the engineer, but a stressed-out Schmidt had to vent to someone. He climbed off the team car and slipped around in the loose rock next to the rails before gaining traction and storming toward the engine. His loud ranting and cussing began with his first step and continued unabated as players, travelers, and newspapermen hung their heads out windows and watched him storm toward the engine. The engineers argued their case: there were too many "specials" and not enough tracks. Schmidt unloaded a large helping of berserk before stalking back to his seat. The players made every effort not to make eye contact with their irrational coach. When the train finally pulled onto the stadium railroad siding only fifteen minutes before kickoff, a veritable jailbreak commenced. Players poured out of the railcar and scrambled up the steep slope between the siding and the stadium. They still had to be taped, had to put on their uniforms, and had to stretch. Schmidt, meanwhile, argued with the referees, seeking a delay to the kickoff. The officials had rules to follow, they claimed, and it was up to Michigan, the host school, to grant leniency. The hosts were not sympathetic and allowed only a five-minute delay.[30]

So it was that the Buckeyes raced onto the field before a delirious crowd of 80,227. Some of the players were not properly taped, and none of them were in their usual game-time mindset, but they had adrenaline and anger working for them, which paid off handsomely. The Buckeyes raced to an early 14–0 lead, both scores coming off forward passes from Don Scott. One was to end Frank Clair and the other was to Vic Marino, a guard who had lined up as an end before drifting to the back of the end zone where he snagged an easy pass thrown against misdirection. The offense was really in synch, but lost fumbles thwarted subsequent scoring chances. On defense the Buckeyes were determined to stop the great Tom Harmon, stacking the line with seven men and daring Harmon to pass. The strategy was initially successful, but Harmon soon found a rhythm and ended up completing 11 of 18, including 1 for a touchdown. He also scored 1 on the ground as the Wolverines fought back to tie the score at 14–14 halfway through the third quarter. The two teams spent the next twenty-five minutes pounding each other with all the dead-legged emotion afforded two bitter enemies, neither getting close to the other's goal. Finally, the Buckeyes mounted a drive, steadily moving through enemy territory and closing in on the game-winning score when Jim Strausbaugh took a vicious hit that caused him to fumble. The ball was recovered by Michigan's Bob Westfall with just over four minutes left in the game. Taking over at their own 37, the Wolverines knew this was probably their last good opportunity and rose to the occasion. Tom

Harmon and Bob Westfall combined to muscle some runs and complete 3 big passes, one of them to Ed Czak, an Ed Yeckley recruit.
With less than two minutes to play, Michigan arrived at the Ohio
6-yard line. It looked like another Buckeye collapse, but Ohio State
refused to roll over to their sworn enemies. They sacked Harmon
twice and forced him out of bounds on a sweep for no gain, leaving
the Wolverines at fourth down and goal from the 24. With less than
a minute left, Fritz Crisler cleverly sent in Bob Ingalls, a center who
reported as quarterback so he could relay the next play to the Michigan players on the field. After breaking huddle, Fred Trosko, the
kick holder, took his place at the 31-yard line, and Tommy Harmon
prepared to attempt the 41-yard game-winning boot. The snap to
Trosko was clean, and the Buckeye front wall did everything they
could to block the kick, but the kick didn't happen. Trosko pulled
the ball away from Harmon's foot, and Harmon—never slowing
down—ran around left end and began blocking down the sideline. The intentional fake caught Ohio State completely off guard,
and Schmidt watched helplessly as Trosko—still holding the ball—
sprinted down the sideline behind a Wolverine blocking contingent that had grown to five men. The Ann Arbor faithful unleashed
a deafening roar as Trosko crossed the goal line with fifty seconds
left in the game. Harmon kicked his third PAT to make the score
21–14 in Michigan's favor.[31]

The easy success of the fake kick should never have been allowed to happen. The center reporting as quarterback should have
sounded alarms for Ohio State, and sending the entire front wall
to try blocking an already high-risk kick left them completely vulnerable. Still, there was a little time left for a possible game-tying
touchdown.

Michigan, trying to keep the ball from being returned, ended up
kicking out of bounds. Starting at his own 35, Don Scott took what
the Wolverine prevent defense would give and picked up 38 yards

on back-to-back scrambles. There was time for only one more play, and Scott had to make sure his throw reached the end zone. Ohio snapped the ball at Michigan's 23-yard line, and Scott waited for his receivers to flood the end zone before unloading one final heave. Plenty of prospective recipients were waiting as the ball crossed the goal line, but only one man was able to snag it: Bob Westfall of Michigan. The clock ran out almost as he hit the turf, setting off a frenzied celebration amongst the Wolverine faithful in the stands about their first home win over Ohio State in six years.[32]

Statistically, it was a sloppy game as Ohio lost 4 fumbles and Michigan was intercepted 4 times. Both teams missed scoring opportunities throughout, but Michigan had been terrific when it counted, using 12 plays to set up the winning score.[33]

Afterward, Schmidt sat on a bench in the locker room, seemingly in a despondent trance while answering reporters' questions. "We just outfumbled them, that's all," he explained. "You can't do that in a tight ball game and expect to come out on top. As for Michigan, it was the best team we played all year, and you have my word for that."[34]

In the home-team locker room, Fritz Crisler smiled and waved his hands like a conductor as the players half-chanted, half-sung "Yea Harmon" and "Yea Trosko." For some time the room was thick with supporters and laughter before the visitors finally began to trickle out and the players changed clothes. Only then could Crisler talk to reporters. "It certainly was a tough one for the other side to lose," he admitted. "To do it twice in a season, after being out in front by two touchdowns, certainly is tough."[35]

For Ohio State fans, "tough" was an understatement. Not only was this the second time in one season that they had blown a 14–0 lead—something that was simply not done in this era—but this time it had been against archrival Michigan, and it had knocked them into a tie for the Big 10 championship. Iowa (6-1), also with a single conference loss, needed only a win at Northwestern (3-4) to share the crown with the Buckeyes. Half an hour after the Ohio State–Michigan contest had ended, the final report from Evanston arrived: Iowa and Northwestern had played to a 7–7 tie, thus wrecking Iowa's dream and leaving Ohio State the sole conference champion. It was Ohio State's first outright conference football title in nineteen years.

Ohio State had attained its goal. The players and coaches celebrated but also felt a certain amount of restraint. They'd lost to Michigan, and their title had come by way of the back door. Even if they *tried* to see the glass half full, the press made sure to illuminate the void. One wire service recap began by saying, "Ohio State University won the Western Conference football championship today in much the same manner that Max Schmeling won the world heavyweight title—flat on his back." Even in victory, Schmidt could not avoid controversy, but he smiled and thoroughly enjoyed the championship. So did Ohio.[36]

The football banquet, now hosted by a campus booster group called "Ohio Staters, Inc.," was bigger than ever. Rows upon rows of folding tables were set up in the Men's Gym, topped with white linen and surrounded by wooden folding chairs. In all, some 1,100 attended the festivity, a substantial dinner gathering by anyone's definition. Of the players in attendance, 41 of them received small gold footballs suitable for wearing on one's vest chain and emblematic of a Western Conference champion. Schmidt, who also had four tiny gold pants hanging from his vest chain, cleverly told the assembled, "We've got the championship, but unfortunately Michigan stole our pants."[37]

He had to be happy nonetheless—happy that he had pleased Ohio, happy that he had probably salvaged his job, and happy that his team had bounced back from a bad season in 1938. Plus, after having his futuristic system doubted by many, Schmidt was able to have one final laugh. His 1939 Buckeyes led the nation in total yardage. For Schmidt, there was no greater validation than having a team using his system gain more yards per game than any other major college football team in America.

The rest of the statistics were a mixed bag but offered a pretty accurate representation of a team coached by Francis Schmidt. A total of 386,362 spectators had watched Schmidt's boys, which again led the conference, even though the number was the smallest since 1934. Unusually bad weather and the tiny number of attendees (3,000) at Chicago's death watch hadn't helped. On the field, the 1939 Buckeyes led the Big 10 in most yards gained (1730) and fewest yards surrendered (502). The Buckeyes also led two other conference categories that were often seen as benchmarks for the Schmidt system: punting average (42.2) thanks in part to the quick kicking, and number of fumbles (24 total, with 11 lost) due to all the ballhandling.[38]

For those who preferred using comparative game results for measuring things, the bottom line was a bit confusing. In this case, Ohio State (No. 15) had blown 14-point leads and lost to Cornell (No. 4) and Michigan (No. 20), yet they had trounced Missouri (No. 6) and handed Minnesota its first home-conference loss since 1932.

Even with the title, the ranking, and the total-yardage crown, Schmidt and Ohio State were at a crossroads. The second of Schmidt's three-year contracts was just a few months from expiring, and the athletic board now had to consider how they would proceed. They were not inclined to jettison a coach after a championship season, but were they brave enough to commit another three years to man who was getting progressively crazier? School officials had already asked him to "calm down his abusive tactics on the practice field." He was too intense and too caustic for a collegiate setting, and his swearing was such that the school found it uncomfortable to allow any guests to wander near a practice session, let alone view one. Schmidt wasn't particularly close to the players, and his coaches were frustrated at being underutilized. Schmidt's discipline was becoming more erratic, and his paranoia was becoming troublesome. Sure that everyone was out to steal his sacred diagrams, he continued locking them up, not even granting full access to his assistants. He had a way of making people feel confused for loving him. For their part, however, the students had never wavered in their adoration for Schmidt. Following the Michigan loss, one of the local sports editors asked his readers whether they thought Schmidt should be retained. Based on the letters he received, the answer was "ten to one in favor of retaining Francis Schmidt." As for the team's performance, the Buckeyes were always *good* but always lost the big games that kept them from being *great*. Then again, Schmidt's offensive scheme was spellbinding, and it drew large crowds, which meant large paydays. And if all this conflicting information wasn't enough to consider, Ohio State's stance was further complicated by the fact that other schools were showing a renewed interest in Schmidt's services.[39]

Of particular note was the flirting between Schmidt and Stanford University. The rumors surfaced two days after the season ended and gained traction during Schmidt's annual trip to the West Coast, where he hobnobbed with other coaches and took in the Rose Bowl game. Stanford wanted Schmidt, and they had plenty to offer. Besides "climactic conditions" that were perfect for razzle-dazzle, there was a five-year contract that included a sizeable increase in salary. Schmidt liked money, and he had a track record for exploring greener pastures every few years, but he was content to remain at Ohio State and offered Stanford only token encouragement. But Schmidt was Stanford's first choice for head coach, and they continued to pursue him throughout his three-week stay on the coast, seeking a final answer one way or the other. Schmidt was in no hurry to decide. You see, St. John and some other Buckeye athletic officials were also part of the traveling party that was soaking up the sunshine, and for leverage reasons, Schmidt was hoping they might take note of Stanford's infatuation. Schmidt used all of his wiles to drag the chase out for three weeks, dropping hints and causing suspicions the whole time. Then just before the Buckeye contingent headed back home, Schmidt finally gave Stanford a flat refusal. When the group arrived back in Ohio, the press asked Schmidt about Stanford. Just as he had in 1937 when Texas pursued him, Schmidt let it be known that he had been stalked by Stanford but wanted to stay in Columbus if the school was interested. The whirling dervish could play coy quite nicely when he needed to. Both parties agreed to a gentleman's pact for three more seasons, but each side knew that the end could come sooner. As for Stanford, they immediately signed their second choice, Clark Shaughnessy. Ironically, it was Shaughnessy's declining of the Ohio State job that had cleared the path for Schmidt. The roles were now reversed, and for Shaughnessy it meant a fortuitous escape from the flatlining Chicago program. One of the first telegrams of congratulations he received was from Schmidt, who claimed that Stanford was "ripe for revival of football."[40]

Shaughnessy would not miss playing Schmidt's Buckeyes on an annual basis, having gone 0-6 and losing by a cumulative score of 238–20. Actually, nobody was particularly enjoying Saturdays with the Scarlet Scourge. So far, in Schmidt's six seasons, the Buckeyes had won 2 conference titles and had finished in second place another 3 times. They had outgained their opponents 307 total yards per game to 175, and had handily outscored them 23 points per game to 6. If the victims found any solace, it's that this entire razzle-dazzle was done in front of an average crowd of 45,543, one of the largest averages in the nation, and thus one of the largest paydays

for opponents. Yet most observers—Ohio fans and enemies alike—
felt like the Buckeyes could be even better and were openly wondering if Schmidt's behavior and his obsession with offensive strategy weren't actually stumbling blocks.[41]

The 1940 football season would determine the fate of Schmidt's
career.

Twelve. The Cost of Odd

J oe Williams, sports editor of the *Syracuse (New York) Herald-Journal,* had just finished covering the World Series in Cincinnati and decided to interrupt his train ride home with a stopover in Columbus. It would be a great chance to check out Ohio State's football program. Not only were Francis Schmidt's Buckeyes one of the most talked-about teams in the nation, but in three weeks they would be in New York, playing a highly anticipated game against Cornell, the team that was ranked No. 1 in the country. It was a perfect opportunity for Williams to gather information for the big game and to finally meet Francis Schmidt, who was "supposed to be the most colorful coach in America." If by "colorful" Williams meant "intense and nearly crazy," he was on the right track. As Williams wandered into the Buckeyes' football locker room he was taken aback by what he saw. It looked like something created by the Mad Hatter. Slowly turning his head to take in each wall, he was amazed to see they were covered with pages and pages of diagrams as though wallpapered.[1]

"There are literally hundreds of these plays hanging on the wall. They are not the conventional black and white creations, either. Mr. Schmidt has the soul of an artist. He enlivens his football doodlings with soft yellows, angry reds, and alluring purples. The effect, if baffling to the mind, is soothing to the eyes. You find yourself thinking of a sunset in the Swiss Alps.

"On one of the wall pieces is a diagram of an old play. It carries the inscription: 'This is the play that cost Ohio State the 1936 championship against Northwestern.' The mistakes that the boys made in the play are sharply indicated. The members of the 1936 varsity have long since passed from the campus, but a detailed record of their crime still hangs on the wall of the dressing room, a static warning to a newer and younger age.

"We were mildly astonished at the easy informality of the place," continued Williams. "Apparently total strangers are not discouraged from strolling into the dressing room and digesting the Schmidt masterpieces at length.

"We commented on this to Lew Byrer, the able local gazetteer. Mr. Byrer shrugged his shoulders. . . . 'Nobody knows what they mean anyway, and I doubt if even Schmidt does.'"[2]

Mr. Williams's confusion is understandable. First, the coaches he knew used only two or three dozen plays. Second, most coaches were reticent about making their plays overtly public. Schmidt also worried about his best plays being seen—even by his own players—and kept them under lock and key. What Joe Williams couldn't know was that most of these hundreds of plays before him were just the leftovers—the old, the incomplete, and the basic. If he thought the amount of plays he was looking at was insane, then the truth would have surely blown his mind.

Still marveling at this diagram gallery, Williams was told by another local reporter that Schmidt was always adding plays to the wall after games, usually with wrathful notations. On a play used during a Michigan game he had scrawled, 'Only a louse would make a play like this.'

Williams knew "it was generally conceded that Mr. Schmidt can rig up the most fantastic plays in football," and he also knew that

"Mr. Schmidt has a gift for the barbed word and the streaming invective," but he had never imagined there was a shrine dedicated to both.[3]

Williams took in one more panoramic glance of the wall-to-wall art before leaving the dressing room and moving on to Schmidt's office, which was adjacent. The Mad Hatter himself was sitting at his desk, studying scouting reports on Northwestern, his upcoming opponent. Williams introduced himself and the paper he worked for. Schmidt, with his large, fake smile welcomed the visitor with all the sincerity he could muster before promptly returning half his attention to the scouting reports. Knowing where the reporter had just come from, Schmidt offered up small talk on the World Series, commenting on the prowess of Reds pitcher Paul Derringer. But he was "giving us one eye and keeping the other on the diagrams," recalled Williams. Their small talk about football continued, and then Schmidt did focus just long enough to unleash a diatribe about his favorite subject: the impossible schedule his boys faced. Ultimately, Williams accepted that he had little command over Schmidt's attention. The coach was preoccupied with diagrams—those formulas that owned his brain—and the forced chitchat was beginning to make him "nervous and fidgety." In an attempt to be properly social, Schmidt was trying to fight his obsessive, impatient nature, but it was almost impossible. Even in the midst of a New York newspaperman who could do more for his reputation than a flock of small-time midwestern sportswriters, Schmidt was unable to prioritize and disengage from his work.

"We sensed he had a lot of things to do," Joe Williams said of Schmidt, "so we paid our respects and moved out quietly. We wish to add, however, that at all times we found him gracious enough. We haven't the slightest doubt that we could have hung around for an hour and bored him with banal questions, and he would have pretended he liked it. In the presence of guests [he is] always smiling—smiling a smile that smokescreens his impatience to get down to the job."[4]

Later, after some more wandering around campus, Williams stopped to watch the Buckeyes practice. He had heard Schmidt was unusual, but as he stood watching the leather-skinned coach direct practice he had time to reflect on just how bizarre Schmidt really was.

"We do not wish to be uncomplimentary to Schmidt," summed up the writer. "Indeed, when we say this we mean just the opposite. His personality seems to personify the kind of wild, lurid, razzle-dazzle football he plays. He looks slightly mad, and hasn't it been said the first mark of genius is madness?"[5]

Call it what you will—madness or genius—but its effects on the program were starting to exhaust those involved. Schmidt was conducting football practice in parts of every month except June, July, and August. The Buckeye football team spent more days practicing than any other team in the conference. Schmidt's combination winter/spring practicing now consumed nearly three months' worth of the early year, and he was becoming more frustrated with those who wanted to play other sports in the "off-season" or—God forbid—just relax without the demands of an athletic training regimen. Unfortunately for him, the boys could only get excited about so much football; they were young and interested in pursuing other things as well. If Schmidt were still coaching a multitude of sports like he did at Tulsa and Arkansas, he'd have agreed with their stance, but as a full-time football coach with no working concept of restraint, he demanded unrealistic commitment to his myopic needs. Realizing they could never please Schmidt, the players simply quit trying in increasing numbers each spring. In 1938 only two of eleven starters (Kaplanoff and Schoenbaum) were available for full spring practice. And in 1940 the situation was worse in that none of his five quarterbacks were available for spring ball. Of the four backup quarterbacks, one was playing on the school golf team, two were ineligible, and Jack Graf was healing from a knee operation. But what really angered Schmidt was Don Scott's decision to join the school's baseball team along with halfback Jim Sexton and others. Don Scott was Schmidt's starting quarterback, an All-American candidate and the main cog in Ohio State's football team. As much as Schmidt's system was built to spread the load, it still functioned best with the right man in the driver's seat. And for a guy with only one year of experience playing quarterback and a multitude of plays to learn, missing spring ball was a killer. Worst of all, from Schmidt's prejudiced standpoint, Scott was being silly, playing on the baseball team after he had skipped it during his first two years of college. Scott, however, just wanted to make the most of his time in college, to experience all that it had to offer. Baseball was fun, and he was good at it. This impasse between coach and player was the beginning of an unexpected year for both.[6]

Perhaps Schmidt wouldn't have been rendered helpless if he'd been able to help himself. Two of his backup quarterbacks' being ineligible was a sin that should never have been committed. There are always players who are going to have academic problems no matter what the coaching staff does, but an organized coach will work to minimize this problem. For boys who never claimed to be scholars-in-training—like Tom Kinkade—a coach must pay extra attention. Left to their own devices, students would usually let studying slide to the bottom of their priority lists. Not surprisingly, Kinkade was another academic casualty who found himself unable to join spring practice in 1940. The *Coshocton (Ohio) Tribune* offered a frank assessment (unusual for the era where a student was concerned) saying, "Kinkade has the ability to become a star if he stays eligible and gets ambition." Unfortunately, Schmidt had been unable to maximize Kinkade's potential the previous season. And

Charley Anderson, the immensely talented end, would flunk out of school in the fall.[7]

Though these problems were not entirely Schmidt's fault, mentoring was definitely not his strength. He tended to view personnel issues from the standpoint of a helpless outsider. Near the end of spring practice, he even complained to reporters, "We're having trouble getting the older boys to come regularly to practice," as though the matter were out of his hands. The threat of discipline may have increased practice attendance, but Schmidt had already proven that his edicts were flimsy. From his first season when he had allowed the players to override his substitution choice during the Iowa game, until last season when he had allowed Frank Smith to return to the team after the players protested his suspension, Schmidt had undermined his own authority.[8]

To be sure, this team could probably survive—if not thrive—on its athleticism and football skill alone. A few days before fall practice opened, Schmidt told sportswriter Fritz Howell, "We'll have a good team this year, and there's no argument about it. We'll be lighter than last year but we'll be more experienced, faster, and trickier. You'll see a lot more razzle-dazzle this year, with plenty of shovel and lateral passing." As fall practice progressed, Schmidt appeared to be in better humor on the practice field than anyone remembered before. "We're going to play wide-open football," he reminded writers a week before the season opened. "We have good ballhandlers. They're fast, too. If we score first and faster they can't beat us." The last sentence was, and always had been, the mission statement for the Schmidt system. Don't worry about field position, or waiting for turnovers, or clock management. Worry about scoring first and fastest.

While it was nice that his grandiose view of himself and his offense had not wavered, there was another side of him—the paranoid and insecure side—that was always prepared for the worst. On this same September day that he was verbally strutting for reporters, a special preseason article he wrote for the UP hit the papers, and it was a dire treatise on Ohio State's prospects for 1940. "We start football at Ohio State this fall under the handicap of having so many people picking us to have an outstanding team. . . . We have had just as big losses from graduation as the other schools in the conference. For example, we lost our two top left ends, one of them All-American Esco Sarkkinen; four senior left guards; two lettermen at center; two lettermen at right halfback; and two good lettermen reserve fullbacks. . . . I might mention here that our freshman team last year was probably the poorest since I came to Ohio State in 1934, and I can't see that any of the sophomores will be good enough for the starting lineup at least early in the season." Of course, it wouldn't be a total apocalypse without that impossibly difficult schedule, and Schmidt sounded like a desperate child when he proclaimed, "The schedule is the toughest we have ever faced, and I really mean this."[9]

Despite Schmidt's recounting of lost players, there was still plenty of experience left in the cupboard. Of the 34 lettermen from last season's Big 10 championship team, 21 were returning, including 7 regulars. Not only that, but Dr. Walter E. Duffee, the team physician, declared this team to be "the finest conditioned squad I've examined in years." This claim would be of significance later.[10]

Once again, fall practice was all about running plays. While Bernie Bierman had his Gophers work on calisthenics and tackling drills on opening day, Schmidt had his boys engaged in full-scale razzle-dazzle from the start. One observer estimated that "two out of every three offensive plays the Bucks brushed up on either started with a lateral or ended with a forward pass." After two days of this, some of the players began hinting that they were ready to do some real hitting, so Schmidt broke tradition and called a scrimmage on the third day, citing their being on a "physical edge." Schmidt much preferred signal drills and stop-action rehearsing of plays. Scrimmages, where the team split up and played realistic games against one another, wore players down, especially in the September heat. And worst of all, they greatly increased the risk of injuries. As a matter of fact, Schmidt usually stopped allowing scrimmages one week before the season started so his players would be healthy and fresh when the action counted.[11]

So it was, as fall practice neared its completion, that Schmidt had the boys scrimmage one last time. And just as Schmidt feared, there was an injury. Jim Strausbaugh, the "Chillicothe Comet" who had battled with the books to stay eligible, severely sprained his ankle. It meant the loss of the Buckeyes' best halfback for the near future. Kinkade was the obvious choice to replace him, but he was also in Schmidt's doghouse for missing spring training due to grades. For now, Strausbaugh's vacancy would be filled by several backs.

The team seemed deep enough to withstand a couple of typical football setbacks, and Schmidt continued plotting his wide-open offense. Schmidt's master playbook, which was already considered obscene for its size in 1934, had grown substantially over the past six years and now included over 500 plays. At the final fall practice Schmidt was seen smiling as he sat on the grass, going through his "fat briefcase of State plays" like a kid rummaging through a toy chest. After much rustling, pulling, and stuffing he selected a few tricky ones and had the boys run them for his delight. The only thing keeping his euphoria in check was the infernal schedule that haunted his mind day and night. "Sure, things are shaping up all right," Schmidt told reporters after practice. "But don't you forget that we're up against one hell of a tough team."[12]

The team he was referencing was the University of Pittsburgh, and the reason he had to remind reporters to be nervous was because this was not the same Panther program that had run roughshod over opponents for twenty-five years. Pitt was still a national behemoth when the 1940 schedule was crafted a couple years earlier, but subsequent internal events had knocked the program off its pedestal. After years of enduring scorn for their semiprofessional approach (players received actual cash to help allay housing and academic expenses), Pitt's new president had decided to deemphasize football. This was not to say they would starve the sport like Chicago did, but it did mean that restoring the school's academic reputation was the new priority. Jock Sutherland had seen the writing on the wall and with great indignation had bailed after the 1938 season. It was all or nothing for the competitive Scotsman. After taking a year off, he had recently cast his lot as an NFL head coach for the Brooklyn Dodgers. Pundits sarcastically wondered if it would be a challenge for him to train lesser-paid players. Without Sutherland's discipline, and their recruiting undermined, Pitt instantly joined the ranks of the mediocre, finishing 5-4 in 1939. It appeared the "new" Panthers were toothless, but Schmidt had a real fear that emotions would rule the day when two neighboring enemies squared off. And besides regional pride, both teams also had long-standing streaks to protect. Pittsburgh had not lost an opening game since 1902, and Ohio State had started with a win every season since 1895. Times were changing, and somebody's streak was going to end on September 28, 1940.

Even after the two teams had played the first half, there were still questions as to their true capabilities. Ohio's razzle-dazzle had garnered a tiny 3–0 lead. Was Pitt really better than everyone thought or was Ohio State really this bland? After a halftime of anticipation, the questions were instantly put to rest. In the first minute of the third quarter, Charley Maag blocked a punt deep in Pittsburgh territory, recovering it himself and running to the 4-yard line. Captain Jim Langhurst scored on the next play. By the end of the quarter, the Buckeyes had scored 2 more touchdowns, and Schmidt was on a substituting binge. The final score was Ohio State 30, Pittsburgh 7. It was the first time the Panthers had given up 30 or more points since getting blown out by USC in the Rose Bowl following the 1933 season. During Jock Sutherland's brilliant fifteen-year run at Pitt, his squads had given up an average of only 44 points *per season*. Followers of the Buckeyes celebrated the win as though they had beaten the old Pitt, but the reality was that this squad represented the end of a great Pitt regime. The 1940 Panthers would finish 3-4-1, their first losing season since 1912. The school would not make a splash on the national scene until Johnny Major's hiring in the 1970s. Schmidt, who had struggled mightily to beat big opponents, was pleased to beat a big name even if it was simply beating the ghost of a dynasty, but he didn't allow himself much time to enjoy it. How could he, with that damned schedule hanging over his head?[13]

Following Monday's practice, Schmidt told reporters the victory would only inspire his opponents. "They've all been 'laying for us' because we're Big 10 champions, and now they'll point at us more than ever because they'll figure we must be pretty tough to beat Pitt like that. Look at what Purdue did to Butler, Minnesota did to Washington, and Michigan did to California Saturday. We have to meet all those winners. Why, we won't have time to take a breath between now and the end of the season." Then, four days later, Schmidt assured reporters, "We'll take care of those Purduers." Two elements of his personality—victor and victim—were widening under the pressure.[14]

At home against Purdue, the Buckeyes got off to a good start. For the third time in their last seven games, Ohio State led 14-0, but just as they had in the other instances, Ohio gave the lead away. The linemen, sloppy against Pitt, had not shown much improvement, especially on defense. Schmidt substituted liberally, trying to regain the momentum that had carried his team to an early lead, but nothing seemed to work. Late in the fourth quarter, with more

Ohio State backups in the lineup than the fans would have liked, Purdue scored to tie the game 14–14. Schmidt sent more of his starters back in the game, and it looked like their time on the bench had inspired them. The Buckeyes were on the move. Don Scott and Charley Anderson hooked up on a huge 35-yard reception. But when Anderson reached Purdue's 15-yard line, Boilermaker halfback Mike Byelene—a former high school teammate of Anderson—drilled him, causing a fumble that Purdue recovered.[15]

Adding insult to injurious turnover was the fact that Byelene was one of six native Ohioans playing for Purdue, and as noted earlier, one of several who had been part of Paul Brown's Massillon pipeline to Purdue. Brown had even transported Byelene on a recruiting trip to Purdue along with Don Scott. Even though Schmidt was adamant that all Ohio schoolboys should stay in state (and play at OSU if they were blue chip), his sloppy program was hurting his wishes and, in this case, diverting good players out of state.[16]

This time, the damage was only temporary. Following Byelene's forced fumble, Ohio State stopped Purdue dead in their tracks, forcing a punt. The suddenly resurgent Buckeyes took possession and stormed inside Purdue's 15-yard line with less than a minute remaining. Ohio State called one more running play with Tom Kinkade carrying the ball to the center of the field where he allowed himself to be tackled, setting up a game-deciding field-goal attempt from straight-on. Charley Maag, the big, blonde tackle stepped out of the line and prepared to kick. He had already connected on a long field goal against Pitt, and today all of his kickoffs had been beauties that carried into the end zone. The ball was snapped to Scott who caught it cleanly and placed it on the 12-yard line as Maag's right foot began its downward arc. The ball cleared the linemen, spinning end-over-end and arcing forward. There were twenty-one seconds left in the game when Maag's kick split the uprights, giving Ohio State a 17–14 decision. The home crowd was awash in joy and relief. For the first time in Schmidt's seven years at Ohio State the Buckeyes had come from behind to win a game they had once led.[17]

It was during the week following this game that Joe Williams, the New York sportswriter, had visited Schmidt's locker room and had been astonished by the panorama of diagrams. After Williams had watched Schmidt run practice for awhile and had decided that Schmidt was half mad he went up to St. John's office to see what he thought about the coach.

"How do you like Schmidt?" Williams asked him point-blank.

"All right," responded St. John. "I picked him, and he does a good job, and the players go for him. Last year he won the conference championship for us. Of course he didn't beat Michigan. You know we operate on a budget, so we have to keep a close eye on finances. Every year Schmidt has been here with one exception we have played to increasingly bigger crowds as you'll note here by the gate receipts." St. John pulled a sheet with some figures from his desk, and he now handed it to his visitor. "You know they are trying to get started with professional football around here," continued St. John between puffs from his pipe, "but they aren't making much success, and I think Schmidt is the reason. The pros can't put on as good a show as he does, so the people don't go out for the games."[18]

Williams left Columbus with a better idea as to why Schmidt had such an interesting reputation. What Williams didn't know was that he had just seen the coach in the final days before his coaching career stumbled for good. After winning the Big 10 title in 1939 and thumping the renowned Pitt Panthers, nobody would have guessed that Schmidt was about to be permanently undone by a spat of controversy and misfortune.

The Buckeyes were now entering the part of the schedule that made Schmidt even more uptight than usual. First a game at Northwestern, the conference dark horse, then Minnesota, the conference favorite, followed by Cornell, the best team in the East. Each squad was seemingly tougher than the last. This was an all-important stretch for Schmidt. If his team were to lose two of these and end the season with a loss to Michigan, his situation would be shaky. If he could win all three, his reputation would regain its luster.

A couple days before Ohio State left for Northwestern, the first visible crack in Schmidt's program appeared. On one of the few spaces in the dressing room walls where a diagram wasn't hanging, there were signs displaying some of Schmidt's inspirational phrases. One sign that Schmidt had hung early on proclaimed, "The only team that can beat Ohio State is Ohio State." It had now been revised by the hand of a player to read, "The only team that can beat Ohio State is the Ohio State coaching staff."[19]

Upon arriving in Chicago, Schmidt and his thirty-six lads checked into the Edgewater Beach Hotel on the shoreline of Lake Michigan before running a quick practice at nearby Loyola University. Schmidt was becoming alarmed at the lack of progress from his linemen and wanted to do some extra work with them. As a unit they were big and heavy, outweighing all of the lines they would oppose in 1940, but they were slow reactors. Schmidt preferred fast and smart linemen to big and strong linemen, although, like all coaches, he dreamed of huskies that were a combination of all those traits. So far, the linemen were keeping the offense from synchronizing, and the uber razzle-dazzle that Schmidt had dreamt of during fall practice had not had the chance to fully materialize.

Unfortunately, the line continued wreaking havoc with plans. Northwestern stopped Ohio's running game cold, allowing it to net only 8 yards. On defense these same linemen couldn't stop the run, giving up 198 yards rushing to Northwestern. Still, neither team could dent the end zone. Unable to run, the Buckeyes attempted 21 passes, and one of them led to a field goal by Maag, his fifth consecutive successful boot going back to the previous season. The slim 3–0 advantage held through three quarters before razzle-dazzle bit them coming and going. On the second play of the final quarter, Northwestern quick kicked, catching Ohio State unprepared for one of their own favorite tricks. The 52-yard boot rolled all the way to Ohio's 20-yard line. Having possession and the lead, traditional football called for the Buckeyes to play safely, punt, and play defense. In the fourth quarter a lead is a lead, and that's what you hang your hat on. Schmidt, however, believed differently, and though it's hard to say if Don Scott was specifically encouraged to do so by Schmidt, he called for a forward pass deep in his own territory. No one knew it at the time, but this play initiated Schmidt's downward spiral, a death spin from which he would never recover. Paul Heimenz, a 182-pound center making his third career varsity start for Northwestern, drifted into the throw's path and intercepted, returning the ball to Ohio's 18-yard line. Two plays later Bill DeCorrevont pounded it home for the game's only touchdown and a 6–3 Northwestern triumph. Razzle-dazzle, the great architect of leads, proved again that it was equally adept at destroying them. The 1935 Notre Dame game had showcased this in the most dramatic of ways, and lesser examples were now beginning to pile up as well. For Ohio State fans, it didn't sting anymore as much as it ached. But the fallout from this loss to Northwestern cut much more deeply than did citizen discontent. Schmidt was about to catch hell from every angle, beginning immediately after the game.[20]

In the locker room, players told reporters they had been unable to hold up during the second half due in part to their poor condition. The players' names were never mentioned, but more than one of them brought it up to reporters, meaning that it had probably been a source of contention amongst the squad before the game.[21]

Physical conditioning was, and still is, a crucial facet of football. In this era the need for stamina was at a premium. Players—especially starters—were expected to play long stretches as part of the offense, defense, and special teams. Besides that, games involved far less passing, meaning players stayed closer to the line and regrouped sooner for the next play. The clock was seemingly always on the move. A typical Big 10 football game in 1940 lasted 2.32 hours and involved about 145 plays (.097 plays per real minute), whereas a 2007 Big 10 game lasted almost an hour longer but yielded only 20-some extra plays (.071 plays per real minute). The pace of the game, the minimal amount of substituting, and the absence of television timeouts meant that physical stamina was a huge issue during Schmidt's era. Coaches like Jock Sutherland and Bernie Bierman put it at a premium much more so than did Schmidt. Because he substituted so much, perhaps Schmidt thought it was an issue less meaningful to his system.[22]

The real question, though, was whether the Ohio State players—particularly the poorly performing linemen—really were out of shape or whether they were looking to excuse their poor performance by hinting that the coaches were at fault. For the moment their complaining was an ominous rumbling from within. Two days later it became a minor earthquake.

After practice Monday night, captain Jim Langhurst called an emergency players-only team meeting. For an hour the fifty-five players vented their frustrations and discussed remedies before agreeing that Langhurst should present the coaching staff with some pointed demands. It turned out that stamina was only part of their complaint; the team desired an emphasis on hardiness as well. They felt the Northwestern defeat was the result of "too much offensive training and not enough contact and defensive work." They

wanted more scrimmages—at least two a week—and more blocking and tackling drills. "We've all made up our minds that we'll ask
the coach for more hard work during the week," announced Langhurst. "We just don't have enough hard work and bodily contact
during the weekly practices. The result is that we aren't ready for
tough games on Saturday." Langhurst then added one final note,
which showed that Schmidt had indeed lost control: "The players-
only team meetings will be held *weekly* to "iron out difficulties."[23]

The team was breaking up into three camps: the players who
were now stepping in to dictate practices; the assistant coaches who
were loyal to Schmidt but also helpless and embarrassed because
of him; and Schmidt himself, a complex man trapped by his hypomanic obsessions, denial, and mistrust.

The boys loved Schmidt, and they were in awe of his large landscape of plays, but his fixation with offense was getting worse instead of better. Like a dog chasing its tail, the more plays they devoted energy to learning, the worse things seemed to get. Weary of
Schmidt's capricious substituting, the players didn't think they were
getting enough individual playing time, and the relentless substitutions weren't helping the timing of their plays either.

The coaches tried to work on fundamentals, but Schmidt was
running the show, and he wanted more strategy. The head coach
and his assistants argued—sometimes in front of the players—
which created an awkward situation for everyone involved with the
program. As one writer put it, "Northwestern showed Ohio State
more fundamental football in one hour than the Buckeyes had absorbed in forty practices."[24]

Schmidt did not understand how they could be complaining. He
worked long and hard. He spent countless hours working on strategy to help them win. And if he avoided giving them excessive physical contact in practice, it was to keep them fresh and to help them
avert injuries. The players were not just second-guessing practice

methods, they were second-guessing Francis Schmidt. He was now faced with a most pivotal decision concerning the future of his program at Ohio State. If he acquiesced to the players' demands he would be admitting his system was flawed (which it was) and he would be letting the inmates run the asylum. If he denied their requests he would alienate the players, ensure a ruinous season, and lose the job he had worked so hard to secure.

More than anything, it was the second-guessing from his players that really bothered him, and starting with the next practice Schmidt decided that if they wanted contact, he would give them contact. He had the team scrimmage three days in a row. And if they wanted tough, he could deliver tough, declaring that he was no longer tolerating "loafers" and "cry babies." Tackling and blocking still required mundane, time-consuming work that bored him, so he declared a convenient edict: "Every man must hit the blocking and tackling dummies at least four times before every workout." Schmidt had staved off a coup, but it had cost him more of his dwindling power. Perhaps he saw it as a pragmatic trade between men. He gave them some of what they clamored for, and on Friday he got what he wanted, giving the players new plays to digest less than twenty-four hours before game time. He still believed in his system even if no one else understood its intricate beauty.[25]

As the three sides worked under an uneasy cease-fire that week, Schmidt was blindsided by another problem. After studying game film of Purdue's loss to osu in week two of the season, Gordon Graham, sports editor of the *Lafayette (Indiana) Journal & Courier*, reported that Charley Maag, the big blonde who had kicked the winning field goal, had been illegally substituted earlier in the game, meaning that he should have been disqualified from playing and attempting the winning kick. During this era, a player who was replaced could not return to the game during the same quarter. Maag had left the game early in the second quarter and had returned with just forty-one seconds before halftime to aid Ohio State in scoring a touchdown from the 3-yard line. The ramifications were huge. If Maag had been caught, there would have been a 15-yard penalty, which would have taken them out of scoring range. Even if they had scored, Maag would have been unavailable to attempt the winning field goal later because he would already have been disqualified from the game. And the Buckeyes had no other players who rivaled Maag's talent for field-goal kicking. In essence, strict adherence to the penalization of Maag's crime would almost surely have caused Ohio's losing to Purdue instead of winning. Commissioner Griffith claimed there was nothing he could do. "Big 10 coaches have been using a so-called 'honor system' on their substitutions the last three or four years. We found when coaches inserted entire teams it slowed up the game considerably since the umpire had to check the names of all substitutes against a list he carried. Umpires have plenty else to do. We figured we would lighten their job by having coaches keep track of their own men." Based on a study conducted by the Big 10, the field officials combined to make an average of five hundred decisions a game, of which five or six were erroneous. Trying to keep track of the comings and goings of some eighty players during each game would only add to the difficulty of their jobs. Appropriately, the "zebras" were the only ones who were spared in Schmidt's rambling explanation of the Maag incident:[26]

> Generally we make it a rule to ask the boys if they've been in the game, but I guess we slipped up in Maag's case. There was no action on plays while he was in there, but the substitution was illegal, and I'm taking the blame for it. We had used Maag just a play or two in the second period, and when we got to the last part of the quarter, Charley was sitting next to Ernie [Godfrey] on the bench. There were only two plays left so we sent him in. Ernie actually made the substitution, and it was

absolutely unintentional. But I'm the coach and I was responsible. Ernie must have said, "Let's put Maag in," and I probably
said, "Okay." It was an oversight and purely unintentional.[27]

Yes, and Schmidt's mea culpa was purely Schmidt. He claims the
blame twice but also makes it clear that Ernie Godfrey and Maag
were the culprits. Either way, Ohio State's reputation was suffering
additional damage.

The best way to heal a fractured football team is to win a big
game, and such a golden opportunity had arrived in Columbus.
The Minnesota Golden Gophers (they added the "golden" part
during the 1930s because Bierman dressed them in all-gold uniforms) were in town seeking revenge for the previous season's
loss. This was their first visit to Columbus since 1921, a staggering
length of time for conference mates. They were currently ranked
No. 7 in the nation and were fully rested, coming off a bye week. It
was the eighth straight season that Bierman had scheduled a week
off in the middle of the season to regroup, rest, and prepare for a
big opponent. He'd thought about traveling to Chicago and scouting osu but decided instead to stay in Minneapolis, work on his
own team, and read scouting reports from his assistants. Given the
chance, Schmidt would never have passed on an opportunity to
watch a game, especially if staying at home and working on fundamentals was the alternative. Because Schmidt rarely had an open
weekend he had to send assistants to do almost all of his scouting,
and this season it was Sid Gillman's job to scout Minnesota. Gillman
had a great mind for football strategy, and Schmidt trusted him as
much as he was capable of trusting anyone. What Sid had to say this
week was not what Schmidt wanted to hear: "If Minnesota doesn't
bring the best team that's played in Ohio Stadium, I miss my guess,"
reported Sid. Minnesota was deep—really deep. Their running
game used more deception, and Bierman had them using multiple

formations, a strategy that most teams who had faced Schmidt were starting to implement.[28]

Rain, never a friend of razzle-dazzle, visited Ohio Stadium once again, but 63,199 of the expected 72,000 fans willingly traded saturation for spectacle. The contrasting styles of the two teams were evident from the outset. Ohio State quick kicked to the Gophers, who used 7 straight runs to methodically move 55 yards for a score and a 6–0 lead. As a matter of fact, the Gophers did not throw a pass the entire game, content to pound away at the Buckeyes' suspect line. When Ohio State had the ball, they repeatedly drove deep into Gopher territory. The first visit resulted in a Charley Anderson touchdown off a daring fourth-down lateral-forward pass combination. A converted extra point gave Ohio a 7–6 lead. Two more Buckeye drives made it inside Minnesota's 10, but both ended with incomplete passes. It was the same old story of the Buckeyes' failure to finish, and it left them trailing 13–7 late in the fourth quarter with only enough time left for one more drive. The rain had now stopped, and Ohio State desperately opened things up. They ran when they were expected to pass and passed when they should have run. They connected on four intricate pass plays in a row. The last, involving two backs swinging out of the backfield, had Don Scott completing a wheel route to Tom Kinkade, who in turn completed a perfectly timed lateral to Les Horvath, putting the ball on Minnesota's 6-yard line. With less than two minutes left in the game, Don Scott called a play for himself. At one point in the drive, with the nerve of a jewel thief, he'd called a delayed draw play for himself, gaining 6 yards on fourth and five. Now, again needing crucial yards, he called on himself once more and powered his way to the 1-yard line. The Buckeyes were 1 yard and a Charley Maag extra point away from a huge victory when disaster struck. Claude White, the center who had brilliantly passed a slippery ball all day, lost his grip on the most crucial hike of all, sending the ball squirting along the ground, evading possession until Jim Langhurst dropped on it at the 13-yard line. Ohio State's momentum died. The simple touchdown and extra-point kick never happened, and the Gophers were 13–7 winners. It was their narrowest escape on the way to an undefeated season that culminated with another national championship.[29]

Ohio State had won almost every single statistical category, including total yards (385–231), first downs (16–10) and turnovers (0–3), but a single miscue at the wrong time had doomed them. Schmidt and his boys had lost yet another big game by yet another means—this one coming just days after the players' uprising and the accusations of cheating. Now they were hitting the rails, headed to New York to play the top-ranked team in America. Maybe Schmidt wasn't paranoid after all.[30]

In anticipation of a visit from the famous Scarlet Scourge, Cornell University had sold out Schoellkopf Stadium a full month before the game, the earliest it had ever done so. They had even erected temporary bleachers, and the two schools split the cost. The expected crowd of 33,400 would be an all-time record. Only 3000 tickets had been allotted to OSU, and they could have sold many more. Tom Kinkade, who always asked for his full allotment of complimentary tickets and then scalped them, thought this game's popularity would work to his advantage. "I got four passes and I figured if I could get $20 a piece for 'em in Columbus, I could get $40 each in Ithaca. So I saved mine, but never did get a chance to get those damn things sold."[31]

Eastern spectators had heard all sorts of stories about Schmidt's unorthodox strategy, and they were barely seated for the big game when they witnessed their first proof. Schmidt had twenty-two of his players huddle on the field as they prepared to kick off. After breaking huddle, half of them lined up on one side of the kicker and the other half on the other side. Then, as the kicker signaled ready, half of them calmly stepped off the field. It was a harmless parlor trick, but it let the fans know they might be in for some fun. When the Buckeyes got the ball back, they had the first bit of fun, traipsing 89 yards, scoring, and converting to lead 7–0. On the ensuing kickoff, Cornell's return man fumbled, and Frank Clair recovered for Ohio. The Buckeyes responded to this huge break by spending "too much time in the huddle," which cost them a 5-yard penalty. It was all downhill from there. Cornell was just too good and looked every bit the part of a first-ranked team. They pulled away in the second half to win 21–7. This was Schmidt's fifty-third game as coach at Ohio State, and the 14-point margin of loss was the worst he had experienced in that run. Having already played poorly in front of the eastern writers, Ohio State then compounded their bad press by immediately telling reporters that Cornell's head coach had cheated throughout the game.[32]

Supposedly, Schmidt and St. John had received letters weeks before the game warning them that Carl Snavely was notorious for illegally signaling plays, a practice known to be more common in the South where Snavely had come from. Wallace Wade (Duke University) had warned of Snavely's practices as early as 1935, practices that included water boys' and trainers' mumbling plays as they attended to players. Schmidt told the officials before the Ohio State–Cornell game to watch Snavely, and he even claimed he said something directly to Snavely about the rumors. At some point during the game, a few players on the Ohio State bench alerted their coaches that they thought Snavely was signaling, and they even claimed to have broken his code. They shouted to their teammates on the field what they believed to be coming based on these signals. Schmidt spent the first half with one eye on the field and one on Snavely. At halftime he cornered St. John and informed him of this egregious situation, asking him to study it as well. By game's end, both were certain that Snavely was cheating. Afterward, Schmidt accused Snavely of having a "lack of ethics and poor sportsman-ship." At the crux of the damnation was Snavely's use of a "light-col-ored cylinder," perhaps a rolled-up program, to signal play choices to his team. Schmidt, who for years had ached to signal play selec-tions, went further by saying, "It was a (expletive) crime, but it was so obvious and so amateurish that we had to laugh. We finally got to the place where we could just about call practically every play. Snavely's actions were so bald-faced. Some guys are foxy about pull-ing stuff like that, but everyone in the stadium could see this. Every time he sent in a sub, the sub's shoe was untied. And as he knelt to tie it, someone on his team would kneel down to help him. I guess the sub did a lot of against-the-rules talking while his friend helped him tie the shoes."[33]

If it was true that Ohio State could predict Cornell's plays, there seemed to be a large difference between knowing what was coming and stopping it, because Ohio had been outplayed most of the day. They may have even psyched themselves out instead of concentrat-ing on their own work. Then again, there seemed to be some con-fusion as to the code they had broken. St. John had cracked a code whereby grasping the cylinder at the bottom meant "pass," grasp-ing it at the middle meant "sweep," and grasping it with both hands meant "line smash." Claude White, starting center, claimed that the bottom meant "single wing right," the top meant "single wing left," and the middle meant, predictably, "middle." Both agreed he called for kicks by swinging one foot while sitting on the bench cross-legged. Muddying the conspiracy pool even further, Ernie Godfrey protested the oddity that every Cornell lineman had his right hand taped, to which the Cornell trainer later responded by explaining that they *all* had right-hand injuries. As for William Frie-sell Jr., the game's referee, he claimed to know nothing about cheat-ing, as he was "too busy watching twenty-two players to pay much attention to what was transpiring on the bench." Upon returning to Columbus, St. John filed a protest with the Eastern Athletic Association, accusing Snavely of a "gross violation of the official football rules."[34]

The powerful East Coast media was outraged by all this. It sounded like sour grapes coming from a team that had now lost 3 straight games. And furthermore, wasn't it a bit sanctimonious for Schmidt to be bringing accusations just three weeks after benefiting from an undetected illegality to beat Purdue? Back home, the sportswriters weren't happy either, but for another reason. Two Columbus beat writers felt like St. John gave his initial, exclusive comments on the subject to one particular paper, causing them and their papers to scramble. With attacks coming from every side, the troubled Ohio State program needed to regroup and unify—easier said than done where Schmidt was involved, as he was usually the one keeping everything off balance.[35]

This mess was no exception. On the same day St. John was filing a protest with the Eastern Athletic Association and going public about it, Schmidt completely reversed field on the question of Snavely's cheating: "I don't think he did and in fact I know he didn't." It's difficult to believe that Schmidt sincerely meant this. Perhaps he was giving peace a chance as he never was good at staying angry with anyone. Maybe a confidante had told him it was making him look bad to complain given the events of the past few weeks. Whatever the reason, Schmidt still managed to take a shot at Snavely by claiming Cornell could win just as easily without Snavely present: "Oh, Carl's boys were a bit puzzled at first, but don't worry, that Cornell club doesn't need any bench coaching and didn't on Saturday. He's got a great machine there and a wonderful team on the field. They would have beaten us if he had been back at North Carolina on Saturday." Whatever the truth might have been, Schmidt had publicly proven his lack of political savvy by foolishly leaving his boss hanging out to dry all alone in the ill wind.[36]

The Buckeye program was so fractionalized that even its sports publicist was turning on Schmidt. Instead of putting a glossy finish on the team's troubles—as was his job—Jim Renick was stoking the fire. Speaking to an alumni group the day after Schmidt's recanting, Renick used some of his time to rehash the team's conditioning controversy. "Our team is poorly conditioned," he told them. "Why that is true I don't know. Our boys seem to lack the pep to play more than half a game at high speed. It may be a lack of scrimmage or some other reason. I do know the physical condition of the squad is poor." How the non-doctor knew this for certain is unknown. Perhaps he figured that their having blown leads in four straight games was unequivocal proof. Perhaps he was taking the word of a player. Until this season, the talented Renick had been a great Schmidt supporter, calling him the "most football-minded coach I ever saw" and happily relating stories such as the time Schmidt was riding in Renick's car on a freezing winter day, drawing plays with his finger on the frost-covered windows. Now he was yet another of the program's members who had chosen to broadcast an opinion that should have stayed in-house.[37]

Reportedly furious by this betrayal, Schmidt told reporters two days later that his team's problem was not conditioning but rather a lack of depth, especially amongst sophomores, forcing juniors and seniors to carry a larger portion of the burden. "You got to have two or three teams of equal worth when you play a schedule like ours."[38]

While all this was going on, Schmidt was busy trying to salvage the season by preparing for Indiana. Always the master of extremism, Schmidt replaced six of the seven starters on his line in one fell swoop. The new starters were lighter, faster, and hopefully hungrier than the deposed. Half the backfield was changed at the same time. Strausbaugh was now healthy enough to start, and Tom Kinkade had earned a starting berth with some hell-bent blocking of late.

All told, only three starters were keeping their jobs: center Claude White, fullback Jim Langhurst, and quarterback Don Scott. Of the three, Scott was causing the most concern among Buckeye followers because everyone's preseason All-American was having a rather bland season.

Observers thought he was too aggressive when he should be cautious and too cautious when he should be aggressive. What they didn't know was that his play selection was partly the result of his losing control of the huddle. A quarterback who calls his own plays needs time to think between plays, and he needs respect and quiet in the huddle. Scott was getting none of this. The huddle had become the place to "air grievances, to haggle with teammates, to yell and howl and rave." Everyone had an opinion about the next play. It didn't help that Schmidt had so many hundreds of plays and that everyone had a "special" one in mind. Scott was a conscientious young man who didn't enjoy being a dictator or an arbitrator. He was also a great runner, and the fans and media called for him to be more selfish, to call his own number more often. Schmidt felt it was a matter of Scott's not having a strong enough grip on the system, something that took a lot of work and commitment. Scott's decision to play baseball in the spring rather than gain experience in Schmidt's complex system had angered the coach. Worse yet, some of Scott's poor prioritization was continuing unabated.[39]

"We had jobs," recalls Jack Graf, the backup quarterback, "and he had a job selling shoes at the houses. He would get to practice late then he would leave practice early so he could get to the fraternities and sororities who had just finished eating dinner and hadn't scattered yet. He had to be there to sell those shoes." Surely Schmidt understood that earning money was important, especially during the Depression. But couldn't Schmidt have arranged for Scott to find more advantageous employment? Or did Scott's lack of commitment keep him from seeking another job? Because

Scott's playing was sub par, everything he did both on and off the field was under scrutiny.[40]

Along with his wholesale personnel changes, Schmidt now made Jim Langhurst the primary signal caller from his fullback position. He also pulled John Hallabrin aside and asked him if he'd like to switch from fullback to backup quarterback behind Scott and Graf, but Hallabrin saw what it had done to Scott and declined, not wishing to become yet another "goat."[41]

To avoid a complete implosion, the Buckeyes *had* to win against Indiana, and they did so by the score of 21–6. Ohio State unloaded its pent-up fury early and quickly, scoring a pair of first-quarter touchdowns in a nine-play span. They tacked on another in the opening moments of the second quarter and then called it a day on offense. It's what a normal team would have done in this era, and the Buckeye signal callers were determined not to create any new controversy. Focusing on defense and forcing the opponent into errors was the Victorian way of handling a lead. For the rest of the game the fans were treated to the spectacle of Indiana's repeatedly threatening to score but managing to fall short by numerous methods including downs, fumbles, interceptions, and penalties.[42]

After disposing of the Hoosiers, the Buckeyes had the following Saturday off—only the second time during Schmidt's reign that this had happened. The first time, in 1937, was because of the long train trip home from Los Angeles. This time it was because Chicago had officially dropped its football program to the relief of everyone who had watched it wither away to its death. President Hutchins had worked tirelessly following the 1939 season to press the school's board of trustees into euthanizing the intercollegiate football program. When he appeared before the student body in the fall (for the first time in five years), he explained the program's demise as the price for integrity, declaring that there is only "one way in which we could win. We could subsidize players or encourage our alumni to do so. Many of the students and alumni with whom I have talked have urged upon me what they call 'legitimate' subsidization. I am sorry to tell you that there is no such thing under the Big 10 rules. The university could not break the rule." The new plan was for Chicago to place more emphasis on intramural competition as well as some other intercollegiate sports that received less interest but also required less effort. "I say that a university must emphasize education and not athletics and social life," Hutchins added. "Even apart from athletics, undergraduate life at the university is so lovely that I don't see how you get any studying done. I know from sad experience with some of you that there actually are students who don't get any done." It's probably a good thing he didn't live to witness the "sad experience" of kegs and STDs floating around campuses like spring pollen. It would have been enough to make him long for the discreetly corruptive influence of big-time football.[43]

Chicago's absence left a hole in the Buckeyes' schedule, and in January they had made inquiries to possible replacement schools. An invitation was supposed to have been given to Colorado, the Big 7 champs, but they had a game scheduled with rival Missouri on that date, so the validity of or logic behind this invitation is questionable. There was even talk of moving dates and perhaps getting Texas A&M, the SWC champ, to play OSU in October. None of these high-profile gems came to fruition (probably to the relief of Schmidt, who was only one accomplished opponent away from an aneurysm). Instead the Buckeyes chose to stick with the break in the schedule and replaced Chicago's spot with a grateful Indiana on another weekend. All told, in Schmidt's seven seasons the Hoosiers and Buckeyes played every year, six times at Ohio and only once at Indiana.[44]

Schmidt was pleased to have a break in the middle of the season, not because he wanted to rest but because he loved watching other games, especially those involving upcoming opponents. In this case he took the long train ride to Minneapolis so he could scout Michigan's game against the Golden Gophers. It might have made more sense to watch the Illinois game since they were Ohio's next opponent, but Schmidt knew the Michigan game was the one that would make or break his season. Plus, it didn't really look like Illinois needed to be scouted. It was Zuppke's second-to-last season, and things were no longer fun in Champaign. After beating Bradley in their opener, Illinois had lost 5 straight by a combined 27–112.

Two weeks later, when the Buckeye team arrived in Champaign, they were greeted by freezing temperatures that thinned an already apathetic collection of fans down to a smallish crowd of 15,571. Those who were brave enough to suffer through the bone-chilling conditions were not rewarded with much excitement. It was not a day conducive to razzle-dazzle, and neither team opened up. Ohio State scored on the opening drive of the game and again early in the second half. They attempted just 4 passes, all in the first quarter and all incomplete. They stuck to the ground game, rushed for 201 yards, and won a simple 14–6 game wherein Don Scott scored both touchdowns.[45]

Ohio State was now 4-3—their first winning record since the second week of the season—but the program was still a fragile entity. Too much had happened in the interim. Rumors were rampant that Schmidt might be done at the end of this disappointing season. Schmidt *had* to beat Michigan if he wanted to keep his job.

It wouldn't be easy. The Wolverines were once again a powerhouse. And much to Schmidt's chagrin—and perhaps because of him—one of Michigan's strengths was the number of quality Ohio schoolboys they had successfully recruited. As one newspaperman pointed out to the public, eight members of the Wolverine team were from Ohio, including two prominent starters that Schmidt had lost through poor politics. Even the University of Tennessee had five Ohioans, including All-American guard Ed Molinski. The fact that so many quality home boys were choosing out-of-state schools did not reflect well upon Schmidt's program.[46]

Michigan arrived in Columbus with a 6-1 record and a national ranking of No. 7. Their only loss had been a 1-point heartbreaker to top-ranked Minnesota. This return to glory for the Wolverines could be traced to 1938 when they hired Fritz Crisler as their head coach. Crisler was very good, but he had also lucked out by inheriting a strong group of players, the greatest of which was Tom Harmon. Each season Harmon had improved, surpassing even the lofty expectations that had been placed on him right out of high school. He was a superstar and the first back to have proven himself genuinely worthy of the Red Grange comparisons that were annually affixed to some Big 10 newcomer. As a matter of fact, Harmon's 30 touchdowns during three years of conference play left him trailing Grange's all-time record by 1, with this one final game remaining in his illustrious career.

In Ohio's dressing room Francis Schmidt had finished his talk, full of strategy and well-worn reminders, and turned the floor over to Ernie Godfrey, the designated motivator. Godfrey was a genuine man, and his passion came easily. Today his eyes were wet as he implored the boys to give their best effort toward beating their archrival. Normally the motivation to slay Michigan was easily tapped, but this had been an exhausting season, and the players' emotions were running low. Some were ready for the season to be over. Even the conditions on the field seemed to capture this somberness; it was wet, gray, and cold. A heavy, swirling mist combined with the breath of 71,648 fans to create a murky effect that made everything seem ghostly and surreal.[47]

The only thing wetter than the fans was the turf, but Michigan didn't seem to notice. After stopping Ohio State's opening drive, the Wolverines took possession of the punt on their own 20. A few minutes, 11 plays, and 80 yards later it was 7–0 Michigan. Tom Harmon took it the last 8 yards to tie Grange's Big 10 touchdown record. Three minutes after that it was 13–0 following a scintillating 81-yard punt return by none other than Paul Kroner, one of the gifted Ohio schoolboys that Schmidt's program had failed to recruit. Meanwhile, the Buckeyes could get nothing going on offense. The Wolverines dominated Ohio's line, slipping into the backfield at will. The pregame strategy began to give way to desperation and shock. Ohio State tried everything within reason, but there just wasn't enough time for the plays to develop before a marauding Wolverine would destroy any semblance of timing. Michigan continued controlling the game throughout the first half, and behind the brilliant all-around play of Tom Harmon they took a 20–0 lead going into halftime, the last touchdown being scored on a pass thrown by Harmon, who also kicked the extra point.[48]

Such a halftime deficit was practically unknown to Ohio State. Certainly in Schmidt's regime such lopsided scores had always been in favor of the Buckeyes and never in favor of the enemy. What could be done here? Schmidt's game plan was in shambles, and Godfrey had already shed his last tear. Realistically, only two questions remained: How badly was Shut-the-Gates-of-Mercy Schmidt going to be paid back, and would Harmon be able to break Grange's record?

Harmon answered the latter question late in the third quarter when he swept around end and galloped 18 yards for his record-setting touchdown. He'd already passed for another touchdown earlier in the quarter, meaning the Wolverines were now up 33–0. The Buckeyes were miserable. Their jerseys were saturated and heavy. Blades of grass clung to their skin. The visitors were superior in every way today, and Ohio had no fight left. Tom Kinkade, usually excited about the prospect of playing all sixty minutes, was not enjoying that rare circumstance today and found himself wondering when he'd be replaced. As the game closed in on a merciful finish, Michigan left no doubt that Schmidt was being paid in full for his merciless ways. Harmon faked a pass and then ran 6 yards for the game's final touchdown with just 38 seconds remaining, making the score 40–0. It was the fifth touchdown accounted for by Harmon, and as he trotted toward the sidelines for the final time in his collegiate career, the Ohio Stadium crowd—many of them standing—cheered long and hard. Even a bitter enemy had to respect such greatness.[49]

Schmidt and his drenched bow tie sat on the bench, nowhere to hide. Here, on Ohio turf, during homecoming weekend, his archrivals had run up the score on him, and their star had been lauded like a war hero. The scoreboard, standing tall and unblinking in the mist, declared Ohio the loser by the appalling count of 40–0—the worst beating the Buckeyes had suffered in thirty-five years. Schmidt's offense had been stifled, outgained 447 yards to 120. They had entered Michigan territory only three times and had never seriously threatened. In the second half it appeared that some of his players had quit on him, giving only mock effort. It was an almost inconceivable nightmare, the type of overwhelming loss that is never forgotten by those involved.[50]

With three straight losses to Michigan ringing in his head, sportswriter Larry Newman could no longer hide his frustration: "Where Ohio State attempted everything from the Statue of Liberty to the third lesson from Madam Lazongs, Michigan depended on four or five simple plays. It has been generally known around these parts for six years that the Schmidt system is a little too complicated for its own good. The boys have a couple of hundred too many plays to learn and too many assignments to memorize on defense to bother with good old-fashioned blocking and tackling." In reality it was Schmidt's poor implementation of his strategies that cost his team wins, but the media and alumni were already gathering pitchfork and torch and were in no mood for details.[51]

Ohio State had finished 4-4 overall and 3-3 in the Big 10. Thanks to the blowout loss against Michigan, the Buckeyes were outscored for the season, the first time this had occurred since 1924. For Schmidt, being outscored was the cruelest of all possible blows. It had never happened to him in all his years of college coaching.

The razzle-dazzle may have failed because of a suspect line, but folks had still poured through the turnstiles to watch Schmidt and the boys try. For the fourth year in a row, the Buckeyes had played before an average crowd of nearly 50,000 (one of the best draws in the nation), and, despite a poor record, the home games had drawn 60,189 per contest, the second highest attendance in school history, topped only by the 1938 numbers. But if there was one set of numbers that Schmidt would have insisted on pointing out, it would have been the final national rankings of the teams Ohio State was victim to in 1940: Minnesota (No. 1), Michigan (No. 3), Northwestern (No. 8) and Cornell (No. 15). It had indeed been a murderous schedule, just as Schmidt had endlessly pointed out. The trouble is, a coach's legacy is built on winning big games against big teams. Not every time, but often enough to spend a reasonable amount of time at the top of the heap where the air is good, the silhouette is dramatic, and the writers and fans can get a good, long, memorable look. Schmidt's Buckeye teams had lost nearly every crucial game, shared one conference title, and backed into the other on the last day of the season. Definitely not the stuff of legend.[52]

On Monday morning St. John and George Trautman headed to Lake Erie for some duck hunting and conversation. Where Buckeye football was concerned, these two men carried substantial weight, and they wanted to make sure it was being wielded in concert. The deluge of opinions from pigskin reactionaries had already begun, and the two men were wise to get their "no comments" in order.[53]

That night, both men attended the annual football banquet along with eight hundred other guests. It was a smaller crowd than was present for last year's championship soiree, and the atmosphere for this one was awkward and full of tension. Before it even started, Schmidt told reporters, "I'm not going to resign, much as some of you newspapermen would like me to. I'm still Ohio State's football coach, and until Mr. St. John tells me they don't want me around here anymore, I'm not going to look for another job. Let's not have any postmortems," he urged. During the banquet, some of the speakers mentioned the Michigan blowout that was on everyone's minds. Fritz Mackey, the freshman coach, "made some thinly disguised remarks that reproached certain members of the varsity squad concerning conditioning and cooperation." The sophomore class that Schmidt had called the worst in OSU history walked away with one solitary letter—Les Horvath, future Heisman trophy winner. Ohio governor John Bricker only offered: "We can't all win." Lineman Jack Stephenson was elected captain for 1941 and, instead of delivering the usual speech full of optimistic platitudes for the next season, immediately condemned the current wreck of a team by declaring that "politics, gangs, favorites, and everything else has got to be forgotten" in the coming season. Players who "don't give everything they've got will be kicked off the team," he concluded. It was a strong indictment of Schmidt, hinting that the coach had been unable to inspire his players. Worse yet, his next captain was now taking ownership of team discipline.[54]

As the banquet shuffled on toward closure, Schmidt's oddly tuned brain began to surrender. The damning speeches, the horrible season, the stress, and that horrendous schedule were simply too much to bear. When Jim Langhurst, the departing captain, presented a gold trophy to Schmidt "in appreciation of your efforts," a stunned crowd watched as "Schmidt accepted the trophy with trembling hands and then broke into convulsive sobs as he attempted to talk." He cried seven years' worth of tears—shaking and inconsolable. It was an unimaginable collapse to those who knew him as the loud, comical bull on the practice field. Players and guests sat in uncomfortable silence, waiting for him to regroup at the lectern as his small, but very public, nervous breakdown played out. Finally, after what seemed like an eternity, he was able to whisper, "This gets my goat. It really means a helluva lot to me. . . . I made mistakes, and the team made mistakes. But we'll show them next year. . . . This is the happiest moment of my life."[55]

Nobody could know the pressure that Francis Schmidt put on himself every day as his mind relentlessly churned and spun. The failure of the just-concluded season had overwhelmed his psyche in a way that few people could understand. And a little gold trophy from a forgiving group of boys had been a gift more precious than he could bear.

The next day the university board of athletic control declared that there should be a cooling-off period before the football program was evaluated. The board's spokesman took the misguided step of saying he believed Schmidt would get another year but offered no concrete promise. But the following day an "unimpeachable source" told editor Robert E. Hooey of the *Ohio State Journal* (Columbus) that Schmidt would not be rehired, not because of his record or the loss to Michigan but because "on frequent occasions and especially during the last three seasons, Schmidt has been the storm center of numerous arguments throughout the coaching and player ranks." The university immediately denied the story. Schmidt, who had already begun his postseason alumni banquet tour, told a gathering of Cleveland alumni that it was a "cock and bull story," and then at a dinner in Detroit he reminded guests that his future would be decided by the board, not by newspapermen. Meanwhile, the sportswriters smelled blood, and they were already

floating rumors about Schmidt's possible successors. Jock Sutherland and Earl "Red" Blaik were the two most common speculations.
As for St. John, he was supposed to have been part of Schmidt's
banquet caravan but had instead stayed in Columbus where he remained unusually quiet.[56]

After his speaking tour was finished, Schmidt took off for the
West Coast to scout USC during their game against Notre Dame.
The Trojans were on Ohio State's schedule for 1941. The decision
to attend the game meant he would miss attending the annual postseason Western Conference meeting. It was just as well since the
fragile state of his employment would have made the situation a bit
awkward. In light of Schmidt's absence, however, athletic directors
and coaches were free to discuss the topic, and by most accounts
Schmidt was the No. 1 subject of unofficial conversation.

Some took Schmidt's trip to California as a sign that he was confident; some thought he was in denial. He was neither. While riding
the train west, he wrote one of his hurried, nearly illegible letters
to St. John. In this one he promised, "I am going to try my best this
year to do the best job of coaching I have ever done, to prove your
confidence in me was not misplaced (assuming of course things go
OK at Ohio State for me)." The question was whether he fully understood what needed improving.[57]

While Schmidt was on the coast, the athletic board conducted
their next meeting on Monday, December 9. Everyone held their
breath for news concerning Schmidt, but the board wisely refused
to make a hasty decision. To do so would only embolden the media, fans, and wolves into thinking they could dictate the agenda.
Instead, the board discussed other pending matters, such as the
approval of one of the three proposed sites for building a giant,
new field house. Only later in the evening's proceedings was the
Schmidt issue introduced, and even then it was dealt with patiently.
On the advice of St. John it was decided to form a committee to

look into the "football situation." The committee was comprised of three people: a representative for the faculty, one for alumni, and a student to represent the school's young scholars. The new committee was instructed to "take its time and dig deeply." They were also presented with three loosely constructed scenarios: get rid of the entire football staff, force Schmidt to resign but keep the coaches, or keep Schmidt and lose the coaches. As one "prominent alumnus" put it: "The board—and St. John—has taken the pressure off itself and placed it on two men and a boy. Whatever comes out of this, this committee is in for the greatest pressuring in Ohio State athletic history."[58]

Many Buckeye fans wanted a new coach, but it seemed that the clear majority still believed in Schmidt. They thought he was charismatic and his football was lurid. They hadn't been privy to all the disorganization transpiring behind the scenes, but they figured Schmidt's brilliant football mind was what mattered most. Whether they were for Schmidt or against him, the mainstream supporters tended to agree that it was best for the program to either give the man a vote of confidence—so he could get on with his job—or cut him loose before all the good replacements were hired by other schools. The High Street crowd—the wolves—simply demanded Schmidt's head immediately.

Schmidt tried to keep abreast of developments during his stay in California, but this was long before the information age, and details were difficult to unearth when one was two thousand miles from home. St. John had been Schmidt's friend and conduit for seven years, but Saint was loyal to himself and Ohio State first, and he wasn't offering Schmidt much in the way of insider knowledge. St. John's aloofness should have been Schmidt's first clue that the party was over.

When Schmidt arrived back in Columbus late on Sunday, December 15, he contacted his few confidantes and found the situation to be absolutely dire. Apparently the special committee assigned to the football situation was recommending wholesale change. Schmidt's entire coaching staff had already handed their resignations to St. John on Thursday, and the athletic director held them privately, awaiting Schmidt's return. The next morning Schmidt went to his office, wrote a letter of resignation and delivered it to St. John. The final scene began to unfold rapidly. Throughout the afternoon phone calls were made to members of the athletic board, setting up an emergency special session in which the board would decide whether to accept the resignations.[59]

That evening as the board huddled, a crestfallen Schmidt stood on a sidewalk outside, waiting to hear his fate. That he even considered it a real possibility for the board to reject his resignation showed how naïve Schmidt could be. He sounded like a hurt child as he shared his despair with the reporters who were gathered around him, awaiting the official news. "I had a pleasant time here and I might just as well sever my relations as they (the athletic board) are not satisfied. I would much rather do this than impose myself upon them any longer. . . . This is a new experience for me. Always before I have been promoted. Now I don't know what to do. But I'll get along. Why didn't they let me out a year ago after I won a championship? There were plenty of good jobs for me then. I could have had a good place on the Pacific Coast. . . . Some of the folks around here evidently don't believe that football teams have their ups and downs. Every coach in the country has had poor seasons. In judging a coach, you have to take a long-range look at his record." He recounted the problems of 1940: weak material, spring no-shows, injuries, and of course the schedule from hell. "The fans don't figure all these things," he said.[60]

It tumbled out of him in one disjointed stream—his insecurities, the plea for understanding, the need for pity. It was the remains of his public vulnerability, the leftovers from his banquet breakdown.

Now, having exposed his pain and realizing that it would do him no good, Schmidt decided he couldn't stand there like a jilted lover, waiting for the affection that would never come. The athletic board, the fans, and the reporters were already more interested in his replacement. Schmidt took one more glance at the illuminated windows of the athletic director's office where the board's final decision would be officially delivered, then started to walk away. As he moved on he told the reporters, "The board doesn't want anything more from me. Mrs. Schmidt and I are going out for the evening." The news photographers asked him to stop for a picture. "Aw, you fellows have plenty of pictures of me in your files," he responded. "Just dig one of them out and use it. And say," he added before disappearing into the night, "beneath it will you print 'Rest in Peace?'"[61]

After meeting for two-and-a-half hours the board finally decided to accept Schmidt's resignation, pending approval from the university president and the board of trustees. It had been a long meeting, but most of it was spent making sure they had their stories straight as well as discussing the near future. The other resignations accepted along with Schmidt's were those of assistants Sid Gillman, Gomer Jones, and Ernie Godfrey. Two other coaches, Ed Bickle and Fritz Mackey, were retained for use in other sports. A statement was released, thanking them for their "loyal service to the university." The board had spoken.[62]

Two days later the students spoke. A large 5-by-10 foot sign that faced the main campus entrance at High and Fifteenth read, "Up with Schmidt, down with St. Johnny, no house is clean without a clean floor." The hastily produced sign lasted but a couple hours before it was removed by school officials. Students on fraternity row agreed almost unanimously with the sign's message when quizzed by one local reporter. Perhaps Schmidt saw the sign—he only lived half a block away—but it was too late to help his cause. He was unemployed for the first time since he was a young man, fresh out of the University of Nebraska.[63]

The sportswriters who covered Buckeye football were in agreement on their postmortem analysis. They thought Schmidt was brilliant, but his bombastic personality had been too much. Bill McKinnon of the *Columbus (Ohio) Dispatch* probably summed it up best:

> I have long believed Schmidt footballed his players to the point of ennui. Winter, spring, summer, fall, day, and night he dreamed football, ate it, worked at it, talked it, crammed it into his players every waking moment he was with them. Such diet often becomes revolting.
>
> On the bench he seemed more interested in charts and diagrams than in his athletes. He had the fire of a zealot but not the understanding of the foibles, the weaknesses, the problems of boys. Too much he was a man aloof in his own thoughts—not purposely, but more likely because he never let down in his desire to win.[64]

Call it what you will—craziness, eccentricity, hypomania—the thing about Schmidt that makes him such a vital influence on today's football is also the same thing that cost him his biggest job and broke his heart into pieces. As one reporter put it, "Francis Schmidt leaves Ohio State a martyr to his own zealousness."[65]

The tragic analysis of Schmidt's fall didn't last long. While Schmidt considered his next move, the frenzy over who would replace him at Ohio State immediately became the hottest topic among fans and supporters. The usual big-time names led all discussions, but the name that kept popping up as a dark horse was Paul Brown, Schmidt's antithesis. What had been Schmidt's sins were Brown's strengths, making him the perfect replacement in the eyes of many. Brown had visited Columbus before Schmidt's resignation, and he visited again soon after. While High Street continued to cry for a big name, fearful that a high school coach would be in over his head at a football circus like Ohio State, a surprising slice of the fan base were staunchly in favor of the Massillon coach and hinted that their support—financial and otherwise—might be tied to his hiring. In a showing of Ohio solidarity, the members of the state's high school coaches' association—some four hundred strong—voted to endorse Brown as the next Buckeye coach. St. John, never one who enjoyed being bullied, coolly began conducting interviews with several coaches, including Schmidt's protégé, Bear Wolf. But, in the end, the drumbeat for Brown had grown too strong, and Saint, knowing what was good for him, recommended the high school mentor. On January 29, Brown was named the new head coach at Ohio State University.[66]

During the period between Schmidt's exit and Brown's entrance, Buckeye team captain Jack Stephenson announced that the team would continue the tradition of winter practice; however, it was hardly a tip of the cap to Schmidt. "Most of our indoor work, if we are compelled to 'go it alone,' will consist of conditioning exercises aimed at keeping our weight down and preparing us for the spring outdoor training grind," said Stephenson. "The new coach probably will have new charging, blocking, and tackling methods for us to learn, so we may as well hold off on that stuff until he arrives." Conspicuously absent was any mention of plays, diagrams, or razzle-dazzle.[67]

It took a few days for Schmidt's resignation to work its way through official channels, but it was accepted at every stop along the way. The final version of the resignation was set to take effect June 30, 1941, the same date Schmidt's contract would have expired had he not "quit." It was a form of severance. He was granted a leave of absence for the winter and spring quarters, thus tying a final, neat bow on Francis Schmidt's Ohio State career.

Schmidt attended the national coaches' convention in New York at the end of the year—a popular venue for divorced coaches to begin building new relationships. The stories were almost always the same. One coach would replace another coach amid much fanfare, have some good seasons, have some bad seasons, and then be replaced with a coach who had experienced the same thing at another school. It was like a never-ending garage sale where all the houses in the neighborhood repeatedly bought and sold the same items, never finding satisfaction, but never giving up hope that one team's trash was indeed another team's treasure. On the final day of the convention the rumors were white hot with news that Schmidt would end up at one of his old haunts—perhaps Tulsa or Arkansas—but nothing happened. There was also some talk of his becoming an NFL coach—something he was probably better suited for. The Detroit Lions were mentioned most frequently, but it was just talk, and nothing happened on that front either.[68]

After a fruitless convention, Schmidt officially began to apply at schools with coaching vacancies. He applied at Dartmouth but lost the job to Tuss McLaughry, thus denying observers the comic possibilities of Schmidt's being turned loose on the Ivy League. Marquette interviewed him in early January but didn't choose him either. Out of ninety coaches who applied for the job at the University of Colorado, Schmidt was among the final five but advanced no closer. The Buffaloes decided to rent something newer and went with Jim Yeager, a thirty-one-year-old who had coached at Iowa State. At one point it seemed as though Schmidt was a lock for the Tulsa job. The idea of his returning to his roots was a romantic notion, but on the same weekend Colorado signed their boy wonder, Tulsa choose to go with Henry Frnka, a hot young commodity from Temple. Once the young "Miracle Man," Schmidt was now the veteran attempting to rebound from failure.[69]

Schmidt began feeling frustrated and awkward. He had always been the object of pursuit, never the pursuer. The ugly ending at

Ohio State had given his résumé a black eye. The quirks that were once lovable accoutrements to his winning methods were now seen as liabilities. And the consistent losses in big games gave the appearance that there was a ceiling to Schmidt's magic. At fifty-four years of age, Schmidt was no longer the rising star.

Francis and Evelyn continued to maintain their home on Fifteenth Street in Columbus, just across from the main entrance of the school that had discarded them. Schmidt was surrounded by Ohio State's excitement in choosing his replacement and pursuing a future that once belonged to him. He spent a great deal of time upstairs in his office, waiting for telegrams and working on football plays for his next team. The number of job possibilities was dwindling as schools rushed to lock up new mentors in time for spring practice. In late January when the head coaching job opened up at Oklahoma, it was reported nationally that Schmidt was the first to officially apply for the position, making him look desperate, which he was. And when a post at Baylor opened up in early February, he applied the day after it was vacated. Neither school offered him employment.[70]

Schmidt's pride was in tatters. The year before, he'd been stalked by Stanford, but now he was being categorically ignored. Schmidt *had* to coach football. It was all that kept him reasonably grounded. As February turned to March there was virtually nothing remaining in the way of major coaching positions. Those remaining coaches without jobs were the ugly and the damned, ready to jump at the next opening like wolves on a rabbit. When the University of Idaho suddenly put out a late help-wanted sign, the whole desperate lot of them leapt.

Thirteen. The Final Act

The University of Idaho quickly narrowed the pool of candidates for their vacant head coaching position. There were six in the final cut, including Francis Schmidt. If this one didn't work out, Schmidt would probably have to wait another year before any other decent college jobs opened up. Thankfully for Schmidt, that scenario never became a reality. The board of regents chose him as Idaho's new head coach of football on March 16, 1941. The position paid $4,500 annually, a large drop from the $8,100 Schmidt was making at Ohio State in 1940 and a long fall from grace. The Moscow, Idaho, school had only thirty-six hundred students, and their stadium held but twelve thousand. They didn't have much tradition in the way of excellence on the football field. In fact, Schmidt's 166 career wins were more than the Vandals' entire program had achieved in forty-eight years. The Vandal squad from the previous season had not scored a single point until their seventh game! If ever a program could use a coach who was fanatical about offense, it was this one.

The timing and the coaching selection seemed to be perfect. Schmidt had previously led three smaller programs to glory, and Idaho was about to enter a phase of unlimited possibility. They were only a year away from rejoining the Pacific Coast Conference

(PCC) as full-fledged members. From 1936 through 1941 Idaho
and Montana were known as "semi-members" or "little brothers"
of the PCC (known today as the Pac Ten) with no rights to titles
or Rose Bowl appearances. They were rarely granted conference
games, and those they got were almost always on the road. With full
membership just around the corner, Idaho was already thinking
big. Though they were the smallest school in the conference, they
figured the right coach might be able to pull off a miracle. And
because Schmidt had made so much of so little in the Southwest,
Idaho was already dreaming about the fame and riches that their
new coach would generate.[1]

Schmidt dove head-first into his new position. He immediately
announced that spring practice would start the following week.
That weekend he traveled to Boise for the state high school basketball tournament. Later, he and his coaching staff went on a whirlwind state tour, visiting prospective recruits and urging them to
go to school in-state and play for the Vandals. It wasn't until late
May that Schmidt and his wife found time to return to Columbus and pack up their belongings. Secure in his new job, Schmidt
was relaxed and playful with the Columbus reporters. He laughed
about his latest post with the Vandals and noted that it fit with the
list of odd nicknames he'd represented: "I've been a Razorback, a
Horned Frog, a Golden Hurricane, a Buckeye, and now I'm a rob-
ber." When asked about whether or not he planned to implement
his razzle-dazzle in Idaho, he replied with a grin: "We'll try to score
if we can."[2]

He returned west in time to attend the PCC spring meeting. Here
it was decided that from now on the conference would adopt the
"literal interpretation" of the football rules, bringing an end to the
practice of exceptions and special interpretations. It was also decided that for all night games an orange ball would be used and

that teams would be required to tell their opponents which uniforms they would be wearing at home.[3]

Of greatest consequence to Schmidt and Idaho was a new crackdown on recruiting practices whereby schools were forbidden from contacting high school students before they had officially registered at a college. The conference schools had been warned previously that violations would be dealt with harshly, but Idaho, in the midst of a complete staff turnover, apparently had not understood this new edict or had not properly communicated it to Schmidt and his assistants. Because Schmidt's statewide publicity tour in the spring was technically illegal, Idaho now faced the possibility that eleven of their freshman would be declared ineligible. Schmidt argued that he hadn't understood the new rule, and, besides, the nearby Rocky Mountain schools had no such recruiting restrictions and were raiding southern Idaho. He singled out Utah as being particularly guilty. Conference administrators withheld a final judgment pending review.[4]

At Idaho, Schmidt had only two assistants: Walter Price, the former freshman coach, and J. A. "Babe" Brown, who had been newly hired away from his position as head coach at Moscow High. Since Schmidt didn't use his staff much anyway, fall practice was conducted similarly to all his others. On the first day of practice he spent the entire time running plays and working on the backfield.

As Schmidt had done in every other town he had invaded, he instantly won the love of the players and locals. Moscow was no different, and before the Vandals' first game under Schmidt, the citizens, students, and faculty showed their support for "the most famous wearer of bow ties in sportsdom" by wearing bow ties to class on Friday. Stores ran out of them, and one employed a seamstress to make more out of leftover dress material. Even the town's lamp posts were adorned with bow ties.[5]

Schmidt warned the fans not to get their hopes too high. The squad he inherited was lacking in speed and ballhandling skills. While he still ran plays from his collection of formations, he was forced to accommodate the squad's weaknesses by scaling back on the openness of their play.

The season got off to a bad start. First they hosted Utah, the team Schmidt had accused of thieving three months earlier, and lost 26–7. This was followed by Schmidt's first conference game, a 21–7 loss at the hands of the Oregon Ducks.

The Vandals finally entered the win column with an authoritative 21–7 win over Gonzaga. By unleashing some razzle-dazzle, including a lateraled interception return for a touchdown, the Vandals thrilled the 6,000 fans in attendance. The Bulldogs only score came on an interception return with three minutes left in the game. Throwing with a 3-touchdown lead late in the contest was pure Shut-the-Gates-of-Mercy Schmidt. Two weeks later 1,200 souls enjoyed Dads' Day in Moscow as they watched the Vandals toy with Willamette (Oregon), winning 33–6.[6]

All in all, the season turned out much as Schmidt had expected. The Vandals finished 4-5 and led the PCC in passes attempted and completed. They scored four times as many points (123) as had the previous year's team (30). The Vandals' freshman team went undefeated, and Schmidt claimed they could compete on even terms with Ohio State's freshmen. The program had momentum, and the timing was perfect. They would be hitting 1942 in full stride, just in time to make the most of becoming full-fledged members of the PCC.

Following the season, the PCC met to begin planning for 1942's new order. They drafted an initial "round-robin schedule" that heavily favored the California schools since they had bigger stadiums, bigger crowds, and thus bigger gates. Not long afterward, Schmidt, speaking to the Moscow chamber of conference, gave his opinion on the round-robin schedule. "As I see it," he told the audience, "we go around and they do the robbin'. We might have to just practice on Sunday, Monday, and Tuesday because we'll be traveling about every week." And just in case those gathered weren't impressed with a tough schedule—the followers never were—he added that it might also be a problem if "the army catches too many of my seasoned men."[7]

The army's catching young men had become a recent threat with the introduction of the draft. The process had been necessitated by Germany's two years of war against Europe, an ugly scene that beckoned America's presence. The U.S. military was preparing to step in when needed. Already, before the season had even ended, the Vandals had lost their starting left guard, Bill Lockey. He had a commitment to the air force, and they had come calling the week before Thanksgiving. Nobody could have predicted that the Japanese would bomb Pearl Harbor less than a month later, turning everybody's plans upside down.[8]

America's entry into World War II meant that young men were desperately needed everywhere. They weren't only being drafted into the military; they were taking jobs in support of the war effort. All of this was leaving college football rather thin, and some schools were hurt more than others. Idaho, the smallest school in the conference—and not a hotbed of talent to begin with—suffered immediately. When Schmidt opened spring practice on March 27, 1942, only sixteen men "turned out" and only one of them, Earl Chandler, was a returning letterman. Needless to say, it was the school's smallest turnout in modern-day history. A few more trickled in, but if Schmidt was going to maintain any sense of momentum it would be solely by virtue of a Herculean effort in fall practice.[9]

Five months later, as the little program began planning for fall practice, the other shoe dropped. PCC commissioner Edwin N. Atherton did declare that eleven of the Vandal's sophomores were ineligible for 1942 as a result of Schmidt's recruiting violations

during his first few months working for the school. Most of the ineligible group had been starters on the undefeated freshman team of
1941 and were the key to the program's immediate hopes. Schmidt
was outraged, but George Greene, Idaho's athletic director, didn't
want to rock the boat. There were already grumblings that Idaho
and Montana shouldn't be full-fledged members of the conference.
"We were too enthusiastic," admitted Greene. "A rule is a rule, and
we are going to abide by the rules. We are not protesting the findings." At this point, all hope for a good season seemed lost.[10]

Fullback William Miklick, who had led the PCC in scoring, had
been drafted by the Marines, and Fred Nichols, the tough right
half, had joined the Naval Air Reserve. Schmidt invited thirty-five
men to fall practice, but only half were there when camp opened.
Assistant Babe Brown played center since one hadn't shown up yet.
A few more trickled in, but many of last year's lettermen had taken
summer jobs that ended up paying so much—more than Schmidt
made in some cases—that they didn't even bother returning to college. Left half Ray Davis was one of the handful that tried to balance
money and football. He'd earned enough money doing defense
work over the summer that he could pay tuition for his entire senior
year. Howard Manson, who had led the PCC in pass completions in
1941, helped build liberty ships on the coast during the summer
and, much to Schmidt's relief, had decided to return. Some of the
players returned the same week of the opening game.[11]

It was an odd season. Idaho's motley crew began with Oregon
State and took a 32–0 beating before hosting the 2nd Air Force
company and losing 14–0. Their first road game of the season was
moved from Saturday to Friday with two days' notice, and they traveled to eastern Washington in station wagons. A 28–7 victory made
the logistical problems more palatable. The Vandals made their
first trip to California under Schmidt when they visited Stanford
on October 17. Only 2,500 students showed up to watch Stanford

pummel Idaho 54–7. Some fistfights broke out near the end, and one Vandal was ejected. A writer noted that Stanford's head coach, "Marchy" Schwartz, had been an assistant at the University of Chicago when Schmidt and the Scarlet Scourge were running up huge scores on them. One can assume Schwartz felt no guilt in abusing Shut-the-Gates-of-Mercy Schmidt and his Vandals.[12]

As Schmidt and company battled through an impossible situation, Schmidt certainly couldn't help but notice that Paul Brown and the Buckeyes were putting together a great wartime season, a season that would end at 9-1 and a national championship. He must have shaken his head, remembering his pair of one-loss seasons at OSU that didn't even result in an outright conference title. The previous season, Ohio had finished 6-1-1 as Brown began the process of building a program built on organization and fundamentals. The wayward Tom Kinkade had played his best ball, and Jack Graf emerged from Don Scott's shadow to be named the Big 10 MVP.

A merciful end to Idaho's season (3-7 overall) came on December 5, 1942, when the Vandals visited UCLA at the Los Angeles Coliseum. It was the same stadium where the annual Rose Bowl was held, which was the biggest game in all of football, and one Schmidt traveled cross country to see every year. On these hallowed grounds, with nothing to lose, Schmidt had his boys shoot the works. But in the end, it didn't matter. UCLA was on their way to a PCC championship, and with Bob Waterfield starring at quarterback, the Bruins beat the Vandals 40–13. Schmidt and his boys were horribly outclassed in terms of material but they never gave up playing razzle-dazzle all afternoon, much to the delight of the 25,000 fans who were treated to the Vandals' "tricky forwards, laterals, hidden ball plays, and runs from fake punts." Idaho attempted a whopping 34 passes, completing 18 for 209 yards and both of their touchdowns, the last coming on a beautiful 44-yarder near the end of the game. There were too many penalties and some "stiff body punching," but the AP reporter covering the contest declared that "it was a wide-open game all the way and one of the best of the season here, so far as the crowd was concerned."[13]

It was the final game of football that Schmidt ever coached. Shooting the works—thus thrilling the fans—was the perfect way to end his career. Those two elements were the benchmarks on which he based his obsessive love of football.

Schmidt didn't know this was the last game of his career, though he suspected it might be his last for some time. America was getting more deeply involved in the war, and his fragile program was feeling it more than most. Also, travel was being restricted in order to preserve resources, and schools in the Northwest didn't have a lot of nearby competition, or at least the kind that could draw a crowd big enough to justify the journey. Even huge California schools like Stanford and Cal were talking about staying local through the rest of the war. There had been a time when it looked as though Idaho's 1942 season might not happen, and now, with things getting even worse, what were the odds that a team would actually be fielded in 1943?[14]

Spring practice was cancelled. There were not enough players, and the campus facilities and equipment were now being devoted to a government-mandated physical-fitness program. Schmidt, the former bayonet instructor, now devoted his time to preparing young men for possible duty in the war by focusing on their physical training.[15]

Any hope of salvaging a season evaporated in September when Idaho, Washington State, and Oregon State officially dropped wartime football. Schmidt's contract, which ran through May of the next year, was retained, but only so that he might continue the work of physical training, which included a football program for military trainees on campus.

Although Schmidt took pride in helping his country, a part of him was dying. The football coaching career he cherished had been reduced to scraps. With the benefit of hindsight, one can speculate that it wasn't even the war that had inflicted Schmidt's wounds. Maybe it started in November of 1935 when his Buckeyes lost the game of the century to Notre Dame. That was the day when his system had first been questioned. Despite all Schmidt's brilliance and influential strategy that followed, his reputation never fully recovered, and the end had been steeper and darker than anyone would have predicted. Just thirteen months after giving Ohio State their first outright conference title in nearly two decades, he had practically begged for a coaching job, somewhere, anywhere. He'd been exiled back to the small time. And then, before he could even start fixing this broken-down little program, the war had completely stolen football from him. Football had served as the medication for his hypomania. Without this balm, all was a dead end. Schmidt was just going through the motions, waiting for his contract to end, waiting for yet another football team.

All of this wasted time was destroying the vitality and impatience that had once marked Schmidt. His bluster and humor had been stifled. On top of it all, as he waited, some of his players were being silenced. Bill Lockey, the guard taken from Schmidt's squad two years earlier, was now dead. He had been killed piloting a pursuit ship in the southwest Pacific. Schmidt received a letter from him that arrived a week after his death. Don Scott, Schmidt's marvelous quarterback at Ohio State, was dead. He was the commanding officer of a bomber and died in a crash at an England airfield, leaving behind a pregnant widow who was expecting any day.[16]

Schmidt was "not surprised" when he was told on February 26, 1944, that his contract would not be renewed when it expired the following month. Realizing that another college gig would be nearly impossible to land, Schmidt let it be known that he was available for any pro teams including several that were joining a new West Coast league called the American Professional Football League. He hunkered down in Moscow, "sending out feelers" to franchises, but nothing materialized.[17]

Schmidt began to weaken emotionally, and as the spring progressed, his physical condition gradually deteriorated as well. He had looked thinner near the end of his Idaho tenure, but now he was looking sickly and gaunt. In early September, about the time he would normally open fall practice, Schmidt was moved eighty miles west to St. Luke's hospital in Spokane, Washington. He was reported to be "gravely ill." A week later, on the evening of September 19, 1944, he was dead. He was fifty-eight years old.[18]

A heartbroken Evelyn Schmidt arranged for his body to be transported to Arkansas City, Kansas, for burial. Schmidt didn't really have a home, but his parents were buried in the Riverview Cemetery, and so was Francis on Sunday, September 24, 1944. Evelyn would live another forty-seven years, and during that time she never stopped telling her nieces and nephews how much she loved her unforgettable husband. She never remarried. Who could possibly have followed an act like Francis?[19]

Where Francis Schmidt was concerned, no one was ever sure what was real and what was myth. In fact, his death only amplified the uncertainty. After his passing had been reported nationally, it was instantly rumored that Schmidt's death was the result of his no longer coaching football. The man who was obsessed with the game had died of a broken heart. Or so they say.

Fourteen. The Schmidt Effect

Decades after Francis Schmidt's death, some of his protégés still marveled at their teacher's vision, imagination, and
influence.

"Francis Schmidt was the greatest coach who ever lived—he was
years ahead of his time," proclaimed Sid Gillman.[1]

"Francis Schmidt had to be the most fantastic coach in the country. He was, at that point—I don't think there is any doubt about
it, it is a matter of record—way ahead of everybody offensively," declared John Vaught.[2]

Although football coaches and pundits in the 1930s knew that
Schmidt was the *de facto* leader of the open-game movement, they
could not possibly understand how he would affect the future of
football for decades to come. Such recognition requires context,
and in this case context required time. As purveyors of cutting-edge
offense in the 1960s and 1970s, Gillman and Vaught had a unique
appreciation for the man who had influenced them. Even as they
were being considered ahead of their time, they were more aware
than ever of what a head start they had been given by learning at
the feet of Francis Schmidt.

Schmidt had his team learning five hundred plays when other
teams were using thirty, and he was using eight or more formations

as a standard practice while others dared not implement more than three. But those are just the facts used for easy reference. Schmidt was not only ahead of his time in actual practice, he was ahead of his time in vision. There was a difference between the modicum of restraint he was forced to cede to his era and what he saw as standard practice in the future. And he wasn't just speculating. He was certain.

"Every team must have a running attack," said Schmidt, "but you can't rely on that alone. In fact, the open style of offense, with passes being tossed on unorthodox downs and from unusual places, will gradually push the running attack into the background. I expect to see the time, before many years, when forward and lateral passes will make up the greatest part of the offense, with the running attack just something to fall back upon. The wide-open, chance-taking game is the style the fans want to see. The day of having a fullback plunge into the center of the line for a yard or 2 at a time is rapidly passing."[3]

Speed, versatility, and deception would be the hallmarks of the game that thrilled future fans, and the completeness of their implementation was "the goal toward which he [was] working."[4]

This vision seems rather pedestrian today, but Schmidt spoke these words in 1936, when major college teams scored less than 12 points per game, threw for less than 70 yards per game, and ran versus passed at a 3:1 ratio. Speed, versatility, and deception were his obsessions in an era that focused almost exclusively on size, strength, and safety. "Schmidt would do anything to move the ball, using every kind of offense in the world," recalled Vaught. Indeed, it's not that *everything* worked in Schmidt's system. It's that he *would do just about anything to move the ball.*[5]

The laterals that Schmidt was so fond of might occur three

separate times in plays he'd drawn up. They might happen off a completed pass downfield and they might happen off an interception on defense. Eventually, they were deemed too risky for downfield use by the football establishment, but laterals have lived on as a main component of option offenses where they get tossed to trailing backs on nearly every other play. The shovel pass, for which Schmidt had dozens of variations, is not a staple today, but it is still featured in nearly every scheme and still quickens pulses. If anything, Schmidt would perhaps be disappointed at the dearth of wide-open ballhandling today.

Remember the three plays Boise State sprung on Oklahoma in the 2006 Fiesta Bowl? Football fans talked about them for weeks afterward. Even today they are the plays people reference when reaching for an example of football at its most thrilling. One play was a hook and lateral, one was a Statue of Liberty, and one was a pass thrown by a wide receiver. All three were part of Schmidt's standard repertoire. As a matter of fact, if one of Schmidt's peak Ohio State teams were to perform today, fans would be dumbfounded at the audacious plays unfolding before them. As popular as football is right now, it only showcases a percentage of Schmidt's razzle-dazzle. "If this man [Schmidt] were alive today," said Sid Gillman decades after Schmidt's death, "I wonder what advances he would be making in offensive football because he had no peer in this category."[6]

Where football has *fully* fulfilled Schmidt's vision is in its abundant use of the forward pass. It easily makes up "the greatest part of the offense" these days, as Schmidt predicted it would clear back in 1936. Here again Schmidt proved to be influential with his array of schemes. The short game inspired Dutch Meyer, and the vertical game inspired Sid Gillman. Schmidt used wheel routes, screens, short crossing patterns, and end delays. He loved involving eligible linemen on the receiving end and unexpected backfield men on the throwing end. And just to keep things stirred up, he loved to see a throw from any part of the field on any down so that the defense could never be certain what to expect.

Isn't that what today's football is all about? Isn't that why offenses and defenses study each other on film for hour upon hour each week? Isn't that why football is the mammoth spectator sport that millions of fans excitedly watch every weekend during the fall?

Francis Schmidt is not solely responsible for the runaway success of modern football, but as the man who was uniquely instrumental in creating and displaying the wide-open spectrum of offensive football, his influence on the game is undeniable. Many call it the Schmidt effect, and it is ubiquitous, influencing modern football in games both big and small. Connect the dots and you will see how it has come to be present in every football game you watch.

Nobody could possibly have been a closer disciple of Schmidt than Sid Gillman. In terms of work ethic, love of football strategy, and a stubborn belief in imagination, Schmidt and Gillman were perfectly matched. They had even traveled down the same path academically, both planning on careers in law. Fate had ended Schmidt's law career before it even started, and in 1934 Schmidt *was* the fate that ended Gillman's law career.

The newly hired Schmidt had been impressed with Gillman from their first meeting, and when Schmidt got the Ohio State job he asked Gillman if he would help out as an assistant during spring practice. Gillman, who had just finished his playing career with the Buckeyes a few months earlier and was nearing graduation, agreed to help. He loved football, and the extra money would help him pay for law school, which he intended to begin in the fall. But just as it had with Schmidt, the football bug bit Gillman deeply, and everything else faded away. His decision to accept Schmidt's offer changed everything. "I went back and I haven't seen a law school yet. I wasn't interested in anything else after that."

After that spring, Gillman took assistant work at smaller Ohio colleges, but he continued to work part-time with Schmidt until Schmidt finally got the okay to hire him full-time in 1938. Gillman, with his fertile mind and his passion for football, had been teamed with the perfect teacher, and his education in offensive football had just begun. "He [Schmidt] was the worker and he enjoyed having me around because I worked right with him," recalled Gillman. They were both obsessed with football strategy and could spend hours toying with the Xs and Os. Schmidt's idea of "scoring first" and playing aggressive open football resonated with Gillman. As a former pass-catching end, Gillman was particularly fascinated with the forward-passing portion of Schmidt's system. "It is something I learned right away. . . . Schmidt, my coach, was pass-oriented. It started kind of with him and the fascination myself. You can score faster, quicker by throwing the ball than you could any other way. So it was Schmidt that really was the key guy in my thinking."[7]

In all, Gillman studied Schmidt's system for seven years before the disastrous season of 1940 caused both men to resign and seek separate paths; Schmidt was exiled to Idaho, and Gillman set off on a program-hopping journey. After successful stops at Army, Miami (OH), and the University of Cincinnati, Gillman was hired to be the head coach of the NFL's Los Angeles Rams in 1955. Six years later he was named the head coach of the San Diego Chargers, a fledgling team in a fledgling league, the AFL.

The AFL, in an attempt to draw fans and compete with the established NFL, played a more open brand of modern football right from the start. It was an ironic twist, as that was the same strategy the NFL had initially used to compete with the college game and establish itself some thirty years before. Now the venturesome boldness and excitement were being used against the NFL, and nobody in the renegade AFL was more revolutionary than Sid Gillman.

One of Gillman's assistants during those first years with the Chargers was a young man named Al Davis. It didn't take Davis long to be blown away by Gillman's creativity: "Sid opened new avenues for me. Being part of Gillman's organization was like going to a laboratory for the highly developed science of organized football. No question, he was the master of using the field, sideline to sideline. Screens, gadgets—he had 'em all. It was like going into a restaurant: Anything you wanted to eat, he had." Davis not only describes how fascinating it was to learn from Gillman, he also perfectly captures the enduring importance of the Schmidt effect. Schmidt opened the "restaurant" (featuring a menu the size of a telephone book), Gillman perfected it, and Davis was now absorbing the formula of "anything goes," which he would use to establish his own famous brand of football in Oakland.[8]

While those on the inside were focused on learning, those on the outside were content to be entertained. Mike Martz was too young to fully grasp its intricacies, but Gillman's trailblazing offense was an awakening vision: "I was a San Diego high school kid in those days. I used to love to sit in old Balboa Stadium and watch Gillman's offense at work. I mean, it was just so great to look at—Lance Alworth and Gary Garrison and John Hadl throwing the ball all over the place. Paul Lowe and Keith Lincoln running. It was an awesome experience." Martz went on to become an NFL coach known for his highly aggressive offense.[9]

By 1964 Gillman's teachings had become important and were already beginning to alter the shape of then-current offensive strategy. Yet even with his stellar reputation, Gillman still remembered with awe Francis Schmidt, the teacher who had influenced his philosophies, calling him "probably the greatest mind the game has ever known. The basic designs and techniques Schmidt used some twenty years ago are most applicable at the present time." While those in the football community were celebrating Gillman as a trailblazer, Gillman saw himself as only having maintained the momentum he had received from Schmidt. Gillman always wore a bow tie on the sidelines as a tribute to Schmidt, the man responsible for giving him his first big break as well as legitimizing and stoking his extreme passion for football strategy—one that would last a lifetime.[10]

Gillman was spreading Schmidt's influence, but he was also advancing the science of ball movement with his own highly organized approach to imagination. Al Davis was sold on what he had seen. After absorbing the brilliance of Gillman's schematics for three years, Davis was hired as the head coach and general manager of the Oakland Raiders in 1963. Having averaged just 3 wins per season during their existence, the Raiders were desperate enough to hand their two most important jobs to a mere thirty-three-year-old. But Davis came through and, using what he had learned, instantly led the Raiders to a 10-4 season—the first of many seasons of excellence.

Three years later Davis hired an assistant named Bill Walsh, the man who would become synonymous with offense as football eventually entered the twenty-first century. And along with his new system of offense would come bushels of victories for himself and those on his coaching tree—not just regular wins but *big* wins. Besides the three Super Bowl teams that Walsh coached, there were those led by his schematic descendants, including Mike Holmgren (thrice), Sam Wyche, Mike Shanahan (twice), Andy Reid, Tony Dungy, and others. Granted, all of these men have their own playbooks, but the base concepts and the encouragement to experiment are well grounded in Walsh's system. So where did Walsh find the foundation for his own offensive beliefs? In his autobiography, Walsh explains:

> The biggest influence on me was the Raider system I learned as an assistant in 1966—and that system emanated from Sid Gillman. . . . With the Raiders, I learned the Gillman system of football, which became the foundation of my philosophy of offense. . . . Sid Gillman brought refinement to the game. Every technique, every skill was isolated. There were no philosophical barriers to restrict Sid's creativity. The Raiders, under Al Davis, further developed this system.[11]
>
> It was a fully dimensional approach. For instance, Gillman, with Joe Madro, his offensive assistant, had developed a system of offensive-line blocking—which Ollie Spencer used with the Raiders—that employed virtually every conceivable blocking combination. It took a year or two for Raider linemen to develop within the system, but when they learned it, they were equipped to handle any situation.[12]

Later Walsh said: "Sid's system was as complex as any in history. He had a term for every pass pattern for every receiver. It took years for some people to learn."[13]

Walsh's description not only sheds light on his own inspiration, it underscores the strengths and weaknesses of Francis Schmidt. The strengths anchor Schmidt's resonating influence, while the weaknesses help to explain why he was unable to secure the notoriety he deserves.

When Walsh talks about influence in the phrases, "no philosophical barriers to . . . creativity" and "virtually every conceivable . . . combination," he refers to Gillman, but this lasting influence was Schmidt's gift to football. This is why Schmidt was ahead of his time. And this is why he is important. Not because of a single play or formation that he created but because he explored the entire spectrum of strategy and tried *everything.* Schmidt had both the imagination to dream up every conceivable method for gaining ground and the daring to try damn near all of them in a single game. This, along with his theory about scoring first and fastest, is what he passed on to his protégés, and they in turn passed it on to the next wave of coaches who were open-minded enough to recognize Schmidt's brilliance. Bill Walsh's landmark offensive strategy, the misnamed West Coast Offense, is not a replica of anything (although it shares traits with Dutch Meyer's famous Spread Offense and its emphasis on short, secure passing). It is a beautifully designed system sprung from Walsh's own imagination and built upon the foundation of the shoot-the-works philosophy that Schmidt had shared with Gillman, who shared it with Davis, who shared it with Walsh. Together, they helped make football the most popular spectator sport in America.

So why has Schmidt, the founding father of wide-open football, been all but forgotten today? Walsh's preceding description provides a clue; he says it took some players years to absorb the complexities of Sid's system. For Raider linemen, it took a "year or two" to learn the subtleties of the blocking schemes. That's an average of eighteen months for men who were being paid and had unlimited learning resources, time, and experience. Schmidt worked with amateurs whose high school backgrounds had not even begun to prepare them for the complex, futuristic stuff he had in mind. His college players had limited opportunities to watch primitive game films, academic responsibilities, and only eight games per season through which to gain experience. This made it nearly impossible for them to fully absorb Schmidt's endless strategies, let alone the finer points that separate the mediocre from the mind-blowing. In many respects Schmidt was simply too far ahead of his time to properly implement his ideas. The rules committee, technology, and high school football—America's football training ground—trailed far behind his obsessive, relentless mind. But—and this is a big but—Schmidt's own inadequacies actually hurt his cause more profoundly than anything and led to his failure in securing his coaching legacy. His hypomanic mind made him a force that demanded reckoning but also sabotaged his efforts.

The litany of Schmidt's coaching sins has been documented in the proceeding chapters. Among other things, he was unable to bear the boredom of fundamentals. He was too disorganized, his practices were too long, and his teaching manner was too caustic. He may have influenced many assistants but he never fully utilized them on the field. And his paranoia mandated that coaches and players have information withheld *from them* at the very time he was trying to teach that same information *to them.*

Because of these weaknesses, Schmidt was not able to mold his players to the extent needed for them to fully utilize his system. Through raw talent, hard work, and the ability to retain a fraction of Schmidt's system, his teams were successful. But at Ohio State, Schmidt's boys just barely missed attaining a superlative level of success. In the rarified air of big-time football, the margin for error is thin, and Schmidt's weaknesses contributed to more errors than was permissible. The conference titles and statistical victories were not as conspicuous as the blown leads, missed opportunities, and last-minute failures that seemed to earmark all the heavyweight matches during his tenure. Big wins against big teams shape and define a football coach's legacy. Without them, his story is usually reduced to nothing more than a couple of anecdotes and some aggregate type buried deep in a media guide.

Francis Schmidt is too important for the historical fate he dealt himself. It would have been a shame had Schmidt's enormous influence on football been derailed by the very weaknesses that eventually sabotaged his coaching career. Fortunately, for all of us who enjoy watching intriguing football, there have been many organized and calculating men who have harnessed Schmidt's imagination and married it with patience and discipline to help make the game what it is today. Sid Gillman may have been influenced by Schmidt strategically, but Gillman's later associations with Earl Blaik and Paul Brown taught him to use his knowledge wisely. Schmidt's failure at Ohio State was the powerful lesson he had not intended to pass on to Gillman, but Gillman was clever enough to understand what went wrong and to realize how Schmidt's system could be better organized so as to reach its potential. As one of his players, Keith Lincoln, put it, "Gillman is so organized it's unreal."[14]

Bill Walsh never forgot his initial exposure to Gillman's intensity for detail: "My first real experience with Sid was when I was with the Raiders. It was the night before the game, and I turned on *The Sid Gillman Show*. He had [Charger receiver] Lance Alworth on, and [Sid] was talking about the slant pass. He was lecturing like somebody at MIT. Me and a few other people could comprehend it, but that was about it. It was so detailed. Sid was going to coach Alworth all night in that studio."[15]

Gillman and Walsh weren't the only ones to benefit by adding some organization to Schmidt's philosophy. John Vaught, because of his curiosity and intelligence, was one of the few players that Schmidt trusted with his lessons. He played guard for four years (1929–32) under Schmidt at TCU and never forgot his opportunity: "For some reason, he [Schmidt] took a liking to me. In those days we had very little film study, but Schmidt managed to get pictures of some of our games and some of the opposition. I can remember going with him to the physics lab to review them. It wasn't done by squad. It was a privilege to be asked to study films with him. They were dull, dim, no-account films, but I could see their value immediately."[16]

After serving as an assistant to Bear Wolf (another Schmidt grad) at North Carolina, John Vaught ended up as the postwar head coach at Ole Miss. There he remained as the Rebels' leader for the next twenty-four years. During that time, his squads won 6 conference titles, a share of 3 national championships and appeared in 18 bowl games. Not a bad job for someone who shared a conference with Bear Bryant, Robert Neyland, and Bobby Dodd. But, of course, all this football excellence wouldn't be noteworthy if Vaught hadn't accomplished it using a heavy dose of Schmidt's philosophy, which called for an aggressive variety of plays and formations designed to create bad personnel matchups and a tentative mindset for the opponent's defense.

"Offense was always what I loved best," admitted Vaught. "That's what I got the biggest kick out of, trying to outmaneuver the other guy. I always tried to get the other team's defense to line up according to what we were doing, and then we had them."[17]

"'Move the ball. Move the ball.' Francis Schmidt preached that to me at TCU," recalled Vaught in 1970, "and I think the Ole Miss attack since 1947 would put a smile on his face. I still have the playbook he gave me. Ole Miss has used just about everything except the old Swinging Gate formation. Our offense has gotten the job done with the Notre Dame Box, the Split-T, the Winged-T, the I-Formation and our own specialty—the Quarterback Sprint-Out."[18]

It was that last formation that Archie Manning worked from when he played under Vaught. The quarterback, who went on to star for the Saints and sire two of the NFL's best-known current quarterbacks, had chosen Ole Miss in part because Vaught had a "reputation for developing great quarterbacks." He was not disappointed. "Coach Vaught was an offensive genius," recalled Manning. "He devoured everything he could learn about offense and was way ahead of most of those he competed against. It helped that he was an unabashed, unrepentant pirate of other coaches' ideas."[19]

"One of his jobs as Ole Miss's offensive coordinator ordinarily would be to break down the film of an opponent's defense the week of a game to determine how and where to exploit it. But not coach Vaught. He watched the other team's *offense* to find formations and plays he could use himself."[20]

Schmidt would have smiled at that practice. He had piles of notebooks filled with strategies he had observed while watching other teams' games or had learned about during one of the dozens and dozens of clinics he attended. Let's be honest—cataloging the spectrum of offensive football required equal parts imagination and thievery on his part. Schmidt would also have been proud of Vaught's record of offensive success. Between 1948 and 1968 Vaught's Rebels amassed more yardage than any other team in the SEC, averaging 332 yards per game. During that same period, Alabama gained 283 yards per game to earn second place. That's a difference of 15 percent, or as Vaught gauged it: "three country miles."[21]

He may not have used the Swinging Gate Formation, but another former Schmidt assistant imported it to his program. Gomer Jones was glad to introduce it to the Oklahoma Sooners' program where he was the line coach to Bud Wilkinson. Schmidt's imprint could even be found on *those* Sooners—the 1947–59 Sooners who won 13 consecutive conference titles, 3 national championships, and put together a 47-game winning streak that has never been topped.[22]

Jones was the power in front of the throne. He instituted the Sooners' line strategy and taught the linemen during this reign. In all, he developed a staggering sixteen All-American linemen during his seventeen years with Wilkinson. So impressed was Pop Ivy, another Sooner assistant, that when he took his first head-coaching job in 1954 he asked Gomer to join him for the first three weeks of training camp where he installed the basics of his line system. The team was the Edmonton Eskimos of the Canadian Football League, and though line play was surely just one part of the team's improvement, it's worth noting that the Eskimos proceeded to win 3 straight Grey Cup Championships and 5 straight Western Division titles. Ivy got all the credit for those titles, just as Wilkinson got most of the credit for Oklahoma's championships, but both men understood how important Gomer's knowledge was to their prosperity. "Gomer and I work as partners," said Wilkinson. "There is no other term for our relationship. All we do at Oklahoma is as much Gomer's thinking as mine." And yes, the Sooners really did use Francis Schmidt's Swinging Gate formation.[23]

Gomer's classic manifesto, *Offensive and Defensive Line Play*, was published in 1961 and for many years was required reading for anyone interested in building a better line. On the opening page, Jones explained that he had played for Francis Schmidt and later "had the good fortune, after graduation, to be a member of Coach Schmidt's staff and work with Ernie Godfrey, his outstanding line coach. The basis of line play described in this book was learned at that time." It had been more than twenty years since his final exposure to Schmidt, but the futuristic training he received was still relevant enough to anchor Jones's highly regarded book.[24]

Vaught and Jones were part of huge programs, but Schmidt's effect on the game of football resonated off the beaten path, as well. In the very corner of barren west Texas stands the University of Texas at El Paso (UTEP), and it was here that Vaught's good friend and ex-teammate Mike Brumbelow spent seven seasons as the head coach from 1950 to 1957. Implementing what he had learned from practicing under Schmidt, Brumbelow guided UTEP to their best stretch of football ever. His all-time best winning percentage and three bowl appearances have not been topped by another UTEP coach in the half century since.

For an even smaller venue one can turn to Missouri State, where Howard "Red" Blair took over as head coach in 1938 after serving as one of Schmidt's assistants at Ohio State. In the four seasons before

World War II, Blair implemented Schmidt's system to the tune of a 30-6-3 record. Missouri State also averaged 18.5 points per game, which is interesting for two reasons. First, it was well above the national average for the time, and second, it was a full touchdown per game more than had been scored by Blair's teams at Akron, the program he ran *before* learning from Schmidt. In 1947, just as his program was about to return to full postwar manpower, Blair died, leaving us to wonder how he would have fared in the world of unlimited substitution.

Sometimes the Schmidt effect can be found unintentionally. In November of 2004 Jim Tressel made a surprising discovery about Francis Schmidt's relevance. Tressel, the highly successful coach at Ohio State, was visiting Nick Wasylik at the osu hospital where the eighty-nine-year-old was having surgery. They began to discuss football, and Wasylik talked about his days as one of Schmidt's "e-flat" quarterbacks. When the discussion turned to current Buckeye football and its need to utilize uber-talented receiver Ted Ginn, Tressel received some advice that he later related at a press conference:

"He [Wasylik] said, 'You know, the thing I like about Ginn is he runs straight, he runs straight for the goal line. I've got a couple plays from Francis Schmidt that you could use to get Ted the ball.' So, we might use a couple of those that Wasylik suggested," admitted Tressel. Perhaps Tressel was just being nice, but he made a point of considering what he had heard and of telling it to the assembled press. And as for Wasylik, the former Schmidt quarterback felt no risk in offering up seventy-year-old plays because those plays were now just as relevant, if not more so, than the day he learned them.[25]

Sometimes you can realize the Schmidt effect in the unlikeliest of places. Consider the power sweep on which Vince Lombardi built his legend. As the play's title suggests, it is a forceful running maneuver—one that is extreme in that it uses nearly every offensive player to generate a wave of momentous destruction around the tackle. It immediately appealed to Lombardi as a statement run. And its inspiration came to him while watching game film of the 1955 Los Angeles Rams. The power sweep that he saw was so perfectly executed that the core of his iconic offensive philosophy was born within. The man who installed that tremendous sweep for the 1955 Rams was none other than their new head coach, Sid Gillman.[26]

Yes, Gillman was known for his open-game rather than for strong-armed running tactics, but anybody who learned from Schmidt learned that sheer variety is what makes an offense truly spectacular. That, and the willingness to attempt anything during live games, which leads to one final story.

You see, sometimes the Schmidt effect can be found in the wrong place at the wrong time, but because it's so memorable you enjoy it anyhow. Sort of like the 1935 Ohio State–Notre Dame game.

One such occasion was the NFL's 1945 championship game—its first post–World War II title contest and the hesitant new beginning of a second modern period. Appropriately, it featured the old versus the new—the Cleveland Rams versus the Washington Redskins. The Rams were the league's newest member, having joined a couple years before the war. The Redskins were veterans, and successful veterans at that. They were led by the legendary Sammy Baugh, while the Rams were led by rookie quarterback Bob Waterfield—a recent UCLA graduate. Two future hall-of-fame inductees at different stages of their career, with decidedly different backgrounds.

Slingin' Sammy Baugh, now thirty-one years old, was finishing his ninth professional season. He'd already played in four championship games and had been named All-Pro seven times, but 1945 had been his finest year. The Skins had switched to the T-Formation (something he had desired for years), and he had responded by completing 128 of 182 passes. This completion percentage of 70.3 percent remained an NFL record for thirty-seven years. Although the lanky Baugh had battled injury issues during his pro career, he had remained the vanguard passer who was setting the standards for the next modern period. His unique throwing skills combined with the advanced open-game training he had received from Schmidt protégée Dutch Meyer had given him an advantage that was only now being challenged by the likes of Sid Luckman.

Young Bob Waterfield hadn't been so blessed. Even though he had a marvelous arm, he had played traditional football from the single wing at UCLA, which did little to equip him for the slightly more open pro game. Unlike Baugh, he hadn't learned cutting-edge strategy that he could bring with him and install with his new NFL team. Fortunately, one of his teammates had been a beneficiary of the Schmidt effect.

Jim Benton, the team's star receiver, had been schooled at the University of Arkansas under former Schmidt assistant Fred Thomsen. So great was Thomsen's reputation for playing open football that it was the deciding factor in Benton's enrolling at Arkansas. Once there, Benton received one of the finest educations available in forward passing, and he got far more repetitions than he might have anywhere else. He learned route-running skills when route running was not even a widely accepted term. He caught 48 balls in 1937, a conference record that stood for twenty-six years.[27]

Now in 1945, he was passing his training on to Waterfield, the rookie quarterback. "I didn't call the plays," recalled Waterfield of his rookie season. "He [Benton] did. He'd tell me what he was going to run and I'd say 'okay.' He was all moves. He had no speed. He used to get caught from behind all the time. . . . He'd tell me he was going to get open on a hook, a corner, or an out. And I believed him. When I got ready to throw, sure enough, he was open." This trust in Benton's understanding led to an unforgettable game against Detroit earlier that season, when the two men hooked up ten times for 303 yards. Benton's receiving yardage smashed Don Hutson's league record for a single game and would not be topped for forty years.[28]

Riding the improvised passing feats of Benton and Waterfield, the Rams not only posted their first winning record in franchise history, they won their division. The championship game against the Redskins was held in Cleveland's Municipal Stadium on December 16, but the weather couldn't have been less inviting. As Benton recalled, "It was only about five degrees above zero. They had put hay on the field and a tarp on top of that for about two weeks before the game to keep the field from freezing. They removed it just before the game but by the first quarter the open end, the one near Lake Erie, was frozen, and by the second half the field was totally frozen."[29]

The weather wasn't the only disappointment. In the second quarter, Sammy Baugh was forced out of the game due to bruised ribs. All was not lost, however. His replacement, Frank Filchock, took over and threw for 2 touchdowns. That matched the 2 touchdown throws tossed by Bob Waterfield, including a 37-yarder to Jim Benton, who ended the game with 9 catches for 125 yards.

The final outcome of the game really came down to two plays involving the goalposts. During this era, the NFL rules dictated that the goalposts be placed at the front of the end zone on the goal line, not at the back as they are today. This meant the goalposts would occasionally disrupt player movement, even if the real purpose behind their placement was to eliminate tie games by making field goals and extra points easier to convert. Following Benton's touchdown catch, Waterfield's extra-point attempt was partially blocked, and it landed softly on the crossbar where it swayed a moment before dropping over successfully. The Rams, who misfired on an extra-point attempt later in the game, would have lost 14–13 if not for the other play involving the goalposts—a play that will never be duplicated.

In the first quarter, with the Redskins in possession of the ball on their *own* 5-yard line, Baugh decided it was the sort of spot where the Rams would least expect a forward pass, so, naturally, that's what he called for. He dropped back, looking for an open receiver, and then dropped back some more to buy time as the pass rushers fought their way closer. Finally, Baugh saw something deep down the middle, and he unleashed his magic arm. But the ball never made it—never even made it out of the end zone. It slammed into the goalpost and ricocheted to the turf, never having crossed the goal line. Today it would simply have been considered an incomplete pass, but in 1945 this unfortunate mishap was still penalized with a safety. Owner George Preston Marshall was so miffed that at a subsequent owners' meeting he bullied the others into changing that rule for good. But at the time of the game, he was helpless just like the rest of the Redskins. Worse yet, those 2 points ended up being *the* difference as Cleveland won 15–14.

One might assume the Schmidt effect can be found in Jim Benton's helping his rookie quarterback win the league MVP award on the way to the championship. And while that would make for a happy ending to this book, it's Baugh's boomerang pass that really captures the essence of Schmidt. For one thing, that rejected pass was the deciding factor in a heavyweight battle, one that the Redskins just barely lost. How many big games did Schmidt lose at Ohio State by the thinnest of margins? Nearly all of them? No matter how many wins and titles he had garnered pre–Ohio State, his seven frustrating years in Columbus would never be forgotten. Just hanging on and beating Notre Dame in 1935 would probably have assured Schmidt and the Buckeyes a national championship. It might have saved his reputation, as well.

The ricocheted Baugh pass was rare, odd, and unexpected.

428 THE SCHMIDT EFFECT

And for all of its potential to develop into a famous play, it ended up nothing more than a curious, bittersweet footnote, not unlike Schmidt's coaching career. Francis Schmidt and the pass that hit the goalpost are also connected in an obvious way: The ball was thrown by Sam Baugh of Sweetwater, Texas—the most gifted of all the players who benefited from exposure to Schmidt's offense.

But that play holds an even more fitting tribute to Schmidt, and especially to his effect: How deep was Sammy in his own end zone that he was able to hit the goalpost? In Schmidt's era, throwing from inside your own 20-yard line was damn near forbidden by the coaching establishment. Throwing from inside your own end zone was one step below dating your own sister and would have been punishable by jail time had it been left up to the era's hard-line coaches.

Here was Baugh, winging a pass from the worst possible spot, in the worst cold imaginable, in the biggest game of the year. It was an exponential sin, and its consequences were exactly what old timers warned of. But for Schmidt and those who believed in his philosophies, bouncing a ball off the goalpost was simply one of the costs of daring to go where the game of football had never gone before. It was a badge of progress. Maybe the next throw from the end zone would result in a touchdown of over 90 yards. Either way, Schmidt's system used every bullet, and, either way, spectators always walked away with thrilling memories. "Football isn't football unless it's wide open," Schmidt once declared. No one else really agreed at the time, but his influence is such that his statement is validated and gains veracity with every passing football season.[30]

If you look closely, you can see traces of Schmidt's overworked thoughts in nearly every game and every program today. Start by connecting the dots from Schmidt to Gillman to Walsh. The idea of the Schmidt effect is not to take away from the hard work and brilliant thinking of Gillman, Walsh, Vaught, Jones, Meyer, or any other coach, but rather to simply note where beautiful football started and then to celebrate its improvement along the way. If you set aside traditional loyalty to a single team or program and consider the open-game philosophy as something that everyone can appreciate, only then can you relax and enjoy the refined shades of Schmidt's influence. Look closely enough and you'll see the unmistakable image of razzle-dazzle in the next game of football you watch.

As for Schmidt himself, he leaves no simple legacy, no refined version, no single descendent. All that remains is the almost unbelievable vision of the capricious bow tie–wearing prairie tornado who swept through a distant era, disappearing almost as quickly as he had touched down, leaving bewilderment and wide-eyed amazement scattered in his wake. Francis Schmidt was an event, an occurrence, a phenomenon who couldn't be replicated if one tried. But Schmidt was more than just a hypomanic coach who did everything to excess. He was someone who understood possibilities and the imagination necessary to bring them to fruition. He not only opened up the game of football, he opened the minds of fans to the game's possibilities. He opened their hearts to the crazy joy that could be delivered by twenty-two scrambled men and one restless football. Football gripped his soul, and he was excited about the day when the game would reach its full potential—the day when a nation of spectators would not just enjoy the competition and pageantry of football but would be forced to the edge of their seats, thrilled with expectation to see what might transpire with each play. His legacy will live on the next time a fantastic play unfolds during a game you watch. As you roar with the crowd, imagine him smiling his own smile of mad genius. It won't be difficult to feel his presence. After all, it would take more than death to keep Frantic Francis from a football game.[31]

EPILOGUE

Schmidt from the Players' View

Laughter and Language

TIPPY DYE: All the players liked Schmidt. He was funny as the dickens the whole time. There was a lot of laughing.[1]

JACK GRAF: When you were with him [Schmidt] at a party or something, he played the banjo, sang, and all that other stuff. He was one of the guys. But on the field he was all business, and if you messed up you were a horse's ass.

CAMPBELL GRAF: His wife, Evelyn, was a wonderful person. She was very quiet. You couldn't figure out how the two of them ever married, how she ever put up with his rambunctious style or cussing or whatever the moment called for.

JACK GRAF: Evelyn was a nice gal, very pleasant. But a lot of times, when Francis would get off base, she would straighten him out.

TOM KINKADE: You know, his language was atrocious. He talked to us like he was talking to men his own age. I'd never heard anything like it. Oh, he was terrible. I remember a bird flew over us at practice one time and crapped on one of his papers—one of his plays—and he looked up at the bird and said "It's a damn good thing cows can't fly." He was funny. He was really funny and not always on purpose. The guys liked him.

CAMPBELL GRAF: He had a lot of nasty language and it came out of him without any effort. He didn't know he was funny. Stuff just flowed out of him that made people laugh. It was so angry and unique. And he got upset about crazy things. The band would march at halftime on the wet field, and Francis would blow his top. As though anyone would stop the band.

TIPPY DYE: One night at practice—it was a Friday—St. John brought some ladies down to watch us practice. He got Schmidt aside and told him what was happening and told him to be sure and watch his language. He was a little better that night, but the ladies got a big kick out of it.

JACK GRAF: He was a little wild at times. The pressure would get to him. Most of the players laughed at his humor, but if it was centered at you, you didn't laugh so much. I remember we would be practicing on the old field out behind the stadium, and Schmidt's wife, Evelyn, would show up to watch. He'd gather the players together and tell them, "Mrs. Schmidt is here so everybody watch their language." And he was serious. We just looked at each other because he was the only one that did any swearing, and lots of it.

CAMPBELL GRAF: He had several sayings, some of which he would post. He had others he used on the practice field, one of which I still remember well: "If brains were shit, you wouldn't even stink."

CECIL CY SOUDERS: My freshman year we were working against the varsity one afternoon. I was playing end on defense and having great fun. I must have stopped about six plays in a row, and Schmidt yells, "Goddamnit, who is this kid? Get him the hell out of here, he's ruining my practice!"

Practice, Plays, and Paranoia

CAMPBELL GRAF: Francis would come out to the field early, like four o'clock, and as players trickled out onto the field he would start putting together an offensive lineup and begin running plays regardless of who they were or even what position they played. Then we would all stand in a bunch, and he would filter players in and out of his plays. Even as a lineman you stood with the whole team while Schmidt coached the whole thing. He was a one-man show and he hardly knew what it was to assign responsibilities to his assistants. When you see all the players standing around in one group, that's not the way it should be done. He wanted control and just didn't feel like he had time to explain things to his assistants. He did all the coaching hands-on. It was incredible how he saw everything at once, watching and criticizing if they did it wrong. If he had been better able to manage a staff, he'd have made a record nobody would have touched.

JACK GRAF: Schmidt did it all. Ernie Godfrey was the line coach and he would call a guy over to show him how to block or something and Schmidt would yell "Goddamnit Ernie, get him over here where he's gonna learn something!" The assistants just stood around out there. Schmidt ran the whole thing, no question about it. They [the assistants] didn't even have all the plays. He had them on big pads of paper and at lunch when he went over to the Faculty Club, they'd sneak in and look because they didn't always know what was coming that afternoon. They all got along with him, but he was very secretive. He thought everyone was cheating him, was afraid someone was gonna steal his offense.

ESCO SARKKINEN: He [Schmidt] zealously guarded his offensive plays, almost to the point of paranoia. Under lock and key in the physical education building (later named Larkins Hall), access to the master play collection was limited to Coach Schmidt and his coaching staff. The playbooks given to Buckeye players were sparse and coded. In my end book, for example, a page would give the number of the play and just a few Xs and Os on the action I was to take. As a consequence, it was impossible for me to compile information on the OSU offense from my own playbook.

CAMPBELL GRAF: The playbook he gave me would only cover my position. He didn't want the wrong person to get hold of his full plays. There were a few, like my brother who was a quarterback, who had the whole schematics, and we figured out one time that there were over five hundred plays in the main playbook. And he changed them all the time, even when you had a playbook. But I do think that fear of somebody stealing his plays was one of his limitations.

ESCO SARKKINEN: After finishing my last season, I got a coaching job at Lancaster High, not far from Columbus, but after three years under Coach Schmidt, I had no offensive system to take with me. I took my dilemma to Sid Gillman, my former ends coach, and we schemed together on how to get the offensive system needed for my new job. Sid came up with the solution. "The Old Man goes to lunch every day between twelve and two o'clock. Come around Monday during that time and I'll get the master plays from his office for you to copy." At the beginning of the week, Sid and I went to work but made little progress during long lunches—it took more than a week to copy the plays I needed. Although there were many anxious moments, I finally had an offensive system ready for my new job.

TOM KINKADE: At practice he would have plays sticking out of his belt and pockets and everywhere. He was just nuts about football. He loved it. At a banquet he'd be writing plays, or I'd see him on campus walking through a flowerbed looking at his plays. He was a little crazy. And he wasn't organized and he had too much stuff. He'd never get anything pinned down before moving on to the next play. He was ready to go on, but the team wasn't. I didn't know all the plays. Nobody did.

TIPPY DYE: We didn't play much defense at practice. We ran offense all night for two or three hours. And even then he was always scribbling something. Notes, plays, diagrams, whatever. Even at his own games.

CAMPBELL GRAF: He had his own office upstairs at the top of his house on Fifteenth Avenue, and if I drove by his house at midnight, he'd still be working with the office light on. He didn't seem to need much sleep.

Game Time

TOM KINKADE: On Friday nights before home games, we'd go out to the country club and spend the night. You'd get a real good steak there. And Schmidt would still be talking about strategy. He seemed to be under immense pressure. The next day, motorcycle cops would drive us to the stadium, and there would be people— fans—hollering the whole way.

JACK GRAF: Earlier in the week, he gave the quarterbacks a card with plays on them that he thought would work against that week's opponent. There would be over a hundred on them and they were the best plays for this particular team. Then before the game he would give you more plays. A lot of the things he gave you had "confidential" or "secret" written on them or a note about returning them to him.

CAMPBELL GRAF: He threw the ball a lot, and the principles behind it were different from others. For example, there was a series of pass plays where he would have the quarterback take one quick step back and throw directly over the line to an end that was crossing. And Francis taught the end that if he had room in front of him to keep running, but if he saw a tackler approaching, to find a trailer in case a lateral would work.

CAMPBELL GRAF: Ernie Godfrey would sit up in the press box and he'd telephone down to Schmidt who sat on the bench. You'd watch Schmidt listen to Ernie for a second and then he'd yell into the phone, "Goddamnit, Ernie, tell me something I don't know!" Sometimes he'd throw down the phone. Ernie was a character himself, and he put up with all that crap and was a key part of what we had there.

JACK GRAF: We were at Minnesota once, and there was a guy on our team, Ross Bartschy, who played end. He was always trying to sell his cause and, in this one particular game, he was sitting on the bench next to Schmidt and he kept telling Schmidt he should put him in the game. Well, Schmidt had enough of this and he walked down to the end of the bench and sat down. A minute later he walked back and said, "Goddamnit Bartschy, I'm the coach. You go sit on the end of the bench!"

CAMPBELL GRAF: Francis wasn't very social—or good at communicating sometimes. I think a lot of the players criticized him when they didn't get used as much.

TOM KINKADE: Most of the players liked Schmidt, but he substituted an awful lot, and that troubled some of 'em. They couldn't figure out why they were in and out. And there were some on the lower end that didn't think he gave them enough chance in practice or game.

TIPPY DYE: On most of the plays we had there was a guy following the ball. Sometimes we had too many guys following and not enough blocking.

JACK GRAF: People loved to watch Schmidt's system. It was different from everything else.

CAMPBELL GRAF: I think we never really appreciated how great he was. He was way ahead of his time. Later you heard about coaches broadening the base and playing sideline to sideline or the quick passes over the middle. He was doing that way before anyone else.

TIPPY DYE: He kept adding plays and working on formations all the time. Never stopped. He didn't use the T-formation, but he used three-man backfields, and the quarterback handled the ball on nearly all plays just like today. As a quarterback, I never really ran with the ball, to speak of. Every once in awhile when someone would forget to take the ball I'd have to run with it, but that was unusual.

Behind the Wheel

CAMPBELL GRAF: There was an All-Star game in Chicago every year, and Francis would take my dad and me along. Francis would drive his Cadillac. He'd have pieces of paper with plays written on them all over the back seat of the car. One time he came up to a railroad crossing and swerved around the crossing guard—the guy with a sign—and Francis yells, "You nut, keep out of the middle of the road!" I'm sure the guard thought he was nuts. During the game he would take notes upon notes, and after the game, on the way home, he would sit in the back seat and make one of us drive while he sorted his notes out.

CECIL SOUDERS: I rode with Schmidt one time in his Cadillac, along with Ernie Godfrey. We were going downtown to have lunch, and with great speed he was avoiding cars while dodging to the right of streetcars and dodging to the left of streetcars. And he was cussing the whole time.

CAMPBELL GRAF: If he were going up a hill where somebody was going too slow, he'd pull up next to them and yell, "Get off the road, dumbass!" It wasn't something he took lightly. He was known to have blown his horn at train crossings to get them to speed up.

Simply Put

TIPPY DYE: He was so much different than anybody else I ever knew.

TOM KINKADE: He was unique in every way imaginable.

LON EVANS: He was dynamic and personally spectacular without intending to be.

JOHN VAUGHT: Francis Schmidt had to be the most fantastic coach in the country.

APPENDIX

1919 Tulsa 8-0-1 (5-0-1, first place)

Sep. 27	Oklahoma Baptist	W	152	0
Oct. 04	East Central OK	W	60	0
Oct. 11	at Oklahoma	W	27	0
Oct. 18	Central Oklahoma	W	67	6
Oct. 25	Northwestern Oklahoma State	W	75	0
Nov. 01	at Arkansas	W	63	7
Nov. 08	Trinity TX	W	70	0
Nov. 15	Burleson College TX	W	70	7
Nov. 21	at Oklahoma A&M	T	7	7

1920 Tulsa 10-0-1 (6-0-1, first place)

Sep. 25	Saint Gregory's OK	W	121	0
Sep. 29	Northeast Oklahoma A&M	W	151	0
Oct. 02	Chilocco Indian School	W	88	0
Oct. 07	Oklahoma A&M	W	20	14
Oct. 16	at East Central OK	W	10	0
Oct. 23	at Central Oklahoma	W	3	0
Oct. 30	Northwestern Oklahoma State	W	14	7
Nov. 06	Oklahoma Baptist	W	81	0
Nov. 11	Kingfisher OK	W	88	0
Nov. 19	at Phillips OK	T	0	0
Nov. 26	Missouri–Rolla	W	45	0

1921 Tulsa 6-3-0 (5-1-0, second place)

Oct. 01	East Central OK	W	92	0
Oct. 08	Chilocco Indian School	W	75	13
Oct. 15	Northwestern Oklahoma State	W	17	7
Oct. 21	at Texas Christian	L	0	16
Oct. 29	at Haskell Institute KS	L	0	21

Nov. 04	at Oklahoma Baptist	W	28	0
Nov. 11	Central Oklahoma	L	0	21
Nov. 19	Kingfisher OK	W	24	7
Nov. 24	Phillips OK	W	21	10

1922 Arkansas 4-5-0 (1-3-0, sixth place)

Sep. 30	Hendrix AR	W	39	0
Oct. 07	Drury MO	W	22	0
Oct. 14	at Ouachita Baptist AR	L	7	13
Oct. 21	at Baylor	L	13	60
Oct. 28	at Louisiana State	W	40	6
Nov. 04	Tulsa	L[1]	6	13
Nov. 11	at Rice	L	7	31
Nov. 18	Southern Methodist	W	9	0
Nov. 30	Oklahoma A&M	L	0	13

1923 Arkansas 6-2-1 (2-2-0, fourth place)

Sep. 29	Arkansas State Normal	W	32	0
Oct. 06	Drury MO	W	26	0
Oct. 13	Rice	W	23	0
Oct. 20	Baylor	L	0	14
Oct. 27	at Louisiana State	W	26	13
Nov. 03	Ouachita Baptist AR	T	0	0
Nov. 10	at Southern Methodist	L	6	13
Nov. 24	at Phillips OK	W	32	0
Dec. 01	Oklahoma State	W	13	0

1924 Arkansas 7-2-1 (1-2-1, seventh place)

Sep. 27	Northeastern State OK	W	54	6
Oct. 04	sw Missouri State	W	47	0
Oct. 11	Hendrix AR	W	34	3
Oct. 18	at Baylor	L	0	13
Oct. 25	Mississippi	W	20	0
Nov. 01	at Louisiana State	W	10	7
Nov. 08	Southern Methodist	T	14	14
Nov. 15	Phillips OK	W	28	6
Nov. 21	at Oklahoma A&M	L	0	20
Nov. 27	Texas Christian	W	20	0

1925 Arkansas 4-4-1 (2-2-1, fourth place — tied)

Oct. 03	at Iowa	L	0	26
Oct. 10	Oklahoma Baptist	L	0	6
Oct. 17	at Rice	L	9	13
Oct. 24	Phillips OK	W	45	0
Oct. 31	at Louisiana State	W	12	0
Nov. 07	at Southern Methodist	T	0	0
Nov. 14	at Texas Christian	L	0	3
Nov. 21	Oklahoma A&M	W	9	7
Nov. 27	at Tulsa	W	20	7

1926 Arkansas 5-5-0 (2-2-0, third place — tied)

Sep. 26	Arkansas State Teachers	W	60	0
Oct. 02	Mississippi	W	21	6
Oct. 09	at Oklahoma	L	6	13
Oct. 16	Hendrix AR	W	14	7
Oct. 23	Centenary LA	W	33	6
Oct. 30	at Kansas State	L	7	16
Nov. 06	at Louisiana State	L	0	14
Nov. 12	Texas Christian	L	7	10
Nov. 19	at Oklahoma A&M	W	24	2
Nov. 25	at Tulsa	L	7	14

1927 Arkansas 8-1-0 (3-1-0, third place — tied)

Oct. 01	School of the Ozarks AR	W	32	0
Oct. 08	Baylor	W	13	6
Oct. 15	at Texas A&M	L	6	40
Oct. 22	Missouri–Rolla	W	34	0
Oct. 29	at Louisiana State	W	28	0
Nov. 05	at Texas Christian	W	10	3
Nov. 12	Oklahoma A&M	W	33	20
Nov. 19	Austin College TX	W	42	0
Nov. 26	Hendrix AR	W	20	7

1928 Arkansas 7-2-0 (3-1-0, second place)

Sep. 29	at Mississippi	L	0	25
Oct. 06	School of the Ozarks AR	W	21	0
Oct. 13	Baylor	W	14	0

Oct. 20	at Texas	L	7	20
Oct. 29	Texas A&M	W	27	12
Nov. 03	at Louisiana State	W	7	0
Nov. 17	Missouri–Rolla	W	45	6
Nov. 24	Oklahoma Baptist	W	57	0
Nov. 29	Southwestern TX	W	73	0

1929 Texas Christian 9-0-1 (4-0-1, first place)

Sep. 28	Daniel Baker TX	W	61	0
Oct. 05	at Hardin-Simmons TX	W	20	0
Oct. 12	at Centenary LA	W	28	0
Oct. 19	Texas A&M	W	13	7
Oct. 26	at Texas Tech	W	22	0
Nov. 02	North Texas	W	25	0
Nov. 09	Rice	W	24	0
Nov. 16	at Texas	W	15	12
Nov. 23	at Baylor	W	34	7
Nov. 30	Southern Methodist	T	7	7

1930 Texas Christian 9-2-1 (4-2-0, third place)

Sep. 19	at North Texas State	W	47	0
Sep. 20	East Texas State	W	40	0
Sep. 27	Austin TX	W	33	7
Oct. 04	at Simmons TX	T	0	0
Oct. 11	Arkansas	W	40	0
Oct. 18	at Texas A&M	W	3	0
Oct. 25	Texas Tech	W	26	0
Nov. 01	Abilene Christian TX	W	62	0
Nov. 08	at Rice	W	20	0
Nov. 15	Texas	L	0	7
Nov. 22	Baylor	L	14	35
Nov. 29	Southern Methodist	W	13	0

1931 Texas Christian 8-2-1 (4-1-1, second place)[2]

Sep. 19	North Texas State	W	33	6
Sep. 26	Louisiana State	W	3	0
Oct. 03	at Tulsa	L	0	13
Oct. 10	Austin TX	W	38	0

Oct. 17	Texas A&M	W	6	0
Oct. 23	at Simmons TX	W	6	0
Oct. 31	at Arkansas	W	7	0
Nov. 07	Rice	W	7	6
Nov. 14	at Texas	L	0	10
Nov. 21	at Baylor	W	19	6
Nov. 28	Southern Methodist	T	0	0

1932 Texas Christian 10-0-1 (6-0-0, first place)

Sep. 17	North Texas State	W	14	2
Sep. 24	at Louisiana State	T	3	3
Oct. 01	Daniel Baker TX	W	55	0
Oct. 08	Arkansas	W	34	12
Oct. 15	at Texas A&M	W	17	0
Oct. 22	Austin TX	W	68	0
Oct. 29	Baylor	W	27	0
Nov. 04	at Simmons TX	W	27	0
Nov. 11	Texas	W	14	0
Nov. 19	at Rice	W	16	6
Nov. 26	at Southern Methodist	W	8	0

1933 Texas Christian 9-2-1 (4-2-0, second place — tied)

Sep. 16	at Austin TX	W	33	0
Sep. 23	at Daniel Baker TX	W	28	6
Sep. 29	at North Texas State	W	13	0
Oct. 07	at Arkansas	L[3]	0	13
Oct. 14	Simmons TX	W	20	0
Oct. 21	Texas A&M	W	13	7
Oct. 28	at Centenary LA	T	0	0
Nov. 04	at Baylor	L	0	7
Nov. 11	North Dakota	W	19	7
Nov. 18	at Texas	W	30	0
Nov. 25	Rice	W	26	3
Dec. 02	Southern Methodist	W	26	6

1934 Ohio State 7-1-0 (5-1-0, second place)

Oct. 06	Indiana	W	33	0
Oct. 13	at Illinois	L	13	14

Oct. 20	Colgate	W	10	7
Oct. 27	at Northwestern	W	28	6
Nov. 03	at Western Reserve OH	W	76	0
Nov. 10	Chicago	W	33	0
Nov. 17	Michigan	W	34	0
Nov. 24	Iowa	W	40	7

1935 Ohio State 7-0-1 (5-0-1, first place — tied)

Oct. 05	Kentucky	W	19	6
Oct. 12	Drake	W	85	7
Oct. 19	Northwestern	W	28	7
Oct. 26	at Indiana	W	28	6
Nov. 02	Notre Dame	L	13	18
Nov. 09	at Chicago	W	20	13
Nov. 16	Illinois	W	6	0
Nov. 23	at Michigan	W	38	0

1936 Ohio State 5-3-0 (4-1-0, second place)

Oct. 03	New York University	W	60	0
Oct. 10	Pittsburgh	L	0	6
Oct. 17	at Northwestern	L	13	14
Oct. 24	Indiana	W	7	0
Oct. 31	at Notre Dame	L	2	7
Nov. 07	Chicago	W	44	0
Nov. 14	at Illinois	W	13	0
Nov. 21	Michigan	W	21	0

1937 Ohio State 6-2-0 (5-1-0, second place)

Sep. 25	Texas Christian	W	14	0
Oct. 02	Purdue	W	13	0
Oct. 09	at Southern California	L	12	13
Oct. 23	Northwestern	W	7	0
Oct. 30	at Chicago	W	39	0
Nov. 06	Indiana	L	0	10
Nov. 13	Illinois	W	19	0
Nov. 20	at Michigan	W	21	0

1938 Ohio State 4-3-1 (3-2-1, sixth place)

Oct. 01	Indiana	W	6	0
Oct. 08	Southern California	L	7	14
Oct. 15	at Northwestern	T	0	0
Oct. 22	Chicago	W	42	7
Oct. 29	at New York University	W	32	0
Nov. 05	Purdue	L	0	12
Nov. 12	at Illinois	W	32	14
Nov. 19	Michigan	L	0	18

1939 Ohio State 6-2-0 (5-1-0, first place)

Oct. 07	Missouri	W	19	0
Oct. 14	Northwestern	W	13	0
Oct. 21	at Minnesota	W	23	20
Oct. 28	Cornell	L	14	23
Nov. 04	Indiana	W	24	0
Nov. 11	at Chicago	W	61	0
Nov. 18	Illinois	W	21	0
Nov. 25	at Michigan	L	14	21

1940 Ohio State 4-4-0 (3-3-0, fourth place — tied)

Sep. 28	Pittsburgh	W	30	7
Oct. 05	Purdue	W	17	14
Oct. 12	at Northwestern	L	3	6
Oct. 19	Minnesota	L	7	13
Oct. 26	at Cornell	L	7	21
Nov. 02	Indiana	W	21	6
Nov. 16	at Illinois	W	14	6
Nov. 23	Michigan	L	0	40

1941 Idaho 4-5-0 (0-4-0, tenth place)

Sep. 27	Utah	L	7	26
Oct. 03	at Oregon	L	7	21
Oct. 10	at Gonzaga WA	W	21	7
Oct. 18	at Utah State	W	16	0
Oct. 25	Willamette OR	W	33	6
Nov. 01	at Oregon State	L	0	33
Nov. 08	at Washington State	L	0	26

Nov. 15	Montana	L	0	16
Nov. 22	Boise State	W	39	0

1942 Idaho 3-7-0 (1-5-0, ninth place)

Sep. 26	Oregon State	L	0	32
Oct. 03	Second Air Force co	L	0	14
Oct. 10	at Eastern Washington	W	28	7
Oct. 17	at Stanford	L	7	54
Oct. 24	at Oregon	L	0	28
Oct. 31	at Montana	W	21	0
Nov. 14	Washington State	L	0	7
Nov. 21	Portland	W	20	14
Nov. 26	at Utah	L	7	13
Dec. 05	at UCLA	L	13	40

NOTES

Abbreviations:

OSU-DA = The Ohio State University Archives, Director of Athletics Collection.

OSU-BF = The Ohio State University Archives, biographical file.

One. Something Stirring on the Prairie

1. OSU-DA, "Schmidt, Francis A.: 1933–34"; "TCU Signs Schmidt for 3 More Years," *San Antonio (TX) Light,* February 19, 1933.

2. "Prexy forced to Use Window," *Mexia (TX) Weekly Herald,* November 18, 1932. Recognized media rankings began in 1936 with the first AP poll; prior to that there were a variety of little-recognized rankings, all of which were Issued after the season. TCU's 1932 team was ranked No. 4 by the *Illustrated Football Annual* for 1933.

3. "Schmidt Gets Revenge," *Columbus (OH) Dispatch,* March 1, 1934; Jenkins, *Greatest Moments in TCU Football History,* 44–45.

4. SWC Scoring statistics based on archival scores at College Football Data Warehouse, *cfbdatawarehouse.com;* "TCU leads nation in scoring," *Syracuse (NY) Herald-Journal,* December 1, 1932.

5. Freund, *The Purple Lawman,* 15.

6. Canning, *Sam Baugh,* 63.

7. Tips, *Football Texas Style,* 232–33; Cope, *The Game That Was,* 163.

8. Tips, *Football Texas Style,* 233.

9. Cope, *The Game That Was,* 163–64; Canning, *Sam Baugh,* 22–23.

10. Canning, *Sam Baugh,* 23.

11. Whittingham, *What a Game They Played,* 171.

12. "Slingin' Sammy Baugh Tells It Like It Is," Sammy Baugh to Dennis Tuttle, NFL.com, http://www.nfl.com/news/hof/40baugh.html.

13. Canning, *Sam Baugh,* 24.

14. Cope, *The Game That Was,* 164.

15. SWC scoring statistics based on archival scores at College Football Data Warehouse, cfbdatawarehouse.com.

16. Oscar Ruhl, "The Tip-Off," *Mansfield (OH) News-Journal*, September 1, 1934.

17. "Missouri Offers Schmidt Coach Job," *San Antonio (TX) Light*, December 4, 1933; OSU-DA, "Schmidt, Francis A.: 1933–34"; "Frogs Break Own Scoring Records," *San Antonio (TX) Express*, February 26, 1933; "TCU Signs Schmidt for 3 More Years," *San Antonio (TX) Light*, February 19, 1933.

Two. Frantic Francis

1. Robert W. Beach, "Buck Coach Observing Birthday Anniversary Today," *Ohio State Journal*, December 3, 1937.

2. Beach, *Ohio State Journal*, December 3, 1937; "It's First Defeat," *Fairbury (NE) Journal*, November 29, 1902.

3. "Class Day Exercises," *Fairbury (NE) Journal*, May 30, 1903; "Class Graduates," *Fairbury (NE) Journal*, June 6, 1903.

4. University of Nebraska–Lincoln, academic transcript, microfilmed October 8, 1970.

5. "Recalls Younger Days," *Lima (OH) News*, April 9, 1934.

6. Nebraska baseball all-time letter winners, NU Media Relations, huskers.com, February 11, 2008.

7. University of Nebraska–Lincoln, academic transcript, microfilmed October 8, 1970.

8. "New Ohio State Football Mentor," *Lincoln (NE) Star*, March 17, 1934.

9. *The Mirror*, 1909.

10. "New Ohio State Football Mentor," *Lincoln (NE) Star*, March 17, 1934.

11. *The Mirror*, 1913.

12. "Record-Breaking Cages Specialty of TCU Coach," *Galveston (TX) Daily News*, February 14, 1932.

13. Rutland, *The Golden Hurricane*, 5–6.

14. Rutland, *The Golden Hurricane*, 12.

15. Barry Lewis, "McBirney Paved Way at TU: Coaching Great to be Honored," *Tulsa (OK) Tribune*, February 26, 1992.

16. Rutland, *The Golden Hurricane*, 13.

17. The Ohio State University Archives, Biographical file (hereafter OSU-BF, "Schmidt, Francis Albert"; Robert W. Beach, "Schmidt Continues Gridiron Activities After World War," *Ohio State Journal*, December 4, 1937.

18. Barry Lewis, "When TU was King: 1922 Ballclub Was Undefeated," *Tulsa (OK) Tribune*, October 11, 1991.

19. OSU-DA, "Schmidt, Francis A.: 1933–34."

20. "The Tulsa Race Riot," Tulsa Historical Society, http://www.tulsahistory .org/learn/riot.htm.

21. "Schmidt Built Great Team at Tulsa University," *Fayetteville (AR) Daily Democrat*, March 24, 1922.

22. "Coach F. A. Schmidt of Kendall College to Pilot Razorbacks," *Fayetteville (AR) Daily Democrat*, March 21, 1922.

23. "Schmidt Built Great Team at Tulsa University," *Fayetteville (AR) Daily Democrat*, March 24, 1922.

24. "960 Are Registered at the University," *Fayetteville (AR) Daily Democrat*, September 22, 1922.

25. "Season Tickets to Ball Games Placed on Sale," *Fayetteville (AR) Daily Democrat*, September 22, 1922.

26. "Prospective Grid Men Want Jobs," *Fayetteville (AR) Daily Democrat*, June 28, 1922.

27. "Baylor Triumphs Over Razorbacks by 60–13 Score," *Fayetteville (AR) Daily Democrat*, October 23, 1922.

28. "Coleman Is Elected Razorback Captain," *Fayetteville (AR) Daily Democrat*, December 13, 1922.

29. "Basketball at UA in January if Fund for Court Is Raised," *Fayetteville (AR) Daily Democrat*, November 14, 1922.

30. "Track Meet of All NW High Schools Here Early in April," *Fayetteville (AR) Daily Democrat*, December 18, 1922.

31. "Plan UA Game at Little Rock Next November," *Fayetteville (AR) Daily Democrat*, November 19, 1923.

32. Henry, *The Razorbacks*, 50.

33. Fritz Howell, "Staying Young? That's Simple! Listen to Coach Schmidt's Wife," *Hamilton (OH) Journal-News*, November 6, 1934; "Mrs. Schmidt Finds Life Perilous in Grid Season," *San Antonio (TX) Light*, November 6, 1934.

34. Serving as Schmidt's assistant for two years between Grove and Thomsen was Harrison Barnes, a recent graduate of the University of Chicago. Barnes had apprenticed under Stagg and was unprepared for Schmidt's unorganized madness. They parted amicably.

35. Stall ball is in "Hogs May Meet Big 6 Champs," *Galveston (TX) Daily News*, February 9, 1929. Scoring marks are in "Porkers Set New Scoring Record," *Galveston (TZ) Daily News*, January 20, 1929.

36. Harold V. Ratliff, "Schmidt's Death Recalls Stories of Grid Career," *Galveston (TX) Daily News*, September 21, 1944; "Coaching Courtsters Is Relaxation After Grid Season, Says Schmidt," *Evening Tribune* (Albert Lea MN), February 10, 1936.

37. Glen Rose claims "those stands and bleachers wouldn't seat but 2,500," but announced figures were given as being between 4,000 and 6,000. The difference was split. Either way, its capacity was woefully small relative to other schools in the SWC. Seating capacity and substitute SWC games in Henry, *The Razorbacks*, 59.

38. "Strong Rumors Link Schmidt, Arkansas Mentor, with TCU," *Dallas (TX) Morning News*, February 8, 1929; "Schmidt Leaving Arkansas to be Athletic Director at TCU, says *Dispatch*," *Fayetteville (AR) Daily Democrat*, February 8, 1929; "Francis Schmidt Named Successor to Matty Bell as TCU's Head Coach," *Dallas (TX) Morning News*, February 9, 1929.

39. "Porker Letter Athletes Back Fred Thomsen," *Dallas (TX) Morning News*, February 13, 1929.

40. "Francis Schmidt Starts Spring Work at TCU," *Galveston (TX) Daily News*, March 5, 1929; George White, "Sport Broadcast," *Dallas (TX) Morning News*, April 12, 1929.

41. Robert W. Madry, "Carolina's New Grid Mentor Hailed as 'Regular Fellow, Popular, Hard Worker,'" *Burlington (NC) Daily Times-News*, May 26, 1936; Felix R. McKnight, "Sports Notes," *Port Arthur (TX) News*, May 8, 1936.

42. "Francis Schmidt Starts Spring Work at TCU," *Galveston (TX) Daily News*, March 5, 1929; George White, "Sport Broadcast," *Dallas (TX) Morning News*, April 12, 1929.

43. "Mrs. J. H. Keesee Dies," *Dallas (TX) Morning News*, April 1, 1930; The Ohio State University Archives, Biographical File, "Schmidt, Francis Albert."

44. "Hot Shots from the Gridiron," *Amarillo (TX) Globe*, September 17, 1929.

45. "Frogs Hop All Over Baker," *San Antonio (TX) Light*, September 29, 1929.

46. George White, "Sport Broadcast," *Dallas (TX) Morning News*, October 24, 1929.

47. "Last Half Splurge Gives TCU 13–7 Victory Over Texas Aggies," *Dallas (TX) Morning News*, October 20, 1929; George White, "Sport Broadcast," *Dallas (TX) Morning News*, May 13, 1930.

48. "TCU Scores First Victory in History Over Texas Longhorns, 15–12," *Dallas (TX) Morning News*, November 17, 1929.

49. George White, "Sport Broadcast," *Dallas (TX) Morning News*, November 19, 1929.

50. Gayle Talbot Jr., "Frogs and Ponies Battle for Championship Today," *Galveston (TX) Daily News*, November 30, 1929; Gayle Talbot Jr., "TCU's 7–7 Tie with SMU Bags Southwest Title," *Abilene (TX) Reporter-News*, December 1, 1929.

51. "Frog Basketball Practice Begins," *Galveston (TX) Daily News*, December 5, 1929.

52. George White, "Mustangs Bow 37–29 as Horned Frogs Win Conference Cage Championship," *Dallas (TX) Morning News*, March 4, 1931.

53. Freund, *The Purple Lawman*, 15.

54. "Schmidt May Be Poison to Other Grid Coaches, But His Boys Think He's OK," *Waterloo (IA) Daily Courier*, October 24, 1935.

55. "Arkansas University Student Paper Carries Warm Reply to Frog Coach," *Dallas (TX) Morning News*, November 24, 1933; "Arkansas Will Not Voluntarily Forfeit Games in Which Schleuter Played," *Dallas (TX) Morning News*, November 22, 1933.

56. Vaught, *Rebel Coach*, 23–24.

57. Based on the official 2007–8 media guides of the respective schools.

58. Based on the official 2007–8 media guides of the respective schools; "TCU Leads Nation in Scoring," *Syracuse (NY) Herald-Journal*, December 1, 1932; "Few Gridsters Reporting for TCU's Squad," *Galveston (TX) Daily News*, September 11, 1932.

Three. The Man from Nowhere

1. Unemployment rate from U.S. Department of Labor, Bureau of Labor Statistics. http://www.bls.gov/opub/cwc/cm20030124ar03p1.htm.

2. *The Ohio State University Monthly* vol. 26, no. 2 (November 1934).

3. Reduction statistics from the *Ohio State University Monthly*, vol. 27, no. 9 (June 1935); new teachers quote from OSU-DA RG 9/e–1/18, "Presidents Communication and Correspondence: 1934–36."

4. "Ohio State Forced to Curtail Athletic Expenditures," *Zanesville (OH) Times-Signal*, January 31, 1932; "Football No Longer Big Brother to Minor Sports in Charity Way," *Waterloo (IA) Daily Courier*, November 23, 1932.

5. Henry McLemore, "Today's Sport Parade," *Coshocton (OH) Tribune*, October 27, 1939.

6. "Students Rush Movie Theatre," *Hammond (IN) Times*, November 23, 1936.

7. Park, *The Official Ohio State Football Encyclopedia*, 118, 139.

8. OSU-DA RG 9/e–1/7, "Football: Coaching Situation: 1933–34."

9. OSU-DA RG 9/e–1/7, "Football: Coaching Situation: 1933–34"; "Ohio Satisfied with Its Staff," *Charleston (WV) Gazette*, December 31, 1932.

10. OSU-DA RG 9/e–1/7, "Football: Coaching Situation: 1933–34."

11. OSU-DA RG 9/e–1/7, "Football: Coaching Situation: 1933–34."

12. Joe Williams, "Sports Roundup," *Syracuse (NY) Herald-Journal*, December 18, 1940; OSU-DA RG 9/e–1/7, "Football: Coaching Situation: 1933–34."

13. "Willaman to Quit, Claim," *Circleville (OH) Herald*, January 31, 1934

14. OSU-DA RG 9/e–1/7, "Football: Coaching Position Application: Shaughnessy, Clark D.: 1934."

15. OSU-DA RG 9/e–1/7, "Football: Coaching Position Application: Shaughnessy, Clark D.: 1934."

16. OSU-DA RG 9/e–1/7, "Football: Coaching Position Application: Shaughnessy, Clark D.: 1934."

17. "Kizer Denies Ohio Offer," *Zanesville (OH) Times-Signal*, February 21, 1934; "Purdue Alumni Protest OSU Bid for Kizer," *Massillon (OH) Evening Independent*, February 22, 1934.

18. Campbell Graf interview by author, Wilmington OH, June 16, 2007; "Schmidt Says New Cage Rule to Pass," *San Antonio (TX) Light*, April 6, 1932.

19. OSU-DA RG 9/e–1/19, "Schmidt, Francis A.: 1933–34."

20. OSU-DA RG 9/e–1/19, "Schmidt, Francis A.: 1933–34."

21. OSU-DA RG 9/e–1/19, "Schmidt, Francis A.: 1933–34."

22. "Willaman Gives Own Version," *Portsmouth (OH) Times*, November 28, 1933.

23. OSU-DA RG 9/e–1/19, "Schmidt, Francis A.: 1933–34."

24. OSU-DA RG 9/e–1/19, "Schmidt, Francis A.: 1933–34."

25. "Ohio State University after TCU Coach," *Brownsville (TX) Herald*, February 25, 1934; "Francis Schmidt Leaves for Ohio," *San Antonio (TX) Express*, February 28, 1934.

26. "Schmidt Receives Welcome at Ohio," *San Antonio (TX) Express*, March 1, 1934.

27. Ed Penisten, "Francis Schmidt Can Give It as Well as Take It," *Columbus (OH) Dispatch*, March 1, 1934.

28. Ed Penisten, "Francis Schmidt Can Give It as Well as Take It," *Columbus (OH) Dispatch*, March 1, 1934.

29. Ed Penisten, "Francis Schmidt Can Give It as Well as Take It," *Columbus (OH) Dispatch*, March 1, 1934.

30. "St. John Seeks Approval of Schmidt Again Today," *Coshocton (OH) Tribune*, March 2, 1934; "Nothing Doing," *Piqua (OH) Daily Call*, March 1, 1934.

31. "Schmidt Sold on Ohio State," *Mansfield (OH) News-Journal*, March 2, 1934.

32. Oscar Ruhl, "The Tip-Off," *Mansfield (OH) News-Journal*, March 3, 1934; three-year contract confirmed by St. John in "Schmidt Signs to Coach Ohio; to Pick Aides," *Circleville (OH) Herald*, March 3, 1934.

33. OSU-DA RG 9/e–1/7, "Football: Coaching Position Application: Shaughnessy, Clark D.: 1934."

34. OSU-DA RG 9/e–1/19, "Schmidt, Francis A.: 1933–34."

35. Bill Snypp, "Snypp's Sports Snacks," *Lima (OH) News*, March 2, 1934.

36. OSU-DA RG 9/e–1/19, "Schmidt, Francis A: 1933–34."

37. Flem R. Hall, "New Ohio State Coach Hailed as Human Dynamo on Football Field," *Fort Worth (TX) Star-Telegram*, March 3, 1934.

38. Roberts, *The Big Nine*, 16.

39. Enrollment figures are from *School and Society Magazine*, December 1937. This survey being conducted at the midpoint of Schmidt's OSU tenure gives a balanced idea of conference enrollment. The national rank and number of full-time students in residence for those Big 10 schools in the top twenty were: Minnesota (3rd: 13,691), Illinois (4th: 13,647), Ohio State (6th: 12,744), Michigan (7th: 10,952), Wisconsin (8th: 10,864), Northwestern (15th: 6,221), and Chicago (18th: 6,035).

40. Roberts, *The Big Nine*, 3.

41. "Schmidt Frowns at Schedule," *Lima (OH) News*, March 4, 1934.

42. "Schmidt Frowns at Schedule," *Lima (OH) News*, March 4, 1934.

43. "Schmidt Frowns at Schedule," *Lima (OH) News*, March 4, 1934; "Schmidt Signs to Coach Ohio; to Pick Aides," *Circleville (OH) Herald*, March 3, 1934.

44. "Schmidt Frowns at Schedule," *Lima (OH) News*, March 4, 1934; "New Coach Isn't Afraid of Michigan," *Mansfield (OH) News-Journal*, March 3, 1934.

45. "Schmidt Frowns at Schedule," *Lima (OH) News*, March 4, 1934.

46. "Schmidt Frowns at Schedule," *Lima (OH) News*, March 4, 1934.

47. The *Ohio State University Monthly*, April 1934, vol. 25, no. 7.

48. OSU-DA RG 9/e–1/19, "Schmidt, Francis A.: 1933–34."

49. OSU-DA RG 9/e–1/19, "Schmidt, Francis A.: 1933–34."

50. OSU-DA RG 9/e–1/19, "Schmidt, Francis A.: 1933–34."

51. OSU-DA RG 9/e–1/19, "Schmidt, Francis A.: 1933–34."

52. "Low Mark Set in College Football Scoring," *New York Times*, November 14, 1933.

Four. The Open-Game Movement

1. "The Game of Football," *Decatur (IL) Daily Republican*, August 8, 1893.

2. "Sporting Notes," *Decatur (IL) Herald-Dispatch*, January 24, 1897; Davis, *Football*, 111–13.

3. Baker, *Football*, 537–49.

4. John Whitaker, "Speculating in Sports," *Hammond (IN) Times*, October 28, 1935.

5. Weyand, *The Saga of American Football*, 84; Baker, *Football*, 540.

6. "1939 Official Intercollegiate Football Statistical Summary," The American Football Statistical Bureau (Seattle, 1940).

7. Whittingham, *What a Game They Played*, 175.

8. Warner, *Football for Coaches and Players*, 62–64.

9. Knute K. Rockne, *Coaching*, 44; Heisman, *Principles of Football*, 122, 319.

10. Danzig, *Oh, How They Played the Game*, 318–23. The actual length of Mueller's pass in the air has been estimated as anywhere from 50 to 63 yards. Suffice to say, observers were amazed to see the era's chubby ball thrown so far, especially off a trick play in the biggest of all games. More on Oberlander's huge day can be found in *Swede: The Will to Win* by David Holman Oberlander; 1939 statistics from "1939 Official Intercollegiate Football Statistical Summary."

11. Bynum, *Pop Warner*, 141.

12. Grange, *Zuppke of Illinois*, 149–51.

13. Tips, *Football Texas Style*, 32–34; Freeman, *That Good Old Baylor Line*, 29–31.

14. Tips, *Football Texas Style*, 220.

15. Pouncey, *Mustang Mania*, 58–61.

16. Tippy Dye, a quarterback for Schmidt from 1934 to 1936, claims their Ohio State playbook required him to memorize 312 plays from seven formations, the *Ohio State University Monthly*, March 1951, 15; Campbell and Jack Graf (lineman and quarterback) counted over 500 plays in 1939, interviews by author; Jones, *Football for the Fan*, 40–41; Little, *How to Watch Football*, 43; Camp, *How to Play Football*, 107–14; Warner, *Football for Coaches and Players*, 133; Heisman, *Principles of Football*, 205–206.

17. "Francis Schmidt Hopes for Color and Deception in New Grid Setting at Ohio State," *Galveston (TX) Daily News*, September 26, 1934; Bill Parker, "Schmidt Predicts Frogs Will Have Great Eleven," *Brownsville (TX) Herald*, September 13, 1933.

18. Rick Snider, "Links of a Chain," *Washington (DC) Times*, October 22, 2003.

19. "Low Mark Set in College Football Scoring," *New York Times*, November 14, 1933.

20. "Pros Agree to New Sideline Grid Rule," *Oakland (CA) Tribune*, February 27, 1933; "Offense Gets Big Break in New Grid Code," *Hammond (IN) Times*, February 12, 1934; Baker, *Football*, 540.

21. Al Mitchell, "Out of the Pressbox," *Mason City (IA) Globe-Gazette*, January 11, 1935.

Five. Razzle-Dazzle

1. "Mrs. Schmidt Finds Life Perilous in Grid Season," *San Antonio (TX) Light*, November 6, 1934.

2. Gartner, *The Hypomanic Edge*, 8–11.

3. James L. Renick, "Schmidt Busy Diagramming Plays for State Squad," *Massillon (OH) Evening Independent*, April 12, 1934; Bob Ingram, "Schmidt Brainy Mentor," *El Paso (TX) Herald Post*, January 2, 1941.

4. "Portfolio Coach Takes Grid Notes Any Time, Place," *Evening Tribune* (Albert Lea MN), June 25, 1935.

5. "Coach Schmidt Faces Task of Replacing 7 Regulars," *Coshocton (OH) Tribune*, September 14, 1934.

6. James L. Renick, "Schmidt Is Enthusiastic over Buckeye Grid Squad," *Lima (OH) News*, April 12, 1934.

7. Fritz Howell, "Ohio State Gridders Given Hard Opening-Day Workout," *Lima (OH) News*, September 16, 1934; "Ohio State Grid Team Will Start Practice Today," *Zanesville (OH) Times-Signal*, September 15, 1934.

8. "Ohio State Gridders to Have New Type Uniform," *Chronicle-Telegram* (Elyria OH), August 3, 1934.

9. Fritz Howell, "Ohio State Gridders Given Hard Opening-Day Workout," *Lima (OH) News*, September 16, 1934.

10. "Football Coach Gives Fine Talk at Rotary Club," *Zanesville (OH) Times-Recorder*, September 5, 1934.

11. *The Ohio State Monthly* vol. 26, no. 1 (October 1934).

12. Tommy Devine, "Fate Sent Pincura to Ohio State," *Stevens Point (WI) Daily Journal*, October 16, 1935.

13. Tippy Dye interview by author, Camptonville CA, March 14, 2007.

14. Tippy Dye interview by author, Camptonville CA, March 14, 2007.

15. "200 Freshmen Out at State," *Massillon (OH) Evening Independent*, October 3, 1934.

16. "200 Freshmen Out at State," *Massillon (OH) Evening Independent*, October 3, 1934.

17. Fritz Howell, "Schmidt on Spot as He Drills Ohio State Gridders for Big 10 Campaign," *Massillon (OH) Evening Independent*, September 26, 1934.

18. Tippy Dye interview by author, Camptonville CA, March 14, 2007; Tom Kinkade interview by author, Indio Springs CA, January 20, 2005.

19. "Bucks Turn On Power to Crush Indiana, 33–0, in Opener," *Lima (OH) News*, October 7, 1934.

20. "Ohio State Reserves Given Train Ride," *Syracuse (NY) Herald-Journal*, November 2, 1934.

21. "Schmidt Alters Buckeye Eleven," *Circleville (OH) Herald*, October 12, 1934; "Ohio State Eleven Views Night Game," *Mansfield (OH) News-Journal*, October 13, 1934.

22. *The Ohio State University Monthly* vol. 26, no. 2 (November 1934).

23. "Ohio State Drops Wild Grid Game to Illinois, 14–13," *Zanesville (OH) Times-Signal*, October 14, 1934.

24. "Ohio State Drops Wild Grid Game to Illinois, 14–13," *Zanesville (OH) Times-Signal*, October 14, 1934; "Schmidt Figures Illinois May Vote Honorary Block Letters to Some of Ohio State's Backs," *Syracuse (NY) Herald-Journal*, November 2, 1934.

25. "Schmidt Figures Illinois May Vote Honorary Block Letters to Some of Ohio State's Backs," *Syracuse (NY) Herald-Journal*, November 2, 1934; Tippy Dye interview by author, Camptonville CA, March 14, 2007; "Ohio State's Belated Drive Defeats Colgate 10–7," *Zanesville (OH) Times-Signal*, October 21, 1934.

26. "Schmidt May Be Poison to Other Grid Coaches, But His Boys Think He's OK," *Waterloo (IA) Daily Courier*, October 24, 1935.

27. Buckeye Eleven Rallies to Trounce Northwestern 28–6," *Lima (OH) News*, October 28, 1934.

28. "Ohio State Works against Fumbles," *Mansfield (OH) News-Journal*, October 31, 1934.

29. Oscar Ruhl, "The Tip-Off," *Mansfield (OH) News-Journal*, October 31, 1934.

30. The *Ohio State University Monthly* vol. 26, no. 2 (November 1934).

31. The *Ohio State University Monthly* vol. 26, no. 2 (November 1934).

32. The *Ohio State University Monthly* vol. 26, no. 2 (November 1934).

33. Oscar Ruhl, "The Tip-Off," *Mansfield (OH) News-Journal*, November 9, 1934.

34. Scott, *Jock Sutherland*, 128–30.

35. "Chicago Trampled by Ohio State in Game at Columbus," *Galveston (TX) Daily News*, November 11, 1934; Oscar Ruhl, "The Tip-Off," *Mansfield (OH) News-Journal*, November 12, 1934.

36. William Weekes, "Buckeyes Seeking Revenge in Tilt with Wolverines," *La Crosse (WI) Tribune and Leader-Press*, November 13, 1934; Harry Kippke, "Kippke Expects Thundering Herd to Set New Record for Production of Grid Tallies," *Massillon (OH) Evening Independent*, November 16, 1934.

37. Fritz Howell, "70,000 to Watch Buckeyes and Wolverines at Columbus," *Massillon (OH) Evening Independent*, November 16, 1934.

38. "Schmidt Expects Terrific Scrap," *Zanesville (OH) Times-Signal*, November 15, 1934.

39. "Schmidt Is Not Satisfied with Buckeyes' Play," *Zanesville (OH) Times-Recorder*, November 13, 1934.

40. "Michigan Outclassed by Flashy Ohio Eleven, 34–0," *Lima (OH) News*, November 18, 1934.

41. Harry Kippke, "Kippke Calls Ohio State, Minnesota Best Teams in Big 10," *Massillon (OH) Evening Independent*, November 20, 1934; "Buckeyes Start, Finish With Dye in This Dizzy Deal," *Ironwood (MI) Daily Globe*, November 26, 1934.

42. Tippy Dye interview by author, Camptonville CA, March 14, 2007.

43. "Michigan Outclassed by Flashy Ohio Eleven, 34–0," *Lima (OH) News*, November 18, 1934.

44. "Badgers Get New Plays for Gopher Tilt," *Evening Tribune* (Albert Lea MN), November 20, 1934.

45. "Schmidt forgets Michigan Game, Thinking of Iowa," *Zanesville (OH) Times-Recorder*, November 19, 1934; the *Ohio State University Monthly* vol. 26, no. 3 (December 1934).

46. "Colored Comet of Hawkeyes Feared by Big 10 Schools," *Bismarck (North Dakota) Tribune*, October 18, 1934; Winthrop Lyman, "Oze Simmons Rated Best in Middlewest," *Vidette-Messenger* (Valparaiso IN), November 7, 1935; Edwin Moore Jr., "Off the Cuff," *Waterloo (IA) Daily Courier*, October 11, 1934.

47. "Ohio State Humbles Hawkeyes, 40–7," *Waterloo (IA) Daily Courier*, November 25, 1934.

48. Bill Snypp, "Snypp's Sport Snacks," *Lima (OH) News*, November 26, 1934.

49. "Gomer Jones to Head Ohio State Squad," *Circleville (OH) Herald*, November 28, 1934.

50. *The Ohio State University Monthly* vol. 26, no. 3 (December 1934); Ralph

Teatsworth, "Grid Coffers of Ohio State Full from Big Gates," *Piqua (OH) Daily Call,* November 23, 1934.

51. Ralph Teatsworth, "Ohio State Closes Fine Grid Season," *Chronicle-Telegram* (Elyria OH), November 26, 1934.

52. Ralph Teatsworth, "Ohio State Closes Fine Grid Season," *Chronicle-Telegram* (Elyria OH), November 26, 1934.

53. Snyder quote in the *Ohio State University Monthly* vol. 26, no. 3 (December 1934); Morrill quote in the *Ohio State University Monthly* vol. 26, no. 9 (June 1935).

54. Francis A. Schmidt and Harold A. Fitzgerald, "The New Open Game," *Saturday Evening Post,* October 5, 1935.

Six. The Game

1. "Buckeye Gridmen Are Called for Indoor Practice," *Newark (OH) Advocate,* February 1, 1935; "Pincura Among Buckeye Group of Athletes," *Hamilton (OH) Journal-News,* June 18, 1935.

2. "Schmidt Drills Buckeye Eleven for '35 Season," *Piqua (OH) Daily Call,* March 22, 1935.

3. "Portfolio Coach Takes Grid Notes Any Time, Place," *Evening Tribune* (Albert Lea MN), June 25, 1935.

4. "Francis Schmidt to Teach Basketball," *Lima (OH) News,* February 8, 1935; "Skidding the Sport Field with Skid," *Syracuse (NY) Herald-Journal,* August 10, 1935.

5. "Grid Practice Starts Next Week but Francis Schmidt Has Been at It All Summer," *Zanesville (OH) Times-Recorder,* September 4, 1935.

6. "Buckeye Coach Watches Many Grid Prospects," *Circleville (OH) Herald,* March 31, 1935; "Big 10 Teams Hold Initial Drills Today," *Chronicle-Telegram* (Elyria OH), September 10, 1935.

7. "Schmidt Tells Bucks to 'Forget Championship,'" *Lima (OH) News,* September 11, 1935.

8. "Schmidt Sends Buck Gridders through Paces," *Hamilton (OH) Journal-News,* September 10, 1935.

9. Grantland Rice, "The Sportlight," *Syracuse (NY) Herald-Journal,* November 2, 1937.

10. Sperber, *Shake Down the Thunder,* 3–20.

11. Carey, *Catholics in America,* 79; http://www.americamagazine.org/content/article.cfm?article_id=1245.

12. 2007 Notre Dame Football Media Guide.

13. "Ohio State Eleven Is Extended to Beat Kentucky, 19–6," *Lima (OH) News*, October 7, 1935.

14. "Grid Notes," *Mansfield (OH) News-Journal*, October 9, 1935.

15. The *Ohio State University Monthly* vol. 27, no. 1 (October 1935); "Ohio State Crushes Drake Under 85–7 Score," *Zanesville (OH) Times-Signal*, October 13, 1935.

16. Bill Braucher, "Francis Schmidt, Ohio State Grid Tutor, One Coach Who Is Willing to Gamble," *Massillon (OH) Evening Independent*, October 23, 1935.

17. "Gridders Just after Position," *Circleville (OH) Herald*, October 17, 1935.

18. John F. Kenny, "The Lookout," *Lowell (MA) Sun*, November 5, 1935.

19. John Whitaker, "Speculating in Sports," *Hammond (IN) Times*, October 18, 1935.

20. Tommy Devine, "Rate Williams Best Buck Bet on Saturday," *Hammond (IN) Times*, October 29, 1935.

21. The *Ohio State University Monthly* vol. 27, no. 1 (October 1935).

22. Harry Grayson, "First Down—and Then Some," *Frederick (MD) Daily News*, October 30, 1935.

23. The *Ohio State University Monthly* vol. 27, no. 2 (November 1935); "Late Scoring Spree Gives Bucks Victory Over Indiana," *Lima (OH) News*, October 27, 1935.

24. "First Down—and Then Some," *Indiana Evening Gazette*, November 5, 1935; "Big Scores Feature 1935 Grid Campaign," *Charleston (WV) Gazette*, October 31, 1935.

25. "Big Crowds to Attend Games," *Ogden (UT) Standard-Examiner*, October 28, 1935.

26. "Schmidt Fails to Predict Outcome of Saturday Tilt," *Zanesville (OH) Times-Recorder*, October 28, 1935.

27. "State May Employ New Offense for Notre Dame Game," *Zanesville (OH) Times-Recorder*, October 29, 1935; Notre Dame statistics in Alan Gould, "State–Notre Dame at Columbus Is No. 1 Test of Season for Both Teams," *Zanesville (OH) Times-Recorder*, October 29, 1935.

28. "Frosh Use Ohio State Plays to Score on Varsity," *Zanesville (OH) Times-Recorder*, October 31, 1935.

29. "Irish Practice on Defense Measures; Layden in Lineup," *Marion (OH) Star*, October 30, 1935; "Few Irishmen on Irish '11'" *Massillon (OH) Evening Independent*, October 31, 1935.

30. Layden, *It Was a Different Game*, 107; Paul Mickelson, "Notre Dame to Point New Men at Ohio State," *Evening Tribune* (Albert Lea MN), October 31, 1935.

31. Joe Williams, "Sports Roundup," *Syracuse (NY) Herald-Journal*, October 28, 1935.

32. John C. Hoffman, "Make Buckeyes 5 to 3 Favorite Over Irish," *Hammond (IN) Times*, October 28, 1935; "Grid Fans to Spend Million at Ohio Event," *Ogden (UT) Standard-Examiner*, October 31, 1935.

33. Fritz Howell, "80,000 to See Ohio State, Irish Clash, *Titusville (PA) Herald*, November 2, 1935; "Notre Dame Pass Play Fools Bucks," *Zanesville (OH) Times-Signal*, October 31, 1935; "Low Traffic toll Sought," *Mansfield (OH) News-Journal*, November 1, 1935; "Special Trains Carry Fans to Football Classic, *Zanesville (OH) Times-Recorder*, November 1, 1935.

34. Shep Sheppard, "fore and Aft," *Port Arthur (TX) News*, October 29, 1935.

35. John Whitaker, "Speculating in Sports," *Hammond (IN) Times*, October 29, 1935.

36. Train delay in *Chronicle-Telegram* (Elyria OH), November 1, 1935; Layden, *It Was a Different Game*, 108; Bob Logan, "Notre Dame 18, Ohio State 13," *Chicago Daily Herald*, September 30, 1995.

37. Henry McLemore, "Mac Picks 'Em," *Dunkirk (NY) Evening Observer*, November 2, 1935.

38. Henry McLemore, "Today's Sports Parade," *Syracuse (NY) Herald-Journal*, November 2, 1935.

39. Francis A. Schmidt and Harold A. Fitzgerald, "The New Open Game," *Saturday Evening Post*, October 5, 1935.

40. Henry McLemore, "Notre Dame Defeats Ohio State in All-Time Thriller," *Waterloo (IA) Daily Courier*, November 3, 1935.

41. *Ohio State University Monthly* vol. 27, no. 2 (November 1935); Henry McLemore, "Notre Dame Stages Great Rally to Defeat Ohio State," *Oakland (CA) Tribune*, November 3, 1935; "Buckeyes Unable to Stave Off Final Rally," *Columbus (OH) Dispatch*, November 3, 1935.

42. Grantland Rice, "The Sportlight," *Syracuse (NY) Herald-Journal*, November 4, 1935.

43. Layden, *It Was a Different Game*, 110; the *Ohio State University Monthly* vol. 27, no. 1 (November 1935).

44. Oscar Ruhl, "Random Shots," *Mansfield (OH) News-Journal*, November 7, 1935.

45. Henry McLemore, "Notre Dame Defeats Ohio State in All-Time Thriller," *Waterloo (IA) Daily Courier*, November 3, 1935.

46. Layden, *It Was a Different Game*, 112.

47. John Whitaker, "Speculating in Sports," *Hammond (IN) Times*, November 5, 1935.

48. Layden, *It Was a Different Game*, 112.

49. Layden, *It Was a Different Game*, 112–13.

50. Curran, *Pro Football's Rag Days*, 143; "Notre Dame Stages Great Rally to Beat Ohio State," *Oakland (CA) Tribune*, November 3, 1935.

51. Henry McLemore, "Today's Sports Parade," *Oakland (CA) Tribune*, November 4, 1935.

52. Bob Logan, "Key Fumble Now a Distant Memory to OSU's Beltz," *Chicago Daily Herald*, September 30, 1995; Layden, *It Was a Different Game*, 113.

53. "Buckeyes Unable to Stave Off Final Rally," *Columbus (OH) Dispatch*, November 3, 1935.

54. "Ohio State's 85–7 Victim Lauds Notre Dame," *Evening Tribune* (Albert Lea MN), November 12, 1935.

55. Henry McLemore, "Today's Sports Parade," *Oakland (CA) Tribune*, November 4, 1935.

56. "No Important Changes for Buck Lineup," *Zanesville (OH) Times-Recorder*, November 4, 1935.

57. Oscar Ruhl, "Random Shots," *Mansfield (OH) News-Journal*, November 7, 1935; "Deny Time Discrepancies in Ohio-Irish Battle," *Mansfield (OH) News-Journal*, November 6, 1935.

58. "Man Dies as He Listens to Notre Dame Game," *Syracuse (NY) Herald-Journal*, November 4, 1935; "A Tough Game," *Jefferson City (MO) Post-Tribune*, November 5, 1935.

59. Layden, *It Was a Different Game*, 104, 113.

60. Clarence Young, "Inwoods's 'Deadwood' to Mates on Ohio 11 but Dynamite to Foes," *Ohio State Journal*, November 5, 1935; "Buckeye Gridders Drill Despite Rain," *Mansfield (OH) News-Journal*, November 6, 1935.

61. *Ohio State University Monthly* vol. 27, no. 2 (November 1935).

62. *Ohio State University Monthly* vol. 27, no. 2 (Novembe 1935).

63. Gomer Jones biography, College Football Hall of Fame, *www.collegefoot ball.org*.

64. "Buckeye Quarterback Is Outstanding Pass Tosser," *Kokomo (IN) Tribune*, October 16, 1935; "Ohio State Is Hard Pressed to Beat Illinois 6–0," *Zanesville (OH) Times-Signal*, November 17, 1935.

65. George Kirksey, "Wolves Yoke of Defeat Is Finally Lifted," *Wisconsin State Journal,* January 23, 1935.

66. Tippy Dye interview by author, Camptonville CA, March 14, 2007.

67. The *Ohio State University Monthly* vol. 27, no. 2 (November 1935).

68. "Ohio Staters Finish in Tie with Minnesota," *Syracuse (NY) Herald-Journal,* November 24, 1935.

69. "More Than 353,000 See Buckeyes in Action," *Mansfield (OH) News-Journal,* November 26, 1935.

70. "Wendt Named to Captaincy of Ohio Team," *Mansfield (OH) News-Journal,* November 26, 1935.

71. The *Ohio State University Monthly* vol. 27, no. 1 (October 1935); the *Ohio State University Monthly* vol. 27, no. 3 (December 1935).

Seven. The Immovable Object

1. "Grid Coach at Ohio State Is Speaker Here," *Newark (OH) Advocate,* January 15, 1936.

2. "Ohio State Bans Sponsored Grid Game Broadcasts," *Coshocton (OH) Tribune,* September 22, 1936; OSU-DA RG 9/e–1/7, "Football: Financial Report: 1940."

3. "Grid Coach at Ohio State Is Speaker Here," *Newark (OH) Advocate,* January 15, 1936; Steve Snider, "Golden Gophers and Scarlet Scourge to Rule Again, Belief," *Oshkosh (WI) Northwestern,* April 21, 1936; Fritz Howell, "Scarlet Scourge '36 Eleven Will Be Light, Speedy Club," *Lancaster (OH) Eagle-Gazette,* April 13, 1936.

4. "Ohio State Gridders Begin Work Sept. 10," *Massillon (OH) Evening Independent,* August 21, 1936.

5. "16 Lettermen to Tote Ohio Burden," *Bismarck (ND) Tribune,* September 4, 1936.

6. "Howard Blair New End Coach at State," *Portsmouth (OH) Times,* June 6, 1936.

7. Fritz Howell, "Ohio State Coaches to Waste Little Time on Rudiments in Opening Drill," *Mansfield (OH) News-Journal,* September 9, 1936.

8. Bill Snypp, "Schmidt Drills Squad of 64 as Bucks Open Football Practice," *Lima (OH) News,* September 11, 1936.

9. "Bettridge Leads Bucks in Sprints," *Coshocton (OH) Tribune,* September 16, 1936.

10. "Rabb's Return Important to Hopes of Buck Eleven," *Daily Herald* (Circleville OH), September 28, 1939.

11. George Kirksey, "Coaches Pep Up Practice with Favorite Wisecracks," *Hammond (IN) Times*, November 10, 1937.

12. Tippy Dye interview by author, Camptonville CA, March 14, 2007.

13. Tippy Dye interview by author, Camptonville CA, March 14, 2007.

14. "State Varsity Scores Five Times In Scrimmage," *Portsmouth (OH) Times*, September 20, 1936.

15. Scott, *Jock Sutherland*, 142.

16. Scott, *Jock Sutherland*, 142.

17. Bill Snypp, "Snypp's Sports Snacks," *Lima (OH) News*, September 28, 1936; Fritz Howell, "Ohio State Chances Rest on Shoulders of Sophomores," *Oshkosh (WI) Northwestern*, September 4, 1936.

18. "Bucks Smother NYU Under Barrage of 9 touchdowns," *Lima (OH) News*, October 4, 1936; *Ohio State University Monthly* vol. 30, no. 2 (November 1938).

19. Herbert W. Barker, "Ohio-Pittsburgh Game Heads Bill," *Mansfield (OH) News-Journal*, October 5, 1936.

20. The *Ohio State University Monthly* vol. 28, no. 2 (November 1936).

21. Jock Sutherland, "Pitt Coach Fears His Eleven Won't Match Ohio State," *Syracuse (NY) Herald-Journal*, October 6, 1936.

22. The *Ohio State University Monthly* vol. 28, no. 2 (November 1936).

23. Pete Minego, "Sport Gossip," *Portsmouth (OH) Times*, October 13, 1936; "Pitt Panthers Overpower Ohio State and Win 6–0," *Zanesville (OH) Times-Signal*, October 11, 1936.

24. The *Ohio State University Monthly* vol. 28, no. 2 (November 1936).

25. "OSU Fans Surprised by Failure of Offense," *Daily Herald* (Circleville OH), October 12, 1936.

26. Fritz Howell, "State Has Edge on Wildcats; Schmidt Defends His System," *Piqua (OH) Daily Call*, October 16, 1936.

27. Dean Watkeys, "SMU's Pass Is Boomerang in New York," *Syracuse (NY) Herald-Journal*, October 11, 1936.

28. Charles Grumich, "Waldorf Is Pleased with Wildcat Team," *Lincoln (NE) Star*, January 20, 1935.

29. Tippy Dye interview by author, Camptonville CA, March 14, 2007.

30. The *Ohio State University Monthly* vol. 28, no. 2 (November 1936).

31. George Kirksey, "Northwestern Downs OSU, 14–13," *Coshocton (OH) Tribune*, October 18, 1936.

32. "Ohio State's Aerial Attack Beats Indiana 7–0," *Zanesville (OH) Times-*

Signal, October 25, 1936; the *Ohio State University Monthly* vol. 28, no. 2 (November 1936).

33. Schmidt Calls Buckeye-Irish Game Toss Up," *Coshocton (OH) Tribune,* October 30, 1936; "Bucks Leave for Scene of Battle with Notre Dame," *Newark (OH) Advocate,* October 30, 1936; 2007 Notre Dame Football Media Guide.

34. "Notre Dame Is Again Victorious over Ohio State," *Zanesville (OH) Times-Signal,* November 1, 1936.

35. Tippy Dye interview by author, Camptonville CA, March 14, 2007.

36. "Notre Dame Is Again Victorious over Ohio State," *Zanesville (OH) Times-Signal,* November 1, 1936.

37. OSU-DA RG 9/e–1/14, "Notre Dame University: Resumption of the OSU–Notre Dame Football Relations: 1940."

38. OSU-DA RG 9/e–1/14, "Notre Dame University: Resumption of the OSU–Notre Dame Football Relations: 1940."

39. OSU-DA RG 9/e–1/14, "Notre Dame University: Resumption of the OSU–Notre Dame Football Relations: 1940."

40. OSU-DA RG 9e–1/9), "Intercollegiate Conference: Commissioner (Griffith): Correspondence: 1938–39."

41. Hutchins, *University of Utopia.*

42. The *Ohio State University Monthly* vol. 28, no. 3 (December 1936).

43. "Sophs Star as Bucks Beat Chicago," *Lima (OH) News,* November 8, 1936.

44. "Ohio State Wins from Illinois, 13–0," *Coshocton (OH) Tribune,"* November 15, 1936.

45. "Rabb's Return Important to Hopes of Buck Eleven," *Circleville (OH) Herald,* September 28, 1939.

46. "Ohio Prepares for Grid Battle with Michigan," *Lima (OH) News,* November 16, 1936.

47. The *Ohio State University Monthly* vol. 28, no. 3 (December 1936); "Michigan Bows to Ohio Power and Passes," *Lima (OH) News,* November 22, 1936.

48. "Grid Receipts Tell Story of 'Better Times, '" *New Castle (PA) News,* November 25, 1936.

49. "Schmidt to Coach at OSU 3 More Years," *Massillon (OH) Evening Independent,* November 24, 1936.

50. "Schmidt Given Bid from Texas Alumni," *Portsmouth (OH) Times,* November 19, 1936; "Schmidt Not Planning to Accept Texas Post," *Zanesville (OH) Times-Recorder,* November 20, 1936.

51. "Football Practice to Begin Jan. 11 at Ohio State," *Zanesville (OH) Times-Signal,* December 20, 1936.

52. "Schmidt Plans Winter Drill for Grid Squad," *Portsmouth (OH) Times,* December 20, 1936.

53. "Grid Practice at OSU," *Marion (OH) Star,* January 9, 1937.

54. "Buckeye Leaders," *Piqua (OH) Daily Call,* October 19, 1937.

55. Tippy Dye interview by author, Camptonville CA, March 14, 2007.

56. Wilton Hazzard, "The Stars of '36," *Illustrated Football Annual 1936,* 11; Canning, *Sam Baugh,* 157.

8. Slingin' for Dollars

1. Canning, *Sam Baugh,* 67; Cope, *The Game That Was,* 164.

2. Palmer, *The ESPN Pro Football Encyclopedia,* 1036–44.

3. Cope, *The Game That Was,* 164.

4. The *Ohio State University Monthly* vol. 31, no. 1 (October 1939).

5. Stagg, *Touchdown!,* 294–96.

6. "Sammy Baugh Phoenix Coach," *San Antonio (TX) Light,* January 30, 1937; Canning, *Sam Baugh,* 65.

7. Canning, *Sam Baugh,* 65–66.

8. John Bentley, "I May Be Wrong," *Lincoln (NE) State Journal,* September 3, 1937.

9. Cope, *The Game That Was,* 164–65.

10. Charles Dunkley, "'Slingin Sam' Baugh Hurls All-Star Mates to Victory Over Professionals, 6–0," *Galveston (TX) Daily News,* September 2, 1937; "Slingin' Sammy Baugh Passes All-Stars to 6–0 Victory Over Packers," *Lincoln (NE) State Journal,* September 2, 1937.

11. "Baugh Status Is Undecided," *El Paso (TX) Herald-Post,* February 5, 1937; "Sammy Baugh, Phoenix Coach," *San Antonio (TX) Light,* January 30, 1937; Canning, *Sam Baugh,* 67.

12. Canning, *Sam Baugh,* 71.

13. Canning, *Sam Baugh,* 71.

14. Povich, "No Boredom or Blacks Allowed," *Redskins,* 18–22.

15. "Redskins Win Opener at DC before 24,942," *Frederick (MD) Post,* September 17, 1937.

16. "Redskins Win Opener at DC before 24,942," *Frederick (MD) Post,* September 17, 1937; Palmer, *The ESPN Pro Football Encyclopedia,* 1044–45; "Baugh Stars as Redskins Down Giants," *Syracuse (NY) Herald-Journal,* September 17, 1937.

17. Henry McLemore, "Marshall Has a New Idea for Pro Football," *Uniontown (PA) News Standard*, September 17, 1937.

18. Henry McLemore, "Today's Sports Parade," *Yuma (AZ) Daily Sun*, September 18, 1937.

19. Henry McLemore, "Today's Sports Parade," *Yuma (AZ) Daily Sun*, September 18, 1937.

20. Tommy Devine, "Free-Scoring Plea Gets 'No' From Schmidt," *Wisconsin State Journal*, November 24, 1937; Grange quote from Davis, *Pictorial Encyclopedia of Football* from Arch Ward article in the *Chicago Tribune*, November 30, 1933.

21. Joe Williams, "Sports Roundup," *Syracuse (NY) Herald-Journal*, November 18, 1937; Ziemba, *When Football Was Football*, 183.

22. Palmer, *The ESPN Pro Football Encyclopedia*, 1038–44.

23. Henry McLemore, "Today's Sports Parade," *Yuma (AZ) Daily Sun*, September 18, 1937.

24. Henry McLemore, "Today's Sports Parade," *Yuma (AZ) Daily Sun*, September 18, 1937.

25. Peterson, *Pigskin*, 96–97; Ziemba, *When Football Was Football*, 184; Cope, *The Game That Was*, 91–92.

26. Joe F. Carr, "Pro Grid Game Enjoys Its Greatest Year in History," *Sheboygan (MI) Press*, January 5, 1939.

27. *The NFL's Official Encyclopedic History of Professional Football*, 103.

28. Sammy Baugh to Dennis Tuttle, "'Slingin' Sammy Baugh Tells It Like It Is," *nfl.com*, February 5, 2003.

Nine. On the Edge

1. Paul Mickelson, "Down the Sports Trail," *Titusville (PA) Herald*, October 26, 1938.

2. Fritz Howell, "St. John, Godfrey Keep Eye on Schmidt to Prevent Another Pursuit this Year," *Newark (OH) Advocate*, August 8, 1938.

3. Cohane, *Great College Football Coaches*, 174.

4. Cohane, *Great College Football Coaches*, 174.

5. George Kirksey, "Coaches Pep Up Practice with Favorite Wisecracks," *Hammond (IN) Times*, November 10, 1937.

6. "Joe Williams, Ohio Grid Star, Out of School," *Circleville (OH) Herald*, July 14, 1937; "Schmidt Calls Riddled Buck Squad; Texas Christian Opener Is Sept. 25," *Lima (OH) News*, September 9, 1937.

7. The *Ohio State University Monthly* vol. 29, no. 1 (October 1937).

8. "Ohio State Coach Sticks Up for 'Razzle-Dazzle' Football," *Zanesville (OH) Times-Recorder*, October 16, 1936; Schmidt's take on seniors in Oscar Ruhl, "Random Shots," *Mansfield (OH) News-Journal*, December 16, 1938.

9. Felix R. McKnight, "If Dutch Meyer Is Pessimistic He Conceals It," *Abilene (TX) Reporter-News*, September 11, 1937.

10. "TCU Coaches Begin Planning for Ohio State," *Ogden (UT) Standard-Examiner*, July 25, 1937.

11. The *Ohio State University Monthly* vol. 29, no. 1 (October 1937); Park, *The Official Ohio State Football Encyclopedia*, 162.

12. "Ohio State Triumphs Over Texas Christian," *Zanesville (OH) Times-Signal*, September 26, 1937.

13. "Downpour Prevents Foes from Using Trick Plays; Texans' Record Smeared," *Galveston (TX) Daily News*, September 26, 1937.

14. Oscar Ruhl, "The Tip-Off," *Mansfield (OH) News-Journal*, June 23, 1934.

15. Steve Snider, "Carl Dahlbeck, Purdue Guard, Dies of Burns," *Wisconsin State Journal*, September 14, 1936; Pete Minego, "Sports Gossip," *Portsmouth (OH) Times*, October 7, 1937.

16. "Bucks Halt Purdue's Aerial Attack and Win 13–0," *Zanesville (OH) Times-Signal*, October 3, 1937.

17. "Buckeyes Leave Omaha for Final Hop to Coast," *Lima (OH) News*, "October 7, 1937.

18. "Irish Will Play Arizona in 1940," *Oakland (CA) Tribune*, September 20, 1937. Initially, the Wildcats were scheduled for October 5, 1940, but this was changed to September 27, 1941.

19. "Buckeyes Arrive for Trojan Game," *Newark (OH) Advocate*, October 8, 1937.

20. Jack Cuddy, "Sports Parade," *Nevada State Journal*, May 30, 1937.

21. "Rabb's Return Important to Buck Eleven," *Circleville (OH) Herald*, September 28, 1939.

22. The *Ohio State University Monthly* vol. 29, no. 2 (November 1937).

23. Ronald Wagoner, "'Jittery' Trojans Nose Out Ohio State, 13–12," *Oakland (CA) Tribune*, October 10, 1937.

24. "Zadworney, Sophomore, to Start for Buckeyes against Wildcats," *Circleville (OH) Herald*, October 21, 1937.

25. The *Ohio State University Monthly* vol. 29, no. 2 (November 1937).

26. "Schindler Is Nightmare to Homeward Bucks Team," *Coshocton (OH) Tribune*, October 11, 1937.

27. "Schmidt Calls Wildcats Lucky," *Chronicle-Telegram* (Elyria OH), October 18, 1937.

28. Tommy Devine, "Ohio State Blasts Wildcat Title Hopes with 7-0 Triumph," *Wisconsin State Journal*, October 24, 1937; the *Ohio State University Monthly* vol. 29, no. 2 (November 1937).

29. OSU-DA RG 9/e-1/7, "Football: Drinking at Games: 1935-37"; George Kirksey, "Drinking on Wane at Big 10 Games, Survey Discloses," *Oshkosh (WI) Northwestern*, October 19, 1937.

30. "Regulars to Open for Ohio Against 'Chi '" *Lima (OH) News*, October 26, 1937.

31. "Bucks, After Slow Start, Ramble to 39-0 Victory Over Maroon of Chicago," *Lima (OH) News*, October 31, 1937.

32. "Ohio State Winds Up Season as Best Defensive Club in Big 10," *Coshocton (OH) Tribune*, November 24, 1937; the *Ohio State University Monthly* vol. 29, no. 3 (December 1937).

33. "Ohio State's Big 10 Title Hopes Blasted by Indiana," *Zanesville (OH) Times-Signal*, November 8, 1937.

34. OSU-DA RG 9/e-1/9, "Intercollegiate Conference: Athletic Director's Correspondence: 1938-40"; "Willingness to Help Rival May Cost Bucks Title," *Mansfield (OH) News-Journal*, November 4, 1937.

35. "Ohio Grid Shorts," *Coshocton (OH) Tribune*, November 10, 1937; "Bucks Title Hopes Dashed by Indiana," *Mansfield (OH) News-Journal*, November 8, 1937.

36. "Bucks Title Hopes Dashed by Indiana," *Mansfield (OH) News-Journal*, November 8, 1937.

37. "Ohio Morale at Low Ebb After Indiana Defeat," *Chronicle-Telegram* (Elyria OH), November 10, 1937.

38. Oscar Ruhl, "Random Shots," *Mansfield (OH) News-Journal*, December 1, 1937.

39. John Whitaker, "Speculating in Sports," *Hammond (IN) Times*, December 3, 1937.

40. The *Ohio State University Monthly* vol. 29, no. 3 (December 1937).

41. The *Ohio State University Monthly* vol. 29, no. 3 (December 1937).

42. "Ohio State Rises from Dust to Lick Hapless Illinois Warriors 19-0, *Portsmouth (OH) Times*, November 14, 1937.

43. "Buckeyes to Name Leader of '38 Buckeye Eleven," *Lima (OH) News*, November 22, 1937; "Ohio State Beats Michigan 21-0 in Final Game," *Zanesville (OH) Times-Signal*, November 21, 1937.

44. "Ohio State Winds Up Season as Best Defensive Club in Big 10," *Coshocton (OH) Tribune*, November 24, 1937; the *Ohio State University Monthly* vol. 29, no. 3 (December 1937); Herbert W. Barker, "Bear's Home Crowds Gain," *Oakland (CA) Tribune*, December 6, 1937.

45. "Bucks Select Two Stars as 1938 Leaders," *Piqua (OH) Daily Call*, November 23, 1937.

Ten. Spreading the Message

1. "Little Labels Football Systems as Bunk," *Evening Huronite* (Huron SD), October 14, 1936.

2. MacCambridge, *ESPN College Football Encyclopedia*, 1168–72; Henry, *The Razorbacks*, 76.

3. Henry, *The Razorbacks*, 76.

4. "Myer [*sic*] Reveals His Secret of Success: He Outscores Them," *Brownsville (TX) Herald*, October 12, 1937; MacCambridge, *ESPN College Football Encyclopedia*, 1173–75.

5. "Southwestern Teams Rely on Pass Attack," *Syracuse (NY) Herald-Journal*, october 25, 1938; official Intercollegiate Football Statistical Summary, Season of 1939.

6. The *Ohio State University Monthly* vol. 28, no. 8 (May 1936); "New Offer Is Made to Wolf," *Daily Herald* (Big Spring TX), April 12, 1936; MacCambridge, *ESPN College Football Encyclopedia*, 601, 1170–72.

7. Cleveland, *Vaught*, 4–5.

8. "Former Buckeyes Barred by Loop," *Zanesville (OH) Times-Signal*, August 2, 1937.

9. Phil Barber, "Gillman Laid Foundation for All Who Followed," *Official Game Program of Super Bowl XXXII*, January 25, 1998; OSU-DA RG 9/e–1/1, "Athletic Board: Minutes: 1934–40."

10. "Grid Coaches Use Colorful Expressions," *Wisconsin State Journal*, November 10, 1937.

11. OSU-BF, "Schmidt, Francis Albert."

12. The Ninth Annual Ohio State Football Clinic Handbook, May 3–4, 1940; Luther Emery, "Ohio Coaches Back Brown for Ohio State, *Massillon (OH) Evening Independent*, December 23, 1940.

13. Brown, *PB: The Paul Brown Story*, 72; Luther Emery, "Massillon Honors Champion Tigers Tonight," *Massillon (OH) Evening Independent*, December 5, 1939.

14. Fritz Howell, "Chuck Mather Scores Big Hit as Humorous Speaker," *Newark (OH) Advocate*, May 11, 1953.

15. Russ Davies, "Rustling through Sports," *Chronicle-Telegram* (Elyria OH), January 3, 1939; Capel McNash, "Bucks 'Scout' Sends Kroner to Michigan," *Coshocton (OH) Tribune*, November 22, 1938.

16. Freund, *The Purple Lawman*, 16.

17. OSU-DA RG 9/e–1/9, "Intercollegiate Conference: Athletic Director's Correspondence: 1938–40"

18. OSU-DA RG 9/e–1/9, "Intercollegiate Conference: Commissioner (Griffith): Correspondence: 1937–38."

19. The *Ohio State University Monthly* vol. 30, no. 3 (December 1938).

20. Tom Kinkade interview by author, Indio Springs CA, January 20, 2005.

21. Tom Kinkade interview by author, Indio Springs CA, January 20, 2005; Offer from Pitt in "Report on Interviews with Ohio State Freshmen" found in OSU-DA RG 9/e–1/9, "Intercollegiate Conference: Commissioner (Griffith): Correspondence: 1938–39."

22. Tom Kinkade interview by author, Indio Springs CA, January 20, 2005.

23. Tom Kinkade interview by author, Indio Springs CA, January 20, 2005.

24. Tom Kinkade interview by author, Indio Springs CA, January 20, 2005.

25. Tom Kinkade interview by author, Indio Springs CA, January 20, 2005.

26. Freund, *The Purple Lawman*, 16.

27. OSU-DA, RG 9/e–1/19, "'S' Correspondence: General: 1938–42."

28. "Ohio State Due for Powerhouse," *Galveston (TX) Daily News*, September 13, 1938; "Schmidt's Grid Squad Starts Year's Drills," *Circleville (OH) Herald*, September 10, 1938.

29. "Bucks Begin Preparations for Tough Schedule," *Zanesville (OH) Times-Signal*, September 11, 1938.

30. "Rabb's Return Important to Hopes of Bucks," *Circleville (OH) Herald*, September 28, 1939.

31. Fritz Howell, "Ohio State to Try Backward Style This Year," *Portsmouth (OH) Times*, September 29, 1938.

32. Fritz Howell, "Southern California Checks Ohio State March 14 to 7," *Lima (OH) News*, October 9, 1938; "Crowd of 73,000 Pack Stadium for Buck-USC Game," *Coshocton (OH) Tribune*, October 8, 1938.

33. "Maag's Kicking Attracts Attention of Grid World, *Circleville (OH) Herald*, October 16, 1940.

34. Fritz Howell, "Langhurst Is Star of Ohio State's 42–7 Romp Over Chicago Maroon," *Portsmouth (OH) Times*, October 23, 1938.

35. "Bucks Click in Easy Win over Violet," *Coshocton (OH) Tribune*, October 30, 1938.

36. "Purdue Scores Late to Beat Favored Ohio State, 12–0," *Lima (OH) News*, November 6, 1938.

37. "Buckeyes Wary as They Entrain for Game with Illinois," *Zanesville (OH) Times-Signal*, November 11, 1938.

38. "Virginia Star Punches Fan," *Oakland (CA) Tribune*, December 8, 1938.

39. The *Ohio State University Monthly*, December 1938, vol. 30, no. 3.

40. Fritz Howell, "Grid Fans Fight after Michigan Whips Buckeyes," *Galveston (TX) Daily News*, November 20, 1938.

41. The *Ohio State University Monthly*, December 1938, vol. 30, no. 3; "Coaches Pleased With Results of '38 Campaign," *Zanesville (OH) Times-Recorder*, November 23, 1938.

42. Paul Mickelson, "The Sports Trail," *San Antonio (TX) Express*, October 26, 1938.

43. Park, *The Official Ohio State Football Encyclopedia*, 168.

Eleven. The Magic Remains

1. Jack Graf interview by author, Columbus OH, June 16, 2007.

2. Jim Emerson, "Hallabrin Figures in Schmidt's Plans," *Mansfield (OH) News-Journal*, September 8, 1939.

3. Campbell Graf interview by author, Wilmington OH, June 16, 2007.

4. "Charley Goes to Ohio State," *Massillon (OH) Evening Independent*, September 14, 1938; Jim Emerson, "Hallabrin Figures in Schmidt's Plans," *Mansfield (OH) News-Journal*, September 8, 1939; "Steve Andrako, 1938 Sub Center, to Lead Buckeyes in Next Campaign," *Circleville (OH) Herald*, November 22, 1938.

5. Non-Ohioans in "'College Spirit' Brings Buckeye Football Crew to Nation's Top Ranks," *Coshocton (OH) Tribune*, October 25, 1939; "Buck Gridders Sign Pledge to Plug for Team," *Coshocton (OH) Tribune*, September 14, 1939.

6. "Buckeyes Wind Up Spring Grid Work," *Zanesville (OH) Times-Signal*, May 7, 1939.

7. "Jim Strausbaugh Buckeye's Fastest," *Coshocton (OH) Tribune*, September 19, 1939; the *Ohio State University Monthly*, October 1939, vol. 31, no. 1.

8. "Schmidt Might Be Poison to Other Grid Coaches, But His Boys Think He's OK," *Waterloo (IA) Daily Courier*, October 24, 1935.

9. Campbell Graf interview by author, Wilmington OH, June 16, 2007; Harper, *An Ohio State Man*, 24.

10. "Injury to Put Maag on Bench for Inaugural," *Mansfield (OH) News-Journal*, October 3, 1939.

11. The *Ohio State University Monthly*, November 1939, vol. 31, no. 2; "Ohio State Has Chance to Give Sophs Workout in Impressive 19–0 Win," *Portsmouth (OH) Times*, October 8, 1939.

12. Enrollment statistics are from *School and Society Magazine*, December 1937. Based on full-time students in residence, Minnesota ranked third nationally (13,691) while Ohio State ranked sixth (12,744).

13. Quirk, *Minnesota Football*, 41.

14. Bernie Bierman, "Razzle-Dazzle Is Side Issue Which Must be Handled Intelligently," *Gastonia (NC) Daily Gazette*, October 14, 1937.

15. "Gophers Confident on Eve of Buck Tilt," *Zanesville (OH) Times-Signal*, October 20, 1939; "Football Briefs," *Logansport (PA) Press*, October 20, 1939.

16. Tom Kinkade interview by author, Indio Springs CA, January 20, 2005; "Ohio State's Aerial Weapons May Turn Tide Against Gophers," *Mansfield (OH) News-Journal*, October 20, 1939.

17. "Buckeye Aerial Attack Beats Minnesota 23–20," *Lima (OH) News*, October 22, 1939.

18. "Buckeye Aerial Attack Beats Minnesota 23–20," *Lima (OH) News*, October 22, 1939; the *Ohio State University Monthly*, November 1939, vol. 31, no. 2; "'Bucks' We-Won't-Be-Beaten' Spirit to Be Tested," *Mansfield (OH) News-Journal*, October 23, 1939.

19. "McCullough, Cornell's Halfback, May Cause Ohio State Trouble," *Mansfield (OH) News-Journal*, October 24, 1939.

20. Oscar Ruhl, "In the Ruhl Book," *Mansfield (OH) News-Journal*, October 24, 1939; "Unbeaten Ohio and Cornell Teams Collide," *Lima (OH) News*, October 28, 1939.

21. Henry McLemore, "Success of Ohio State Due to New Spirit of Players," *Corpus Christi (TX) Times*, October 27, 1939.

22. Steve Snider, "Cornell Game Big Test for Buckeye Team," *Piqua (OH) Daily Call*, October 24, 1939.

23. The *Ohio State University Monthly*, November 1939, vol. 31, no. 2.

24. Bill Snypp, "Snypp's Sports Snacks," *Lima (OH) News*, October 30, 1939; Henry McLemore, "Cornell Downs Ohio State in Sensational Game, 23–14" *Syracuse (NY) Herald-Journal*, October 29, 1939.

25. "Buckeyes Slap Indiana 24–0," *Lincoln (NE) Star*, November 5, 1939.

26. Jerry Brondfield, "Best Since Harley, Say Buckeye Fans of Don Scott, Nation's Most Versatile Back," *Burlington (NC) Daily Times-News*, September 30, 1940.

27. "Buckeyes to Use Fourth Stringers Against Maroons," *Coshocton (OH) Tribune*, November 9, 1939.

28. "Ohio State on Scoring Spree to Crush Hapless Maroons, 61–0," *Zanesville (OH) Times-Signal*, November 12, 1939.

29. Fritz Howell, "Buckeyes Clinch Share in Big 10 Championship," *Lima (OH) News*, November 19, 1939; the *Ohio State University Monthly*, vol. 31, no. 3.

30. Tom Kinkade interview by author, Indio Springs CA, January 20, 2005; Roberts, *The Big Nine*, 232–33.

31. "Ohio State 'Backs-In' to Big 10 Championship," *Zanesville (OH) Times-Signal*, November 26, 1939.

32. "Ohio State Loses to Michigan, 21–14, but Wins Big 10 Title," *Lima (OH) News*, November 26, 1939.

33. "Ohio State Loses to Michigan, 21–14, but Wins Big 10 Title," *Lima (OH) News*, November 26, 1939.

34. "Crisler Praises Players; Schmidt Blames Fumbles," *Portsmouth (OH) Times*, November 26, 1939.

35. "Crisler Praises Players; Schmidt Blames Fumbles," *Portsmouth (OH) Times*, November 26, 1939.

36. "Ohio State Wins Crown," *Paris (TX) News*, November 26, 1939.

37. The *Ohio State University Monthly* vol. 31, no. 3 (December 1939).

38. Paul R. Allerup, "Statistics Prove Ohio Best Team in League," *Circleville (OH) Herald*, November 28, 1939.

39. Jim Maher, "Schmidt Bitter as He Resigns at OSU," *Coshocton (OH) Tribune*, December 17, 1940; "AAU Gets No Takers on Track, Field Championship," *Ogden (UT) Standard-Examiner*, December 14, 1939.

40. Bill McKinnon, "Truth About Schmidt, Stanford," *Columbus (OH) Dispatch*, January 15, 1940; "Report Stanford May Seek Schmidt," *Massillon (OH) Evening Independent*, November 30, 1939.

41. Fritz Howell, "Schmidt Is Actually Optimistic," *Zanesville (OH) Times-Recorder*, September 6, 1940.

Twelve. The Cost of Odd

1. Joe Williams, "Sports Roundup," *Syracuse (NY) Herald-Journal*, October 11, 1940.

2. Joe Williams, "Sports Roundup," *Syracuse (NY) Herald-Journal*, October 11, 1940.

3. Joe Williams, "Sports Roundup," *Syracuse (NY) Herald-Journal*, October 11, 1940.

4. Joe Williams, "Sports Roundup," *Syracuse (NY) Herald-Journal*, October 11, 1940.

5. Joe Williams, "Sports Roundup," *Syracuse (NY) Herald-Journal*, October 11, 1940.

6. Coach Francis Schmidt 'Resigns, '" *Galveston (TX) Daily News*, December 17, 1940.

7. Jim Emerson, "Francis Schmidt Unable to Frown about Bucks' Grid Prospects for 1940, *Coshocton (OH) Tribune*, May 3, 1940.

8. Jim Emerson, "Francis Schmidt Unable to Frown about Bucks' Grid Prospects for 1940, *Coshocton (OH) Tribune*, May 3, 1940.

9. Fritz Howell, "Schmidt Is Actually Optimistic," *Zanesville (OH) Times-Recorder*, September 6, 1940; Bill McKinnon, "Schmidt Sounds Pleased," *Columbus (OH) Dispatch*, September 16, 1940; Francis A. Schmidt, "Pick Ohio as Outstanding Team; But Coach Schmidt Bemoans Loss of Regulars," *Vidette Messenger* (Valparaiso IN), September 21, 1940.

10. "Top Conditioned State Squad Set for 1st Workout," *Piqua (OH) Daily Call*, September 10, 1940.

11. "Buckeye Squad Confident of Good Football Season," *Lima (OH) News*, September 11, 1940; "Bucks Ready to Go," *Mansfield (OH) News-Journal*, September 12, 1940.

12. "Pitt First Test of Buckeye Grid Eleven Saturday," *Piqua (OH) Daily Call*, September 27, 1940; Campbell Graf interview by author, Wilmington OH, June 16, 2007.

13. The *Ohio State University Monthly* vol. 32, no. 2 (November 1940).

14. Fritz Howell, "Schmidt Worrying Despite Plenty of Talent for Gridiron," *Marion (OH) Star*, October 1, 1940; Larry Newman, "Big 10 Crown Goes on the Line," *Circleville (OH) Herald*, October 5, 1940.

15. "Maag's Field Goal Beats Purdue, 17–14," *Lima (OH) News*, October 6, 1940.

16. OSU-DA RG 9/e–1/9, "Intercollegiate Conference: Communications (Griffith): Correspondence: 1937–38."

17. "Maag's Field Goal Beats Purdue, 17–14," *Lima (OH) News*, October 6, 1940.

18. Joe Williams, "Sports Roundup," *Syracuse (NY) Herald-Journal*, December 18, 1940.

19. "Ohio State in Market for New Coach," *Hammond (IN) Times*, December 18, 1940.

20. Boyd Lewis, "The Day's Biggest Upset: Wildcats 6, Buckeyes 3," *Wisconsin State Journal*, October 13, 1940.

21. "Bucks Too Soft so Team Demands Work," *Circleville (OH) Herald*, October 15, 1940.

22. OSU-DA RG 9/e–1/9, Intercollegiate Conference: Commissioner (Griffith), Correspondence: 1940–41 (Folder 2 of 2)"; "2005–2007 Network Broadcast Data," *cfbdatawarehouse.com*, February 18, 2008.

23. "Bucks Too Soft so Team Demands Work," *Circleville (OH) Herald*, October 15, 1940.

24. Eddie Brietz, "The Sports Roundup," *Ironwood (MI) Daily Globe*, October 17, 1940.

25. "Buckeyes to Be Hard for Duel with Minnesota," *Circleville (OH) Herald*, October 16, 1940; "Punts and Passes," *Reno (NV) Evening Gazette*, October 15, 1940; Eddie Brietz, "Sports Gossip," *Mansfield (OH) News-Journal*, November 27, 1940.

26. "Illegal Substitution by OSU Stirs Flareup on Campus at Purdue," *Portsmouth (OH) Times*, October 17, 1940; "Disputed Purdue Game Stands," *Mason City (IA) Globe-Gazette*, October 18, 1940; "Officiating Can't Be Perfect, Says Big 10 Boss," *Helena (Montana) Daily Independent*, November 29, 1936.

27. "Big 10 Boss Rules Score Is Still Official," *Mansfield (OH) News-Journal*, October 18, 1940.

28. "Ohio State Will Test Minnesota 'Open Date' Plan," *Piqua (OH) Daily Call*, October 18, 1940; "Ohio State Hunts Spark Plug Performer," *Piqua (OH) Daily Call*, October 16, 1940.

29. Fritz Howell, "Minnesota Wrecks Buckeyes' Title Hopes with 13–7 Triumph," *Portsmouth (OH) Times*, October 20, 1940; the *Ohio State University Monthly* vol. 32, no. 2 (November 1940).

30. "Gophers Outplay Buckeyes for 13–7 Victory," *Lima (OH) News*, October 20, 1940.

31. "Cornell Record," *Coshocton (OH) Tribune*, November 9, 1940; "Ohio State Heads East with Three Full Grid Teams," *Syracuse (NY) Herald-Journal*, October 24, 1940; Tom Kinkade interview by author, Indio Springs CA, January 20, 2005.

32. "Field Goals, Conversions Deciding More Big Games than in Many Seasons," *Nevada State Journal*, October 31, 1940.

33. Wade accusation claimed in OSU-DA RG 9/e–1/9, "Intercollegiate Con-

ference: Athletic Director's Correspondence: 1938–40"; Schmidt quotes in Fritz Howell, "Buck Officials Admit Snavely Is a 'Pretty Fair Quarterback,'" *Portsmouth (OH) Times*, October 28, 1940.

34. Don Smith, "White Backs Up L. W. St. John on Charges against Snavely," *Portsmouth (OH) Times*, November 10, 1940; "Buckeye Leader Pushing Charge against Mentor," *Cumberland (MD) Evening Times*, October 29, 1940; "Ohio Protest of Snavely Carried to Eastern-Assn," *Lima (OH) News*, October 29, 1940.

35. John Bentley, "I May Be Wrong," *Nebraska State Journal*, November 9, 1940.

36. "You Don't Say!" *Dunkirk (NY) Evening Observer*, October 29, 1940.

37. "Buck Publicity Head Says Team Lacks Pep to Keep Steam Up over Half Game," *Daily Times-Bulletin* (Van Wert OH), October 30, 1940; Paul Mickelson, "World Is Getting Better in Opinion of Press Agent for Buck Grid Team," *Reno (NV) Evening Gazette*, October 26, 1938.

38. "Schmidt Defends Team," *Charleroi (PA) Mail*, November 1, 1940.

39. Rex Hess, "Sports Podge," *Mansfield (OH) News-Journal*, October 18, 1941.

40. Jack Graf interview by author, Columbus OH, June 16, 2007.

41. Rex Hess, "Sports Podge," *Mansfield (OH) News-Journal*, October 18, 1941.

42. The *Ohio State University Monthly*, December 1940, vol. 32, no. 3.

43. "Chicago Was Unwilling to Buy Winning Eleven," *Oakland (CA) Tribune*, January 13, 1940.

44. "Colorado Uses New Stunt," *Ogden (UT) Standard-Examiner*, January 24, 1940.

45. "Scott Stars as Buckeyes Win From Illinois, 14–6," *Lima (OH) News*, November 17, 1940.

46. Harry Snyder, "Ohio Big Factor in Tennessee's Success," *Massillon (OH) Evening Independent*, November 13, 1940; "Bucks Aiming at Tom Harmon; Awaiting Test," *Circleville (OH) Herald*, November 20, 1940.

47. Tom Kinkade interview by author, Indio Springs CA, January 20, 2005.

48. "Buckeyes Routed by Michigan Attack, 40–0," *Lima (OH) News*, November 24, 1940.

49. Tom Kinkade interview by author, Indio Springs CA, January 20, 2005.

50. Fritz Howell, "Michigan Humiliates Ohio State with 40–0 Homecoming Victory," *Portsmouth (OH) Times*, November 24, 1940.

51. Larry Newman, "Names of Harmon and Schmidt Get Attention," *Circleville (OH) Herald*, November 25, 1940.

52. Park, *The Official Ohio State Football Encyclopedia*, 180.

53. Fritz Howell, "See Shakeup at OSU," *Zanesville (OH) Times-Recorder*, November 26, 1940.

54. "Schmidt Insists He Is Still Coach of Bucks," *Portsmouth (OH) Times*, November 26, 1940; the *Ohio State University Monthly* vol. 32, no. 3 (December 1940); "Paper Says Schmidt Is Through as Mentor of Ohio State Grid Teams," *Portsmouth (OH) Times*, November 27, 1940.

55. "Schmidt Gets Appreciation Gift of Club," *Coshocton (OH) Tribune*, November 26, 1940; the *Ohio State University Monthly* vol. 32, no. 3 (December 1940); Tom Kinkade interview by author, Indio Springs CA, January 20, 2005.

56. "Marion Athlete to Lead Bucks Next Season," *Circleville (OH) Herald*, November 26, 1940; "Schmidt Silent Concerning His Status at OSU," *Circleville (OH) Herald*, November 27, 1940; "Schmidt Through at OSU, Says Columbus Report," *Massillon (OH) Evening Independent*, November 27, 1940; "Schmidt Plans to Coach at Ohio in 1941," *News-Palladium* (Benton Harbor MI), November 28, 1940.

57. OSU-DA RG 9/e–1/19, "'S' Correspondence: General: 1938–42"

58. Larry Newman, "University Puts Fate of Schmidt and Aides in Hands of Three Men," *Circleville (OH) Herald*, December 10, 1940.

59. Fritz Howell, "Schmidt and Five assistants Resign Ohio State Job," *Massillon (OH) Evening Independent*, December 17, 1940.

60. Jim Maher, "Schmidt Bitter as He Resigns at OSU," *Coshocton (OH) Tribune*, December 17, 1940; "Schmidt Resigns at Ohio State," *Nebraska State Journal*, December 17, 1940.

61. "Four Other Members of Buckeye Football Staff Quit Jobs with 'Razzle-Dazzle' Introducer," *Zanesville (OH) Times-Recorder*, December 17, 1940; "Schmidt Leaves with Wise Crack," *Massillon (OH) Evening Independent*, December 17, 1940.

62. Jim Maher, "Schmidt Bitter as He Resigns at OSU," *Coshocton (OH) Tribune*, December 17, 1940.

63. Jim Maher, "'Down with St. Johnny' Reads Sign Hung on OSU Campus—Students Agree," *Coshocton (OH) Tribune*, December 19, 1940.

64. Bill McKinnon, "Schmidt's Time Was Up," *Columbus (OH) Dispatch*, December 19, 1940.

65. Henry J. McCormick, "No Foolin,'" *Wisconsin State Journal*, December 20, 1940.

66. Jerry Brondfield, "Massillon Coach Feels He's Capable of Doing Good Job at Ohio State," *Circleville (OH) Herald*, December 20, 1940; "Coaching Rumors Pervade Meet," *Albuquerque (NM) Journal*, December 31, 1940.

67. Fritz Howell, "Stephenson to Direct Winter Grid practice," *Massillon (OH) Evening Independent*, December 19, 1940.

68. Sid Feder, "Francis Schmidt Rumored about to Return to Southwest School," *Galveston (TX) Daily News*, December 31, 1940; Eddie Brietz, "Sports Roundup," *Ironwood (MI) Daily Globe*, December 31, 1940.

69. Larry Newman, "Ex-Buck Mentor Still Seeking Job Post," *Circleville (OH) Herald*, January 27, 1941.

70. Austin Bealmear, "Schmidt First Applicant for Oklahoma Job," *Abilene (TX) Reporter-News*, January 26, 1941; "Thornhill and Schmidt Reported Seeking Baylor Post; Morley Jennings Says Good-Bye," *Galveston (TX) Daily News*, February 8, 1941.

Thirteen. The Final Act

1. "Francis Schmidt Is Named Idaho Football Coach," *Fresno (CA) Bee*, March 17, 1941; "Francis Schmidt Find Football at Low Ebb in Idaho University," *Charleroi (PA) Mail*, April 30, 1941.

2. "Idaho Court Teams Open Play in State Tournament," *Ogden (UT) Standard-Examiner*, March 20, 1941; Schmidt's return to Columbus in *Coshocton (OH) Tribune*, May 20, 1941.

3. "Idaho Complains Mountain Schools 'Raiding' Talent," *Nevada State Journal*, June 8, 1941.

4. "Idaho Complains Mountain Schools 'Raiding' Talent," *Nevada State Journal*, June 8, 1941.

5. "It's Bow Tie Day in Moscow, Idaho," *Oakland (CA) Tribune*, September 22, 1941; "AAU Gets No Takers on National Track, Field Championship," *Ogden (UT) Standard-Examiner*, December 14, 1939.

6. "Idaho Bewilders Gonzaga, 21–7," *Nevada State Journal*, October 12, 1941.

7. "Idaho Has Little Round-Robin Hope," *Montana Standard*, November 28, 1941.

8. "Idaho Guard in Air Service," *Oakland (CA) Tribune*, November 14, 1941.

9. "16 Turn Out," *Nevada State Journal*, March 27, 1942.

10. "Vandals Lose Eleven Stars," *Ogden (UT) Standard-Examiner*, August 22, 1942.

11. Victor Dallaire, "Idaho Gridders Face Stumbling Blocks in 1942 Campaign," *Ogden (UT) Standard-Examiner*, August 9, 1942; "Idaho's Chances for Coast Wins Remain Doubtful," *Nevada State Journal*, September 20, 1942.

12. Alan Ward, "Fawcett Paces Tribe Attack," *Oakland (CA) Tribune*, October 18, 1942.

13. Frank Frawley, "UCLAns Spank Idaho Vandals before 25,000," *Ogden (UT) Standard-Examiner*, December 6, 1942.

14. Dan McGuire, "Problems Face Coast Conference," *Modesto (CA) Bee*, December 14, 1942.

15. "Idaho Announces Abandonment of Spring Grid," *Helena (MT) Daily Independent*, February 24, 1943.

16. "Idaho Gridder Killed in Action," *Reno (NV) Evening Gazette*, July 3, 1943; "Noted Ohio State Athlete Killed in Plane Accident," *Marysville (OH) Evening Tribune*, October 4, 1943.

17. "Schmidt Out as Coach at Idaho University," *San Antonio (TX) Light*, February 27, 1944; Hugh Fullerton Jr., "Chain Store Baseball Is Focal Point," *Council Bluffs (IA) Nonpareil*, January 19, 1944; "Schmidt, Ex-Idaho Coach, Seeks New Grid Birth," *Fresno (CA) Bee*, March 23, 1944.

18. "Francis Schmidt Ill," *Oakland (CA) Tribune*, September 9, 1944; "Francis Schmidt Dies Ending Career of Roving Coach," *Ada (OK) Evening News*, September 20, 1944.

19. "Francis Schmidt Will Be Buried in Arkansas City," *San Antonio (TX) Express*, September 21, 1944; "Schmidt's Funeral in Arkansas City," *San Antonio (TX) Light*, September 25, 1944.

Fourteen. The Schmidt Effect

1. Sid Gillman, *San Diego (CA) Union*, August 22, 1965.

2. Vaught, *Rebel Coach*, 18.

3. Fritz Howell, "Schmidt Says Football to Be Wide Open in 1936," *Zanesville (OH) Times-Signal*, April 5, 1936.

4. Fritz Howell, "Schmidt Says Football to Be Wide Open in 1936," *Zanesville (OH) Times-Signal*, April 5, 1936.

5. Vaught, *Rebel Coach*, 18.

6. Gillman, *San Diego Chargers Strength Program*, foreword.

7. Sid Gillman interview by Todd Tobias on December 16, 1998.

8. Ed Levitt, "Al Talks about Sid," *Oakland (CA) Tribune*, November 16, 1969; Phil Barber, "Gillman Laid Foundation for All Who Followed," Official program for Super Bowl XXXII, January 25, 1998.

9. Paul Zimmerman, "The Real West Coast Offense," *Sports Illustrated* online, October 29, 1999, sportsillustrated.cnn.com/inside_game/dr_z/news/1999/10/28/inside_football/.

10. Gillman, *San Diego Chargers Strength Program*, foreword.

11. Walsh, *Building a Champion*, 33.

12. Walsh, *Building a Champion*, 33.

13. Pont, *Fields of Honor*, 108.

14. Jack Murphy, *San Diego (CA) Union*, December 5, 1968.

15. Sam Farmer, "Coach Revolutionized Offenses in Football," *Los Angeles Times*, January 4, 2003.

16. Vaught, *Rebel Coach*, 19–20.

17. Cleveland, *Vaught*, 9.

18. Vaught, *Rebel Coach*, 95.

19. Manning, *Manning*, 37, 50.

20. Manning, *Manning*, 50.

21. Vaught, *Rebel Coach*, 19.

22. King, *An Autumn Remembered*, 57.

23. "Another Sooner," *Lethbridge (Alberta) Herald*, April 29, 1954; "Oklahoma's Little Round Coach," Al Dewlen, *Saturday Evening Post*, November 3, 1956.

24. Jones, *Offensive and Defensive Line Play*, vii–viii.

25. Jim Tressel, Ohio State Football Press Luncheon, November 9, 2004. http://www.buckeyeplanet.com/forum/content/25849-transcript-november-9th-ohio-state-football-press-luncheon-jim-tressel.html.

26. Maraniss, *When Pride Still Mattered*, 168.

27. Whittingham, *What a Game They Played*, 185.

28. Bisheff, *Los Angeles Rams*, 133.

29. Whittingham, *What a Game They Played*, 191.

30. "Ohio State Gridders Begin Work Sept. 10," *Massillon (OH) Evening Independent*, August 21, 1936.

31. Campbell Graf interview by author, Wilmington OH, June 16, 2007.

Epilogue

1. Tippy Dye interview by author, Camptonville CA, March 14, 2007; Campbell Graf interview by author, Wilmington OH, June 16, 2007; Jack Graf interview by author, Columbus OH, June 16, 2007; Tom Kinkade interview by author, Indio Springs CA, January 20, 2005; Cecil Souders telephone interview by

author, July 12, 2006; Harper, *An Ohio State Man*, 24–26; Vaught, *Rebel Coach*, 18; Freund, *The Purple Lawman*, 15.

Appendix

1. Arkansas still claims to have won this game based on forfeit. Previous to the game, it had been announced that Tulsa's star quarterback, Rex Thomas, played professional baseball for his hometown's minor league team during the summer, a violation of Oklahoma Intercollegiate Conference (OIC) rules. Thomas claimed to have received no money nor to have been on the official roster, and while the conference reviewed the evidence, Schmidt and Arkansas agreed to play Tulsa *with* Thomas, eventually losing to the Hurricanes 13–6. The next week, Oklahoma A&M refused to play Tulsa if they used Thomas, and Tulsa refused to play without him. The game was declared a forfeit in Oklahoma A&M's favor. When the conference finally ruled against Tulsa with regard to Thomas, there was a fine and penalties, but the OIC had no jurisdiction over the nonconference Arkansas–Tulsa game. To this day, each school claims to have won the game. It is the author's position that Tulsa was the better team that day, and considering the eligibility tricks employed by Schmidt, it would seem disingenuous to claim a victory based on a minor nonfootball technicality.

2. Texas Christian still claims a record of 9-2-1 for 1931, based on an extra victory over Texas Military College (40–0) on September 18. However, Texas Military was a junior college, which would seem to make this game ineligible for consideration. Granted, this era was more lenient in its definitions of competition, and many schools claim wins from earlier decades against high schools, college freshmen teams, and athletic clubs. And, even taking into consideration some of the other lightweight teams that TCU used for warm-up fodder during a typical September in the 1930s, it is still difficult to justify claiming an official win over a junior college with less than two hundred students. This one seems to be more of a scrimmage with a paid attendance.

3. Texas Christian still claims a forfeit victory Arkansas. The Razorbacks appeared to have won their first-ever conference title in 1933, but it was discovered they had used an ineligible player (Ulysses "Dutch" Schleuter) for a few minutes covering three games, including one against TCU. At season's end, the SWC penalized Arkansas by denying them the claim of a conference title. None was awarded. And though TCU and Schmidt implored the conference to force Arkansas to forfeit the games in which Schleuter was used, the SWC never took this action. It would seem that the loss of a title is punishment enough for using an inconsequential substitute for mere minutes and that Arkansas earned their victory over TCU.

BIBLIOGRAPHY

Manuscripts and Archives

Jack Graf. Personal collection of playbooks, notes, signal cards, and charts from his days as a quarterback in Schmidt's system at Ohio State University, 1938–40.

The Ohio State University Archives, The Ohio State University, Columbus OH.

Director of Athletics Collection (OSU-DA).

Biographical file (OSU-BF).

University of Nebraska–Lincoln, academic transcript for Francis Albert Schmidt. Microfilmed October 8, 1970.

University of Tulsa, McFarlin Library, Department of Special Collections and University Archives, "Tulsa Race Riot of 1921," collection 1984-004.

Books

Akers, Charles W., and John W. Carter. *Bo McMillin: Man and Legend.* Louisville KY: Sulgrave, 1989.

Baker, L. H. (pseudonym of Louis Henry Levy). *Football: Facts and Figures.* New York: Rinehart, 1945.

Bierman, B. W. "Bernie." *Winning Football.* New York: McGraw-Hill, 1937.

Bisheff, Steve. *Los Angeles Rams.* New York: Macmillan, 1973.

Brown, Paul, and Jack Clary. *PB: The Paul Brown Story.* New York: Atheneum, 1979.

Bynum, Mike, ed. *Pop Warner, Football's Greatest Teacher: The Epic Autobiography of Major College Football's Winningest Coach, Glenn S. "Pop" Warner.* N.p.: Gridiron Football Properties, 1993.

Camp, Walter. *How to Play Football.* New York: American Sports, 1921.

Canning, Whit, and Dan Jenkins, ed. *Sam Baugh: Best There Ever Was.* Dallas TX: Masters Press, 1997.

Carey, Patrick W. *Catholics in America: A History.* Westport CT: Greenwood, 2004.

Carroll, John M. *Red Grange and the Rise of Modern Football.* Carbondale: University of Illinois Press, 1999.

Claassen, Harold "Spike." *The History of Professional Football.* Englewood Cliffs NJ: Prentice-Hall, 1963.

Cleveland, Rick. *Vaught: The Man and His Legacy.* N.p.: Epic Sports, 2000.

Cohane, Tim. *Great College Football Coaches of the Twenties and Thirties.* New Rochelle NY: Arlington, 1973.

Cope, Myron. *The Game That Was.* New York: World, 1970.

Curran, Bob. *Pro Football's Rag Days.* New York: Bonanza, 1969.

Danzig, Allison. *Oh, How They Played the Game: The Early Days of Football and the Heroes Who Made it Great.* New York: Macmillan, 1971.

Davis, Parke H. *Football: The American Intercollegiate Game.* New York: Scribner's, 1911.

Davis, Willard, ed. *Pictorial Encyclopedia of Football.* N.p.: Castle, 1974.

Freeman, Denne H. *That Good Old Baylor Line.* Huntsville AL: Strode, 1975.

Freund, Carl, and Louie Hulme and D. Kent Pingel and Kitty Evans Loveless, eds. *The Purple Lawman: From Horned Frog to High Sheriff.* Fort Worth: Summit, 1990.

Gartner, John D. *The Hypomanic Edge: The Link Between (A Little) Craziness and (A Lot) of Success in America.* New York: Simon & Schuster, 2005.

Gillman, Sid, and Alvin Roy. *San Diego Chargers Strength Program In and Out of Season.* N.p.: Gillman-Roy, 1964.

Grange, Harold E. "Red." *Zuppke of Illinois.* Chicago: Glaser, 1937.

Halas, George S., and Gwen Morgan and Arthur Veysey. *Halas: An Autobiography.* Chicago: Bonus, 1986.

Harper, William L. *An Ohio State Man: Coach Esco Sarkkinen Remembers OSU Football.* Columbus OH: Anthea, 2000.

Heisman, John. *Principles of Football.* St. Louis: Sports Publishing, 1922.

Henry, Orville, and Jim Bailey. *The Razorbacks: A Story of Arkansas Football.* Huntsville AL: Strode, 1973.

Hutchins, R. M. *University of Utopia.* Chicago: University of Chicago Press, 1953.

Jenkins, Dan and Francis J. Fitzgerald, eds. *Greatest Moments in TCU Football History.* Louisville KY: AdCraft, 1996.

Jones, Gomer. *Offensive and Defensive Line Play.* Englewood Cliffs NJ: Prentice-Hall, 1961.

Jones, Howard H., and Alfred Wesson. *Football for the Fan.* Los Angeles: Times-Mirror, 1929.

Keith, Harold. *Forty-Seven Straight: The Wilkinson Era at Oklahoma.* Norman: University of Oklahoma Press, 1984.

Kurz, Bob. *Miami of Ohio: The Cradle of Coaches.* Troy OH: Troy Daily News, 1983.

Layden, Elmer, and Ed Snyder. *It Was a Different Game: The Elmer Layden Story.* Englewood Cliffs NJ: Prentice-Hall, 1969.

Little, Lou. *How to Watch Football: The Spectator's Guide.* New York: McGraw-Hill, 1935.

MacCambridge, Michael, ed. *ESPN College Football Encyclopedia: The Complete History of the Game.* New York: ESPN, 2005.

Manning, Archie, and Peyton Manning and John Underwood. *Manning.* New York: Harper, 2000.

Maraniss, David. *When Pride Still Mattered: A Life of Vince Lombardi.* New York: Simon & Schuster, 1999.

Meyer, L. R. "Dutch." *Spread Formation Football.* New York: Prentice-Hall, 1952.

The Mirror. Arkansas City High School yearbook. Arkansas City KS, 1909-15.

The NFL's Official Encyclopedic History of Professional Football. New York: Macmillan, 1973.

Oberlander, David Holman. *Swede: The Will to Win.* Kearney NE: Morris, 1996.

Oriard, Michael. *King Football: Sport and Spectacle in the Golden Age of Radio and Newsreels, Movies and Magazines, the Weekly and the Daily Press.* Chapel Hill: University of North Carolina Press, 2001.

Owen, Steve and Joe King, eds. *My Kind of Football.* New York: David McKay, 1952.

Palmer, Pete. *The ESPN Pro Football Encyclopedia.* New York: Sterling, 2007.

Park, Jack. *The Official Ohio State Football Encyclopedia.* St. Louis: Sports Publishing, 2003.

Peterson, Robert W. *Pigskin: The Early Years of Pro Football.* New York: Oxford University Press, 1997.

Pont, Sally. *Fields of Honor: The Golden Age of College Football and the Men Who Created It.* New York: Harcourt, 2001.

Pope, Edwin. *Football's Greatest Coaches.* Atlanta: Tupper & Love, 1955.

Pouncey, Temple. *Mustang Mania: SMU Football.* Huntsville AL: Strode, 1981.

Povich, Shirley. "No Boredom or Blacks Allowed," *Redskins: A History of Washington's Team.* Washington DC: Washington Post, 2007.

Quirk, James P. *Minnesota Football: The Golden Years 1932–41.* N.p.: Quirk, 1984.

Roberts, Howard. *The Big Nine: The Story of Football in the Western Conference*. New York: Putnam's, 1948.

_____. *The Story of Pro Football*. Rand McNally, 1953.

Rockne, Knute K. *Coaching*. New York: Devin-Adair, 1928.

Roper, William W. *Football: Today and Tomorrow*. New York: Duffield, 1927.

Rutland, Robert. *The Golden Hurricane: Fifty Years of Football at the University of Tulsa*. Tulsa Quarterback Club, 1952.

Scott, Harry G. *Jock Sutherland: Architect of Men*. New York: Exposition, 1954.

Smith, Myron J. Jr. *The College Football Bibliography*. Westport CT: Greenwood, 1994.

Sperber, Murray. *Shake Down the Thunder: The Creation of Notre Dame Football*. New York: Henry Holt, 1993.

Stagg, A. A., and W. W. Stout. *Touchdown!* New York: Longmans, Green, 1927.

Steinberg, Donald M. D. *Expanding Your Horizons: Collegiate Football's Greatest Team*. N.p.: Steinberg, 1992.

Tips, Kern. *Football Texas Style: An Illustrated History of the Southwest Conference*. New York: Doubleday, 1964.

Vaught, John. *Rebel Coach*. Memphis: Memphis State University Press, 1971.

Walsh, Bill, and Glenn Dickey. *Building a Champion: On Football and the Making of the 49ers*. New York: St. Martin's, 1990.

Warner, Glenn Scobey. *Football for Coaches and Players*. Palo Alto CA: Stanford University Press, 1927.

_____. *The Saga of American Football*. New York: Macmillan, 1955.

Washington Post, The. *Redskins: A History of Washington's Team*. Washington DC: Washington Post Books, 2000.

Watterson, John Sayle. *College Football: History, Spectacle, Controversy*. Baltimore: Johns Hopkins University Press, 2000.

Weyand, Alexander M. *American Football: Its History and Development*. New York: Appleton, 1926.

Whittingham, Richard. *What a Game They Played: An Inside Look at the Golden Era of Pro Football*. Lincoln: University of Nebraska Press, 2001.

Ziemba, Joe. *When Football Was Football*. Chicago: Triumph, 1999.

INDEX

310–11; restrictions placed on
Schmidt, 310; by Schmidt, 152,
313–14; Schmidt's failures, 307–9,
384–85; tradition as draw, 311–12

Reid, Andy, 415

Renfro, Elza, 35

Renick, Jim, 112, 259, 380

reputation: for caustic personality,
53–55; factors affecting, ix; fading
of, 417–18; and job offer from
Henry Kendall College, 25; and
job offer from Ohio State, 70; rise
and fall of, 407; for running up
scores, 29, 137; TSU success and,
53

restlessness, 13, 14, 21, 33. *See also*
manic temperament

Rice, Grantland, 175, 177, 250

Rice University, 73, 156

Richards, Dick, 256–57

Rickey, Branch, 243

Rightmire, George W., 69, 83

risk-taking, Schmidt's love of, 112,
428

Robbins, Jack, 296

Robinson, James L., 305

Rockne, Knute, 95, 96, 155–56, 162,
167, 172, 187, 309

Rose, Glen, 40, 297

Rose Bowl (1920), 95

Rose Bowl (1942), 405

Ruhl, Oscar, 134, 288

rules: easing of restrictions on
forward pass, 105–6; efforts to
increase offense, 86, 89, 104,
105–6; 4 downs/10 yard rule, 18,
89; introduction of modern game,
89–90; legalization of forward

pass, 18, 89, 90; NFL changes to
increase excitement, 254–55;
outlawing of Tower play, 26; on
signaling plays, 118; on substitutions, 206, 372–73

running up scores: contemporary
views on, 29; at Henry Kendall
College, 26, 29; at Ohio State,
133, 136–37, 145–46, 282; press
on, 134, 136–37, 160–61, 162–63;
Schmidt on, 29–30, 161–62

Russell, Dorothy, 234

Russell, Mary Kennedy, 119–20,
207, 221, 234

St. John, Lynn Wilbur "Saint":
concerns about Schmidt, 81, 110,
122, 202; and Cornell play-signal-
ing scandal, 377–79; and decision
to dismiss Schmidt, 388, 391–92;
feedback on Schmidt hire, 83–84;
and Ohio State schedule, 81, 114,
198–201, 222–24, 286; postal
miscommunications with Schmidt,
84–85; recruiting restrictions on
Schmidt, 310; removal of Willaman, 63–65; on Schmidt, 367;
Schmidt's salary and, 77; and
Schmidt's staff, 202; search for
head coach, 62, 67–73, 76; search
for Schmidt replacement, 396;
vacations/travel with Schmidt,
258–61, 354

St. Louis Cardinals, 243

salaries: of coach *vs.* professor,
77–78; in NFL, 238–39, 246–47

salary, of Schmidt: at Ohio State, 77;
Schmidt's refusal to haggle over,